The Great Consolidation

The Great Consolidation

Reconciling the Family of God

by

Duane Andry

Copyright 2005 Duane Andry

This document is copyrighted material. Under copyright law, no parts of this document may be reproduced without the expressed permission of the author.

Unless otherwise indicated, Bible quotations are taken from the King James Version of the Bible.

No Copyright. Public Domain.

ISBN 978-0-9798444-2-3

Preface

There came a man Jesus. He was conceived by the overshadowing of the Holy Ghost and born of a virgin named Mary, who, along with Joseph her husband, is of the seed of David the king.

This same man, Jesus, was sanctified by God with the filling of the Holy Ghost, which remained upon him. At this time he was announced to those with him, and thus to the world, as being the beloved Son of God. At that time, we were directed by the voice of God to "hear ye him". This is the one called, the Son of man, and the Son of God.

This same man, Jesus, after the anointing of the Holy Ghost, continued his ministry on the earth with mighty signs and wonders. Because of these signs he engendered the displeasure of the religious/political powers of his day. They, thinking to rid the world of this *nuisance*, crucified and killed this body on the cross. By so doing, they brought into effect God's will for the salvation of mankind and for the return of all His children to Him. Jesus Christ, the Lamb of God, is the last sacrifice sanctioned by God to carry away the sins of the world through the blood. "It is finished."

This same man, Jesus, is spoken of throughout the pages of the Bible, the Holy Word of God. And this Bible was transcribed by holy men moved by the Spirit of God. And this Bible is sealed until the time of the end of this current earthly reality. It is in the light of this Bible that I present this message; for the remission of sin and the salvation of mankind.

Introduction

Hello.
How are you today?

I pray that you are well and that you are moving of one accord with the Almighty. Let it be so that you increase in understanding of God's way and of His kingdom; LORD willing.

I truly thank you for obtaining this book. I pray to the Father that as you read it, your world will be transformed by an even closer walk with Him.

Today there are many religions, with many sects and denominations of these religions. The multiplication effect of these two, gives us thousands of religious practices from which to choose. Add to this, the effect of tradition, and the number of ways to worship the Almighty can quickly rise to the millions. We will not even mention the effect of individual preferences. Even so, there is still, by definition and by fact, only one Almighty.

There is, of course, room for other mighties, but there can be only one Almighty. Whether one is a monotheist or a polytheist, there is still only one Almighty. Even those who believe in a trinity, with three parts, strive to place them under one power source, the Almighty. No matter how we look at it, there will still only be One.

> *Hear, O Israel: The LORD our God is one LORD: And thou shalt love the LORD thy God with all thine heart, and with all thy soul, and with all thy might.*
>
> (Deuteronomy 6:4-5)

The best statement of the Most High status of the Almighty comes from words attributed to the Almighty.

> *I am the LORD, and there is none else, there is no God beside me: I girded thee, though thou hast not known me: That they may know from the rising of the sun, and from the west, that there is none beside me. I am the LORD, and there is none else.*
>
> (Isaiah 45:5-6)

In this document, I will refer to the Almighty as, LORD, God, Him, He, Himself, or His; to reduce the high level of formality that the word Almighty conjures up.

I believe that it is time for all mankind to grasp this basic concept: it is past time that mankind, in religions within nations, understand that what they say about the Almighty is a very precious thing. It can also be very dangerous, if it is mishandled for personal gain; individual or governmental. Words about the Almighty are not said in isolation. This is true not just on the earth, but it is true throughout the universe. Please understand that the Almighty is listening and watching. His agents are also poised to protect His reputation and His honor among men. No man ever born, or who will ever be born, is as powerful as the Almighty: and there is nothing that can ever exceed Him in power.

The LORD has tolerated much from mankind; but woe unto you who think that He will tolerate anything. Our environmental atrocities should give us a clear indication of the tolerance of God. He has allowed mankind a very broad slate of power in the world; not unrestricted, just broad.

> *And God said, Let us make man in our image, after our likeness: and let them have dominion over the fish of the sea, and over the fowl of the air, and over the cattle, and over all the earth, and over every creeping thing that creepeth upon the earth. So God created man in his own image, in the image of God created he him; male and female created he them. And God blessed them, and God said unto them, Be fruitful, and multiply, and replenish the earth, and subdue it: and have dominion over the fish of the sea, and over the fowl of the air, and over every living thing that moveth upon the earth.*

(Genesis 1:26-28)

Read the above Scripture, very carefully. In it, God does not give man dominion over the environment.

On a more somber note, neither does the Scripture give any nation or group of people dominion over all other nations or peoples. Dominion over the nations is reserved for God, and His chosen representatives. He has allowed us presidents, kings, dictators, prime ministers, and other high governmental officials to work with us on a regional basis.

There is, however, a representative of God who is above all governmental officials on this earth. This is he who stands in a chosen position to rule on a global level. He is the one who comes to show us The Way. He is the one who has the promise of God to inherit the kingdoms of the earth. All religions know of him, and all are awaiting the manifestation of his eternal reign. This one was crafted and equipped personally by the Almighty.

That there is one, who was crafted and equipped personally by the Almighty, should not surprise us. On this earth we are accustomed to powerful men hand-picking and grooming their successors. Why should the most powerful being in the universe not do so? As a matter of fact, where do you think we learned how to do what we do?

It has been, and will continue to be, my constant attempt, in presenting the information that is contained in these pages, to persuade the Almighty and His chosen guide to mankind to share with me some key secrets. I am not referring to new things about reality, but, rather, to new methods. I am asking God to show me ways to pierce the clouds of misunderstanding and variance from the truth of the Bible. These are the clouds that are becoming thicker and thicker, over all mankind.

The knowledge that I request, is not intended for me to be able to say that I know, and leave it at that. It is my intention to share all the secrets that I am told by God; however little or however much that may be.

The world needs a refreshing shot of divinity in its relational veins: individual and institutional; religious and secular. The nations, as the representatives of the power of God, need to understand their responsibilities. They can no longer blame the children (citizens) of the nation for being unruly and uncontrollable. They can no longer say that they have shown proper restraint: they have not. God is the standard of proper restraint, and God is Tolerance.

To kill in anger will never be tolerance. To indiscriminately kill is nothing less than murder. To kill in revenge is nothing less than unrighteous slaughter. It is time for the leaders of the nations to follow God, or stop calling themselves people of God. Too many leaders, in too many nations, are turning a blind eye to suppression and killing among the people of their nation. There are too many episodes of angry people, killing in anger. One of the most common excuses that they use is that they are purifying the nation. Scripture rebuts that contention.

> *To me belongeth vengeance, and recompense; their foot shall slide in due time: for the day of their calamity is at hand, and the things that shall come upon them make haste. For the LORD shall judge his people, and repent himself for his servants, when he seeth that their power is gone, and there is none shut up, or left.*
>
> (Deuteronomy 32:35-36)

> *Dearly beloved, avenge not yourselves, but rather give place unto wrath: for it is written, Vengeance is mine; I will repay, saith the Lord.*
>
> (Romans 12:19)

For a nation to say that "such is our traditions", is irrelevant. God does not embed Himself in your traditions. God is not subject to tradition. All your traditions are subject to God. All priests, prophets, pastors, apostles, scholars, scribes, Pharisees, bishops, popes, as well as all other religious officers, are subject to God. There is none so blessed as to be able to modify God's rules of behavior. This is the example given to us by the life of the greatest among prophets--Moses. Even he was subject to God's will, and when he did not perform his duties as required by God, he was chastened by God.

> *And the LORD spake unto Moses that selfsame day, saying, Get thee up into this mountain Abarim, unto mount Nebo, which is in the land of Moab, that is over against Jericho; and behold the land of Canaan, which I give unto the children of Israel for a possession: And die in the mount whither thou goest up, and be gathered unto thy people; as Aaron thy brother died in mount Hor, and was gathered unto his people: Because ye trespassed against me among the children of Israel at the waters of Meribah-Kadesh, in the wilderness of Zin; because ye sanctified me not in the midst of the children of Israel. Yet thou shalt see the land before thee; but thou shalt not go thither unto the land which I give the children of Israel.*
>
> (Deuteronomy 32:48-52)

We can learn much from Moses, on many matters; and especially, on matters of devotion to God. We know from his life, what God does when we do not live according to His way and His will. Moses' life also shows us what we are capable of doing when we are at our best before God.

Moses was very diligent about guarding both his own reputation and the reputation of God. He did not spend much, if any, time concentrating n the reputations of men; this is a wise thing for us to do. When one concentrates on guarding the reputation of men, no matter how noble or seemingly close to God the person may be; they will discover that God is unimpressed by our effort. In fact, they will discover that God is displeased with their focus on a person, and not on Him; even when we focus on our self.

One of the lessons that God presented to Moses, was to show him just how far he had developed in his relationship with Him. By asking Moses if he wanted to take over the position as the father of the chosen people, God was causing Moses to look deeply within himself. Would he choose fame, or would he choose to protect the reputation of God?

Moses response shows us how we should behave. Moses' choice was, to protect God's reputation.

> *And the LORD said unto Moses, I have seen this people, and, behold, it is a stiffnecked people: Now therefore let me alone, that my wrath may wax hot against them, and that I may consume them: and I will make of thee a great nation.*
>
> *And Moses besought the LORD his God, and said, LORD, why doth thy wrath wax hot against thy people, which thou hast brought forth out of the land of Egypt with great power, and with a mighty hand? Wherefore should the Egyptians speak, and say, For mischief did he bring them out, to slay them in the mountains, and to consume them from the face of the earth? Turn from thy fierce wrath, and repent of this evil against thy people. Remember Abraham, Isaac, and Israel, thy servants, to whom thou swarest by thine own self, and saidst unto them, I will multiply your seed as the stars of heaven, and all this land that I have spoken of will I give unto your seed, and they shall inherit it for ever.*

(Exodus 32:9-13)

When God has established a nation, or allowed a nation to exist, who are we to decide that it should not?

In like manner, the selective slaughter of certain groups of people within a nation is in direct defiance to the ways of God. It should not be tolerated by any government on this earth. The nation that cannot rise to the level shown by the one man, Moses, is not fit to call itself a nation of God.

Moses sought peace; over destruction. He promoted God's ability to heal and redeem; over the ability to destroy and enslave. The nation that cannot do this, among all people within its borders, is unfit, and must turn to God for refreshing. Nations must absorb and activate the Law, as given by God to the children of Israel.

> *All that are born of the country shall do these things after this manner, in offering an offering made by fire, of a sweet savour unto the LORD. And if a stranger sojourn with you, or whosoever be among you in your generations, and will offer an offering made by fire, of a sweet savour unto the LORD; as ye do, so he shall do. One ordinance shall be both for you of the congregation, and also for the stranger that sojourneth with you, an ordinance for ever in your generations: as ye are, so shall the stranger be before the LORD. One law and one manner shall be for you, and for the stranger that sojourneth with you.*

(Numbers 15:13-16)

It is my prayer that God gives us the insight that we need, to develop for Him the message of tolerance; to represent it to one another. This is my request to Him for this book. It is time for the great consolidation of all religions around God. This does not mean that mankind must be forced to choose one religion, now. There will be one religion soon enough; and it will be at God's timing. At the time of the earthly rule of the Messiah, there will be one world religion: it will not happen until then. This is, instead, a call for a consolidation in sharing, with others, the tolerance that the LORD shows us. This is a call for all nations to diligently seek God.

> *But without faith it is impossible to please him: for he that cometh to God must believe that he is, and that he is a rewarder of them that diligently seek him.*

(Hebrews 11:6)

Always remember that we are tolerated as individuals, and as nations, because God has not charged our sin to our account.

> *If thou, LORD, shouldest mark iniquities, O Lord, who shall stand? But there is forgiveness with thee, that thou mayest be feared.*
>
> (Psalm 130:3-4)

We are definitely not deserving of tolerance, within ourselves and by our own actions.

> *But now the righteousness of God without the law is manifested, being witnessed by the law and the prophets; Even the righteousness of God which is by faith of Jesus Christ unto all and upon all them that believe: for there is no difference: For all have sinned, and come short of the glory of God; Being justified freely by his grace through the redemption that is in Christ Jesus: Whom God hath set forth to be a propitiation through faith in his blood, to declare his righteousness for the remission of sins that are past, through the forbearance of God; To declare, I say, at this time his righteousness: that he might be just, and the justifier of him which believeth in Jesus.*
>
> (Romans 3:21-26)

Please, let us honor God, as best we can, in His power; by embracing His nature.

> *Ask, and it shall be given you; seek, and ye shall find; knock, and it shall be opened unto you: For every one that asketh receiveth; and he that seeketh findeth; and to him that knocketh it shall be opened. Or what man is there of you, whom if his son ask bread, will he give him a stone? Or if he ask a fish, will he give him a serpent? If ye then, being evil, know how to give good gifts unto your children, how much more shall your Father which is in heaven give good things to them that ask him?*
>
> (Matthew 7:7-11)

Remember that we all are living because of the grace of God. Please do not provoke Him.

For we know him that hath said, Vengeance belongeth unto me, I will recompense, saith the Lord. And again, The Lord shall judge his people.

It is a fearful thing to fall into the hands of the living God.

(Hebrews 10:30-31)

*Just as I am
Without one plea,
Is a maxim with which
I surely agree.*

*It is from the beginning
That we all must start,
In the search for truth
That lies at the heart*

*Of God's total plan
For all mankind;
The one his servants
Will help us find.*

*We want to be one
Of those that know
Just THE way
Mankind must go.*

*Each religion says
I have the way;
Follow me;
You will prosper, today.*

*Some religions say
That they have the right
To physically damage
And others give flight.*

*God is not found
In religions of the lands;
Above us all
His majesty stands*

*With arms outstretched,
In a gesture of love;
Extended to all
By the Saviour, above.*

*No, it is not for men
To give us the sky;*

God will do this,
By and by.

Our purpose is not enhanced
By how many we kill;
But, by righteous living,
As we do God's will.

Contents

Preface		v
Introduction		vii
The Word from the Bible		1
1.	*Start of Worship*	5
1a.	*Why Bother?*	15
2.	Recognition of God	23
2a.	*The Mechanics of Heaven*	43
3.	Impossible to Restore	55
3a.	*Piercing To The Dividing*	65
4.	Just Shall Live by Faith	75
4a.	*Everything Comes From God*	85
5.	Period of refreshing	97
5a.	*Positive = Negative*	109
6.	The Natures of Man	123
6a.	*Sending Forth vs Making*	133
7.	The Branching of Nations	143
7a.	*Before the Foundation*	175
8.	No Respect of Persons	187
8a.	*The First Sending Forth (the being, Christ)*	203
9.	The Power of Prophecy	213
9a.	*The Pattern of the First*	225

10.	Separation of a People	243
10a.	*The Godhead Complete*	257
11.	Provision for the Others	279
11a.	*The Child is Born*	287
12.	Laying Out the Journey	309
12a.	*If They Will Not Hear*	327
13.	The Great Consolidation	343
13a.	*The Spirit descends like a dove*	359
14.	The Pedal to the Metal	377
14a.	*My Bewildered Prayer*	389

In My Conclusion (Almost) 393

Ramblings 409
   A Matter of Obedience 409
   Why I Can't Sing 425
   As the Lightning Cometh 431
   The Two Fires 449
   The World to Come 471

The Word from the Bible

Genesis 2:4-9

These are the generations of the heavens and of the earth when they were created, in the day that the LORD God made the earth and the heavens, And every plant of the field before it was in the earth, and every herb of the field before it grew: for the LORD God had not caused it to rain upon the earth, and there was not a man to till the ground. But there went up a mist from the earth, and watered the whole face of the ground. And the LORD God formed man of the dust of the ground, and breathed into his nostrils the breath of life; and man became a living soul. And the LORD God planted a garden eastward in Eden; and there he put the man whom he had formed. And out of the ground made the LORD God to grow every tree that is pleasant to the sight, and good for food; the tree of life also in the midst of the garden, and the tree of knowledge of good and evil.

Genesis 2:15-17

And the LORD God took the man, and put him into the garden of Eden to dress it and to keep it. And the LORD God commanded the man, saying, Of every tree of the garden thou mayest freely eat: But of the tree of the knowledge of good and evil, thou shalt not eat of it: for in the day that thou eatest thereof thou shalt surely die.

Genesis 2:21-25

And the LORD God caused a deep sleep to fall upon Adam, and he slept: and he took one of his ribs, and closed up the flesh instead thereof; And the rib, which the LORD God had taken from man, made he a woman, and brought her unto the man. And Adam said, This is now bone of my bones, and flesh of my flesh: she shall be called Woman, because she was taken out of Man. Therefore shall a man leave his father and his mother, and shall cleave unto his wife: and they shall be one flesh. And they were both naked, the man and his wife, and were not ashamed.

Genesis 3:1-7

Now the serpent was more subtle than any beast of the field which the LORD God had made. And he said unto the woman, Yea, hath God said, Ye shall not eat of every tree of the garden?

And the woman said unto the serpent, We may eat of the fruit of the trees of the garden: But of the fruit of the tree which is in the midst of the garden, God hath said, Ye shall not eat of it, neither shall ye touch it, lest ye die.

And the serpent said unto the woman, Ye shall not surely die: For God doth know that in the day ye eat thereof, then your eyes shall be opened, and ye shall be as gods, knowing good and evil.

And when the woman saw that the tree was good for food, and that it was pleasant to the eyes, and a tree to be desired to make one wise, she took of the fruit thereof, and did eat, and gave also unto her husband with her; and he did eat. And the eyes of them both were opened, and they knew that they were naked; and they sewed fig leaves together, and made themselves aprons.

Genesis 3:8-11

And they heard the voice of the LORD God walking in the garden in the cool of the day: and Adam and his wife hid themselves from the presence of the LORD God amongst the trees of the garden. And the LORD God called unto Adam, and said unto him, Where art thou?

And he said, I heard thy voice in the garden, and I was afraid, because I was naked; and I hid myself.

And he said, Who told thee that thou wast naked? Hast thou eaten of the tree, whereof I commanded thee that thou shouldest not eat?

Genesis 3:21-24

Unto Adam also and to his wife did the LORD God make coats of skins, and clothed them.

And the LORD God said, Behold, the man is become as one of us, to know good and evil: and now, lest he put forth his hand, and take also of the tree of life, and eat, and live for ever: Therefore the LORD God sent him forth from the garden of Eden, to till the ground from whence he was taken.

So he drove out the man; and he placed at the east of the garden of Eden Cherubims, and a flaming sword which turned every way, to keep the way of the tree of life.

Chapter One

Start of Worship

We are going on a search for the nature of our relationship with God. This is the relationship with God as He sees it, and not as we would like to have it. For some, we will not start early enough in many sections. For others, we will start too early. To both I say, please evaluate the whole message before making a judgment on the part. Where one starts is not as important as that one starts somewhere. With this in mind, let us get started.

First we will bypass a major chunk of science, as it is being described at this time. It is not of any significance whether there was or was not a Big Bang. It does not matter for the worship of God, whether evolution is a factual methodology of God. Intellectually, we can accept it as a product of man's desire to capture the brilliance of Creation. However, for purposes of worship of God, it is enough that man is here and that God Is.

We will also not, now, ponder where God came from, or how He got His power. Some have stated that God was reverse engineered out of the mind of man. Later on we will show why this is somewhat ridiculous, considering man's understanding of cause and effect in the universe. For now, however, we will let the mind wander on this notion; or even, just drop it: we recommend the latter. It is enough for our discussion that worship exists.

All people worship. Some people worship one another exclusively. This type of worship is seen in the worship of young couples for one another; as well as many not so young couples. Some broaden their worship to include their friends: some only worship their friends. Others worship only those who give advantage and favors to them.

The vast majority of mankind, however, is attempting to extend its worship to encompass things greater than its self. Among these things is science, the collective mind, and, yes, even God. We know that all mankind worships something; and that something, at some point, will become their god. We will explore how one moves from worshipping god, to worshipping **the** God. That is, taking some insight from the apostle Paul, as written in the Bible, we will show you how to transcend worshipping the movable or unknown god.

> *Then Paul stood in the midst of Mars' hill, and said, Ye men of Athens, I perceive that in all things ye are too superstitious. For as I passed by, and beheld your devotions, I found an altar with this inscription, TO THE UNKNOWN GOD. Whom therefore ye ignorantly worship, him declare I unto you.*
>
> *God that made the world and all things therein, seeing that he is Lord of heaven and earth, dwelleth not in temples made with hands; Neither is worshipped with men's hands, as though he needed any thing, seeing he giveth to all life, and breath, and all things; And hath made of one blood all nations of men for to dwell on all the face of the earth, and hath determined the times before appointed, and the bounds of their habitation; That they should seek the Lord, if haply they might feel after him, and find him, though he be not far from every one of us: For in him we live, and move, and have our being; as certain also of your own poets have said, For we are also his offspring.*
>
> (Acts 17:22-28)

+=+=+=+=+=+=+=+=+=+=+=+=+=+=+=+=+=+

Worship of God can be divided into two types. The first type of worship is thought to be based on the works of man for God. The second type is thought to be based on the works of God for man. It is, however, not that simple. Yes, the worship of God is of two basic types, but they are not as described above.

The first type of worship is based on the physical works of man for God. This says that God requires that certain things be created; such as the construction of temples, or the tooling of idols. Those things that are built by the hand of man can even be conjured up from the reputation of another man. These things are often held in reverence and treated as a substitute for God. They are given supernatural honor; and the performance of certain works with and within them is necessary for pleasing the god of the religion. The failure to properly reverence the object, or perform the act, sometimes carries a death sentence. Alternatively, it is believed that the proper performance of these actions leads to eternal benefit. This is set forth by the leaders of the religion. It is sometimes based on actual writings attributed to God, but in most cases it is based on tradition.

The second type of worship is based on psychological works of man for God. Words such as belief, love and faith come to mind. They are pushed forth as a work that man must accomplish, distinct from the god to whom they are to be given. This is the *price* that man must pay for the benefits that they expect to receive from the god that they serve. The giving of this type of worship is sometimes routed through human intermediaries. These things are to be held in reverence, and they are treated as a substitute for God. They are given supernatural honor; and the performance of these psychological works is necessary for pleasing the god of the religion. The failure to properly perform the act sometimes carries a death sentence. However, the proper performance of these actions may leads to eternal benefit. This is set forth by the leaders of the religion. It is sometimes based on actual writings attributed to God, but in most cases it is based on tradition. Yes, the practice is the same for both activities.

Every man who worships God believes that God created man. Furthermore, the worshippers are convinced, and rightly so, that God can destroy man at any time. A simple well placed solar flare, into some of our larger stockpiles of weapons, could take care of that, if He so chose. However, it is not God's intention to create just to destroy-- this is what man does. Even so, the man who worships God has a deep respect for the power that is within God; which is the power to do whatever He wills. Those who worship God know that the life of mankind and the stasis of the universe are allowances from Him.

So, what is man to do about these two?

Well, it is surely nice for us to make *pretty* things for Him. We, who are human, are pleased when we have a lot of *pretty* stuff. So, to give a lot to God seems reasonable. But these are only the results of worship, and not the root of it. We need only consider some basic facts about God to see where these are insufficient to complete worship.

Considering the matter of giving God lots of stuff, some of those who worshipped Him were told the futility of trying to bribe Him in this fashion.

> *I will take no bullock out of thy house, nor he goats out of thy folds. For every beast of the forest is mine, and the cattle upon a thousand hills. I know all the fowls of the mountains: and the wild beasts of the field are mine. If I were hungry, I would not tell thee: for the world is mine, and the fulness thereof. Will I eat the flesh of bulls, or drink the blood of goats? Offer unto God thanksgiving; and pay thy vows unto the most High: And call upon me in the day of trouble: I will deliver thee, and thou shalt glorify me.*

(Psalm 50:9-15)

As far as pretty things, Jesus of Nazareth told us of natural beauty created by God; and not, by man.

> *And why take ye thought for raiment? Consider the lilies of the field, how they grow; they toil not, neither do they spin: And yet I say unto you, That even Solomon in all his glory was not arrayed like one of these.*

(Matthew 6:28-29)

Even if we should choose, as some have, to give these things as a sacrifice, for their own sake; we must understand that there is a wrong way, and a righteous way to do things. This is described by Samuel, the prophet of God, in a discussion with king Saul.

> *Wherefore then didst thou not obey the voice of the LORD, but didst fly upon the spoil, and didst evil in the sight of the LORD?*
>
> *And Saul said unto Samuel, Yea, I have obeyed the voice of the LORD, and have gone the way which the LORD sent me, and have brought Agag the king of Amalek, and have utterly destroyed the Amalekites. But the people took of the spoil, sheep and oxen, the chief of the things which should have been utterly destroyed, to sacrifice unto the LORD thy God in Gilgal.*
>
> *And Samuel said, Hath the LORD as great delight in burnt offerings and sacrifices, as in obeying the voice of the LORD? Behold, to obey is better than sacrifice, and to hearken than the fat of rams. For rebellion is as the sin of witchcraft, and stubbornness is as iniquity and idolatry.*

> *Because thou hast rejected the word of the LORD, he hath also rejected thee from being king.*
>
> *And Saul said unto Samuel, I have sinned: for I have transgressed the commandment of the LORD, and thy words: because I feared the people, and obeyed their voice.*

(1 Samuel 15:19-24)

To summarize: God can make as much stuff as He wills; in the same way and just as pretty as He made it before.

So what does God want?

He wants obedience. This means that physical works without psychological works are worthless as gifts to God.

But why doesn't God just "make me do it"?

Because!

God presents to mankind the gift of a relationship with Him. This is clearly seen in the Garden of Eden when He came for a walk. God did not just stroll along in His own *space*. During His walk, God sought out Adam. It was in the Garden that the full nature of the ideal relationship between God and man was first revealed.

Adam knew that God was someone to be respected. Adam knew this so well that he hid in shame from God. Was the shame because he had eaten the forbidden apple? Probably not. Even though he now knew good and evil, he did not seem to have made the connection between his actions and the consequences. After all, in his mind he might have thought that the consequences stated had not been fulfilled; he was still alive.

What struck Adam most was his nakedness. He now realized that he was unfit to stand in the presence of God. Adam could no longer see God as just "one of the boys" in the Garden of Eden. He even knew that God was not just his Creator; not just the Father: he now knew that God is good. Adam now understood the message that is given to us by Jesus of Nazareth.

> *And, behold, one came and said unto him, Good Master, what good thing shall I do, that I may have eternal life?*
>
> *And he said unto him, Why callest thou me good? there is none good but one, that is, God: but if thou wilt enter into life, keep the commandments.*

(Matthew 19:16-17)

In knowing, this Adam finally realized that he had quite a huge debt to pay to God. Adam knew that he owed God respect; which, as displayed by man, is too often done in raw, cringing fear. Adam hid himself because he knew he could not stand in the presence of God. Adam answered the call of God because he knew that he needed God for all things. That Adam felt insufficient to be in the relationship, is not the point. That God established the relationship is.

Physical works of man for God; psychological works of man for God: two types of worship. There is a third type of worship of God. In this type of worship it is accepted that a human has no way of living up to the standards of righteousness in God. A seeker of God once told me that he just did not see how in the eighty or so years we live on this earth there can be anything that we can do to merit eternal benefit. This is the idea that drives the third type of worship. It is akin to the child who understands that nothing they do on this earth can ever be repayment for the time their mother carried them to term: our relationship with God is akin to this; but very much more intense.

The third type of worship may seem like a "why bother" type of worship. If there is nothing that we can do in our life to earn eternity, then why should we do anything?

On the one side of the equation are those who say that we are all doomed anyway (except maybe a few really special people). On the other side of the equation are those who say that we will all receive benefit from God, no matter what we do (except maybe a few really evil people).

There is, of course, a middle ground. This is the one where we accept the gift of peaceful eternity, as having its origin from the Creator of the universe. This is the place where God gives us eternity not based on what we do, or even on what we believe; but based on how we love. Now, do not misunderstand me; the proof of our love is displayed through not just what we do, but also what we believe. Belief and faith are the evidences of our love. Works of righteousness and thanksgiving to God through worship are evidences of our faith. The first hurdle, however, is love. This was neatly summed up by Jesus of Nazareth.

> *But when the Pharisees had heard that he had put the Sadducees to silence, they were gathered together. Then*

one of them, which was a lawyer, asked him a question, tempting him, and saying, Master, which is the great commandment in the law?

Jesus said unto him, Thou shalt love the Lord thy God with all thy heart, and with all thy soul, and with all thy mind. This is the first and great commandment. And the second is like unto it, Thou shalt love thy neighbour as thyself. On these two commandments hang all the law and the prophets.

(Matthew 22:34-40)

The apostle Paul, as they say, *brought it home*.

Though I speak with the tongues of men and of angels, and have not charity, I am become as sounding brass, or a tinkling cymbal. And though I have the gift of prophecy, and understand all mysteries, and all knowledge; and though I have all faith, so that I could remove mountains, and have not charity, I am nothing. And though I bestow all my goods to feed the poor, and though I give my body to be burned, and have not charity, it profiteth me nothing.

Charity suffereth long, and is kind; charity envieth not; charity vaunteth not itself, is not puffed up, Doth not behave itself unseemly, seeketh not her own, is not easily provoked, thinketh no evil; Rejoiceth not in iniquity, but rejoiceth in the truth; Beareth all things, believeth all things, hopeth all things, endureth all things.

Charity never faileth: but whether there be prophecies, they shall fail; whether there be tongues, they shall cease; whether there be knowledge, it shall vanish away.

(1 Corinthians 13:1-8)

And now abideth faith, hope, charity, these three; but the greatest of these is charity.

(1 Corinthians 13:13)

Jesus, the Son of God, a great scholar and lover of mankind, told us how this *love* thing works.

> *If ye love me, keep my commandments. And I will pray the Father, and he shall give you another Comforter, that he may abide with you for ever; Even the Spirit of truth; whom the world cannot receive, because it seeth him not, neither knoweth him: but ye know him; for he dwelleth with you, and shall be in you.*
>
> (John 14:15-17)

Please note that the above quote is not a bi-directional one. In other words, we do not prove our love just because we keep the commandments. The keeping of the commandments can be done either out of greed or fear, as well as love. Love, as humans generally express it, is based on fear, giving and reciprocity. We fear the loss of this love, unless we give things unto someone or something, for which we expect reciprocal acts from those to whom we give. This is not the love that God requires.

> *And we have known and believed the love that God hath to us. God is love; and he that dwelleth in love dwelleth in God, and God in him. Herein is our love made perfect, that we may have boldness in the day of judgment: because as he is, so are we in this world. There is no fear in love; but perfect love casteth out fear: because fear hath torment. He that feareth is not made perfect in love.*
>
> *We love him, because he first loved us.*
>
> (1 John 4:16-19)

True love flows in only one direction. First it exists, and then as a result of its existence we do those things that are for the benefit of another, such as keeping commandments. It has been said that, love is giving to the needs of another without expecting anything in return. This is how we must approach God. This type of love is true, and it is the start of worship.

> *But without faith it is impossible to please him: for he that cometh to God must believe that he is, and that he is a rewarder of them that diligently seek him.*
>
> (Hebrews 11:6)

Our desire is to please Him,
This is certainly true;
But sometimes we just
Don't know what to do.

So many choices;
Which one is right?
Which one is truly
The path to the light?

We know that God
Has a plan and a Way
To keep mankind
From going astray;

But we hear this,
And we're told that,
Till the words just
Begin to all fall flat.

No sonorous tones
Fall upon our ear,
To tell us of God
And truth most dear.

So we search and search
Throughout our land:
There must be truth here
On which we can stand.

There must be someone
Who has a full plan
For the unity of nations,
For peace among man.

Then just when we cry
That we'll never find love,
A voice persuades us
To look above;

To focus our minds
To hear God's command,

*As His love proclaims,
"Before you were, I AM".*

*So into His grace
We, our whole self, dip;
Acknowledging love as
The start of worship.*

Chapter 1a

Why Bother?

God stands in the void, alone. He wills that certain things come into existence. Why does He bother?

Because He is Pure Creativity, and that is what Creativity does; it calls things into being.

Among the first of the products of His will, are the Heavenly beings. These are beings whose sole job is to serve God. In Christianity and Judaism--the religions I know a little something about--and in some others, we call them angels. These are beings that are specialists. Some are good at delivering messages, some are good at war, some are good at nation building, and some are good at construction; while others are very good at destruction. For the most part they do not cross the lines of their specialty.

How much more breathtaking would it be if God could have beings that would cross the lines? What about beings that would do so in totally non-angelic patterns? How about also giving them a little of the knowledge of God. Let us say, God allows them to obtain the knowledge of good and evil. Maybe, even, God would allow them to obtain a measure of divinity.

> *And the LORD God said, Behold, the man is become as one of us, to know good and evil: and now, lest he put forth his hand, and take also of the tree of life, and eat, and live for ever:*
>
> (Genesis 3:22)

Surely, such a being, a being with attitude, would show forth the confidence and majesty of God. Surely, this would be one of the best ways to teach the universe how to tolerate differences. I can visualize the celestial byline:

"God takes another step toward universal unity. He creates a being different from Himself. He creates a being that is allowed to behave contrary to Him. He creates a being with attitude. He calls it Adam (mankind). He creates a place for Adam, and even gives the first assignment. Stay tuned, O universe, to this station! There is much more to come!"

Hold on there! Is God going to just shoot this being out into existence and do nothing after that?

Not so. When this Adam performs the functions that are assigned to it, God will continue to bless him with the fruit of the earth; as He stated when he created him.

> *And God said, Behold, I have given you every herb bearing seed, which is upon the face of all the earth, and every tree, in the which is the fruit of a tree yielding seed; to you it shall be for meat. And to every beast of the earth, and to every fowl of the air, and to every thing that creepeth upon the earth, wherein there is life, I have given every green herb for meat: and it was so.*
>
> (Genesis 1:29-30)

We heard that God assigned Adam a task to do, but what is it?

Well it would not be, to destroy itself and the other physical creations made for its benefit; would it?

No, it is not.

Is Adam supposed to be greedy and want for more than he needs? No!

The task God gave to Adam is **not** to conquer all, for Him: God already owns all that is, and He has no need for a conqueror. The task is this:

> *And God blessed them, and God said unto them, Be fruitful, and multiply, and replenish the earth, and subdue it: and have dominion over the fish of the sea, and over the fowl of the air, and over every living thing that moveth upon the earth.*
>
> (Genesis 1:28)

Before we can continue with this discussion, we will have to wait one more minute; or in our case, an unknown amount of time. You see,

God decided to do a little *resting* after that *tough* job of willing things into existence.

> *Thus the heavens and the earth were finished, and all the host of them. And on the seventh day God ended his work which he had made; and he rested on the seventh day from all his work which he had made. And God blessed the seventh day, and sanctified it: because that in it he had rested from all his work which God created and made.*

(Genesis 2:1-3)

Ah, now that He has given us an audience again, let us continue with our quest.

So what does God want from this being? What concession is God willing to make to get something from this being? It is well known that Adam expects God to do things for him: this is the nature of Adam.

God has already *proved* Himself by the Creative process. God has shown that He loves Adam. God has created a being that can give Him nothing, but that He has given everything that it has. At this point we will once again introduce the definition of love that says, "Giving unto the need of another without expecting anything in return". By this definition God has surely loved.

There is another statement that was made about man, and all his kind.

> *We love him, because he first loved us. If a man say, I love God, and hateth his brother, he is a liar: for he that loveth not his brother whom he hath seen, how can he love God whom he hath not seen? And this commandment have we from him, That he who loveth God love his brother also.*

(1 John 4:19-21)

Well it seems reasonable to say that it is time for man to step up to the plate, as they say in baseball, and see if he can hit a love homerun out of the park. This is something that mankind must do, so that it can run away from hatred and complacency. The specific way that mankind can accomplish this is clarified by Jesus, the Son of God.

> *And, behold, one came and said unto him, Good Master, what good thing shall I do, that I may have eternal life?*

And he said unto him, Why callest thou me good? there is none good but one, that is, God: but if thou wilt enter into life, keep the commandments.

He saith unto him, Which?

Jesus said, Thou shalt do no murder, Thou shalt not commit adultery, Thou shalt not steal, Thou shalt not bear false witness, Honour thy father and thy mother: and, Thou shalt love thy neighbour as thyself.

(Matthew 19:16-19)

But when the Pharisees had heard that he had put the Sadducees to silence, they were gathered together. Then one of them, which was a lawyer, asked him a question, tempting him, and saying, Master, which is the great commandment in the law?

Jesus said unto him, Thou shalt love the Lord thy God with all thy heart, and with all thy soul, and with all thy mind. This is the first and great commandment. And the second is like unto it, Thou shalt love thy neighbour as thyself. On these two commandments hang all the law and the prophets.

(Matthew 22:34-40)

This seems simple enough, especially since all mankind came from Adam and are the children of Adam (who is the son of God, small *s*). It seems reasonable to ask fathers and mothers to love their children: it seems beyond reasonable; it would seem to be a natural response from even the basest of creatures. Such a thing as, love, should be automatic for mankind.

Every other boy and girl of mankind will be, as a result of the fulfillment of God's gift to man to be fruitful and multiply. Thus, everyone will be Adam's neighbor, and by expansion everyone will be everyone else's neighbor. It really does not matter if our children move around the world, and start a new family there; they are still our children and our neighbors. Thus, the request from God is further summarized as "love everyone as you love yourself". In this way the love of God will be expanded throughout the earth, and even the angels in Heaven will be impressed with this new creation.

To broaden the scope of love in the universe; this is the destiny of mankind. To manifest the expansive glory of God; this is the reason for the creation of mankind. To unfold the matchless power of the Almighty; this is the lesson to be learned from mankind. And all this was, and still is, done with the Purest of Tolerance, by the Almighty. This is why God bothered to make man.

The Word from the Bible

Genesis 4:25-26

And Adam knew his wife again; and she bare a son, and called his name Seth: For God, said she, hath appointed me another seed instead of Abel, whom Cain slew.

And to Seth, to him also there was born a son; and he called his name Enos: then began men to call upon the name of the LORD.

Genesis 5:19-24

And Jared lived after he begat Enoch eight hundred years, and begat sons and daughters: And all the days of Jared were nine hundred sixty and two years: and he died.

And Enoch lived sixty and five years, and begat Methuselah: And Enoch walked with God after he begat Methuselah three hundred years, and begat sons and daughters: And all the days of Enoch were three hundred sixty and five years: And Enoch walked with God: and he was not; for God took him.

Genesis 5:28-32

And Lamech lived an hundred eighty and two years, and begat a son: And he called his name Noah, saying, This same shall comfort us concerning our work and toil of our hands, because of the ground which the LORD hath cursed. And Lamech lived after he begat Noah five hundred ninety and five years, and begat sons and daughters: And all the days of Lamech were seven hundred seventy and seven years: and he died.

And Noah was five hundred years old: and Noah begat Shem, Ham, and Japheth.

Genesis 6:1-3

And it came to pass, when men began to multiply on the face of the earth, and daughters were born unto them, That the sons of God saw the daughters of men that they were fair; and they took them wives of all which they chose.

And the LORD said, My spirit shall not always strive with man, for that he also is flesh: yet his days shall be an hundred and twenty years.

Genesis 6:5-8

And God saw that the wickedness of man was great in the earth, and that every imagination of the thoughts of his heart was only evil continually. And it repented the LORD that he had made man on the earth, and it grieved him at his heart. And the LORD said, I will destroy man whom I have created from the face of the earth; both man, and beast, and the creeping thing, and the fowls of the air; for it repenteth me that I have made them. But Noah found grace in the eyes of the LORD.

Chapter Two

Recognition of God

We, as humans, were built to go beyond ourselves. This does not mean that we are to do things that are impossible for us to do. It does mean that we are to seek the One who can do for us what seems impossible. This is the condition of recognizing that God exists.

> *But without faith it is impossible to please him: for he that cometh to God must believe that he is, ...*
>
> (Hebrews 11:6a)

This recognition is sometimes done in order to get something; namely, from God the continuation of His stream of benefits. Most times, however, it is done to garner some sort of advantage in life from Him. The Scripture supports this desire.

> *... and that he is a rewarder of them that diligently seek him.*
>
> (Hebrews 11:6b)

Wherefore it is both natural and healthy to give recognition to God through prayer and worship. This is one of the major benefits of the Sabbath. The celebration of the Sabbath is done on a certain fixed day of the week; or for certain special occasions. It is the time when many religions recognize God, as a congregation. On this day, and others like it, the collective mind comes forth to give collective recognition to God. It is a day most holy. Often work is stopped. Definitely it is a day when minds focus on God, sometimes exclusively. This is sometimes done for the entire day, and at other times for only a special ceremonial part or parts of the day. But what happens with the remainder of the day, and days?

The answer to this question depends on at least three factors. The first is our personal relationship with God. The second is the relationship of our fellow worshippers with God. Please note that the term *worship* must be thought of in its general sense. In the general sense, we consider it to be the actions of anyone who expresses any kind of similar relationship to God as ours. The relationship is not necessarily a true one or a false one. We are actively attempting to follow two passages of Scripture.

> *Another parable put he forth unto them, saying, The kingdom of heaven is likened unto a man which sowed good seed in his field: But while men slept, his enemy came and sowed tares among the wheat, and went his way. But when the blade was sprung up, and brought forth fruit, then appeared the tares also.*
>
> *So the servants of the householder came and said unto him, Sir, didst not thou sow good seed in thy field? from whence then hath it tares?*
>
> *He said unto them, An enemy hath done this.*
>
> *The servants said unto him, Wilt thou then that we go and gather them up?*
>
> *But he said, Nay; lest while ye gather up the tares, ye root up also the wheat with them. Let both grow together until the harvest: and in the time of harvest I will say to the reapers, Gather ye together first the tares, and bind them in bundles to burn them: but gather the wheat into my barn.*
>
> (Matthew 13:24-30)
>
> *Judge not, and ye shall not be judged: condemn not, and ye shall not be condemned: forgive, and ye shall be forgiven: Give, and it shall be given unto you; good measure, pressed down, and shaken together, and running over, shall men give into your bosom. For with the same measure that ye mete withal it shall be measured to you again.*
>
> (Luke 6:37-38)

The third factor, and by far the largest one in terms of mass, is the remainder of the universe. These intrusions can be anything; from thoughts about the color of our shoes, to the color of the third jewel in the walls of the Heavenly kingdom. Typically these are of such a nature that they are intrusive. We mean by this, that we do not have to actively ponder them; they will interrupt what we are doing and introduce themselves. This is not limited to things, but may include *irritating* or *difficult* people.

All of these factors work together within and around us to affect our recognition of God. However, it is not as individualized as it seems: there are patterns of recognition. By studying the actions of early man, we can see several of these patterns. We have searched the Scripture, and found five patterns to share with you.

+=+=+=+=+=+=+=+=+=+=+=+=+=+=+=+=+=+=+=+

Genesis 4:25-26

> *And Adam knew his wife again; and she bare a son, and called his name Seth: For God, said she, hath appointed me another seed instead of Abel, whom Cain slew. And to Seth, to him also there was born a son; and he called his name Enos: then began men to call upon the name of the LORD.*

The simplest form of recognition of God is simply to call upon His name. This, of course, seems to be something that is very noble, but let us think this through a bit. The text does not say that they worshipped the name of the LORD, but that they called upon Him. This is the first kind of service that is given to God. Once an individual is convicted that they need God, they start to call upon Him for deliverance. This is a blessed thing for some, and a pitfall for others.

The blessing is in the fact that the name of God is being invoked. If this is done long and hard enough, a habit can be formed. As we call upon His name, we begin to place ourselves in His presence. We have the opportunity while there to listen for His voice. We can avail ourselves of His counsel. We can learn the mysteries of life that will allow us to excel in any environment. We can, by little and little, take on parts of the nature of God. This we can do as we start to imitate God. The highest of these imitations of God, is that we love one another.

> *There is no fear in love; but perfect love casteth out fear: because fear hath torment. He that feareth is not made perfect in love. We love him, because he first loved us. If a man say, I love God, and hateth his brother, he is a liar: for he that loveth not his brother whom he hath seen, how can*

> *he love God whom he hath not seen? And this commandment have we from him, That he who loveth God love his brother also.*

(1 John 4:18-21)

We have an excellent opportunity not just to please God, but also to establish a solid relationship with the LORD. Our objective must be to call upon the LORD for understanding. Solomon behaved like this: he asked the LORD for a little, and God gave him even more.

> *And Solomon said, Thou hast showed unto thy servant David my father great mercy, according as he walked before thee in truth, and in righteousness, and in uprightness of heart with thee; and thou hast kept for him this great kindness, that thou hast given him a son to sit on his throne, as it is this day. And now, O LORD my God, thou hast made thy servant king instead of David my father: and I am but a little child: I know not how to go out or come in. And thy servant is in the midst of thy people which thou hast chosen, a great people, that cannot be numbered nor counted for multitude. Give therefore thy servant an understanding heart to judge thy people, that I may discern between good and bad: for who is able to judge this thy so great a people?*
>
> *And the speech pleased the Lord, that Solomon had asked this thing.*
>
> *And God said unto him, Because thou hast asked this thing, and hast not asked for thyself long life; neither hast asked riches for thyself, nor hast asked the life of thine enemies; but hast asked for thyself understanding to discern judgment; Behold, I have done according to thy words: lo, I have given thee a wise and an understanding heart; so that there was none like thee before thee, neither after thee shall any arise like unto thee. And I have also given thee that which thou hast not asked, both riches, and honour: so that there shall not be any among the kings like unto thee all thy days.*

(1 Kings 3:6-13)

We must call upon the name of the LORD for both wisdom and understanding: these are the things of the Kingdom of God. Jesus of Nazareth spoke of how we should seek after the things of God.

> *Therefore take no thought, saying, What shall we eat? or, What shall we drink? or, Wherewithal shall we be clothed? (For after all these things do the Gentiles seek:) for your heavenly Father knoweth that ye have need of all these things. But seek ye first the kingdom of God, and his righteousness; and all these things shall be added unto you. Take therefore no thought for the morrow: for the morrow shall take thought for the things of itself. Sufficient unto the day is the evil thereof.*

(Matthew 6:31-34)

However, if the habit of calling on Him is formed without wisdom and understanding, then the pit starts to open. This is what is happening in many of our assemblies, today. We have multitudes of people calling upon the name of the LORD; however, they are doing so amiss. There are those ones calling on the name of the LORD for material possessions. There are those ones calling on the name of the LORD to take their side in disputes. There are those ones even calling on the name of the LORD for extinction of other nations and cultures. These are part of calling on His name, but these will not be honored by Him without wisdom: indeed some of them will not be honored at all.

Asking for possessions:

> *And when thou prayest, thou shalt not be as the hypocrites are: for they love to pray standing in the synagogues and in the corners of the streets, that they may be seen of men. Verily I say unto you, They have their reward. But thou, when thou prayest, enter into thy closet, and when thou hast shut thy door, pray to thy Father which is in secret; and thy Father which seeth in secret shall reward thee openly. But when ye pray, use not vain repetitions, as the heathen do: for they think that they shall be heard for their much speaking. Be not ye therefore like unto them: for your Father knoweth what things ye have need of, before ye ask him.*

(Matthew 6:5-8)

Most definitely we should ask God for what we need, and even for what we want; but this must be done with wisdom. God is not, nor has he issued, a magic lantern to anyone, which can be rubbed to get things. God is not in the "quid pro quo", "you scratch my back and I'll scratch yours," business. God is in the soul building business. This may mean few possessions; this may mean many possessions. The selection of the level of possessions is up to God. So, yes, ask God for the world, but be willing to accept a place to sleep, if this is all that He knows you need. What you receive is designed to keep you calling upon the name of the LORD; from now until, well, forever.

Seeking dispute resolution:

> *But be not ye called Rabbi: for one is your Master, even Christ; and all ye are brethren. And call no man your father upon the earth: for one is your Father, which is in heaven. Neither be ye called masters: for one is your Master, even Christ. But he that is greatest among you shall be your servant. And whosoever shall exalt himself shall be abased; and he that shall humble himself shall be exalted.*
>
> (Matthew 23:8-12)

It would be a very unusual person who asked for a dispute to be resolved in favor of their adversary. Typically, we are requesting of God that He resolve the dispute in our favor by taking away possession or benefit from another. This "you show them" attitude is not consistent with calling upon the name of the LORD in knowledge.

Moses, the prophets, the apostles, and all other servants of God and of the Lord Jesus Christ, are just that, servants. Even Jesus of Nazareth did not come to earth to be served. Instead he came to provide service to man, and he demonstrated the importance of giving, as opposed to receiving, service when he washed the feet of the disciples. The one that is in a position of leadership must serve those whom they are leading.

> *Jesus knowing that the Father had given all things into his hands, and that he was come from God, and went to God; He riseth from supper, and laid aside his garments; and took a towel, and girded himself. After that he poureth water into a bason, and began to wash the disciples' feet, and to wipe them with the towel wherewith he was girded.*
>
> *Then cometh he to Simon Peter: and Peter saith unto him, Lord, dost thou wash my feet?*

Jesus answered and said unto him, What I do thou knowest not now; but thou shalt know hereafter.

Peter saith unto him, Thou shalt never wash my feet.

Jesus answered him, If I wash thee not, thou hast no part with me.

Simon Peter saith unto him, Lord, not my feet only, but also my hands and my head.

Jesus saith to him, He that is washed needeth not save to wash his feet, but is clean every whit: and ye are clean, but not all. For he knew who should betray him; therefore said he, Ye are not all clean.

So after he had washed their feet, and had taken his garments, and was set down again, he said unto them, Know ye what I have done to you? Ye call me Master and Lord: and ye say well; for so I am. If I then, your Lord and Master, have washed your feet; ye also ought to wash one another's feet. For I have given you an example, that ye should do as I have done to you. Verily, verily, I say unto you, The servant is not greater than his lord; neither he that is sent greater than he that sent him.

(John 13:3-16)

Disposition of nations:

O thou king, the most high God gave Nebuchadnezzar thy father a kingdom, and majesty, and glory, and honour: And for the majesty that he gave him, all people, nations, and languages, trembled and feared before him: whom he would he slew; and whom he would he kept alive; and whom he would he set up; and whom he would he put down. But when his heart was lifted up, and his mind hardened in pride, he was deposed from his kingly throne, and they took his glory from him: And he was driven from the sons of men; and his heart was made like the beasts, and his dwelling was with the wild asses: they fed him with grass like oxen, and his body was wet with the dew of heaven; till he knew that the most high God ruled in the kingdom of men, and that he appointeth over it whomsoever he will.

(Daniel 5:18-21)

I am very, very glad that God does not burden His elect with the knowledge of the contents of anyone else's prayers; except where that affects their mission. If He did so burden them, they might be overwhelmed by the intensity of anger. I can imagine that in some nations, and among the people of God in those nations, there could be as much as ninety percent of the population calling on the name of the LORD in prayer for the destruction of someone or something.

There is, as of this writing, a nation that has publicly called for the extinction of another nation: you know who you are. I pray to God that by the time of the publication of this writing that this public statement has been retracted. This is not what God wants us to spend our time in prayer over. Our prayers must be that God will enable us, not that He will disable anyone else.

> *And why beholdest thou the mote that is in thy brother's eye, but perceivest not the beam that is in thine own eye? Either how canst thou say to thy brother, Brother, let me pull out the mote that is in thine eye, when thou thyself beholdest not the beam that is in thine own eye? Thou hypocrite, cast out first the beam out of thine own eye, and then shalt thou see clearly to pull out the mote that is in thy brother's eye.*
>
> (Luke 6:41-42)

+=+=+=+=+=+=+=+=+=+=+=+=+=+=+=+=+=+=+=+

Genesis 5:19-24

> *And Jared lived after he begat Enoch eight hundred years, and begat sons and daughters: And all the days of Jared were nine hundred sixty and two years: and he died.*
>
> *And Enoch lived sixty and five years, and begat Methuselah: And Enoch walked with God after he begat Methuselah three hundred years, and begat sons and daughters: And all the days of Enoch were three hundred sixty and five years: And Enoch walked with God: and he was not; for God took him.*

This is a most unique type of personality. Enoch's recognition of God was on a personal level, both ways. Enoch did not only enter a closet and pray; he did so everywhere. Enoch's devotion is a powerful recognition of God, and by God; one that would not be seen again until the time of Moses. Even Abraham did not have so conversational a relationship with God. Truly, Abraham believed strongly in the things of God, and his faith was counted to him as righteousness. He was a true servant of God and was selected by God to bless the earth. We are not talking about levels of power, for such is irrelevant to the true servant of God; we are, instead, talking about a form of communion.

From the small amount of writing that is done about Enoch, we come to understand that Enoch viewed God as a friend. This is why we said that his recognition was like the one that Moses grew into. Enoch does not seem to be one who just asked God for things. Nor does he seem to have just asked God to do things. In fact, the image that we have of him is that he really did not ask God for anything.

The conversation between God and Enoch just started, and it must have gotten very interesting. We say this because as we read the account of his time with God, we receive an image of Enoch and God walking in the same spatial reality. As God walks, He continues on from the earth to Heaven, still in conversation with Enoch. Enoch did not pursue entry into Heaven; he was wrapped in the conversation with God. God undoubtedly knew that Enoch was with Him as he entered Heaven. This must have been God's gift to Enoch, for the astounding recognition given by Enoch to Him. This would be a gift that no man would ever want to give back. So Enoch stayed there and *he was not; for God took him.*

This is the same sort of gift that has been given to the world through Christ. When a person becomes a part of Christ through belief in his works and in his mission on the earth, he receives the gift of uninterrupted life. As Enoch was wrapped in the conversation with God, so, too, there are now others who are wrapped in the body of the Son of God.

> *These words spake Jesus, and lifted up his eyes to heaven, and said, Father, the hour is come; glorify thy Son, that thy Son also may glorify thee: As thou hast given him power over all flesh, that he should give eternal life to as many as thou hast given him. And this is life eternal, that they might know thee the only true God, and Jesus Christ, whom thou hast sent.*

(John 17:1-3)

As time goes on, God will continue to commune with the body of the Son of God. The body of the Son of God, the church, will continue on into Heaven, and God will carry, with Him, to His Son, those who are wrapped in His Son. For the ones among us that believe in Christ and have not yet tasted death, there are two ways that we will be joined with the Lord Jesus Christ in paradise.

> *Therefore we are always confident, knowing that, whilst we are at home in the body, we are absent from the Lord: (For we walk by faith, not by sight:) We are confident, I say, and willing rather to be absent from the body, and to be present with the Lord. Wherefore we labour, that, whether present or absent, we may be accepted of him.*

(2 Corinthians 5:6-9)

> *Immediately after the tribulation of those days shall the sun be darkened, and the moon shall not give her light, and the stars shall fall from heaven, and the powers of the heavens shall be shaken: And then shall appear the sign of the Son of man in heaven: and then shall all the tribes of the earth mourn, and they shall see the Son of man coming in the clouds of heaven with power and great glory.*

(Matthew 24:29-30)

This is the message of Enoch, for the age of Christ. Wherefore as Enoch was wrapped in the conversation of recognition of God; so ye, too, must be wrapped in the body of the Son of God. In this way it will be said of each of you, who believe: that *he was not; for God took him.*

+=+=+=+=+=+=+=+=+=+=+=+=+=+=+=+=+=+=+=+

Genesis 5:28-32

> *And Lamech lived an hundred eighty and two years, and begat a son: And he called his name Noah, saying, This same shall comfort us concerning our work and toil of our hands, because of the ground which the LORD hath cursed. And Lamech lived after he begat Noah five hundred ninety and five years, and begat sons and daughters: And all the days of Lamech were seven hundred seventy and seven years: and he died. And Noah was five hundred years old: and Noah begat Shem, Ham, and Japheth.*

We have seen the way of the perfect recognition of God, in Enoch; there are other ways. What of the average man of God? We are not referring here to average in the sense of level of service, but in the sense of that which all men, who truly recognize God, will give to God. This man is a simple family man. Prior to his call by God, there is no indication that he had shaken the world. Up to the time of the call of God, the life that he is living appears to have been a simple life. The most spectacular thing that is reported of him is that he married and had children. However, this family man recognized God as the source. In this, he is an example for all of us, whether married or unmarried. That he was married only sets the stage for our understanding of another form of recognition of God. This is the man, Noah.

This man recognized God as the provider and sustainer of his existence, and subsistence. Apply the following thoughts to anything you have that is of God: Noah did not then consider the grace that he had received from God, as a mere possession to be used by him. Rather, he considered it to be another means of recognition of God, through service to God. That which he received from God, he recognized as unrestrictedly for the service of God. Indeed, because of his standing with God, he could have proclaimed his gift from God as being a good tool for making his life easy; but he did not do that.

He is the type of man who allows God to take the gifts that He has given to him, and sanctify them for the work in His service. Meanwhile, while moving to the time when God brings that gift into His service, the family man will obtain benefit from the gift, too: God is not stingy. But when the gift is called into service, he will willingly release not just the gift, but also whatever other thing God requires. And the gift will surely bring honor to itself, and thus to he who rightly handled the gift, in righteous recognition of God.

> *And Noah did according unto all that the LORD commanded him. And Noah was six hundred years old when the flood of waters was upon the earth. And Noah went in, and his sons, and his wife, and his sons' wives with him, into the ark, because of the waters of the flood. Of clean beasts, and of beasts that are not clean, and of fowls, and of every thing that creepeth upon the earth, There went*

> *in two and two unto Noah into the ark, the male and the female, as God had commanded Noah.*
>
> (Genesis 7:5-9)

+=+=+=+=+=+=+=+=+=+=+=+=+=+=+=+=+=+=+=+

Genesis 6:1-3

> *And it came to pass, when men began to multiply on the face of the earth, and daughters were born unto them, That the sons of God saw the daughters of men that they were fair; and they took them wives of all which they chose.*
>
> *And the LORD said, My spirit shall not always strive with man, for that he also is flesh: yet his days shall be an hundred and twenty years.*

The perfect and the average recognition are both accepted by God. What, therefore, of the sub-standard recognition? In a perfect world it would not be necessary to write this. But, in the perfect world, mankind will not be as we know him now. In our current world, the sub-standard recognition of God seems to be the large majority of the public face of recognition. After all, we have *evolved* to the point where we want what we want, and we want to do only what is pleasing to us.

These are not just the people who say that they reject God. These are the people who are known for their recognition of God; up to a point. Outwardly they take upon themselves the title, *children of God*. Inwardly, however, they have captured neither the wisdom nor the understanding of God.

> *This know also, that in the last days perilous times shall come. For men shall be lovers of their own selves, covetous, boasters, proud, blasphemers, disobedient to parents, unthankful, unholy, Without natural affection, trucebreakers, false accusers, incontinent, fierce, despisers of those that are good, Traitors, heady, highminded, lovers of pleasures more than lovers of God; Having a form of godliness, but denying the power thereof: from such turn away.*
>
> (2 Timothy 3:1-5)

They perform their deeds thinking themselves to be *entitled*. This thought of entitlement is what causes them to seek after their own, and not after God. They do not take their possessions, and in recognition of God, turn them over to Him for His blessing. Indeed they cannot, for their acquisition of them has been in violation of God.

Looking at the case in Genesis 6:1-3; it is not the name of the action that is at fault, but the manner of its performance. Marriage is fine; indiscriminate and parasitic marriage is not. By their position in the world and by their calling upon the name of the LORD, they had received certain insights and directions. They then used these insights to exalt themselves over others. Some of the others were probably children. Many of the others may have been beyond the offender's capacity to rightly serve. Yes, husband, you are required by God to serve your wife; and that service must go well beyond sex. In fact, for one to place sexual *service* as he primary service is equivalent to providing no service, in the sight of the virtuous woman of God.

Those in Genesis 6:1-3 are the prototypes of our *me* generation. It is from such people as these that we receive our examples of unbridled consumption. These are the type that show us the way to the *prosperity gospel*, so called. These are the methods of ones that use the recognition of God as a tool. These are they that recognize God as an employer, and not as LORD. The employer promises wages; the LORD gives according to His knowledge of need and worthiness.

Of course, there is nothing wrong with looking to God for blessings.

> *Bring ye all the tithes into the storehouse, that there may be meat in mine house, and prove me now herewith, saith the LORD of hosts, if I will not open you the windows of heaven, and pour you out a blessing, that there shall not be room enough to receive it. And I will rebuke the devourer for your sakes, and he shall not destroy the fruits of your ground; neither shall your vine cast her fruit before the time in the field, saith the LORD of hosts. And all nations shall call you blessed: for ye shall be a delightsome land, saith the LORD of hosts.*

(Malachi 3:10-12)

But blessings do not equal material things. Blessings can be material things: a place to stay bigger and better than we expected, for instance. But blessings can also be internal human conditionings: such things as, a peace of mind that passes understanding, and knowledge beyond our years. Blessings can be many things; but blessings are not wages.

Furthermore, blessings that are requested because of stated, illusory and manipulative recognition of God will not be given by God. Blessings are not defined by the receiver, but by the giver, God. It is not true recognition of God when we say, "I'll give you this, if you give me that." It is also not true recognition of God when we say, "I'll give you this, so that you will give me that." Again I state: blessings are not prescribed by the receiver but by the giver; especially when the giver is God.

The end result of the misuse of our petition for blessing, on the first level, is a shortening of our assignment from the giver.

> *And the LORD said, My spirit shall not always strive with man, for that he also is flesh: yet his days shall be an hundred and twenty years.*
>
> (Genesis 6:3)

The final result of such continued behavior is far more destructive for us and for our possessions and charges. We will see this in a moment.

+=+=+=+=+=+=+=+=+=+=+=+=+=+=+=+=+=+=+=+

Genesis 6:5-8

> *And God saw that the wickedness of man was great in the earth, and that every imagination of the thoughts of his heart was only evil continually. And it repented the LORD that he had made man on the earth, and it grieved him at his heart. And the LORD said, I will destroy man whom I have created from the face of the earth; both man, and beast, and the creeping thing, and the fowls of the air; for it repenteth me that I have made them. But Noah found grace in the eyes of the LORD.*

The final lesson, during this period of man, in recognition of God by man, is given in the service of the excellent man of God. This man is Noah, beyond his activities as a family man. The result of his recognition of God was that he received from God a very high honor:

he received the grace of God. This is the level that must be sought by any, and every, one called to be in active service for God.

There are quite a few things remarkable about Noah's post-call life; we will only cover a few here. First is the intensity of his devotion to God. Noah was a member of a family, and had family pressures as many of us do also. He was a member of the community, and was subject to the pull and sway of both society and its norms. However, in the midst of the conformance to the world's approach to existence, and in spite of the corruption that was going on around him, he remained true to his recognition of God.

As a result of this true recognition of God, Noah was given an assignment by God.

> *And God said unto Noah, The end of all flesh is come before me; for the earth is filled with violence through them; and, behold, I will destroy them with the earth. Make thee an ark of gopher wood; rooms shalt thou make in the ark, and shalt pitch it within and without with pitch. And this is the fashion which thou shalt make it of: The length of the ark shall be three hundred cubits, the breadth of it fifty cubits, and the height of it thirty cubits. A window shalt thou make to the ark, and in a cubit shalt thou finish it above; and the door of the ark shalt thou set in the side thereof; with lower, second, and third stories shalt thou make it.*

(Genesis 6:13-16)

Noah is also an example of one, who did not wait to obtain credentials or certification before yielding to God. There is no mention of whether Noah actually knew how to build a boat, but we know that he did not say to God, "Wait a decade or so while I study the matter." He immediately set out on the course requested. Besides he had the best credentials available, "God said do it"; and the best certification ever bestowed, "God selected him."

> *Not that we are sufficient of ourselves to think any thing as of ourselves; but our sufficiency is of God;*

(2 Corinthians 3:5)

Noah was also a man of great individual initiative. There is no indication from the writing that he had any help in his task. We know that the community <u>did not</u> take up a fund to support him; nor did it give him any other type of support, physical or moral. There is a strong indication in the Scripture that this was not Noah's only project in life: he still had to raise a family, and a community to hold at bay. Building this boat was not a *money-making venture for Noah; therefore, he still had to obtain sustenance for himself and his family.* He also had to obtain the materials for the project; a boat, a very big boat. Furthermore, building the boat was not his life's mission: that was to come later.

Noah did not even pull the "loneliness card." Considering what he was preparing for, and the final group he would have left, we see that Noah would have no friends--other than the most important one, God. His family would have no next door neighbors. There would be no more rallies to attend; no more community meetings. For Noah, his small family would soon be the community; indeed, it would soon be the entire world of humans.

Within himself and in his recognition of God, Noah had to drive his family through periods of absolute separation. Of course this requires the mighty hand of God on a person (note that Scripture does not indicate that Noah demanded the presence of God, in his midst). Might it be that Noah's recognition of God was such a powerful force that it is the equivalent of the powerful presence of God in ones midst? Might it be that the gift which God gave Noah because of his recognition of Him was so potent that it absorbed his family into it? I think so!

Noah is the kind of person that we all can be; because he is who we all are. Especially, the ones that think that certain matters pass through the human genome should take note. The same genes that made Noah are within the human race today. Yes, they may have been filtered in the individual; but, as a community, we will find that they exist in our midst in an unfiltered fashion. These same motivations that pushed Noah to greatness are a part of us, individually; if we choose to allow God to access them. They are also a part of our communities, corporately; if we allow God to work in the midst of our families and neighborhoods. This is how the message of God must be dispersed among the nations of man.

> *But ye shall receive power, after that the Holy Ghost is come upon you: and ye shall be witnesses unto me both in*

Jerusalem, and in all Judaea, and in Samaria, and unto the uttermost part of the earth.

(Acts 1:8)

+=+

This is the least that the man of God should strive to be: moving through life with the mindset of Noah. You might think of striving for the relationship that Enoch had with God, and this would be good, too. However, in the world as it is structured today, it is very difficult for anyone to be totally oblivious of their surroundings. This was the advantage that Enoch had; he could remove himself from all other cares of the world, even his family, and pursue a relationship with God. However, Noah's time was more like our current time. When God looks at our world now, He indeed sees in each one of us, that *"every imagination of the thoughts of his heart was only evil continually"*. This is the dubious benefit of having advertising.

Therefore, since we are in a world such as Noah had, we call upon the name of the LORD as Noah did. This is the image that we can project as we recognize God. This is the example that we can incorporate into our prayer life, today. This goal for our lives is to be honored, as Noah was, and as stated by God.

> *And God spake unto Noah, and to his sons with him, saying, And I, behold, I establish my covenant with you, and with your seed after you;*

(Genesis 9:8-9)

Furthermore, let us accept as our life's mission that which was given to Noah. Even though we are not called upon to do this for THE world, we can do it for OUR world. Replenish, can not be limited to children; it must encompass everything we touch that promotes the recognition of God.

> *And God blessed Noah and his sons, and said unto them, Be fruitful, and multiply, and replenish the earth. And the fear of you and the dread of you shall be upon every beast of the earth, and upon every fowl of the air, upon all that moveth upon the earth, and upon all the fishes of the sea; into your hand are they delivered.*

(Genesis 9:1-2)

We say we want to be
A part of His plan
To bring out the best
That can come from man.

We say we call Him
Almost every day
To give us the Word,
To show us the Way.

But what is the content
Of the petitioning we do:
Is it seeking God
In a way that is true?

Or, do we only ask
For things we crave,
To elevate our status
Before we see the grave?

Is it about us,
Or is it about Him?
Is the light truly bright,
Or is it depressingly dim?

Let us study the word
To find our course,
To in Him dwell,
To dispel the remorse

That comes when we
Do not get what we ask,
And we wallow in anger,
And in depression bask.

God is Faithful and True
To give us what we need,
When to His way
We surely take heed;

When we recognize
That He is above all,

That held in His hand
We never can fall.

In faith, let us recognize God,
As righteousness doth demand;
In spirit and in truth,
As the Word doth command.

Chapter 2a

The Mechanics of Heaven

Heaven is a spiritual realm: earth is in the physical realm. To say this does not imply mutual exclusion, or isolation of one from the other. There are definitely spirits from Heaven that have visited the earth, according to the Bible. God visited here while creating it, and afterwards; and God is definitely Spirit.

> *But the hour cometh, and now is, when the true worshippers shall worship the Father in spirit and in truth: for the Father seeketh such to worship him. God is a Spirit: and they that worship him must worship him in spirit and in truth.*
>
> (John 4:23-24)

We have the record of Enoch's physical disappearance from the earth.

> *And Enoch lived sixty and five years, and begat Methuselah: And Enoch walked with God after he begat Methuselah three hundred years, and begat sons and daughters: And all the days of Enoch were three hundred sixty and five years: And Enoch walked with God: and he was not; for God took him.*
>
> (Genesis 5:21-24)

We must accept that he entered a different realm, which is not the one associated with the grave. This realm is the spiritual realm. Enoch is believed to have entered that most spiritual of places called Heaven. There are other examples of physical transferences in the pages of the Bible. The prophet Elijah is one of them.

> *And it came to pass, as they still went on, and talked, that, behold, there appeared a chariot of fire, and horses of fire,*

> *and parted them both asunder; and Elijah went up by a whirlwind into heaven. And Elisha saw it, and he cried, My father, my father, the chariot of Israel, and the horsemen thereof. And he saw him no more: and he took hold of his own clothes, and rent them in two pieces.*
>
> (2 Kings 2:11-12)

Men have also visited Heaven in another fashion; however, before introducing this, let us lay some groundwork. Man, though physical, also has a spirit. This was described in relation to Moses and Elijah.

> *And the LORD said unto Moses, Gather unto me seventy men of the elders of Israel, whom thou knowest to be the elders of the people, and officers over them; and bring them unto the tabernacle of the congregation, that they may stand there with thee. And I will come down and talk with thee there: and I will take of the spirit which is upon thee, and will put it upon them; and they shall bear the burden of the people with thee, that thou bear it not thyself alone.*
>
> (Numbers 11:16-17)

> *And it came to pass, when they were gone over, that Elijah said unto Elisha, Ask what I shall do for thee, before I be taken away from thee. And Elisha said, I pray thee, let a double portion of thy spirit be upon me. And he said, Thou hast asked a hard thing: nevertheless, if thou see me when I am taken from thee, it shall be so unto thee; but if not, it shall not be so.*
>
> (2 Kings 2:9-10)

The existence of man's spirit made it possible for the prophets to visit with God, on His level. This was done in the revelations that were given to several kings and prophets of the Bible. There are many examples to relate, but we will only mention one. The last book of the Bible, Revelation, is an account of an encounter with God, on this level.

> *I John, who also am your brother, and companion in tribulation, and in the kingdom and patience of Jesus Christ, was in the isle that is called Patmos, for the word of*

> *God, and for the testimony of Jesus Christ. I was in the Spirit on the Lord's day, and heard behind me a great voice, as of a trumpet, Saying, I am Alpha and Omega, the first and the last: and, What thou seest, write in a book, and send it unto the seven churches which are in Asia; unto Ephesus, and unto Smyrna, and unto Pergamos, and unto Thyatira, and unto Sardis, and unto Philadelphia, and unto Laodicea.*

(Revelation 1:9-11)

It is the spirit of man that is accessed by the spirits of Heaven and by the Holy Ghost, on behalf of the Spirit of God, to effect change in the soul of man. How does this work?

The Scripture teaches about several times when the spirits of men were stirred. The first king of Israel, Saul, had his spirit stirred even though he was in a foul mood and intent on doing mischief. This shows the power of the Spirit of God over the spirit of man: and over any other spirit.

> *So David fled, and escaped, and came to Samuel to Ramah, and told him all that Saul had done to him. And he and Samuel went and dwelt in Naioth.*
>
> *And it was told Saul, saying, Behold, David is at Naioth in Ramah. And Saul sent messengers to take David: and when they saw the company of the prophets prophesying, and Samuel standing as appointed over them, the spirit of God was upon the messengers of Saul, and they also prophesied. And when it was told Saul, he sent other messengers, and they prophesied likewise. And Saul sent messengers again the third time, and they prophesied also. Then went he also to Ramah, and came to a great well that is in Sechu: and he asked and said, Where are Samuel and David? And one said, Behold, they be at Naioth in Ramah. And he went thither to Naioth in Ramah: and the spirit of God was upon him also, and he went on, and prophesied, until he came to Naioth in Ramah. And he stripped off his clothes also, and prophesied before Samuel in like manner, and lay down naked all that day and all that night. Wherefore they say, Is Saul also among the prophets?*

(1 Samuel 19:18-24)

In such cases, we see how the stirring of the spirit of man triggered a change in the behavior of a person. This change in behavior, once internalized by the one changed, becomes a part of the soul. This works in both a positive and a negative way for man. This is because man is subject to both positive and negative spirits. The example of Saul, written above, illustrates this point.

In Heaven the spirits, known as angels, are the major work force. God has willed them into existence to interface with all His creation. The angels do not just move man to perform various actions. The angels can also move the elements, and cross time and space. They seem to be assigned to specific tasks, covering events, individuals, nations and sometimes the entire world. It seems, however, to be only God who moves the universe.

It has always been of some interest to me why God willed into existence so many angels: the answer may be found in their specificity. As there are many, many men and many circumstances that an individual can experience; or a village or a nation, or a world; so, there are many angels to cover all possibilities, across all time. The book of Revelation gives us some numbers to consider.

> *And I beheld, and I heard the voice of many angels round about the throne and the beasts and the elders: and the number of them was ten thousand times ten thousand, and thousands of thousands;*
>
> (Revelation 5:11)
>
> *And the sixth angel sounded, and I heard a voice from the four horns of the golden altar which is before God, Saying to the sixth angel which had the trumpet, Loose the four angels which are bound in the great river Euphrates. And the four angels were loosed, which were prepared for an hour, and a day, and a month, and a year, for to slay the third part of men. And the number of the army of the horsemen were two hundred thousand thousand: and I heard the number of them.*
>
> (Revelation 9:13-16)

No, the angels were not called forth just to praise God; He has no need of praise from anyone or anything, God is extremely confident in what He Is. The angels praise God out of recognition of His majesty, and because they exist. They know that it is the Word of God that sustains them--unlike most humans, they are grateful for just this. It is sufficient to them that He is God; they need no other gift from Him to cause them to perform praise.

Angels also do not try to change their position, or rise above where they are; except for the one that was brought forth for that illustrative purpose. The angels that have the assignment to seek for grandeur were dismissed from Heaven in the last days. They were sent--gasp--to the earth. They were thrown here not to control it (Satan is only called a prince, not a king). Satan and his associates are tools to further refine mankind, toward excellence in God. It may be true that the dismissed angels did not see it that way, but, nonetheless, it is true.

I really should not say that these angels did not see it that way; their concentration is, as is all angels concentration, on the job that they have been assigned. In their operations, dismissed angels do not concentrate on anything other than what they want to do. Man is only an incidental part of their activities. For them, all mankind is collateral damage. Their mission is to strive against God; and mankind just gets in the way. The activity of these angels is also described in the book of Revelation.

> *And there appeared a great wonder in heaven; a woman clothed with the sun, and the moon under her feet, and upon her head a crown of twelve stars: And she being with child cried, travailing in birth, and pained to be delivered. And there appeared another wonder in heaven; and behold a great red dragon, having seven heads and ten horns, and seven crowns upon his heads. And his tail drew the third part of the stars of heaven, and did cast them to the earth: and the dragon stood before the woman which was ready to be delivered, for to devour her child as soon as it was born.*

(Revelation 12:1-4)

All these angels, brought forth in Heaven, and dispatched from Heaven to educate mankind about the ways of God; all these angels, stationed only on the earth, to further refine man and assist in transforming him to the nature of God: such is the mechanics of Heaven. Such is the way of God: messengers and messages to the spirit of man, to refine the soul of man.

Therefore, we can rest in the goodness of God, working to affect the maximal benefit for our soul. Yes, there are both positive and negative spirits, but only God has authority over the soul of man. God alone knows the entire map of human reality. God alone has already written what was, what is and what will be, from a human point of view. There is no need to fear anyone or anything. Only by allowance or direction from God can any other force in the universe move for or against the soul of man.

> *What I tell you in darkness, that speak ye in light: and what ye hear in the ear, that preach ye upon the housetops. And fear not them which kill the body, but are not able to kill the soul: but rather fear him which is able to destroy both soul and body in hell. Are not two sparrows sold for a farthing? and one of them shall not fall on the ground without your Father. But the very hairs of your head are all numbered. Fear ye not therefore, ye are of more value than many sparrows.*
>
> (Matthew 10:27-31)

The spirits can influence what we do, but they cannot force us to do anything. They have no magic that can produce a temptation that we cannot resist; nor can they produce one that we have never seen. The Bible tells us that there is nothing new under the sun. As you read the Bible you will see that all those things that we think are so pitiful today, existed in the time before, and the time before that, and so on down to the creation of mankind. This is one of the reasons that Scripture provides the full, unadulterated story of mankind, and not just the sweetness of our existence. We need to see that God has endured as LORD through ages of man that were at least as *challenging* as ours is; and through some episodes in existence that were more challenging than we will ever have to see. Through it all, we have confidence that we can rest in God.

> *Moreover, brethren, I would not that ye should be ignorant, how that all our fathers were under the cloud, and all passed through the sea; And were all baptized unto Moses in the cloud and in the sea; And did all eat the same spiritual meat; And did all drink the same spiritual drink: for they drank of that spiritual Rock that followed them: and that Rock was Christ. But with many of them God was not well pleased: for they were overthrown in the wilderness. Now these things were our examples, to the*

intent we should not lust after evil things, as they also lusted. Neither be ye idolaters, as were some of them; as it is written, The people sat down to eat and drink, and rose up to play. Neither let us commit fornication, as some of them committed, and fell in one day three and twenty thousand. Neither let us tempt Christ, as some of them also tempted, and were destroyed of serpents. Neither murmur ye, as some of them also murmured, and were destroyed of the destroyer. Now all these things happened unto them for ensamples: and they are written for our admonition, upon whom the ends of the world are come.

Wherefore let him that thinketh he standeth take heed lest he fall. There hath no temptation taken you but such as is common to man: but God is faithful, who will not suffer you to be tempted above that ye are able; but will with the temptation also make a way to escape, that ye may be able to bear it.

(1 Corinthians 10:1-13)

God is Good!

The Word from the Bible

Proverbs 21:1-3

The king's heart is in the hand of the LORD, as the rivers of water: he turneth it whithersoever he will.

Every way of a man is right in his own eyes: but the LORD pondereth the hearts.

To do justice and judgment is more acceptable to the LORD than sacrifice.

Exodus 23:20-24, 32-33

Behold, I send an Angel before thee, to keep thee in the way, and to bring thee into the place which I have prepared. Beware of him, and obey his voice, provoke him not; for he will not pardon your transgressions: for my name is in him. But if thou shalt indeed obey his voice, and do all that I speak; then I will be an enemy unto thine enemies, and an adversary unto thine adversaries. For mine Angel shall go before thee, and bring thee in unto the Amorites, and the Hittites, and the Perizzites, and the Canaanites, the Hivites, and the Jebusites: and I will cut them off.

Thou shalt not bow down to their gods, nor serve them, nor do after their works: but thou shalt utterly overthrow them, and quite break down their images.

Thou shalt make no covenant with them, nor with their gods. They shall not dwell in thy land, lest they make thee sin against me: for if thou serve their gods, it will surely be a snare unto thee.

Numbers 25:1-9, 16-18

And Israel abode in Shittim, and the people began to commit whoredom with the daughters of Moab. And they called the people unto the sacrifices of their gods: and the people did eat, and bowed down to their gods. And Israel joined himself unto Baalpeor: and the anger of the LORD was kindled against Israel.

And the LORD said unto Moses, Take all the heads of the people, and hang them up before the LORD against the sun, that the fierce anger of the LORD may be turned away from Israel.

And Moses said unto the judges of Israel, Slay ye every one his men that were joined unto Baalpeor.

And, behold, one of the children of Israel came and brought unto his brethren a Midianitish woman in the sight of Moses, and in the sight of all the congregation of the children of Israel, who were weeping before the door of the tabernacle of the congregation.

And when Phinehas, the son of Eleazar, the son of Aaron the priest, saw it, he rose up from among the congregation, and took a javelin in his hand; And he went after the man of Israel into the tent, and thrust both of them through, the man of Israel, and the woman through her belly. So the plague was stayed from the children of Israel. And those that died in the plague were twenty and four thousand.

And the LORD spake unto Moses, saying, Vex the Midianites, and smite them: For they vex you with their wiles, wherewith they have beguiled you in the matter of Peor, and in the matter of Cozbi, the daughter of a prince of Midian, their sister, which was slain in the day of the plague for Peor's sake.

Matthew 15:10-14

And he called the multitude, and said unto them, Hear, and understand: Not that which goeth into the mouth defileth a man; but that which cometh out of the mouth, this defileth a man.

Then came his disciples, and said unto him, Knowest thou that the Pharisees were offended, after they heard this saying? But he answered and said, Every plant, which my heavenly Father hath not planted, shall be rooted up. Let them alone: they be blind leaders of the blind. And if the blind lead the blind, both shall fall into the ditch.

Hebrews 6:1-8

Therefore leaving the principles of the doctrine of Christ, let us go on unto perfection; not laying again the foundation of repentance from dead works, and of faith toward God, Of the doctrine of baptisms, and of laying on of hands, and of resurrection of the dead, and of eternal judgment. And this will we do, if God permit. For it is impossible for those who were once enlightened, and have tasted of the heavenly gift, and were made partakers of the Holy Ghost, And have tasted the good word of God, and the powers of the world to come, If they shall fall away, to renew them again unto repentance; seeing they crucify to themselves the Son of God afresh, and put him to an open shame.

For the earth which drinketh in the rain that cometh oft upon it, and bringeth forth herbs meet for them by whom it is dressed, receiveth blessing from God: But that which beareth thorns and briers is rejected, and is nigh unto cursing; whose end is to be burned.

Genesis 6:5-8

And God saw that the wickedness of man was great in the earth, and that every imagination of the thoughts of his heart was only evil continually. And it repented the LORD that he had made man on the earth, and it grieved him at his heart. And the LORD said, I will destroy man whom I have created from the face of the earth; both man, and beast, and the creeping thing, and the fowls of the air; for it repenteth me that I have made them. But Noah found grace in the eyes of the LORD.

Chapter Three

Impossible to Restore

We, in our nations, and in the world, are becoming more and more like the children of the world in Noah's day. We, who call ourselves the servants of God, seem to be missing the mark. We have gone beyond "dropping the ball" in the handling of the things of God; we are changing the game altogether. And, yes, many of those calling themselves servants of God, are playing their relationship with God like a game.

We have started to count success in terms of numbers. How many souls can we convert? How many dollars can we accumulate? How big a tabernacle can we build? How ornate and impressive can we make our services? How many infidels can we destroy? And, yes, even, how many times can we persuade God's Spirit to enter us and performs signs and wonders. This is very much like what they did in Noah's day.

> *And it came to pass, when men began to multiply on the face of the earth, and daughters were born unto them, That the sons of God saw the daughters of men that they were fair; and they took them wives of all which they chose.*
>
> *And the LORD said, My spirit shall not always strive with man, for that he also is flesh: yet his days shall be an hundred and twenty years.*
>
> (Genesis 6:1-3)

But, you say, "I am not a bigamist; I only have one wife;" or none at all.

Indeed! Is that really true?

Maybe it is, and maybe it is not. New expressions have been added to our language, such as "married to the job", which indicate bonding of a different type. The expression, *"that they were fair"*, may also fit other types of competing commitments, as relates to our commitment to God, besides just *the daughters of men*. Additionally, consider these words of the Bible, referring to a certain time of bad behavior of the children of Israel.

> *Moreover thou hast taken thy sons and thy daughters, whom thou hast borne unto me, and these hast thou sacrificed unto them to be devoured. Is this of thy whoredoms a small matter, That thou hast slain my children, and delivered them to cause them to pass through the fire for them? And in all thine abominations and thy whoredoms thou hast not remembered the days of thy youth, when thou wast naked and bare, and wast polluted in thy blood.*
>
> *And it came to pass after all thy wickedness, (woe, woe unto thee! saith the Lord GOD;) That thou hast also built unto thee an eminent place, and hast made thee an high place in every street. Thou hast built thy high place at every head of the way, and hast made thy beauty to be abhorred, and hast opened thy feet to every one that passed by, and multiplied thy whoredoms. Thou hast also committed fornication with the Egyptians thy neighbours, great of flesh; and hast increased thy whoredoms, to provoke me to anger.*
>
> *Behold, therefore I have stretched out my hand over thee, and have diminished thine ordinary food, and delivered thee unto the will of them that hate thee, the daughters of the Philistines, which are ashamed of thy lewd way. Thou hast played the whore also with the Assyrians, because thou wast unsatiable; yea, thou hast played the harlot with them, and yet couldest not be satisfied. Thou hast moreover multiplied thy fornication in the land of Canaan unto Chaldea; and yet thou wast not satisfied herewith.*
>
> *How weak is thine heart, saith the Lord GOD, seeing thou doest all these things, the work of an imperious whorish woman;*

(Ezekiel 16:20-30)

One might say that a nation cannot perform a sex act; but this is not the meaning of the scriptural indictment. The meaning is that when an action is performed that resembles and has the same consequences as another action, then that action can be properly described with the name of the action it imitates. Thus, I say that we in this culture have started to take on many spouses. Among these spouses are friends, pets, jobs and possessions. Yes, there is a more direct term for these things; it is the term, idol. As the children in Noah's day took on many wives, we are taking on many idols. And we are binding ourselves to them as tightly as any marriage. Indeed, many of the marriages among humans are weaker than our bonds to things.

Many religious persons and organizations are married to their numbers. They devote themselves to achieving this number of things and accumulating that number of things. They miss the lesson of the parable told by Jesus of Nazareth.

> *And he spake a parable unto them, saying, The ground of a certain rich man brought forth plentifully: And he thought within himself, saying, What shall I do, because I have no room where to bestow my fruits? And he said, This will I do: I will pull down my barns, and build greater; and there will I bestow all my fruits and my goods. And I will say to my soul, Soul, thou hast much goods laid up for many years; take thine ease, eat, drink, and be merry. But God said unto him, Thou fool, this night thy soul shall be required of thee: then whose shall those things be, which thou hast provided?*
>
> *So is he that layeth up treasure for himself, and is not rich toward God. And he said unto his disciples, Therefore I say unto you, Take no thought for your life, what ye shall eat; neither for the body, what ye shall put on. The life is more than meat, and the body is more than raiment.*

(Luke 12:16-23)

We live in an age in which the marriage to numbers produces a divorce rate, from concepts and principles, which is starting to exceed the rate of divorce between men and women. This is so because once we have satisfied ourselves with one number, it is time to move on to the next number. There is always a new number to be achieved, and a new mark to set. We can not seem to get enough of numbers of stuff.

It is said that of those attending religious rallies, and other numbers type religious gatherings; that a very large percentage of them fall away from following the teaching. This is a direct restatement of a significant portion of another of the parables of Jesus of Nazareth.

> *And he spake many things unto them in parables, saying, Behold, a sower went forth to sow; And when he sowed, some seeds fell by the way side, and the fowls came and devoured them up: Some fell upon stony places, where they had not much earth: and forthwith they sprung up, because they had no deepness of earth: And when the sun was up, they were scorched; and because they had no root, they withered away. And some fell among thorns; and the thorns sprung up, and choked them: But other fell into good ground, and brought forth fruit, some an hundredfold, some sixtyfold, some thirtyfold.*
>
> (Matthew 13:3-8)
>
> *Hear ye therefore the parable of the sower.*
>
> *When any one heareth the word of the kingdom, and understandeth it not, then cometh the wicked one, and catcheth away that which was sown in his heart. This is he which received seed by the way side.*
>
> *But he that received the seed into stony places, the same is he that heareth the word, and anon with joy receiveth it; Yet hath he not root in himself, but dureth for a while: for when tribulation or persecution ariseth because of the word, by and by he is offended.*
>
> *He also that received seed among the thorns is he that heareth the word; and the care of this world, and the deceitfulness of riches, choke the word, and he becometh unfruitful.*
>
> *But he that received seed into the good ground is he that heareth the word, and understandeth it; which also beareth fruit, and bringeth forth, some an hundredfold, some sixty, some thirty.*
>
> (Matthew 13:18-23)

"But, so what," you say, "If even one soul is saved, that's good."

Indeed, every soul that is saved from judgment is a soul that will experience the deeper riches of God's glory. However, the number's attitude is not good.

First, know this: there is none good except God, and that which God says of it, it is good. And know also that we have no right to latch on to the good work of God, bestowed on the life of another. We especially have no right to take these works as our possessions.

Furthermore, we are liable for the damage done to those whose hearts we are hardening by causing them to continually reject the message of God. These are those ones that move forward out of emotion, but when life returns, they move away from God. Each time they do this they are in danger of hardening their heart toward God; this is the example of Pharaoh, as seen in the Bible in the book of Exodus. We have a responsibility to fulfill; not just for selective ones, but to all men.

> *Let us therefore follow after the things which make for peace, and things wherewith one may edify another. For meat destroy not the work of God. All things indeed are pure; but it is evil for that man who eateth with offence. It is good neither to eat flesh, nor to drink wine, nor any thing whereby thy brother stumbleth, or is offended, or is made weak. Hast thou faith? have it to thyself before God. Happy is he that condemneth not himself in that thing which he alloweth. And he that doubteth is damned if he eat, because he eateth not of faith: for whatsoever is not of faith is sin.*

(Romans 14:19-23)

Any *convert* that we think we have made belongs to God. For, we do not make converts; God does. We do not start churches; God does. We can, however, become a stumbling block in the path of one or more of our fellow humans. We need to do the work that is assigned to us, finish the job, plant or water; then leave it to God. Let God give the increase. Let God count the numbers. Let God write their actions in His book. Any book we keep will be irrelevant at the judgment; as it is irrelevant now. Any *convert* we make by force of arms, or guilt, will be in danger of falling away. As such we will have set them up for condemnation, as stated by the apostle Paul.

> *Therefore leaving the principles of the doctrine of Christ, let us go on unto perfection; not laying again the foundation of*

> *repentance from dead works, and of faith toward God, Of the doctrine of baptisms, and of laying on of hands, and of resurrection of the dead, and of eternal judgment. And this will we do, if God permit. For it is impossible for those who were once enlightened, and have tasted of the heavenly gift, and were made partakers of the Holy Ghost, And have tasted the good word of God, and the powers of the world to come, If they shall fall away, to renew them again unto repentance; seeing they crucify to themselves the Son of God afresh, and put him to an open shame.*
>
> (Hebrews 6:1-6)

The area where we can become *impossible to restore* is not just in our belief in the Messiah. The impossibility can flow into any knowledge of the way and will of God. In any of these areas where once we knew and now we ignore, it is possible for us to reach this place of *impossibility*.

It is time to take a new inventory of where we are with the things of God. Let us request of God a stirring of the Spirit within us, and within our nations. Let us turn to him for the revival of trust that allows us to do as Jesus of Nazareth told his disciples.

> *Now the names of the twelve apostles are these; The first, Simon, who is called Peter, and Andrew his brother; James the son of Zebedee, and John his brother; Philip, and Bartholomew; Thomas, and Matthew the publican; James the son of Alphaeus, and Lebbaeus, whose surname was Thaddaeus; Simon the Canaanite, and Judas Iscariot, who also betrayed him. These twelve Jesus sent forth, and commanded them, saying, Go not into the way of the Gentiles, and into any city of the Samaritans enter ye not: But go rather to the lost sheep of the house of Israel.*
>
> *And as ye go, preach, saying, The kingdom of heaven is at hand. Heal the sick, cleanse the lepers, raise the dead, cast out devils: freely ye have received, freely give. Provide neither gold, nor silver, nor brass in your purses, Nor scrip for your journey, neither two coats, neither shoes, nor yet staves: for the workman is worthy of his meat.*
>
> (Matthew 10:2-10)

Above all, let us return to the confidence and peace in God that knows that God will provide. Let us return to the peace that accepts this as true for all workers in the vineyard.

> *After these things the Lord appointed other seventy also, and sent them two and two before his face into every city and place, whither he himself would come. Therefore said he unto them, The harvest truly is great, but the labourers are few: pray ye therefore the Lord of the harvest, that he would send forth labourers into his harvest. Go your ways: behold, I send you forth as lambs among wolves. Carry neither purse, nor scrip, nor shoes: and salute no man by the way.*
>
> (Luke 10:1-4)

Life is a challenge;
This we all know.
So, it seems so simple
To go with the flow.

Why should we
Reinvent the wheel?
Following the crowd
Isn't such a bad deal.

We listen to others,
We see the news;
We too want to excel
Without paying dues.

There must be a shortcut
In the things we see;
It cannot just be
All up to me.

This secular view
Rules our decisions,
Even those that
Are of our religions.

But God is precise,
He does not change;
There is just no way
For us to arrange

Things to get around
His message most true.
Yes, churchman,
This applies to you.

Whether in a church
Or synagogue you kneel;
Yes, even if you
Pray on a hill;

If you choose to ignore
The precision of His word

Because for our times
It just seems absurd,

You may be closing
A most divine door;
Making rest in His will
Impossible to restore.

Chapter 3a

Piercing to the Dividing

Psalm 95:8-11

Harden not your heart, as in the provocation, and as in the day of temptation in the wilderness: When your fathers tempted me, proved me, and saw my work. Forty years long was I grieved with this generation, and said, It is a people that do err in their heart, and they have not known my ways: Unto whom I sware in my wrath that they should not enter into my rest.

Hebrews 4:9-13

There remaineth therefore a rest to the people of God. For he that is entered into his rest, he also hath ceased from his own works, as God did from his.

Let us labour therefore to enter into that rest, lest any man fall after the same example of unbelief. For the word of God is quick, and powerful, and sharper than any twoedged sword, piercing even to the dividing asunder of soul and spirit, and of the joints and marrow, and is a discerner of the thoughts and intents of the heart. Neither is there any creature that is not manifest in his sight: but all things are naked and opened unto the eyes of him with whom we have to do.

Genesis 2:7-8

And the LORD God formed man of the dust of the ground, and breathed into his nostrils the breath of life; and man became a living soul. And the LORD God planted a garden eastward in Eden; and there he put the man whom he had formed.

+=+=+=+=+=+=+=+=+=+=+=+=+=+=+=+=+=+=+=+

The breath of life is the gift of a spirit, which God gave to the man Adam, and thus to all mankind. By giving the spirit, in the breath of life; God activated the living soul of Adam. The spirit and the soul are the components of man that have to be placed in subjection to man by releasing them to God.

The serpent when he came to Eve, knew about the spirit of mankind. It was for this reason that he appealed to the spirit of Eve. The serpent used words that would motivate the spirit to desire stuff that could enhance the soul of mankind. The serpent could not touch the soul of Eve, for this was created and is solely owned by God.

> *Behold, all souls are mine; as the soul of the father, so also the soul of the son is mine: the soul that sinneth, it shall die.*

(Ezekiel 18:4)

At the point of contact with the serpent, Eve had no knowledge of good and evil, and so her soul was still pure. Her spirit, however, was on a quest for more substance to feed the soul. This quest was being undertaken through discovery of the nature of her environment. This the serpent knew, and it was more than willing to provide the stuff that seemed pleasing to the taste of the spirit; however, what the serpent was really providing was stuff that could entrap the soul. This stuff is the knowledge of good and evil.

> *Now we know that what things soever the law saith, it saith to them who are under the law: that every mouth may be stopped, and all the world may become guilty before God. Therefore by the deeds of the law there shall no flesh be justified in his sight: for by the law is the knowledge of sin.*

(Romans 3:19-20)

It is this interaction that provides us with the information that we need, to understand the separation between the soul and the spirit. We will see later how the knowledge of the separation is useful for us in our worship of God, and for dealings with Satan, and other serpents.

The spirit is the driving force behind the collection of experiences. We like to refer to it as the emotional side of man. We speak of someone who has *spirit*, in referring to someone who can use the emotional side in a seemingly powerful way. The spirit of man, however, is not just the emotional side. The spirit of man is also the filter of cognition. We receive information from the outside world through the brain and process this information. First, the information is matched with portions of our existing experiences to filter it. In this filter, certain impressions are formed that match our view of reality.

For example, when the male of the human species sees a woman, he may see someone who is ripe for exploitation. This was the case in the time of Noah. However, another man, such as Noah, operating with a spirit touched by God, will see that to behave in this fashion is to exploit female children. Indeed, God revealed the harm in exploitative actions by men toward women, and He started the solution that had been prepared from before the foundation of the world.

> *And it came to pass, when men began to multiply on the face of the earth, and daughters were born unto them, That the sons of God saw the daughters of men that they were fair; and they took them wives of all which they chose. And the LORD said, My spirit shall not always strive with man, for that he also is flesh: yet his days shall be an hundred and twenty years.*
>
> *There were giants in the earth in those days; and also after that, when the sons of God came in unto the daughters of men, and they bare children to them, the same became mighty men which were of old, men of renown. And God saw that the wickedness of man was great in the earth, and that every imagination of the thoughts of his heart was only evil continually. And it repented the LORD that he had made man on the earth, and it grieved him at his heart.*
>
> *And the LORD said, I will destroy man whom I have created from the face of the earth; both man, and beast, and the creeping thing, and the fowls of the air; for it repenteth me that I have made them. But Noah found grace in the eyes of the LORD.*
>
> (Genesis 6:1-8)

The spirits of the males of that day were receiving visual input from their environment, and processing it through their experience of wantonness, to produce fruit for internal consumption. This fruit was then *fed* to the soul, and thus became a part of the nature of the man. It has been said that *we are what we eat*; and this is true not just in the physical realm, but also in the spiritual realm, as well.

The soul, therefore, is the storage place for all the accepted experiences that we hold to be true and useful. The soul is thus the collection of knowledge, habits, intentions and motives.

What difference does this knowledge make to the future of mankind? Just this: when both the spirit and the soul are operating solely from the standpoint of mankind, then failure is the only option. This is so because mankind is temporary. However, the soul is immortal. When the temporary tries to prepare the eternal, a problem arises. The eternal, in this case the soul, fails to mature properly. The result is that the soul has an eternity to pay the price of this failure; or at least a very long time to recover from the shortfall.

The answer is to have an alliance between the divine Spirit of truth and the natural spirit of man. This is the message of the whole of the Bible, including both the Old Testament and the Old New Testament. Both of these Testaments are the good news of preparing the eternal soul for its final state in eternity. This is the mission of the message of the Bible, and it is the mission of every minister of God.

There is an occasion when the spirit can be quieted in its interactions with the soul; this is the time when the Comforter comes into the life of an individual. It is not that the spirit of the man has been destroyed, but that it has been placed in subjection to the Holy Ghost, the Spirit of Truth. The Comforter comes to mankind from God at the request of the Messiah. As the Bible tells us, the purpose of the Holy Ghost is the same as the purpose of the spirit of man.

> *Judas saith unto him, not Iscariot, Lord, how is it that thou wilt manifest thyself unto us, and not unto the world?*
>
> *Jesus answered and said unto him, If a man love me, he will keep my words: and my Father will love him, and we will come unto him, and make our abode with him. He that loveth me not keepeth not my sayings: and the word which ye hear is not mine, but the Father's which sent me. These things have I spoken unto you, being yet present with you. But the Comforter, which is the Holy Ghost, whom the Father will send in my name, he shall teach you all things, and bring all things to your remembrance, whatsoever I have said unto you.*

> *Peace I leave with you, my peace I give unto you: not as the world giveth, give I unto you. Let not your heart be troubled, neither let it be afraid.*

(John 14:22-27)

The indwelling Spirit of Truth will refresh the soul by feeding it the things of God. Unfortunately, we will still have a measure of rebellion within ourselves. The apostle Paul proclaimed this in his writings.

> *For I know that in me (that is, in my flesh,) dwelleth no good thing: for to will is present with me; but how to perform that which is good I find not. For the good that I would I do not: but the evil which I would not, that I do. Now if I do that I would not, it is no more I that do it, but sin that dwelleth in me. I find then a law, that, when I would do good, evil is present with me. For I delight in the law of God after the inward man: But I see another law in my members, warring against the law of my mind, and bringing me into captivity to the law of sin which is in my members.*

(Romans 7:18-23)

Even with this residual pollution, we will have received from the Spirit of Truth much useful and permanent food for the soul. This food, this information, will remain with us for all time to come.

What of the other stuff that we collected from things pertaining to the world and not from God?

This stuff will pass through the fire and be purged. Again the apostle Paul gives us insight on this matter.

> *For other foundation can no man lay than that is laid, which is Jesus Christ.*
>
> *Now if any man build upon this foundation gold, silver, precious stones, wood, hay, stubble; Every man's work shall be made manifest: for the day shall declare it, because it shall be revealed by fire; and the fire shall try every man's work of what sort it is. If any man's work abide which he hath built thereupon, he shall receive a reward. If any man's work shall be burned, he shall suffer loss: but he himself shall be saved; yet so as by fire.*

(1 Corinthians 3:11-15)

The process of receiving the Spirit of Truth is a very real transformation of our nature, and heightening of our potential. This is the message of the Gospel of Jesus Christ. This is what he told us to accept from God the Father. We do this as stated by Jesus Christ, when we serve God the Father in spirit and in truth.

> *But the hour cometh, and now is, when the true worshippers shall worship the Father in spirit and in truth: for the Father seeketh such to worship him. God is a Spirit: and they that worship him must worship him in spirit and in truth.*
>
> (John 4:23-24)

The apostles of Jesus Christ spoke often of believing in him. We must believe in Jesus because the message that he delivered to us is from God the Father. If we do not believe in him, we will not believe that he has the authority to deliver God's message. God certified Christ by the actions He caused him to perform on this earth. We must hear Jesus, and adhere to his words; because he made a very serious request of us.

> *Philip saith unto him, Lord, show us the Father, and it sufficeth us.*
>
> *Jesus saith unto him, Have I been so long time with you, and yet hast thou not known me, Philip? he that hath seen me hath seen the Father; and how sayest thou then, Show us the Father? Believest thou not that I am in the Father, and the Father in me? the words that I speak unto you I speak not of myself: but the Father that dwelleth in me, he doeth the works.*
>
> *Believe me that I am in the Father, and the Father in me: or else believe me for the very works' sake.*
>
> (John 14:8-11)

Without this belief, an individual will not be saved from the ravages of this life, and will have a very difficult time when the soul enters eternity. The acceptance of salvation, through the works and the message of Christ, is not just for the heavenly time. Salvation is also for the time we live in now, here on this earth. Without the combination of the divine Holy Ghost with the natural soul of man, there will be no advancement of the state of existence of mankind.

It is, and always has been, God's known will to provide the way. Only God can provide the way to the proper state of eternal life that is destined for the soul of man. This way is the mission and the message of the Messiah; and the Messiah has surely come, in the person of Jesus of Nazareth, the Christ, who is the Son of God.

The Word from the Bible

Genesis 4:25-26

And Adam knew his wife again; and she bare a son, and called his name Seth: For God, said she, hath appointed me another seed instead of Abel, whom Cain slew. And to Seth, to him also there was born a son; and he called his name Enos: then began men to call upon the name of the LORD.

Distance from Seth to Noah

Seth	*105 when Enos was born*	*912*
Enos	*90 when Cainan was born*	*905*
Cainan	*70 when Mahalaleel was born*	*910*
Mahalaleel	*65 when Jared was born*	*895*
Jared	*162 when Enoch was born*	*962*
Enoch	*65 when Methuselah was born*	*365*
Methuselah	*187 when Lamech was born*	*969*
	(died when Noah was 600)	
Lamech	*182 when Noah was born*	*777*
	(died when Noah was 595)	
Noah	*500+ when his sons were born*	*950*
	(the flood came when Noah was 600)	

Genesis 6:1-4

And it came to pass, when men began to multiply on the face of the earth, and daughters were born unto them, That the sons of God saw the daughters of men that they were fair; and they took them wives of all which they chose. And the LORD said, My spirit shall not always strive with man, for that he also is flesh: yet his days shall be an hundred and twenty years.

There were giants in the earth in those days; and also after that, when the sons of God came in unto the daughters of men, and they bare children to them, the same became mighty men which were of old, men of renown.

Genesis 6:5-8

And God saw that the wickedness of man was great in the earth, and that every imagination of the thoughts of his heart was only evil continually. And it repented the LORD that he had made man on the earth, and it grieved him at his heart. And the LORD said, I will destroy man whom I have created from the face of the earth; both man, and beast, and the creeping thing, and the fowls of the air; for it repenteth me that I have made them. But Noah found grace in the eyes of the LORD.

Matthew 24:37-39

But as the days of Noe were, so shall also the coming of the Son of man be. For as in the days that were before the flood they were eating and drinking, marrying and giving in marriage, until the day that Noe entered into the ark, And knew not until the flood came, and took them all away; so shall also the coming of the Son of man be.

Luke 18:18-27

And a certain ruler asked him, saying, Good Master, what shall I do to inherit eternal life?

And Jesus said unto him, Why callest thou me good? none is good, save one, that is, God. Thou knowest the commandments, Do not commit adultery, Do not kill, Do not steal, Do not bear false witness, Honour thy father and thy mother.

And he said, All these have I kept from my youth up.

Now when Jesus heard these things, he said unto him, Yet lackest thou one thing: sell all that thou hast, and distribute unto the poor, and thou shalt have treasure in heaven: and come, follow me.

And when he heard this, he was very sorrowful: for he was very rich.

And when Jesus saw that he was very sorrowful, he said, How hardly shall they that have riches enter into the kingdom of God! For it is easier for a camel to go through a needle's eye, than for a rich man to enter into the kingdom of God.

And they that heard it said, Who then can be saved?

And he said, The things which are impossible with men are possible with God.

Chapter Four

Just Shall Live by Faith

Many are familiar with the faith of Abraham as attested to by the apostle Paul.

> *What shall we say then that Abraham our father, as pertaining to the flesh, hath found? For if Abraham were justified by works, he hath whereof to glory; but not before God. For what saith the scripture? Abraham believed God, and it was counted unto him for righteousness. Now to him that worketh is the reward not reckoned of grace, but of debt. But to him that worketh not, but believeth on him that justifieth the ungodly, his faith is counted for righteousness.*
>
> (Romans 4:1-5)

However, Noah was faithful before Abram (who is Abraham) was born. He was told by God to build a boat to preserve life on the earth. Noah believed that God would do what He said He would do. Noah devoted himself to the accomplishment of the mission. Noah's faith is the kind that we also need to imitate in this day. Yes, we must have the faith of Abraham, but we must also have the ability to transform that faith into works as Noah did.

The earth during the time of Noah was a place that is mirrored almost directly in the people of the time of Jesus of Nazareth.

> *Because that, when they knew God, they glorified him not as God, neither were thankful; but became vain in their imaginations, and their foolish heart was darkened. Professing themselves to be wise, they became fools, And changed the glory of the uncorruptible God into an image made like to corruptible man, and to birds, and fourfooted beasts, and creeping things. Wherefore God also gave them up to uncleanness through the lusts of their own hearts, to*

> *dishonour their own bodies between themselves: Who changed the truth of God into a lie, and worshipped and served the creature more than the Creator, who is blessed for ever. Amen.*
>
> (Romans 1:21-25)

The people of that day had reached the lowest point of the brief history of mankind. Corrupt behavior and neglect of the things of God was the order of the day. This was the situation with all families of the earth except one: the family of Noah. That there was only one family selected by God means that all other families of man had either fallen away from God or never completely surrendered to Him. In fact, it was because so many had fallen away that God performed the cleansing of mankind. To preserve the one family that had not fallen away is a significant outcome of God sending the flood. For, it was to set a righteous baseline for all of mankind, that God preserved the remnant.

We are in a time such as Noah's now. The religious community, worldwide, has a choice to make, as stated in the challenges given to the children of Israel.

> *Now therefore fear the LORD, and serve him in sincerity and in truth: and put away the gods which your fathers served on the other side of the flood, and in Egypt; and serve ye the LORD. And if it seem evil unto you to serve the LORD, choose you this day whom ye will serve; whether the gods which your fathers served that were on the other side of the flood, or the gods of the Amorites, in whose land ye dwell: but as for me and my house, we will serve the LORD.*
>
> (Joshua 24:14-15)

> *And Elijah came unto all the people, and said, How long halt ye between two opinions? if the LORD be God, follow him: but if Baal, then follow him. And the people answered him not a word.*
>
> (1 Kings 18:21)

On the other side of the flood is the combined concept of size and possession. It involves the practice of amassing huge quantities of stuff, and not dispensing proper service. It involves looking to each organization's or nation's bottom line conquest. The lie that we tell ourselves is that we are doing it for God. We quote Scripture that says that we must go into the entire world and preach our messages. But we do not read the bold statements in the Bible of continued service, through teaching and follow-up. We just proceed to count numbers, in our vain attempt to add fine print to already sufficient Scripture.

> *And Jesus came and spake unto them, saying, All power is given unto me in heaven and in earth. Go ye therefore, and teach all nations, baptizing them in the name of the Father, and of the Son, and of the Holy Ghost: Teaching them to observe all things whatsoever I have commanded you: and, lo, I am with you alway, even unto the end of the world. Amen.*

(Matthew 28:18-20)

Nowhere in the message, above, is the statement or even the notion that we should count the numbers, or amass the fortunes. In fact, in this matter, one other Scripture might be worth reading.

> *And they continued stedfastly in the apostles' doctrine and fellowship, and in breaking of bread, and in prayers. And fear came upon every soul: and many wonders and signs were done by the apostles. And all that believed were together, and had all things common; And sold their possessions and goods, and parted them to all men, as every man had need. And they, continuing daily with one accord in the temple, and breaking bread from house to house, did eat their meat with gladness and singleness of heart, Praising God, and having favour with all the people. And the Lord added to the church daily such as should be saved.*

(Acts 2:42)

The quick reading of the above degrades it to "all properties in common;" *things*, however, go beyond that. "Things," go to the psychological and spiritual realms. The concept of, *"things common"*, runs across organizations, and even across nations. This concept is the basis of charity. It does not say that nothing is owned by anyone; even the children of Israel were authorized to have boundaries in the possession of their inheritances.

> *Then came the daughters of Zelophehad, the son of Hepher, the son of Gilead, the son of Machir, the son of Manasseh,*

of the families of Manasseh the son of Joseph: and these are the names of his daughters; Mahlah, Noah, and Hoglah, and Milcah, and Tirzah. And they stood before Moses, and before Eleazar the priest, and before the princes and all the congregation, by the door of the tabernacle of the congregation, saying, Our father died in the wilderness, and he was not in the company of them that gathered themselves together against the LORD in the company of Korah; but died in his own sin, and had no sons. Why should the name of our father be done away from among his family, because he hath no son? Give unto us therefore a possession among the brethren of our father.

And Moses brought their cause before the LORD.

And the LORD spake unto Moses, saying, The daughters of Zelophehad speak right: thou shalt surely give them a possession of an inheritance among their father's brethren; and thou shalt cause the inheritance of their father to pass unto them. And thou shalt speak unto the children of Israel, saying, If a man die, and have no son, then ye shall cause his inheritance to pass unto his daughter. And if he have no daughter, then ye shall give his inheritance unto his brethren. And if he have no brethren, then ye shall give his inheritance unto his father's brethren. And if his father have no brethren, then ye shall give his inheritance unto his kinsman that is next to him of his family, and he shall possess it: and it shall be unto the children of Israel a statute of judgment, as the LORD commanded Moses.

(Numbers 27:1-11)

And the chief fathers of the families of the children of Gilead, the son of Machir, the son of Manasseh, of the families of the sons of Joseph, came near, and spake before Moses, and before the princes, the chief fathers of the children of Israel: And they said, The LORD commanded my lord to give the land for an inheritance by lot to the children of Israel: and my lord was commanded by the LORD to give the inheritance of Zelophehad our brother unto his daughters. And if they be married to any of the sons of the other tribes of the children of Israel, then shall their inheritance be taken from the inheritance of our fathers, and shall be put to the inheritance of the tribe whereunto they are received: so shall it be taken from the lot of our inheritance. And when the jubile of the children of Israel shall be, then shall their inheritance be put unto the inheritance of the tribe whereunto they are received: so shall their inheritance be taken away from the inheritance of the tribe of our fathers.

And Moses commanded the children of Israel according to the word of the LORD, saying, The tribe of the sons of Joseph hath said well. This is the thing which the LORD doth command concerning the daughters of Zelophehad, saying, Let them marry to whom they think best; only to the family of the tribe of their father shall they marry. So shall not the inheritance of the children of Israel remove from tribe to tribe: for every one of the children of Israel shall keep himself to the inheritance of the tribe of his fathers. And every daughter, that possesseth an inheritance in any tribe of the children of Israel, shall be wife unto one of the family of the tribe of her father, that the children of Israel may enjoy every man the inheritance of his fathers. Neither shall the inheritance remove from one tribe to another tribe; but every one of the tribes of the children of Israel shall keep himself to his own inheritance.

Even as the LORD commanded Moses, so did the daughters of Zelophehad:

(Numbers 36:1-10)

Though the children of Israel could have boundaries in the possession of their inheritances, they were told that they must all support the common mission of God, above their possessions. This took an extreme act of faith--by modern standards--in God's ability to preserve their families, their lifestyle and their lives. For example:

The children of Gad and the children of Reuben came and spake unto Moses, and to Eleazar the priest, and unto the princes of the congregation, saying, Ataroth, and Dibon, and Jazer, and Nimrah, and Heshbon, and Elealeh, and Shebam, and Nebo, and Beon, Even the country which the LORD smote before the congregation of Israel, is a land for cattle, and thy servants have cattle: Wherefore, said they, if we have found grace in thy sight, let this land be given unto thy servants for a possession, and bring us not over Jordan.

(Numbers 32:2-5)

And they came near unto him, and said, We will build sheepfolds here for our cattle, and cities for our little ones: But we ourselves will go ready armed before the children of Israel, until we have brought them unto their place: and our little ones shall dwell in the fenced cities because of the inhabitants of the land. We will not return unto our houses, until the children of Israel have inherited every man his inheritance. For we will not inherit with them on yonder side Jordan, or forward; because our inheritance is fallen to us on this side Jordan eastward.

And Moses said unto them, If ye will do this thing, if ye will go armed before the LORD to war, And will go all of you armed over Jordan before the LORD, until he hath driven out his enemies from before him, And the land be subdued before the LORD: then afterward ye shall return, and be guiltless before the LORD, and before Israel; and this land shall be your possession before the LORD. But if ye will not do so, behold, ye have sinned against the LORD: and be sure your sin will find you out. Build you cities for your little ones, and folds for your sheep; and do that which hath proceeded out of your mouth.

And the children of Gad and the children of Reuben spake unto Moses, saying, Thy servants will do as my lord commandeth. Our little ones, our wives, our flocks, and all our cattle, shall be there in the cities of Gilead: But thy servants will pass over, every man armed for war, before the LORD to battle, as my lord saith.

(Numbers 32:16-27)

The faith of these tribes of the nation of Israel was evidenced by their works for God, and for His purpose. We must have the same sort of diligence about our works for God. This is the message that the apostle James gives us.

> *What doth it profit, my brethren, though a man say he hath faith, and have not works? can faith save him? If a brother or sister be naked, and destitute of daily food, And one of you say unto them, Depart in peace, be ye warmed and filled; notwithstanding ye give them not those things which are needful to the body; what doth it profit? Even so faith, if it hath not works, is dead, being alone. Yea, a man may say, Thou hast faith, and I have works: show me thy faith without thy works, and I will show thee my faith by my works. Thou believest that there is one God; thou doest well: the devils also believe, and tremble. But wilt thou know, O vain man, that faith without works is dead?*
>
> (James 2:14)

Returning to the example of Noah; this moves us from corporate actions back to individual ones. It is not that Noah's justification before God came because of his works, but that Noah was selected by God for works because of his faith. The Scripture indicates that he found favor with God before he had built the boat. Then, he also blessed us by yielding to the command of God.

It **really** would not have done us any good if Noah had been able to say to God, "Oh yes, I believe that you can destroy all life with a flood, but I really do not want to get involved in your squabble with mankind". No, it *really* would not have done us any good. In exercising his faith through his works, Noah made it possible for me to write this, and for you to read it.

Think, if you will, on what may be perceived to be a smaller level: do we really know what the long-range consequences are of our denial of service to God? Do we really know what worlds this might affect, and what lives it might serve to destroy? Do we really want to damage another human because we do not want to get involved in a matter in which God directed us to intercede? Noah chose not to neglect the call of God. Think seriously about this that you have read, before you choose to neglect even one that God has given to your intervention or care.

> *Therefore take no thought, saying, What shall we eat? or, What shall we drink? or, Wherewithal shall we be clothed? (For after all these things do the Gentiles seek:) for your heavenly Father knoweth that ye have need of all these*

things. But seek ye first the kingdom of God, and his righteousness; and all these things shall be added unto you.

Take therefore no thought for the morrow: for the morrow shall take thought for the things of itself. Sufficient unto the day is the evil thereof.

(Matthew 6:31-34)

I'm on the move,
I'm working my plan;
One of these days,
***I'll** be the man.*

I've read the books,
I'm in with the flow;
I know how this thing
Ought to go.

My jets are roaring;
I've started to burn.
There is nothing new
I have to learn.

My circle is wide,
I've got great fame;
Why I'm in so deep,
They all know my name.

Yes, I've got it all,
I can do what I please;
But something's missing,
I just do not feel at ease.

I tried this religion thing
They're talking about,
But all it did
Was fill me with doubt.

Who is this God?
What did He really say?
Which of these religions
Really knows the way?

I look for answers
From my fellow man,
And all they tell me
Is what they can

Do for me if I walk
Their special line;

*If I do what they say
Things will be just fine.*

*Then God speaks out,
I hear something great:
"Those who would please Me,
The just, shall live by faith".*

Chapter 4a

Everything Comes From God

Please consider the following passage of Scripture.

> *In the beginning was the Word, and the Word was with God, and the Word was God. The same was in the beginning with God. All things were made by him; and without him was not any thing made that was made.*
>
> (John 1:1-3)

I want you to keep the following in mind: *All things were made by him; and without him was not any thing made that was made.* We want to explore just how broad a statement that is. We will do so in seven thoughts.

Thought 1: In the beginning, there is only God

This is a spot somewhere on the line between everlasting and everlasting. It is the time of the establishment of the foundation of the world, which will lead to the creation of the earth. God is present for the entire stream of events. This is the time of the preparation of the raw materials that will be used to construct our universe. The expression "time of the preparation" is not, however, a representation of a process; it is, rather, an expression of the nature of God. The expression "time of the preparation" is only used to place the thought in a human framework.

God has always contained all the resources necessary to build all that is. There is no need for construction within Him, or within His type of *time*. What happens in this *time*, is a revelation of His might and majesty, according to His glory, within frames of activity that we can only grasp as being in time.

A Prayer of Moses the man of God.

> *LORD, thou hast been our dwelling place in all generations. Before the mountains were brought forth, or ever thou hadst formed the earth and the world, even from everlasting to everlasting, thou art God.*
>
> (Psalm 90:1-2)

Thought 2: All that we know unfolds after our beginning

This is a rather obvious statement: when there is no "us", there is no "our knowing". We mention this thought, only to establish that God allows mankind to have the ability to know His essence, works and purpose. Before this universe was, God already is from "Everlasting -->". Then there comes the foundation of the world, and after that, the world, and after that, mankind. The time before mankind is really irrelevant to mankind, as a proof item. Many thinkers spend a lot of time trying to decipher the messages God has placed in His creation, so that they can have a view of the time of "Everlasting --> beginning --> man --". All we really need to know is that the beginning is somewhere on the line between "Everlasting <---> Everlasting".

> *In the beginning God created the heaven and the earth. And the earth was without form, and void; and darkness was upon the face of the deep. And the Spirit of God moved upon the face of the waters. And God said, Let there be light: and there was light. And God saw the light, that it was good: and God divided the light from the darkness. And God called the light Day, and the darkness he called Night. And the evening and the morning were the first day.*
>
> (Genesis 1:1-5)

Any other information about the time before the beginning, other than that God Is, is purely academic and does not enhance the nature of mankind, in any way. In some senses, it detracts from the forward progress of mankind. It does so because it causes mankind to try to second-guess the method God used. By doing this, mankind hopes to create a method that is superior to God's. This cannot be done; for, every method man *creates* is also from God, and belongs to God.

Therefore, it is more productive to accept that we are here, that we did not make ourselves, and the method God used is a *done deal*. However, inquiring minds want to know. God is not displeased at our quest, only at our sometimes arrogance about what we discover.

For the invisible things of him from the creation of the world are clearly seen, being understood by the things that are made, even his eternal power and Godhead; so that they are without excuse: Because that, when they knew God, they glorified him not as God, neither were thankful; but became vain in their imaginations, and their foolish heart was darkened. Professing themselves to be wise, they became fools, And changed the glory of the uncorruptible God into an image made like to corruptible man, and to birds, and fourfooted beasts, and creeping things. Wherefore God also gave them up to uncleanness through the lusts of their own hearts, to dishonour their own bodies between themselves: Who changed the truth of God into a lie, and worshipped and served the creature more than the Creator, who is blessed for ever. Amen.

(Romans 1:20-25)

Thought 3: The only source of what is, is God

The Scripture that we started with stated that *All things were made by him*; this is a seemingly uncomplicated point. However, it is not as simple as it seems, but we will not explore the lack of simplicity, at this time. For now just believe that ALL things were made by Him that exists in the universe of mankind: physical, psychological and spiritual.

The preparations of the heart in man, and the answer of the tongue, is from the LORD. All the ways of a man are clean in his own eyes; but the LORD weigheth the spirits. Commit thy works unto the LORD, and thy thoughts shall be established. The LORD hath made all things for himself: yea, even the wicked for the day of evil.

(Proverbs 16:1)

Thought 4: The I AM'S of God as seen in the Scripture

Thinking in a broad sense about the word, *all*; consider this: even God's image of Himself was created by Him. Such images as "I AM" or "I the LORD thy God am" were made by God. There are other images that were made according to the statement that *without him was not any thing made that was made*. Among these are the images such as the one visualized by Hagar when she viewed God's angel. Though this was not a direct sighting of God, it did cause Hagar to produce an image of God's working with her.

> *And she called the name of the LORD that spake unto her, Thou God seest me: for she said, Have I also here looked after him that seeth me?*
>
> (Genesis 16:13)

There are unfortunately other images that are a composite of errors. These images are produced from the wishes of mankind to have some control over God. However, this too is not as simple as it seems, but we will not explore this lack of simplicity either, at this time. For now, just think of these errors as being ones that are put forth to bring about submission to the rule of men.

> *Then spake Jesus to the multitude, and to his disciples, Saying The scribes and the Pharisees sit in Moses' seat: All therefore whatsoever they bid you observe, that observe and do; but do not ye after their works: for they say, and do not. For they bind heavy burdens and grievous to be borne, and lay them on men's shoulders; but they themselves will not move them with one of their fingers. But all their works they do for to be seen of men: they make broad their phylacteries, and enlarge the borders of their garments, And love the uppermost rooms at feasts, and the chief seats in the synagogues, And greetings in the markets, and to be called of men, Rabbi, Rabbi. But be not ye called Rabbi: for one is your Master, even Christ; and all ye are brethren.*
>
> *And call no man your father upon the earth: for one is your Father, which is in heaven. Neither be ye called masters: for one is your Master, even Christ. But he that is greatest among you shall be your servant. And whosoever shall exalt himself shall be abased; and he that shall humble himself shall be exalted.*
>
> *But woe unto you, scribes and Pharisees, hypocrites! for ye shut up the kingdom of heaven against men: for ye neither go in yourselves, neither suffer ye them that are entering to go in. Woe unto you, scribes and Pharisees, hypocrites! for ye devour widows' houses, and for a pretence make long*

> *prayer: therefore ye shall receive the greater damnation. Woe unto you, scribes and Pharisees, hypocrites! for ye compass sea and land to make one proselyte, and when he is made, ye make him twofold more the child of hell than yourselves.*

(Matthew 23:1-15)

Even in the erroneous creation by humans of an image of God, God is manifested and will be magnified among man. It is not the preferred way, of knowing the good; but knowing what is not good can point the way to that which is good, and can point the way to He who is good.

> *Some indeed preach Christ even of envy and strife; and some also of good will: The one preach Christ of contention, not sincerely, supposing to add affliction to my bonds: But the other of love, knowing that I am set for the defence of the gospel. What then? notwithstanding, every way, whether in pretence, or in truth, Christ is preached; and I therein do rejoice, yea, and will rejoice. For I know that this shall turn to my salvation through your prayer, and the supply of the Spirit of Jesus Christ, According to my earnest expectation and my hope, that in nothing I shall be ashamed, but that with all boldness, as always, so now also Christ shall be magnified in my body, whether it be by life, or by death. For to me to live is Christ, and to die is gain.*

(Philippians 1:15-21)

There is a similar type of presentation of God, which though done in error, is allowed by God. This type of presentation on behalf of God is used to test the faith of the people of God. It is also used to weed out those who would pervert the ways of God. It is described by Moses.

> *If there arise among you a prophet, or a dreamer of dreams, and giveth thee a sign or a wonder, And the sign or the wonder come to pass, whereof he spake unto thee, saying, Let us go after other gods, which thou hast not known, and let us serve them; Thou shalt not hearken unto the words of that prophet, or that dreamer of dreams: for the LORD your God proveth you, to know whether ye love*

> *the LORD your God with all your heart and with all your soul. Ye shall walk after the LORD your God, and fear him, and keep his commandments, and obey his voice, and ye shall serve him, and cleave unto him. And that prophet, or that dreamer of dreams, shall be put to death; because he hath spoken to turn you away from the LORD your God, which brought you out of the land of Egypt, and redeemed you out of the house of bondage, to thrust thee out of the way which the LORD thy God commanded thee to walk in. So shalt thou put the evil away from the midst of thee.*
>
> (Deuteronomy 13:1-5)

And please remember that to ostracize, isolate and confine is also a most effective form of death. It is a death to the spirit of man, a community, a region or even a nation.

Thought 5: Even the "negatives" arise from God in some form

Within some of the images of God are historically negative terms: such as Jealous. If God is willing either to apply them to Himself, or to allow His servants to apply them to Him, they must be owned by Him. All that is owned by Him was created by Him. Thus, God is even the creator of the historically negative terms. This does not mean that God uses them in a negative fashion, only that He does have a use for them in the development of mankind. Consider this most carefully: God is even the author of the concept of sin.

> *For when we were in the flesh, the motions of sins, which were by the law, did work in our members to bring forth fruit unto death. But now we are delivered from the law, that being dead wherein we were held; that we should serve in newness of spirit, and not in the oldness of the letter. What shall we say then? is the law sin? God forbid. Nay, I had not known sin, but by the law: for I had not known lust, except the law had said, Thou shalt not covet.*
>
> (Romans 7:5-7)

However, that does not mean that we just lay down in defeat under the power of sin. We must resist it through the gift of the Holy Ghost, in Jesus Christ.

> *But sin, taking occasion by the commandment, wrought in me all manner of concupiscence. For without the law sin was dead. For I was alive without the law once: but when the commandment came, sin revived, and I died. And the commandment, which was ordained to life, I found to be unto death. For sin, taking occasion by the commandment, deceived me, and by it slew me.*
>
> *Wherefore the law is holy, and the commandment holy, and just, and good. Was then that which is good made death unto me? God forbid. But sin, that it might appear sin, working death in me by that which is good; that sin by the commandment might become exceeding sinful. For we know that the law is spiritual: but I am carnal, sold under sin.*

(Romans 7:8-14)

> *O wretched man that I am! who shall deliver me from the body of this death?*
>
> *I thank God through Jesus Christ our Lord. So then with the mind I myself serve the law of God; but with the flesh the law of sin.*

(Romans 7:24-25)

This concept of sin is very necessary; in order to show mankind that it has an irrevocable need for God. One of the tools of mankind is sin. It is not the preferable tool, but it is a tool. Sin in a man, if rightly visualized, will drive a man directly to God. This is similar to the way a cough, which if it persists, drives a man to a doctor for healing. The cough is not bad; it is a messenger of the true nature of the man.

This type of messenger is especially useful when a formerly dormant birth defect rears its head in later life. This is what happens spiritually, when we reach the point of maturation such that we activate the formerly dormant knowledge of good and evil. God highlighted this in his statement about the condemnation of those who violated His will, as set aside the exemption for those who had no idea of what they were doing.

> *And the LORD spake unto Moses and unto Aaron, saying, How long shall I bear with this evil congregation, which murmur against me? I have heard the murmurings of the children of Israel, which they murmur against me.*

> *Say unto them, As truly as I live, saith the LORD, as ye have spoken in mine ears, so will I do to you: Your carcases shall fall in this wilderness; and all that were numbered of you, according to your whole number, from twenty years old and upward, which have murmured against me, Doubtless ye shall not come into the land, concerning which I sware to make you dwell therein, save Caleb the son of Jephunneh, and Joshua the son of Nun. But your little ones, which ye said should be a prey, them will I bring in, and they shall know the land which ye have despised. But as for you, your carcases, they shall fall in this wilderness.*

(Numbers 14:26-32)

Thought 6: To understand the form is the mission of mankind

All things, including the negatives, were created by God. It is not the thing that is the culprit, but the form of use. We have seen how we can use a negative to cause us to seek the shelter of God. This is no less true when we speak of the positives. These, too, must be passed through the filter of the will of God. The apostle Paul gives us insight on this.

> *Know ye not that the unrighteous shall not inherit the kingdom of God? Be not deceived: neither fornicators, nor idolaters, nor adulterers, nor effeminate, nor abusers of themselves with mankind, Nor thieves, nor covetous, nor drunkards, nor revilers, nor extortioners, shall inherit the kingdom of God. And such were some of you: but ye are washed, but ye are sanctified, but ye are justified in the name of the Lord Jesus, and by the Spirit of our God. All things are lawful unto me, but all things are not expedient: all things are lawful for me, but I will not be brought under the power of any.*

(1 Corinthians 6:9-12)

We need a mediator from God to give us His understanding of the form of the matter, in our spirit, in the Spirit. Human understanding is not sufficient for proper execution of the moral law of God. This Mediator is, and he has been here.

> *Jesus saith unto him, I am the way, the truth, and the life: no man cometh unto the Father, but by me. If ye had known me, ye should have known my Father also: and from henceforth ye know him, and have seen him.*

(John 14:6-7)

It is only through the constancy of the Mediator that we can hope to achieve the understanding of eternal excellence in life.

Thought 7: To yield is the only way to understand the form to use

This is especially true of our use of the blessings in the concepts that have been presented to us by God. The requirement for constant contact is shown in Jesus. He is in singular agreement with the Father; the Father and the Son are one on this matter. This is why he would not leave us unattended: we need the Teacher.

> *If ye love me, keep my commandments. And I will pray the Father, and he shall give you another Comforter, that he may abide with you for ever; Even the Spirit of truth; whom the world cannot receive, because it seeth him not, neither knoweth him: but ye know him; for he dwelleth with you, and shall be in you.*

(John 14:15-17)

Furthermore, the Mediator, Jesus Christ, will return to us again to validate within us his eternal concern for our well-being. For there will come a time when the oppression on earth will rise to such a great level that we will even lose the rational sight of the power of the Comforter, as it impacts all lives. At this time, we will begin to feel comfortless because of circumstances, even in the presence of the Comforter. Then Jesus will fulfill his promise and we will rest in the peace of God in eternity.

> *I will not leave you comfortless: I will come to you.*

(John 14:18)

Then, having understanding of the full circle, we will know that everything which comes from God will also, one day, return to Him. And we will believe that God has final say as to the disposition of all that is.

The Word from the Bible

Genesis 5:28-32

And Lamech lived an hundred eighty and two years, and begat a son: And he called his name Noah, saying, This same shall comfort us concerning our work and toil of our hands, because of the ground which the LORD hath cursed. And Lamech lived after he begat Noah five hundred ninety and five years, and begat sons and daughters: And all the days of Lamech were seven hundred seventy and seven years: and he died.

And Noah was five hundred years old: and Noah begat Shem, Ham, and Japheth.

Genesis 6:11-22

The earth also was corrupt before God, and the earth was filled with violence. And God looked upon the earth, and, behold, it was corrupt; for all flesh had corrupted his way upon the earth.

And God said unto Noah, The end of all flesh is come before me; for the earth is filled with violence through them; and, behold, I will destroy them with the earth. Make thee an ark of gopher wood; rooms shalt thou make in the ark, and shalt pitch it within and without with pitch. And this is the fashion which thou shalt make it of: The length of the ark shall be three hundred cubits, the breadth of it fifty cubits, and the height of it thirty cubits. A window shalt thou make to the ark, and in a cubit shalt thou finish it above; and the door of the ark shalt thou set in the side thereof; with lower, second, and third stories shalt thou make it.

And, behold, I, even I, do bring a flood of waters upon the earth, to destroy all flesh, wherein is the breath of life, from under heaven; and every thing that is in the earth shall die. But with thee will I establish my covenant; and thou shalt come into the ark, thou, and thy sons, and thy wife, and thy sons' wives with thee.

And of every living thing of all flesh, two of every sort shalt thou bring into the ark, to keep them alive with thee; they shall be male and female. Of fowls after their kind, and of cattle after their kind, of every creeping thing of the earth after his kind, two of every sort shall come unto thee, to keep them alive. And take thou unto thee of all food that is eaten, and thou shalt gather it to thee; and it shall be for food for thee, and for them.

Thus did Noah; according to all that God commanded him, so did he.

Genesis 7:6

And Noah was six hundred years old when the flood of waters was upon the earth.

Chapter Five

Period of refreshing

God and Moses had a discovery time, where Moses wanted to know by what authority he was entering Egypt to retrieve the children of Israel.

> *And Moses said unto God, Behold, when I come unto the children of Israel, and shall say unto them, The God of your fathers hath sent me unto you; and they shall say to me, What is his name? what shall I say unto them?*
>
> *And God said unto Moses, I AM THAT I AM: and he said, Thus shalt thou say unto the children of Israel, I AM hath sent me unto you.*
>
> (Exodus 3:13-14)

The LORD did not say to Moses, "And you have to rush; because if you do not get there before this period is gone, you will have to say 'I WAS' sent you." It may seem that I am somewhat irreverent, in saying this. Yes, I do say it to catch your attention. I do so because it is a very serious matter. The matter is this: God is "I AM", across all times. He is the same yesterday, today and forever. So, why is this important?

It is important because it ties in with a notion that is commonly implied, if not directly stated, about the time of Noah. From listening to some of our religious leaders tone, one might get the impression that God was surprised by the events among mankind in the day of Noah. Not so; God is "I AM" in the *time* before the foundation of the world, and He is "I AM" in the time of Noah. Thus, He already knew what happened. One cannot be surprised by what one already knows. And in the case of God, nothing can happen that is not allowed by God: this includes the actions of man.

I say allowed because God does not condone the evil that mankind does; He just does not punish it until He knows it must be addressed. Some would apply the following Scripture to say that God felt He had made a mistake in creating mankind, at least that part of mankind leading up to Noah.

> *And God saw that the wickedness of man was great in the earth, and that every imagination of the thoughts of his heart was only evil continually. And it repented the LORD that he had made man on the earth, and it grieved him at his heart. And the LORD said, I will destroy man whom I have created from the face of the earth; both man, and beast, and the creeping thing, and the fowls of the air; for it repenteth me that I have made them.*

> (Genesis 6:5-7)

The term repented does not carry the same message as man's repentance. Man repents because he has done evil, and must petition God for forgiveness. A part of the forgiveness in repentance is making restitution. An example from the New Testament might clarify this concept.

> *And Jesus entered and passed through Jericho. And, behold, there was a man named Zacchaeus, which was the chief among the publicans, and he was rich. And he sought to see Jesus who he was; and could not for the press, because he was little of stature. And he ran before, and climbed up into a sycomore tree to see him: for he was to pass that way.*

> *And when Jesus came to the place, he looked up, and saw him, and said unto him, Zacchaeus, make haste, and come down; for to day I must abide at thy house. And he made haste, and came down, and received him joyfully.*

> *And when they saw it, they all murmured, saying, That he was gone to be guest with a man that is a sinner. And Zacchaeus stood, and said unto the Lord; Behold, Lord, the half of my goods I give to the poor; and if I have taken any thing from any man by false accusation, I restore him fourfold.*

> (Luke 19:1-8)

Man must constantly repent of evil acts. God, however, does not perform evil acts: God does not make mistakes.

Let no man say when he is tempted, I am tempted of God: for God cannot be tempted with evil, neither tempteth he any man:

(James 1:13)

What God makes, is always good. This includes the creation of man. Six times, plus one, in the creation (recorded in the book of Genesis) He described what He had made as good.

1:4   And God saw the light, that it was good: and God divided the light from the darkness.

1:10   And God called the dry land Earth; and the gathering together of the waters called he Seas: and God saw that it was good.

1:12   And the earth brought forth grass, and herb yielding seed after his kind, and the tree yielding fruit, whose seed was in itself, after his kind: and God saw that it was good.

1:18   And to rule over the day and over the night, and to divide the light from the darkness: and God saw that it was good.

1:21   And God created great whales, and every living creature that moveth, which the waters brought forth abundantly, after their kind, and every winged fowl after his kind: and God saw that it was good.

1:25   And God made the beast of the earth after his kind, and cattle after their kind, and every thing that creepeth upon the earth after his kind: and God saw that it was good.

1:31   And God saw every thing that he had made, and, behold, it was very good. And the evening and the morning were the sixth day.

When God repents, it is a time when He will activate another part of His plan; to correct an error that will, if left unchecked, lead to the destruction of mankind. Such destruction will not happen; because it would defeat His act of creating man. The well-being of mankind will be preserved; even when that means the removal of any *cancer* that is infecting mankind and attempting to go beyond the limits set by God. Jesus of Nazareth gives us an example of God's timing.

> *But pray ye that your flight be not in the winter, neither on the sabbath day: For then shall be great tribulation, such as was not since the beginning of the world to this time, no, nor ever shall be. And except those days should be shortened, there should no flesh be saved: but for the elect's sake those days shall be shortened.*
>
> (Matthew 24:20-22)

Moral laws and the example of Israel

The principle of God's timed tolerance is clearly shown in the Law of Moses, and the separations from the neighbors that were required (this may also be referred to it as, segregation). These separations were such that they would endanger the survival of the nation, by containing the impact of the neighbors. Yes, if integration with the neighbors was left unchecked the people might survive, and they might stay together as a nation under the sun. However, they would not be a nation under God, and they would no longer be a nation fit to carry out the purpose for which they were begotten by God.

> *Now therefore, if ye will obey my voice indeed, and keep my covenant, then ye shall be a peculiar treasure unto me above all people: for all the earth is mine: And ye shall be unto me a kingdom of priests, and an holy nation. These are the words which thou shalt speak unto the children of Israel.*
>
> (Exodus 19:5-6)

Meditation: This is something every nation should take very seriously. When you cease to perform the functions in the world for which God designed you, you are going back to the time of the rebellions of the children of Israel. In fact, you may be returning to the day of Noah. By this return, you make your people eligible for the same recompense God delivered to the people of Noah's day. However, according to Scripture he will not visit it in the same fashion--but there are many other methods that God has to deliver national judgment.

It is not sufficient to God that you manufacture your own purpose. The nation of Israel is witness to the calamity that comes when man, government and religious officials, create a purpose that is not in line with God's purpose. Refer to this nation in the Scripture for lessons on this matter.

As surely as God established physical laws ... He also established moral laws

We seem to be fairly comfortable with the physical laws. I believe this is because they obviously enforce themselves. A rock falling from a ledge will not petition gravity to suspend itself, so that the rock does not crush anything.

The moral laws, however, are another matter. These laws are those that we have the responsibility to enforce on ourselves. On the other hand, we also have the authority to suspend them for our self. We have been given a spirit that may also empower us to suspend the laws for others, on our behalf. This we do, by convincing others that such a suspension is in fact in their best interest; which, generally, it is not. This is what the Moabites did to the Midianites, their brethren of the seed of Abraham, when they wanted to destroy the children of Israel.

> *And the children of Israel set forward, and pitched in the plains of Moab on this side Jordan by Jericho. And Balak the son of Zippor saw all that Israel had done to the Amorites. And Moab was sore afraid of the people, because they were many: and Moab was distressed because of the children of Israel. And Moab said unto the elders of Midian, Now shall this company lick up all that are round about us, as the ox licketh up the grass of the field. And Balak the son of Zippor was king of the Moabites at that time.*

(Numbers 22:1-4)

Moral laws for the preservation of mankind

God established certain moral laws that are for the benefit of individuals. God also has a set of moral laws that are for the benefit of nations. There is even a moral law that is for the benefit of all mankind. Well, actually there are two, but they function as one. These two, which are one, form the basis of all national, regional, religious and individual moral laws.

> *But when the Pharisees had heard that he had put the Sadducees to silence, they were gathered together. Then one of them, which was a lawyer, asked him a question, tempting him, and saying, Master, which is the great commandment in the law?*
>
> *Jesus said unto him, Thou shalt love the Lord thy God with all thy heart, and with all thy soul, and with all thy mind. This is the first and great commandment. And the second is like unto it, Thou shalt love thy neighbour as thyself. On these two commandments hang all the law and the prophets.*

(Matthew 22:34-40)

Critical mass is unknown ... Only the Father knows the time ...

We briefly mentioned a concept that can be summarized as, *critical mass*. What is the mass of violations of God's moral law that triggers direct action from Him? Jesus was asked a question on this order. This same question could have been asked of Noah by his sons, concerning their future, and they could have been given a similar response: *It is not for you to know the times or the seasons, which the Father hath put in his own power.*

> *When they therefore were come together, they asked of him, saying, Lord, wilt thou at this time restore again the kingdom to Israel?*
>
> *And he said unto them, It is not for you to know the times or the seasons, which the Father hath put in his own power. But ye shall receive power, after that the Holy Ghost is come upon you: and ye shall be witnesses unto me both in Jerusalem, and in all Judaea, and in Samaria, and unto the uttermost part of the earth.*

(Acts 1:6-8)

The end does not pertain only to the end of this human system. It can be the end of an age or a period in the human timeline.

Like an earthly parent, it grieves God when He triggers a higher moral law: the term repent.

Let us think in reverse--using human examples--about God's Fatherhood of mankind: I say, "thinking in reverse," because it is God that sets the pattern, which human parents then imitate. We understand that for an earthly father, parts of the concept of repenting are the actions of thinking through what must be done, and understanding that the process of restoration will be a painful one. We are accustomed to this in modern surgical and dental procedures. We know that even when anesthetic is given, it will wear off. At that point, some measure of pain will return. It will be less than not performing the procedure. It will be less, in the long run, than it would have been without anesthetic. Pain, however, will be there.

> *In that day shalt thou not be ashamed for all thy doings, wherein thou hast transgressed against me: for then I will take away out of the midst of thee them that rejoice in thy pride, and thou shalt no more be haughty because of my holy mountain. I will also leave in the midst of thee an afflicted and poor people, and they shall trust in the name of the LORD. The remnant of Israel shall not do iniquity, nor speak lies; neither shall a deceitful tongue be found in their mouth: for they shall feed and lie down, and none shall make them afraid.*
>
> (Zephaniah 3:11-13)

What has always struck me as strange in the days of Noah is that there was no spiritual reawakening by mankind. With the passage of time, in the building of the boat, the state of mankind had still not improved to the point where God turned aside judgment.

> *Even from the days of your fathers ye are gone away from mine ordinances, and have not kept them. Return unto me, and I will return unto you, saith the LORD of hosts. But ye said, Wherein shall we return?*
>
> (Malachi 3:7)

The flood: the highest moral law of God for the preservation of mankind

Think about it for a moment. How much further decayed would be the condition of mankind, if it had been allowed to continue without this key incident? There was a need for a refreshing that only the law of God can accomplish; and this could only be done by starting with a core that loved God. This core was only present in Noah, and, by extension, in his family. This is a serious indicator of the extreme needs of mankind. Other than Noah, all of mankind had become a fulfillment of Scripture. The Scripture was fulfilled during Noah's time, even though it was not revealed on a national level until a time past Noah's: this is the timelessness of God.

> *To the chief Musician, A Psalm of David.*
>
> *The fool hath said in his heart, There is no God. They are corrupt, they have done abominable works, there is none that doeth good. The LORD looked down from heaven upon the children of men, to see if there were any that did understand, and seek God. They are all gone aside, they are all together become filthy: there is none that doeth good, no, not one.*
>
> (Psalm 14:1-3)

A new way is promised

After the refreshing, God established a covenant with all that was, and all those that would come thereafter. However, this meant that God had prepared another technique to deal with man's ignoring of the moral law. This technique is revealed in the Messiah.

> *For, behold, the day cometh, that shall burn as an oven; and all the proud, yea, and all that do wickedly, shall be stubble: and the day that cometh shall burn them up, saith the LORD of hosts, that it shall leave them neither root nor branch. But unto you that fear my name shall the Sun of righteousness arise with healing in his wings; and ye shall go forth, and grow up as calves of the stall. And ye shall tread down the wicked; for they shall be ashes under the soles of your feet in the day that I shall do this, saith the LORD of hosts. Remember ye the law of Moses my servant,*

which I commanded unto him in Horeb for all Israel, with the statutes and judgments.

Behold, I will send you Elijah the prophet before the coming of the great and dreadful day of the LORD: And he shall turn the heart of the fathers to the children, and the heart of the children to their fathers, lest I come and smite the earth with a curse.

(Malachi 4:1-6)

The Messiah is the new way; which will be explored more, further on.

*Sometimes in this life
We hit a wall,
Then its time for
A major overhaul.*

*We fix things here,
We tweak things there;
But finally we admit
It is beyond repair.*

*We search for pieces
That we can save,
Before our strivings
End at the grave.*

*If diligent in our search,
We find something to restore,
Instead of throwing
Everything out the door.*

*But the time does come
When we must begin
To change what is,
To start to amend*

*The ways things are,
To produce what must be;
But the anguish we feel
Is not pretty to see.*

*We separate what is good
From that which remains.
Then, we place our stakes,
And we make our claims.*

*The good we doth prepare
For the time to be revealed;
Eventually, we tear down,
In order to rebuild.*

*The pieces that remain
May be really small,*

*But from these pieces
Grows a thing quite tall.*

*God was faced with
This time most depressing,
And instead of discarding all,
He caused a refreshing.*

Chapter 5a

Positive = Negative

We mostly think of words as positive or negative. On rare occasion we think of some words as being neutral. Words, however, are all neutral. They only gain a character when they are added to expressions. This is especially true of the highly emotional words, such as love, hate, joy, and peace. These words have very little meaning when said alone.

This is a difficult concept for many to accept. Take, for instance, the word *hate*. Most people think of it as being a negative thing. However, consider the following statement: I hate evil and abuse. Is the word *hate* negative in this statement? Actually, not. In this sentence, the word is motivational. The intensity of the statement sets the stage for the reaction that we are willing to give when confronted with the object of the emotion: in this case, evil and abuse.

However, when we hear the statement, *I hate you*, we are generally sure that this is not a good thing. We are not necessarily ready to say that it is a bad thing, but we feel fairly strongly that it is not a positive thing. However, there is a case where it does enter into the category of positive motivation. Add to the statement the following phrase: *when you willingly abuse children*. This, then, gives us a category of person who is worthy of some measure of disdain. However, it really is not complete.

Statements and expressions are only complete when they fully describe the object of the action. In the case of the full sentence above, the hate is actually not of a person, but of a type of behavior. It might be clearer to say "I hate what you do when you abuse children." This more clearly identify the thing that is being hated, and it moves us closer to a position where we can say that something is worthy of that high an emotion. However, we have still not arrived at a complete understanding of the nature of the word, *hate*, and why it can be applied to this action. One question that comes to mind is "What is meant by the term abuse?"

Does the person observing the action of the other see a situation of physical damage, or is it a matter of withholding of privilege? Some feel that it is an abuse of a child if we do not give them what they fervently ask for (also known as whining). This denial is thought, by some, to be psychologically damaging to the child. On a related subject, some people feel that extreme damage is being inflicted on a child being given a spanking. There are many parents, and some legal folk, who have attempted to convert this form of discipline into a criminal action.

So, in light of these nuances of speech, what are we to do with the matter of communication? How do we make sure that what we say is what we mean? Furthermore, how do we make sure that what we mean is appropriate for what we see?

The handling of nuances of speech is an important matter in the field of religion, and in our discussions of the working and way of the LORD. For communication sake, there are many things that have been said about God. We need to be sure that we are conveying the proper message, appropriate for the events that are unfolding, or that are under review. To help us explore this matter further, I will list just a few here. This list will only include those that contain words that may be considered negative.

> *Therefore the LORD, the God of hosts, the Lord, saith thus; Wailing shall be in all streets; and they shall say in all the highways, Alas! alas! and they shall call the husbandman to mourning, and such as are skilful of lamentation to wailing. And in all vineyards shall be wailing: for I will pass through thee, saith the LORD.*

> *Woe unto you that desire the day of the LORD! to what end is it for you? the day of the LORD is darkness, and not light. As if a man did flee from a lion, and a bear met him; or went into the house, and leaned his hand on the wall, and a serpent bit him. Shall not the day of the LORD be darkness, and not light? even very dark, and no brightness in it?*

> *I hate, I despise your feast days, and I will not smell in your solemn assemblies.*

> (Amos 5:16-21)

> *Take heed to thyself, lest thou make a covenant with the inhabitants of the land whither thou goest, lest it be for a*

snare in the midst of thee: But ye shall destroy their altars, break their images, and cut down their groves: For thou shalt worship no other god: for the LORD, whose name is Jealous, is a jealous God: Lest thou make a covenant with the inhabitants of the land, and they go a whoring after their gods, and do sacrifice unto their gods, and one call thee, and thou eat of his sacrifice; And thou take of their daughters unto thy sons, and their daughters go a whoring after their gods, and make thy sons go a whoring after their gods.

(Exodus 34:12-16)

And the LORD said unto Moses, When thou goest to return into Egypt, see that thou do all those wonders before Pharaoh, which I have put in thine hand: but I will harden his heart, that he shall not let the people go.

(Exodus 4:21)

And God saw that the wickedness of man was great in the earth, and that every imagination of the thoughts of his heart was only evil continually. And it repented the LORD that he had made man on the earth, and it grieved him at his heart. And the LORD said, I will destroy man whom I have created from the face of the earth; both man, and beast, and the creeping thing, and the fowls of the air; for it repenteth me that I have made them. But Noah found grace in the eyes of the LORD.

(Genesis 6:5-8)

And Moses said unto them, Have ye saved all the women alive? Behold, these caused the children of Israel, through the counsel of Balaam, to commit trespass against the LORD in the matter of Peor, and there was a plague among the congregation of the LORD. Now therefore kill every male among the little ones, and kill every woman that hath known man by lying with him. But all the women children, that have not known a man by lying with him, keep alive for yourselves.

(Numbers 31:15-18)

We must be careful each time we read one of these statements; we must read all the surrounding matters. This may mean that we will have to read an entire chapter, or in some cases the entire Bible, before we can make a *judgment* about what is appropriate and what is not. There is a statement on the matter of judgment that takes us one step further.

> *Judge not, that ye be not judged. For with what judgment ye judge, ye shall be judged: and with what measure ye mete, it shall be measured to you again.*
>
> *And why beholdest thou the mote that is in thy brother's eye, but considerest not the beam that is in thine own eye? Or how wilt thou say to thy brother, Let me pull out the mote out of thine eye; and, behold, a beam is in thine own eye? Thou hypocrite, first cast out the beam out of thine own eye; and then shalt thou see clearly to cast out the mote out of thy brother's eye.*
>
> (Matthew 7:1-5)

How important is this concept?

Very!

There is only one Being with the breadth of understanding to execute judgment: this is God. Therefore, let judgment rest with God. There is one other person qualified to judge; this is Jesus Christ. However, we must take this concept in stages.

Jesus Christ had to play two roles while he was on the earth. The first role was as a citizen of the nation of Israel, in what we will call his mankind outfit. The second role is as a citizen of Heaven, in what we will call his God-kind outfit. In his God-kind outfit he is known as both the Son of man and the Son of God. Each role has a different relationship with judgment. While Jesus was on the earth, in his mankind outfit, he did not judge.

> *Then spake Jesus again unto them, saying, I am the light of the world: he that followeth me shall not walk in darkness, but shall have the light of life.*
>
> *The Pharisees therefore said unto him, Thou bearest record of thyself; thy record is not true.*
>
> *Jesus answered and said unto them, Though I bear record of myself, yet my record is true: for I know whence I came,*

and whither I go; but ye cannot tell whence I come, and whither I go. Ye judge after the flesh; I judge no man. And yet if I judge, my judgment is true: for I am not alone, but I and the Father that sent me.

(John 8:12-16)

Jesus, while in his God-kind outfit, also known to us as the Son of man, was given an honor that no man ever had, and that no other man would ever have. He was given this honor once he was cloaked with, and begun speaking in, his God-kind outfit. Eventually the mankind outfit was transformed and he was only in the God-kind outfit. This happened at his transfiguration.

And after six days Jesus taketh Peter, James, and John his brother, and bringeth them up into an high mountain apart, And was transfigured before them: and his face did shine as the sun, and his raiment was white as the light. And, behold, there appeared unto them Moses and Elias talking with him.

Then answered Peter, and said unto Jesus, Lord, it is good for us to be here: if thou wilt, let us make here three tabernacles; one for thee, and one for Moses, and one for Elias.

While he yet spake, behold, a bright cloud overshadowed them: and behold a voice out of the cloud, which said, This is my beloved Son, in whom I am well pleased; hear ye him. And when the disciples heard it, they fell on their face, and were sore afraid.

And Jesus came and touched them, and said, Arise, and be not afraid. And when they had lifted up their eyes, they saw no man, save Jesus only.

(Matthew 17:1-8)

The power of the God-kind outfit was demonstrated when he refused to allow death to hold him, and he returned to the natural side of life, to show forth the glory of God.

In the end of the sabbath, as it began to dawn toward the first day of the week, came Mary Magdalene and the other Mary to see the sepulchre. And, behold, there was a great

> *earthquake: for the angel of the Lord descended from heaven, and came and rolled back the stone from the door, and sat upon it. His countenance was like lightning, and his raiment white as snow: And for fear of him the keepers did shake, and became as dead men.*
>
> *And the angel answered and said unto the women, Fear not ye: for I know that ye seek Jesus, which was crucified. He is not here: for he is risen, as he said. Come, see the place where the Lord lay. And go quickly, and tell his disciples that he is risen from the dead; and, behold, he goeth before you into Galilee; there shall ye see him: lo, I have told you.*
>
> *And they departed quickly from the sepulchre with fear and great joy; and did run to bring his disciples word.*

(Matthew 28:1-8)

Furthermore, Jesus of Nazareth was magnificently equipped by God to perform all functions that would ever be required of the Son of God and the Son of man, as Jesus Christ, the Lord.

> *Then the eleven disciples went away into Galilee, into a mountain where Jesus had appointed them. And when they saw him, they worshipped him: but some doubted.*
>
> *And Jesus came and spake unto them, saying, All power is given unto me in heaven and in earth. Go ye therefore, and teach all nations, baptizing them in the name of the Father, and of the Son, and of the Holy Ghost: Teaching them to observe all things whatsoever I have commanded you: and, lo, I am with you alway, even unto the end of the world. Amen.*

(Matthew 28:16-20)

Once Jesus Christ had obtained all power in heaven and earth, bestowed on him by the Father, he was more than qualified to judge both men and angels. Additionally, Jesus Christ was, and still is, authorized, by God, to share his abilities with the ones among the elect of God. The following ones are also given judgmental authority by Christ, in God.

> *Then answered Peter and said unto him, Behold, we have forsaken all, and followed thee; what shall we have therefore?*
>
> *And Jesus said unto them, Verily I say unto you, That ye which have followed me, in the regeneration when the Son of man shall sit in the throne of his glory, ye also shall sit upon twelve thrones, judging the twelve tribes of Israel. And every one that hath forsaken houses, or brethren, or sisters, or father, or mother, or wife, or children, or lands, for my name's sake, shall receive an hundredfold, and shall inherit everlasting life. But many that are first shall be last; and the last shall be first.*
>
> (Matthew 19:27-30)
>
> *And when the people were gathered thick together, he began to say, This is an evil generation: they seek a sign; and there shall no sign be given it, but the sign of Jonas the prophet. For as Jonas was a sign unto the Ninevites, so shall also the Son of man be to this generation. The queen of the south shall rise up in the judgment with the men of this generation, and condemn them: for she came from the utmost parts of the earth to hear the wisdom of Solomon; and, behold, a greater than Solomon is here. The men of Nineve shall rise up in the judgment with this generation, and shall condemn it: for they repented at the preaching of Jonas; and, behold, a greater than Jonas is here.*
>
> (Luke 11:29-32)

However, the judgmental ability of the others was provided to them because they have a God given acquaintance with the people whom they will judge; and they know the glory of God that these people have abused, and some have even rejected. The remainder of humanity will be judged only by the selected Judge from God: this is Jesus Christ.

> *Then answered Jesus and said unto them, Verily, verily, I say unto you, The Son can do nothing of himself, but what he seeth the Father do: for what things soever he doeth, these also doeth the Son likewise. For the Father loveth the Son, and sheweth him all things that himself doeth: and he*

> *will shew him greater works than these, that ye may marvel. For as the Father raiseth up the dead, and quickeneth them; even so the Son quickeneth whom he will.*
>
> *For the Father judgeth no man, but hath committed all judgment unto the Son: That all men should honour the Son, even as they honour the Father. He that honoureth not the Son honoureth not the Father which hath sent him.*
>
> (John 5:19-23)

If we think that we should be included in the ranks of those who are able to judge, then please study these two passages of Scripture; then you will begin to understand how difficult judging can be. Would you judge these statements as evil or righteous, good or bad?

> *And there went great multitudes with him: and he turned, and said unto them, If any man come to me, and hate not his father, and mother, and wife, and children, and brethren, and sisters, yea, and his own life also, he cannot be my disciple. And whosoever doth not bear his cross, and come after me, cannot be my disciple.*
>
> *For which of you, intending to build a tower, sitteth not down first, and counteth the cost, whether he have sufficient to finish it? Lest haply, after he hath laid the foundation, and is not able to finish it, all that behold it begin to mock him, Saying, This man began to build, and was not able to finish.*
>
> *Or what king, going to make war against another king, sitteth not down first, and consulteth whether he be able with ten thousand to meet him that cometh against him with twenty thousand? Or else, while the other is yet a great way off, he sendeth an ambassage, and desireth conditions of peace. So likewise, whosoever he be of you that forsaketh not all that he hath, he cannot be my disciple.*
>
> (Luke 14:25-33)

This Scripture was applied to the apostle who would have the responsibility to participate in the judgment of the tribes of Israel; including the twelve who would be given the authority to do so. The word hate in this expression is invoking an intensity of emotion that places our life, which we have lived up to this point, including our birth and family situation, as something that is in total subjection to the will of God. When we are at this point in life, the work that He calls us to do is of such a high magnitude that if a choice ever arises between our family and God, we will choose God.

Sometimes when we serve God we will find ourselves in situations where we really do not like having been born, and wish that we never existed. This is the intensity that may accompany full service to God. This is not the level that is required of everyone. However, there is a level of devotion to God that is required of all mankind: you can be sure that all are called to accept the salvation that is provided for them in Christ.

> *And as Moses lifted up the serpent in the wilderness, even so must the Son of man be lifted up: That whosoever believeth in him should not perish, but have eternal life. For God so loved the world, that he gave his only begotten Son, that whosoever believeth in him should not perish, but have everlasting life. For God sent not his Son into the world to condemn the world; but that the world through him might be saved. He that believeth on him is not condemned: but he that believeth not is condemned already, because he hath not believed in the name of the only begotten Son of God. And this is the condemnation, that light is come into the world, and men loved darkness rather than light, because their deeds were evil.*
>
> (John 3:14-19)

> *Now is the judgment of this world: now shall the prince of this world be cast out. And I, if I be lifted up from the earth, will draw all men unto me. This he said, signifying what death he should die.*
>
> (John 12:31-33)

Read the text of Luke 14:25-33, above, and you will see the word, disciple. Everyone is not called to be a disciple of Christ; only those ones that can live up to these qualifications. All men will be drawn to God through Jesus, but not all men will be chosen to be disciples.

Yes, discipleship is a matter of selection by God.

No, there is no such thing as an occupation of discipleship. There is no record in Scripture of any apostle who took on the mantle by himself; all were called by Jesus Christ. Pretense is not a wise thing to practice; there is an extreme penalty for pretenders.

> *And when the king came in to see the guests, he saw there a man which had not on a wedding garment: And he saith unto him, Friend, how camest thou in hither not having a wedding garment?*
>
> *And he was speechless.*
>
> *Then said the king to the servants, Bind him hand and foot, and take him away, and cast him into outer darkness, there shall be weeping and gnashing of teeth. For many are called, but few are chosen.*

(Matthew 22:11-14)

The word, disciple, is often generalized to cover anyone who even mentions the name of Jesus. This, however, is merely a convenience for man. When someone states that they are a disciple, we have no authority to question them. However, they know within their heart, and within their relationship with God, whether this mantle fits them. There were many who called themselves disciples, but when they were given a fuller measure of what was required of them, well, they seemed to have other things to do.

> *Many therefore of his disciples, when they had heard this, said, This is an hard saying; who can hear it?*
>
> *When Jesus knew in himself that his disciples murmured at it, he said unto them,*
>
> *Doth this offend you? What and if ye shall see the Son of man ascend up where he was before? It is the spirit that quickeneth; the flesh profiteth nothing: the words that I speak unto you, they are spirit, and they are life. But there are some of you that believe not.*
>
> *For Jesus knew from the beginning who they were that believed not, and who should betray him.*
>
> *And he said, Therefore said I unto you, that no man can come unto me, except it were given unto him of my Father.*

From that time many of his disciples went back, and walked no more with him.

(John 6:60-66)

Again, even though many people have done marvelous works; a portion of these people have done so in their own power, and with their own agenda. The only agenda that Jesus, and his followers, will acknowledge is God's. No matter how magnanimous the actions are; if they are not done for God, they will not last. God will not accept our offerings of works just because they follow the formula of ritual. They must have the seal of faith. The true nature of our service is all important: the title of our service, when standing alone, means nothing.

But without faith it is impossible to please him: for he that cometh to God must believe that he is, and that he is a rewarder of them that diligently seek him.

(Hebrews 11:6)

Only in God can we be sure that our positives are indeed positive and that our negatives are not present. God's world is all positive, never negative. God is good. Wherefore guard yourself against the temptation to accept scenarios where positive cannot be clearly distinguished from negative.

But above all things, my brethren, swear not, neither by heaven, neither by the earth, neither by any other oath: but let your yea be yea; and your nay, nay; lest ye fall into condemnation.

(James 5:12)

The Word from the Bible

Genesis 5:32

And Noah was five hundred years old: and Noah begat Shem, Ham, and Japheth.

Genesis 7:13-14

In the selfsame day entered Noah, and Shem, and Ham, and Japheth, the sons of Noah, and Noah's wife, and the three wives of his sons with them, into the ark; They, and every beast after his kind, and all the cattle after their kind, and every creeping thing that creepeth upon the earth after his kind, and every fowl after his kind, every bird of every sort.

Genesis 9:20-27

And Noah began to be an husbandman, and he planted a vineyard: And he drank of the wine, and was drunken; and he was uncovered within his tent.

And Ham, the father of Canaan, saw the nakedness of his father, and told his two brethren without.

And Shem and Japheth took a garment, and laid it upon both their shoulders, and went backward, and covered the nakedness of their father; and their faces were backward, and they saw not their father's nakedness.

And Noah awoke from his wine, and knew what his younger son had done unto him. And he said, Cursed be Canaan; a servant of servants shall he be unto his brethren. And he said, Blessed be the LORD God of Shem; and Canaan shall be his servant. God shall enlarge Japheth, and he shall dwell in the tents of Shem; and Canaan shall be his servant.

Chapter Six

The Natures of Man

Where we start from will, in large degree, determine where we end up. The world started afresh with the sons of Noah.

> *And the sons of Noah, that went forth of the ark, were Shem, and Ham, and Japheth: and Ham is the father of Canaan. These are the three sons of Noah: and of them was the whole earth overspread.*
>
> (Genesis 9:18-19)

These sons had unique characteristics. Maybe we can understand some of the types of relationships with God in the earth by the nature of these sons. This does not stereotype any person or race of peoples, but is only a search for an understanding of the ground from which mankind restarted. God, of course, shapes the nature of any person, or any nation, to fit His design, or according to their acknowledgement of Him. Conversely, Satan can also contact the spirit of a person, to persuade it to turn away from that which the LORD shows that person or nation God can do. Thus, there is no formula that we have a right to apply, forever and absolutely, to any of the descendants of any the sons. This is just a study of what a nation would look like if it emerged unchanged from what we can determine about the natures of the sons of Noah, from the Bible.

The only incident that gives us any insight into the character of the sons of Noah is described in Genesis 9:20-27. The first part shows their reaction to a potentially stressful situation. There is implied in this account an extreme measure of negativity in what Ham did. We did not learn until the Law of Moses was delivered why this is a violation of God's requirements for mankind, as is also the case with anything like it.

> *None of you shall approach to any that is near of kin to him, to uncover their nakedness: I am the LORD. The nakedness of thy father, or the nakedness of thy mother, shalt thou not uncover: she is thy mother; thou shalt not uncover her nakedness. The nakedness of thy father's wife shalt thou not uncover: it is thy father's nakedness. The nakedness of thy sister, the daughter of thy father, or daughter of thy mother, whether she be born at home, or born abroad, even their nakedness thou shalt not uncover. The nakedness of thy son's daughter, or of thy daughter's daughter, even their nakedness thou shalt not uncover: for theirs is thine own nakedness. The nakedness of thy father's wife's daughter, begotten of thy father, she is thy sister, thou shalt not uncover her nakedness.*
>
> *Thou shalt not uncover the nakedness of thy father's sister: she is thy father's near kinswoman. Thou shalt not uncover the nakedness of thy mother's sister; for she is thy mother's near kinswoman. Thou shalt not uncover the nakedness of thy father's brother, thou shalt not approach to his wife: she is thine aunt. Thou shalt not uncover the nakedness of thy daughter in law: she is thy son's wife; thou shalt not uncover her nakedness. Thou shalt not uncover the nakedness of thy brother's wife: it is thy brother's nakedness.*
>
> *Thou shalt not uncover the nakedness of a woman and her daughter, neither shalt thou take her son's daughter, or her daughter's daughter, to uncover her nakedness; for they are her near kinswomen: it is wickedness. Neither shalt thou take a wife to her sister, to vex her, to uncover her nakedness, beside the other in her life time.*
>
> *Also thou shalt not approach unto a woman to uncover her nakedness, as long as she is put apart for her uncleanness.*
>
> (Leviticus 18:6-19)

There is, however, a little bit of a paradox in this account. If Ham had not come upon his father lying exposed, then there would have been no announcement to the brothers, and there would have been no covering. In a sense, the curse that Noah invoked had already manifested itself in Ham's action; for, Ham, who may have been either mocking his father or just not aware of what to do, became a servant to his brothers by delivering the news. His brothers then became a servant to their father by covering him. Thus, by the flow of the event, Ham became kind of a servant of servants. This is our first peek at the nature of the sons.

I would like to think that Noah would not have been angry at his son for an honest mistake or inability to know how to act. Therefore, there must have been some measure of the Law of Moses instilled in the mind of man, even before the actual introduction of the Law to the children of Israel. This is further substantiated by the offering that Noah made to God; it was a preview of the offerings that God would require of the children of Israel, as written in the Law of Moses.

> *And Noah went forth, and his sons, and his wife, and his sons' wives with him: Every beast, every creeping thing, and every fowl, and whatsoever creepeth upon the earth, after their kinds, went forth out of the ark.*
>
> *And Noah builded an altar unto the LORD; and took of every clean beast, and of every clean fowl, and offered burnt offerings on the altar. And the LORD smelled a sweet savour; and the LORD said in his heart, I will not again curse the ground any more for man's sake; for the imagination of man's heart is evil from his youth; neither will I again smite any more every thing living, as I have done.*

(Genesis 8:18-21)

Therefore, if the rules of conduct which govern these actions toward relatives were already in the heart of those who honored the LORD, then Ham was in violation of one of these rules. This shows us the mindset of a person who, though he knows the rules, will try to circumvent them for his own benefit; which may include his amusement. Furthermore, he will be of the sort that will attempt to build alliances for the sole purpose of furthering the violation of God's law. Such people definitely exist on this earth. Nations of this sort also exist.

The other two sons honored their father and did those things that were pleasing to him. We will see more about the significance of the blessing that was given to them, and some more about the curse that was pronounced against one of the sons of Ham. However, this is as far as we can go with the children of Noah, specifically.

We will now introduce the natures of man, in general. To do so we will first lay a foundation based on human psychology, as it relates to religion. The concepts behind the psychology that we will explore come from the New Testament. They are from the parable known as *The Parable of the Sower*.

> *And he spake many things unto them in parables, saying, Behold, a sower went forth to sow; And when he sowed, some seeds fell by the way side, and the fowls came and devoured them up: Some fell upon stony places, where they had not much earth: and forthwith they sprung up, because they had no deepness of earth: And when the sun was up, they were scorched; and because they had no root, they withered away. And some fell among thorns; and the thorns sprung up, and choked them: But other fell into good ground, and brought forth fruit, some an hundredfold, some sixtyfold, some thirtyfold.*
>
> *Who hath ears to hear, let him hear.*
>
> (Matthew 13:3-9)
>
> *Hear ye therefore the parable of the sower.*
>
> *When any one heareth the word of the kingdom, and understandeth it not, then cometh the wicked one, and catcheth away that which was sown in his heart. This is he which received seed by the way side.*
>
> *But he that received the seed into stony places, the same is he that heareth the word, and anon with joy receiveth it; Yet hath he not root in himself, but dureth for a while: for when tribulation or persecution ariseth because of the word, by and by he is offended.*
>
> *He also that received seed among the thorns is he that heareth the word; and the care of this world, and the deceitfulness of riches, choke the word, and he becometh unfruitful.*
>
> *But he that received seed into the good ground is he that heareth the word, and understandeth it; which also beareth fruit, and bringeth forth, some an hundredfold, some sixty, some thirty.*
>
> (Matthew 13:18-23)

Do not let the success of your relationship with God, as evidenced in the prosperity of your country, go unacknowledged. Do not sit back and think that it was done by you and you alone.

> *When thou hast eaten and art full, then thou shalt bless the LORD thy God for the good land which he hath given thee. Beware that thou forget not the LORD thy God, in not keeping his commandments, and his judgments, and his statutes, which I command thee this day: Lest when thou hast eaten and art full, and hast built goodly houses, and dwelt therein; And when thy herds and thy flocks multiply, and thy silver and thy gold is multiplied, and all that thou hast is multiplied; Then thine heart be lifted up, and thou forget the LORD thy God, which brought thee forth out of the land of Egypt, from the house of bondage; Who led thee through that great and terrible wilderness, wherein were fiery serpents, and scorpions, and drought, where there was no water; who brought thee forth water out of the rock of flint; Who fed thee in the wilderness with manna, which thy fathers knew not, that he might humble thee, and that he might prove thee, to do thee good at thy latter end; And thou say in thine heart, My power and the might of mine hand hath gotten me this wealth.*
>
> *But thou shalt remember the LORD thy God: for it is he that giveth thee power to get wealth, that he may establish his covenant which he sware unto thy fathers, as it is this day. And it shall be, if thou do at all forget the LORD thy God, and walk after other gods, and serve them, and worship them, I testify against you this day that ye shall surely perish.*

(Deuteronomy 8:10-19)

Each of us must follow the Scripture of life, and remember that it is God's benevolence that provides the benefits we enjoy. Continue to serve Him and to lift His name among your people, and among the other nations of the world. Maybe by doing this, you will be the instrument to turn other peoples, and maybe even other nations, to God. This is a very good thing.

> *Behold, I have taught you statutes and judgments, even as the LORD my God commanded me, that ye should do so in*

> *the land whither ye go to possess it. Keep therefore and do them; for this is your wisdom and your understanding in the sight of the nations, which shall hear all these statutes, and say, Surely this great nation is a wise and understanding people. For what nation is there so great, who hath God so nigh unto them, as the LORD our God is in all things that we call upon him for? And what nation is there so great, that hath statutes and judgments so righteous as all this law, which I set before you this day?*
>
> *Only take heed to thyself, and keep thy soul diligently, lest thou forget the things which thine eyes have seen, and lest they depart from thy heart all the days of thy life: but teach them thy sons, and thy sons' sons;*
>
> (Deuteronomy 4:5-9)

The character of the nation is highly intertwined with the people of the nation. For this reason, we have presented the four types of religious individuals. This is the message of the Parable of the Sower. Please absorb this information, and take stock of your own position in God. As we go forward, we will move from the nature of individuals, and flow into a demonstration of how these same natures are represented by the nations of the earth.

God has presented His Gospel to all nations of the earth. However, the way the Gospel had been handled by these nations produced different types. Just as the children of the sons of Noah went on varying routes for their service to God, so also have the nations of the world. We will explore the destinations that nations have reached, as based on the routes they chose. The nation of Israel, in its later life, illustrated the way this can happen. Please read this as a preview to the branching of the nations.

> *And when Joshua had let the people go, the children of Israel went every man unto his inheritance to possess the land. And the people served the LORD all the days of Joshua, and all the days of the elders that outlived Joshua, who had seen all the great works of the LORD, that he did for Israel. And Joshua, the son of Nun, the servant of the LORD, died, being an hundred and ten years old. And they buried him in the border of his inheritance in Timnathheres, in the mount of Ephraim, on the north side of the hill Gaash.*

And also all that generation were gathered unto their fathers: and there arose another generation after them, which knew not the LORD, nor yet the works which he had done for Israel. And the children of Israel did evil in the sight of the LORD, and served Baalim: And they forsook the LORD God of their fathers, which brought them out of the land of Egypt, and followed other gods, of the gods of the people that were round about them, and bowed themselves unto them, and provoked the LORD to anger. And they forsook the LORD, and served Baal and Ashtaroth.

(Judges 2:6-13)

We want to be different;
It's our claim to fame.
We cringe when we think
We might all be the same.

It might please you to know
Your fame is secure,
But your uniqueness
Will only endure

To a certain level;
We are of similar minds:
To God we are all
One of four kinds.

The first is the one
Who hears his word,
And says in their mind
"This is surely absurd.

It is illogical,
Just leave me alone.
Do you think I'm dense,
Like this dead stone?"

Other say, "You know
This just might make sense;
Let me relax just a little
My strong defense.

I think I can believe it;
I'll give it a whirl.
Nah, what's the use:
It does not fit my world."

Some even pretend
To take heed,
But say in their heart,
"The world's all I need".

Then, there's the blessed:
Receiving what He gives,

They merge it in,
Using it to live;

Enjoying rich peace
On a spiritual plain,
By God sheltered
From life's constant drain.

Chapter 6a

Sending Forth vs. Making

There are two concepts that are present in the Kingdom of Heaven: making and sending forth. These two are often merged in the characterizations of the work of God, by mankind. Most of us are aware of God's creative ability; we are comfortable believing that it is a part of God's works from the beginning. It is this creative ability that causes us to call Him Father. God expressed His creative ability at the foundation of the world. But there were other things of God before the foundation of the world.

To understand better where we are, when we arrive at where we must go, keep in mind one word: Authority. This word is often equated with power; but they are not equal. Yes, power is contained in authority, for without "the power to do," the "authority to do" becomes meaningless. Whether this power is currently with us, or whether it is derived or acquired from outside of us, is not the issue. In some form, we must have the power to execute authority, before we can make a change.

Both by definition and by fact, God has All Power and All Authority. This does not mean that the only action done in the universe will be done directly by God. Along with God's Authority He has the power of delegation: this He does, in two forms. One form of delegation is, "sending forth"; the other is, "making".

Sending forth is seen when God, by a statement of His Word, causes an action to occur; or a thing to appear, or be revealed. In the Genesis report of creation, God, by His Word, issued light into the universe.

> *In the beginning God created the heaven and the earth. And the earth was without form, and void; and darkness was upon the face of the deep. And the Spirit of God moved upon the face of the waters. And God said, Let there be*

> light: and there was light. And God saw the light, that it was good: and God divided the light from the darkness. And God called the light Day, and the darkness he called Night. And the evening and the morning were the first day.

> (Genesis 1:1-5)

> And God said, Let there be a firmament in the midst of the waters, and let it divide the waters from the waters. And God made the firmament, and divided the waters which were under the firmament from the waters which were above the firmament: and it was so. And God called the firmament Heaven. And the evening and the morning were the second day.

> (Genesis 1:6-8)

On the other hand, by His authority, God commissioned the making of mankind. God did not say of man, "Let there be", but He said, "Let us make". This started a process that, though it could be accomplished by others, was a direct product of the will of God. As such God is responsible for it, and retains ownership of it.

> And God said, Let us make man in our image, after our likeness: and let them have dominion over the fish of the sea, and over the fowl of the air, and over the cattle, and over all the earth, and over every creeping thing that creepeth upon the earth. So God created man in his own image, in the image of God created he him; male and female created he them.

> (Genesis 1:26-27)

God also presented the concept of His authority by issuing calls to action. He expanded the bounds of this creation by enlisting the creation, on the first level, to bring forth from itself other creations. Even so, God still holds responsibility for the products of the creation.

> And God said, Let the waters under the heaven be gathered together unto one place, and let the dry land appear: and it was so. And God called the dry land Earth; and the gathering together of the waters called he Seas: and God saw that it was good. And God said, Let the earth bring forth grass, the herb yielding seed, and the fruit tree

yielding fruit after his kind, whose seed is in itself, upon the earth: and it was so. And the earth brought forth grass, and herb yielding seed after his kind, and the tree yielding fruit, whose seed was in itself, after his kind: and God saw that it was good.

(Genesis 1:9-12)

And God said, Let the waters bring forth abundantly the moving creature that hath life, and fowl that may fly above the earth in the open firmament of heaven. And God created great whales, and every living creature that moveth, which the waters brought forth abundantly, after their kind, and every winged fowl after his kind: and God saw that it was good.

(Genesis 1:20-21)

And God said, Let the earth bring forth the living creature after his kind, cattle, and creeping thing, and beast of the earth after his kind: and it was so. And God made the beast of the earth after his kind, and cattle after their kind, and every thing that creepeth upon the earth after his kind: and God saw that it was good.

(Genesis 1:24-25)

Then, on the second level, God empowered the creatures to continue the creation process, by making more of their kind.

And God blessed them, saying, Be fruitful, and multiply, and fill the waters in the seas, and let fowl multiply in the earth.

(Genesis 1:22)

And God blessed them, and God said unto them, Be fruitful, and multiply, and replenish the earth, and subdue it: and have dominion over the fish of the sea, and over the fowl of the air, and over every living thing that moveth upon the earth.

(Genesis 1:28)

This is such an important delegation that it is repeated to Noah when God refreshes mankind.

> *And God spake unto Noah, saying, Go forth of the ark, thou, and thy wife, and thy sons, and thy sons' wives with thee. Bring forth with thee every living thing that is with thee, of all flesh, both of fowl, and of cattle, and of every creeping thing that creepeth upon the earth; that they may breed abundantly in the earth, and be fruitful, and multiply upon the earth.*

(Genesis 8:15-17)

As opposed to "making", the ability to send forth is dependent on the Word of God. Therefore, it can only be delegated to those who are of God. This is a power at a level that requires a divine structure, and some serious maturity. It is done only by those ones that are so selected by God because they have been, or are being, equipped, by God, with a necessary level of maturity. The delegation of the authority to make is not so restricted.

To make something can be done by anyone with the ability to make, whether they have the wisdom to manage what they make or not. This is clearly seen in many of the births that occur to teenage girls. This does not mean that anyone, at anytime, can make anything. The ability to make is still under God's control, and is also among those things which are issued from God by His Word. There is no way for any human to acquire this ability on their own. This holds true, especially, for the process of birth.

> *In the beginning was the Word, and the Word was with God, and the Word was God. The same was in the beginning with God. All things were made by him; and without him was not any thing made that was made. In him was life; and the life was the light of men.*

(John 1:1-4)

The whole of existence is by the action and/or the allowance of God.

This brings us to a most important piece of existence: this is the piece known as angels. Angels existed before the foundation of the world. Angels are spirits. God is a Spirit. <u>Angels are not created beings</u>. As spirits, angels must come from God. Remember what God told the earth to do during creation: bring forth after its kind. Remember also that He told the sea to do a like thing. Jesus of Nazareth explained how this occurs in the realm of the Spirit.

> *There was a man of the Pharisees, named Nicodemus, a ruler of the Jews: The same came to Jesus by night, and said unto him, Rabbi, we know that thou art a teacher come from God: for no man can do these miracles that thou doest, except God be with him.*
>
> *Jesus answered and said unto him, Verily, verily, I say unto thee, Except a man be born again, he cannot see the kingdom of God.*
>
> *Nicodemus saith unto him, How can a man be born when he is old? can he enter the second time into his mother's womb, and be born?*
>
> *Jesus answered, Verily, verily, I say unto thee, Except a man be born of water and of the Spirit, he cannot enter into the kingdom of God. That which is born of the flesh is flesh; and that which is born of the Spirit is spirit.*
>
> (John 3:1-6)

This allows us to envision a time when God brought forth, from Himself, the Heavenly hosts, known as angels. There must have been a reason for this. There is.

Looking at the point on the flow of existence where God sees the establishment of the foundation, God set up a workforce. This workforce is the angels. Among this workforce are those angels that we consider to be positive, and those that we consider to be negative.

The negative spirits, which have been labeled demons, were brought forth for proving and refining; chief among these is, Satan. As a piece of sand to an oyster, they exist to cause reality, in general, and mankind, specifically, to create pearls of great price. These pearls are highly treasured; as taught by Jesus of Nazareth.

> *Again, the kingdom of heaven is like unto a merchant man, seeking goodly pearls: Who, when he had found one pearl of great price, went and sold all that he had, and bought it.*
>
> (Matthew 13:45-46)

The positive spirits, which are still called angels, were brought forth for healing and expansion. Chief among these, and chief among all angels, including demons, is the Son of man, also known as, the Son of God. The Son of God is a most powerful Spirit.

Jesus answered and said unto him, Art thou a master of Israel, and knowest not these things? Verily, verily, I say unto thee, We speak that we do know, and testify that we have seen; and ye receive not our witness. If I have told you earthly things, and ye believe not, how shall ye believe, if I tell you of heavenly things? And no man hath ascended up to heaven, but he that came down from heaven, even the Son of man which is in heaven.

(John 3:10-13)

God, who at sundry times and in divers manners spake in time past unto the fathers by the prophets, Hath in these last days spoken unto us by his Son, whom he hath appointed heir of all things, by whom also he made the worlds; Who being the brightness of his glory, and the express image of his person, and upholding all things by the word of his power, when he had by himself purged our sins, sat down on the right hand of the Majesty on high; Being made so much better than the angels, as he hath by inheritance obtained a more excellent name than they.

For unto which of the angels said he at any time, Thou art my Son, this day have I begotten thee? And again, I will be to him a Father, and he shall be to me a Son? And again, when he bringeth in the firstbegotten into the world, he saith, And let all the angels of God worship him.

And of the angels he saith, Who maketh his angels spirits, and his ministers a flame of fire. But unto the Son he saith, Thy throne, O God, is for ever and ever: a sceptre of righteousness is the sceptre of thy kingdom.

(Hebrews 1:1-8)

The subject of Hebrews 1:1-8, is the one that is given custody of and authority over all mankind, by God the Father. The subject is the Christ, who has been sent forth from God to perform His judgment--at the time designated by God the Father. So when you think to condemn anyone or anything; *back off.*

Judge not, that ye be not judged. For with what judgment ye judge, ye shall be judged: and with what measure ye mete, it shall be measured to you again.

> *And why beholdest thou the mote that is in thy brother's eye, but considerest not the beam that is in thine own eye? Or how wilt thou say to thy brother, Let me pull out the mote out of thine eye; and, behold, a beam is in thine own eye?*
>
> (Matthew 7:1-4)

Judgment is reserved to God, and to those designated by Him to do so. As was mentioned before, this is not a matter for beings of our nature; we were created. This is something that requires a being of extreme maturity and strong presence with God; and origin from God. It requires a being that is at once like us and also like God. It requires a being that has been around a very long time. It requires a being that has participated with the Father from the dawn of our time. It requires the Christ.

The one that is sent forth from God is given, by God, the depth and breadth of understanding necessary to perform all actions required of him; chief among which is judgment. However, understanding is not just reserved for the judgment seat of Christ. Those ones sent forth as apostles, pastors, and other spiritual representatives, must have a depth of understanding of the things of God. These ones are sent forth by God; and monitored by God and his Son, through the Holy Ghost.

Everyone in such offices operate under the shadow of the Almighty. It is best that they operate with the indwelling of the Holy Ghost. Indeed it is impossible to be true in judging between one thing and another without the Spirit of Truth, the Holy Ghost. To judge, without the empowerment of the Spirit of truth, degenerates into nothing other than condemnation. If God is not in it, it is not of God. Those ones sent forth by Him know this, and they are known by Him. This is the thought that anyone serving God, or desiring to serve Him, must keep in the forefront of their thoughts. It is the highest motivation for all our actions.

> *Yea doubtless, and I count all things but loss for the excellency of the knowledge of Christ Jesus my Lord: for whom I have suffered the loss of all things, and do count them but dung, that I may win Christ, And be found in him, not having mine own righteousness, which is of the law, but that which is through the faith of Christ, the righteousness which is of God by faith: That I may know him, and the*

power of his resurrection, and the fellowship of his sufferings, being made conformable unto his death; If by any means I might attain unto the resurrection of the dead. Not as though I had already attained, either were already perfect: but I follow after, if that I may apprehend that for which also I am apprehended of Christ Jesus.

Brethren, I count not myself to have apprehended: but this one thing I do, forgetting those things which are behind, and reaching forth unto those things which are before, I press toward the mark for the prize of the high calling of God in Christ Jesus.

(Philippians 3:8-14)

And unto the angel of the church in Smyrna write; These things saith the first and the last, which was dead, and is alive; I know thy works, and tribulation, and poverty, (but thou art rich) and I know the blasphemy of them which say they are Jews, and are not, but are the synagogue of Satan. Fear none of those things which thou shalt suffer: behold, the devil shall cast some of you into prison, that ye may be tried; and ye shall have tribulation ten days: be thou faithful unto death, and I will give thee a crown of life.

He that hath an ear, let him hear what the Spirit saith unto the churches; He that overcometh shall not be hurt of the second death.

(Revelation 2:8-11)

The Word from the Bible

Genesis 9:20-27

And Noah began to be an husbandman, and he planted a vineyard: And he drank of the wine, and was drunken; and he was uncovered within his tent.

And Ham, the father of Canaan, saw the nakedness of his father, and told his two brethren without.

And Shem and Japheth took a garment, and laid it upon both their shoulders, and went backward, and covered the nakedness of their father; and their faces were backward, and they saw not their father's nakedness.

And Noah awoke from his wine, and knew what his younger son had done unto him. And he said, Cursed be Canaan; a servant of servants shall he be unto his brethren. And he said, Blessed be the LORD God of Shem; and Canaan shall be his servant. God shall enlarge Japheth, and he shall dwell in the tents of Shem; and Canaan shall be his servant.

Genesis 10:2

The sons of Japheth;
 Gomer, and Magog, and Madai, and Javan, and Tubal, and Meshech, and Tiras.
And the sons of Gomer;
 Ashkenaz, and Riphath, and Togarmah.
And the sons of Javan;
 Elishah, and Tarshish, Kittim, and Dodanim.
By these were the isles of the Gentiles divided in their lands; every one after his tongue, after their families, in their nations.

Genesis 10:6-20

And the sons of Ham; Cush, and Mizraim, and Phut, and Canaan.
And the sons of Cush;

Seba, and Havilah, and Sabtah, and Raamah, and Sabtechah: and the sons of Raamah; Sheba, and Dedan.

And Cush begat Nimrod: he began to be a mighty one in the earth. He was a mighty hunter before the LORD: wherefore it is said, Even as Nimrod the mighty hunter before the LORD. And the beginning of his kingdom was Babel, and Erech, and Accad, and Calneh, in the land of Shinar. Out of that land went forth Asshur, and builded Nineveh, and the city Rehoboth, and Calah, And Resen between Nineveh and Calah: the same is a great city.

And Mizraim begat Ludim, and Anamim, and Lehabim, and Naphtuhim, And Pathrusim, and Casluhim, (out of whom came Philistim,) and Caphtorim.

And Canaan begat Sidon his firstborn, and Heth, And the Jebusite, and the Amorite, and the Girgasite, And the Hivite, and the Arkite, and the Sinite, And the Arvadite, and the Zemarite, and the Hamathite: and afterward were the families of the Canaanites spread abroad. And the border of the Canaanites was from Sidon, as thou comest to Gerar, unto Gaza; as thou goest, unto Sodom, and Gomorrah, and Admah, and Zeboim, even unto Lasha.

These are the sons of Ham, after their families, after their tongues, in their countries, and in their nations.

Genesis 10:21-31

Unto Shem also, the father of all the children of Eber, the brother of Japheth the elder, even to him were children born. The children of Shem; Elam, and Asshur, and Arphaxad, and Lud, and Aram.

And the children of Aram; Uz, and Hul, and Gether, and Mash.

And Arphaxad begat Salah;
and Salah begat Eber.
And unto Eber were born two sons: the name of one was Peleg; for in his days was the earth divided; and his brother's name was Joktan.

And Joktan begat Almodad, and Sheleph, and Hazarmaveth, and Jerah, And Hadoram, and Uzal, and Diklah, And Obal, and Abimael, and Sheba, And Ophir, and Havilah, and Jobab: all these were the sons of Joktan. And their dwelling was from Mesha, as thou goest unto Sephar a mount of the east.

These are the sons of Shem, after their families, after their tongues, in their lands, after their nations.

Chapter Seven

The Branching of Nations

It is not usually a positive thing to start an enterprise with a negative; but then again, this is not a usual set of information we are presenting. The negative we start with, is that this work is not another confirmation of the general nature of three groups of nations. It is a disavowal of the logic that attempts to categorize all mankind based on the words of Noah in Genesis 9:25-27, written in The Word from the Bible section, before this one. Therefore, let us fragment that message of Noah, starting with the curse.

The curse would not have continued very far without the allowance of God. Furthermore, considering the forbearance of God, it in fact does not proceed very far, at all. We say this because of the limitation of man's punishment for sin, in that time, as declared by God.

> *Thou shalt not make unto thee any graven image, or any likeness of any thing that is in heaven above, or that is in the earth beneath, or that is in the water under the earth. Thou shalt not bow down thyself to them, nor serve them: for I the LORD thy God am a jealous God, visiting the iniquity of the fathers upon the children unto the third and fourth generation of them that hate me;*

(Exodus 20:4-5)

The only way it could have initiated itself, is if the father demonstrated that he hated God. This has already been shown to us as being possible with Ham, but not probable; considering who his father is. However, if such is the case, then it is fitting that it be visited upon Canaan; to the second and third generation, at least. Then, the only way for the curse to continue is for the hateful behavior toward God to continue with the sons of Canaan; and the sons of these sons; and the sons of these sons; and so on until the present generation of modern times. However, if somewhere along the way from Ham to us, a son of Ham turned to the ways of God; then, the curse is released.

> *And shewing mercy unto thousands of them that love me, and keep my commandments.*

> (Exodus 20:6)

The action of Ham, the son of Noah, is one of the illustrations that have been used as the basis for a wide-reaching negative image, in the world. Some have used these words to segregate whole races of peoples; people that were viewed as member of so-called cursed nations. With this segregation, they felt empowered to perform, on God's behalf, what they described as justice. God does not need our help, nor has He authorized such actions as these.

Any action based on the curse by Noah, comes from the hearts and minds of sinful, and, sometimes, just plain evil, people. These ones are either misinformed, or unrighteous in their thinking. For the misinformed ones I say that it is time to drop your ignorance.

> *Forasmuch then as we are the offspring of God, we ought not to think that the Godhead is like unto gold, or silver, or stone, graven by art and man's device. And the times of this ignorance God winked at; but now commandeth all men every where to repent: Because he hath appointed a day, in the which he will judge the world in righteousness by that man whom he hath ordained; whereof he hath given assurance unto all men, in that he hath raised him from the dead.*

> (Acts 17:29-31)

For the evil ones, I remind you of God's view of your actions; whether these actions are in word, or deed.

> *They answered and said unto him, Abraham is our father.*

> *Jesus saith unto them, If ye were Abraham's children, ye would do the works of Abraham. But now ye seek to kill me, a man that hath told you the truth, which I have heard of God: this did not Abraham. Ye do the deeds of your father.*

> *Then said they to him, We be not born of fornication; we have one Father, even God.*

> *Jesus said unto them, If God were your Father, ye would love me: for I proceeded forth and came from God; neither came I of myself, but he sent me. Why do ye not understand my speech? even because ye cannot hear my word. Ye are of your father the devil, and the lusts of your father ye will do. He was a murderer from the beginning, and abode not in the truth, because there is no truth in him. When he speaketh a lie, he speaketh of his own: for he is a liar, and the father of it. And because I tell you the truth, ye believe me not.*

(John 8:39-45)

The curse of Noah was fulfilled in the conquest of the Promised Land by God, on behalf of the children of Israel. At this time, God placed the children of Ham in the line of Canaan under subjection. Those that were not removed became the servants of the nation of Israel; and Israel is a nation that is of the seed of Shem.

> *Behold, I send an Angel before thee, to keep thee in the way, and to bring thee into the place which I have prepared. Beware of him, and obey his voice, provoke him not; for he will not pardon your transgressions: for my name is in him. But if thou shalt indeed obey his voice, and do all that I speak; then I will be an enemy unto thine enemies, and an adversary unto thine adversaries. For mine Angel shall go before thee, and bring thee in unto the Amorites, and the Hittites, and the Perizzites, and the Canaanites, the Hivites, and the Jebusites: and I will cut them off. Thou shalt not bow down to their gods, nor serve them, nor do after their works: but thou shalt utterly overthrow them, and quite break down their images.*

(Exodus 23:20-24)

The final demolition of this curse on Ham's son, Canaan, is done by God. We are each made responsible for our own sin and released from penalty for anyone else's.

> *In those days they shall say no more, The fathers have eaten a sour grape, and the children's teeth are set on edge. But every one shall die for his own iniquity: every man that eateth the sour grape, his teeth shall be set on edge.*

(Jeremiah 31:29-30)

No, the modern spiritual branches of the nations are not the result of Noah's sons. Instead they exist in a fashion like that described in the Parable of the Sower. This parable applies not just to people as individuals, but also to people collected into nations. It applies to all principalities and to powers, as well. All of these have one of four relationships with the things of God, as described in the parable.

> *And he spake many things unto them in parables, saying, Behold, a sower went forth to sow;*
>
> *And when he sowed, some seeds fell by the way side, and the fowls came and devoured them up:*
>
> *Some fell upon stony places, where they had not much earth: and forthwith they sprung up, because they had no deepness of earth: And when the sun was up, they were scorched; and because they had no root, they withered away.*
>
> *And some fell among thorns; and the thorns sprung up, and choked them:*
>
> *But other fell into good ground, and brought forth fruit, some an hundredfold, some sixtyfold, some thirtyfold.*
>
> *Who hath ears to hear, let him hear.*
>
> (Matthew 13:3-9)
>
> *Hear ye therefore the parable of the sower.*
>
> *When any one heareth the word of the kingdom, and understandeth it not, then cometh the wicked one, and catcheth away that which was sown in his heart. This is he which received seed by the way side.*
>
> *But he that received the seed into stony places, the same is he that heareth the word, and anon with joy receiveth it; Yet hath he not root in himself, but dureth for a while: for when tribulation or persecution ariseth because of the word, by and by he is offended.*
>
> *He also that received seed among the thorns is he that heareth the word; and the care of this world, and the deceitfulness of riches, choke the word, and he becometh unfruitful.*

> *But he that received seed into the good ground is he that heareth the word, and understandeth it; which also beareth fruit, and bringeth forth, some an hundredfold, some sixty, some thirty.*

(Matthew 13:18-23)

Jesus gave us this parable to direct our attention to his call for his disciples to work in God's vineyard of souls. It is the mission of Jesus and his apostles, teachers and other workers in the vineyard to present the message, soul to soul. Indeed, the Father's gift of the Comforter is bestowed on individual souls. We know that Jesus delivered this message, which he received from the Father.

> *I have glorified thee on the earth: I have finished the work which thou gavest me to do. And now, O Father, glorify thou me with thine own self with the glory which I had with thee before the world was. I have manifested thy name unto the men which thou gavest me out of the world: thine they were, and thou gavest them me; and they have kept thy word. Now they have known that all things whatsoever thou hast given me are of thee. For I have given unto them the words which thou gavest me; and they have received them, and have known surely that I came out from thee, and they have believed that thou didst send me.*

(John 17:4-8)

The Christ sows the seed of the word of wisdom--truth--among souls. God the Father had already sowed the seed of his presence among the nations. This is the purpose for which the seed of Jacob, who is Israel, was selected. This, they continue to do, by taking the message of Jesus to the people of the nations. The Father works on a macroscopic level to prepare the field for the micromanagement to be done by the Son, with the help of his Holy Ghost filled workers.

> *And Jesus went about all the cities and villages, teaching in their synagogues, and preaching the gospel of the kingdom, and healing every sickness and every disease among the people. But when he saw the multitudes, he was moved with compassion on them, because they fainted, and were scattered abroad, as sheep having no shepherd. Then saith he unto his disciples, The harvest truly is plenteous, but the*

> *labourers are few; Pray ye therefore the Lord of the harvest, that he will send forth labourers into his harvest.*

(Matthew 9:35-38)

So, let us get back to the work of the Father, in defining nations. This was not done from the time of the origins of Noah, alone. The children of Noah were the starters of the nations, but they were not the authors of the final outcome of the nations. This is similar to the outreach of the apostles who introduced Christ to the people. Though they delivered the message of the Gospel of Jesus Christ they did not cause salvation.

> *For ye are yet carnal: for whereas there is among you envying, and strife, and divisions, are ye not carnal, and walk as men? For while one saith, I am of Paul; and another, I am of Apollos; are ye not carnal? Who then is Paul, and who is Apollos, but ministers by whom ye believed, even as the Lord gave to every man? I have planted, Apollos watered; but God gave the increase. So then neither is he that planteth any thing, neither he that watereth; but God that giveth the increase.*

(1 Corinthians 3:3-7)

For the world of nations, God started giving the increase with Abraham. It is from this point that we see the branching of nations. To a degree these branching are mirrored in the words of Noah, as he described the places of service for his sons; but, not totally. Moses also provided some insight on this matter.

> *Remember the days of old, consider the years of many generations: ask thy father, and he will show thee; thy elders, and they will tell thee. When the Most High divided to the nations their inheritance, when he separated the sons of Adam, he set the bounds of the people according to the number of the children of Israel.*

(Deuteronomy 32:7-8)

The words of Noah are not designed, nor are they able, to lock a lineage of peoples into any pattern. God is not restricted by Noah's pronouncement, to eternally act according to Noah's words among all peoples and across all time. This is not in the covenant that God spoke to Noah.

> *And God spake unto Noah, and to his sons with him, saying, And I, behold, I establish my covenant with you, and with your seed after you; And with every living creature that is with you, of the fowl, of the cattle, and of every beast of the earth with you; from all that go out of the ark, to every beast of the earth. And I will establish my covenant with you; neither shall all flesh be cut off any more by the waters of a flood; neither shall there any more be a flood to destroy the earth.*

(Genesis 9:8-11)

Furthermore, when we consider the modern representatives of God, and of His Son, we know that their mission is: to convert individuals and to work through individuals. The conversion of a nation is done through its leaders. Therefore, since we do not know who God will select as the leader of a nation, we must never apply an automatic negative to anyone. We must not consider anyone beyond redemption, or label them as being cursed; this is the origin of unrighteous judgment and condemnation by humans, attempting to stand in the place of God and His Son, who is the only custodian of the judgment of humans.

> *Then answered Jesus and said unto them, Verily, verily, I say unto you, The Son can do nothing of himself, but what he seeth the Father do: for what things soever he doeth, these also doeth the Son likewise. For the Father loveth the Son, and sheweth him all things that himself doeth: and he will shew him greater works than these, that ye may marvel. For as the Father raiseth up the dead, and quickeneth them; even so the Son quickeneth whom he will. For the Father judgeth no man, but hath committed all judgment unto the Son: That all men should honour the Son, even as they honour the Father. He that honoureth not the Son honoureth not the Father which hath sent him.*

(John 5:19-23)

In like manner, we must not place the label of, blessed, on any person or nation, just because of lineage.

> *In those days came John the Baptist, preaching in the wilderness of Judaea, And saying, Repent ye: for the*

> *kingdom of heaven is at hand. For this is he that was spoken of by the prophet Esaias, saying, The voice of one crying in the wilderness, Prepare ye the way of the Lord, make his paths straight. And the same John had his raiment of camel's hair, and a leathern girdle about his loins; and his meat was locusts and wild honey.*
>
> *Then went out to him Jerusalem, and all Judaea, and all the region round about Jordan, And were baptized of him in Jordan, confessing their sins.*
>
> *But when he saw many of the Pharisees and Sadducees come to his baptism, he said unto them, O generation of vipers, who hath warned you to flee from the wrath to come? Bring forth therefore fruits meet for repentance: And think not to say within yourselves, We have Abraham to our father: for I say unto you, that God is able of these stones to raise up children unto Abraham.*
>
> (Matthew 3:1-9)

To apply a *positive* judgment based on nationality, or by recognition of any other human connection type, is to open the door to false prophecy.

> *Not every one that saith unto me, Lord, Lord, shall enter into the kingdom of heaven; but he that doeth the will of my Father which is in heaven. Many will say to me in that day, Lord, Lord, have we not prophesied in thy name? and in thy name have cast out devils? and in thy name done many wonderful works? And then will I profess unto them, I never knew you: depart from me, ye that work iniquity.*
>
> (Matthew 7:21-23)
>
> *Then if any man shall say unto you, Lo, here is Christ, or there; believe it not. For there shall arise false Christs, and false prophets, and shall shew great signs and wonders; insomuch that, if it were possible, they shall deceive the very elect. Behold, I have told you before. Wherefore if they shall say unto you, Behold, he is in the desert; go not forth: behold, he is in the secret chambers; believe it not.*
>
> (Matthew 24:23-26)

In your interactions, let judgment rest solely in the realm of God and His Son. All nations belong to God, and all nations and persons can be heirs to His promise. Only God knows who is who; and when they are what they are.

> *Another parable put he forth unto them, saying, The kingdom of heaven is likened unto a man which sowed good seed in his field: But while men slept, his enemy came and sowed tares among the wheat, and went his way. But when the blade was sprung up, and brought forth fruit, then appeared the tares also.*
>
> *So the servants of the householder came and said unto him, Sir, didst not thou sow good seed in thy field? from whence then hath it tares?*
>
> *He said unto them, An enemy hath done this.*
>
> *The servants said unto him, Wilt thou then that we go and gather them up?*
>
> *But he said, Nay; lest while ye gather up the tares, ye root up also the wheat with them. Let both grow together until the harvest: and in the time of harvest I will say to the reapers, Gather ye together first the tares, and bind them in bundles to burn them: but gather the wheat into my barn.*
>
> (Matthew 13:24-30)
>
> *Then Jesus sent the multitude away, and went into the house: and his disciples came unto him, saying, Declare unto us the parable of the tares of the field.*
>
> *He answered and said unto them, He that soweth the good seed is the Son of man; The field is the world; the good seed are the children of the kingdom; but the tares are the children of the wicked one; The enemy that sowed them is the devil; the harvest is the end of the world; and the reapers are the angels.*
>
> *As therefore the tares are gathered and burned in the fire; so shall it be in the end of this world. The Son of man shall send forth his angels, and they shall gather out of his kingdom all things that offend, and them which do iniquity;*

And shall cast them into a furnace of fire: there shall be wailing and gnashing of teeth.

Then shall the righteous shine forth as the sun in the kingdom of their Father.

Who hath ears to hear, let him hear.

(Matthew 13:36-43)

Judge not, that ye be not judged. For with what judgment ye judge, ye shall be judged: and with what measure ye mete, it shall be measured to you again.

And why beholdest thou the mote that is in thy brother's eye, but considerest not the beam that is in thine own eye? Or how wilt thou say to thy brother, Let me pull out the mote out of thine eye; and, behold, a beam is in thine own eye?

(Matthew 7:1-4)

Let us look, therefore, at a more logical approach to the branching of nations. We will use some of the attributes of the sons of Noah, as a tool for study, but we will not depend totally on Noah's pronouncement. We do not wish to discard any of the words of the chosen servants of God, but we defer directly to God and His Son for the words that guide our understanding of Him.

+=+=+=+=+=+=+=+=+=+=+=+=+=+=+=+=+=+=+

Structure of Nations - Image One

And when he sowed, some seeds fell by the way side, and the fowls came and devoured them up:

Ham was in violation of the rule of God. He had discarded it in favor of his own rules of conduct. His behavior is a preview of the nation that forms alliances for the sole purpose of making war. These wars are not for the benefit of the family of man, but only for the expansion of the warring nation. Promises will be made, and deals cut, that have no real substance beyond the time of the endeavor. And the things of the devil will be willingly appropriated to accomplish the ends of the national leaders, in order to further their agenda.

Those nations which are caught up with these nations will see only a temporary alliance. Once there is an offense of any sort within the alliance, the nation that started the wars will turn and make war with those who were formerly their friends.

+=+=+=+=+=+=+=+=+=+=+=+=+=+=+=+=+=+=+=+

Structure of Nations - Image Two

Image Two - Phase One

Some fell upon stony places, where they had not much earth: and forthwith they sprung up, because they had no deepness of earth: And when the sun was up, they were scorched; and because they had no root, they withered away.

To accept God's way is a tough allowance for the leaders of the nation of today to accept. They want to think that they know how to run a nation, and that they really do not need to *bother* God about day to day operations. This is the start of the slide into another type of image of nations. They are examples of a sort of pattern of the children of Japheth, the sons of Noah. Let us continue our exploration of this example, using techniques of human psychology as it relates to religion, with wisdom from the New Testament. You may recall that this is described in the parable known as, *The Parable of the Sower*: Matthew 13:3-9 and Matthew 13:18-23. This message can be applied to nations, as well.

This type of nation is one that knows the will of God, and starts out to accomplish it, but somewhere along the lines it gets sidetracked. This type of nation is in the pattern of the people of Midian. The people of Midian held a key place in the development of the children of Israel. It started as an offshoot of the man Abraham.

> *Then again Abraham took a wife, and her name was Keturah. And she bare him Zimran, and Jokshan, and Medan, and **Midian**, and Ishbak, and Shuah*

(Genesis 25:1-2)

The Midianites were the instrument to deliver Joseph to Egypt.

> *And Judah said unto his brethren, What profit is it if we slay our brother, and conceal his blood? Come, and let us*

> *sell him to the Ishmeelites, and let not our hand be upon him; for he is our brother and our flesh. And his brethren were content. Then there passed by Midianites merchantmen; and they drew and lifted up Joseph out of the pit, and sold Joseph to the Ishmeelites for twenty pieces of silver: and they brought Joseph into Egypt.*

(Genesis 37:26-28)

In Egypt, Joseph was able to make the preparations for the saving of the people of Israel. Then, the people were gathered together by God into the nation of Israel. By God's divine intervention, the nation was placed on the path of service that started paving the way for one of the greatest demonstrations of God's power on behalf of a nation that is favored by Him. The deliverance of the nation of Israel was one of the early steps in God's flow of events to provide the world with the Messiah.

Image Two - Stage Two

Midian gave us the wife of Moses. It is also the nation of Moses' father-in-law, who was a priest of Midian. Moses' father-in-law was instrumental in directing Moses in the proper management of his burden among the children of Israel.

> *Now when Pharaoh heard this thing, he sought to slay Moses. But Moses fled from the face of Pharaoh, and dwelt in the land of Midian: and he sat down by a well.*
>
> *Now the priest of Midian had seven daughters: and they came and drew water, and filled the troughs to water their father's flock. And the shepherds came and drove them away: but Moses stood up and helped them, and watered their flock.*
>
> *And when they came to Reuel their father, he said, How is it that ye are come so soon to day?*
>
> *And they said, An Egyptian delivered us out of the hand of the shepherds, and also drew water enough for us, and watered the flock.*
>
> *And he said unto his daughters, And where is he? why is it that ye have left the man? call him, that he may eat bread.*

And Moses was content to dwell with the man: and he gave Moses Zipporah his daughter. And she bare him a son, and he called his name Gershom: for he said, I have been a stranger in a strange land.

(Exodus 2:15-22)

And it came to pass on the morrow, that Moses sat to judge the people: and the people stood by Moses from the morning unto the evening. And when Moses' father in law saw all that he did to the people, he said, What is this thing that thou doest to the people? why sittest thou thyself alone, and all the people stand by thee from morning unto even?

And Moses said unto his father in law, Because the people come unto me to enquire of God: When they have a matter, they come unto me; and I judge between one and another, and I do make them know the statutes of God, and his laws.

And Moses' father in law said unto him, The thing that thou doest is not good. Thou wilt surely wear away, both thou, and this people that is with thee: for this thing is too heavy for thee; thou art not able to perform it thyself alone.

Hearken now unto my voice, I will give thee counsel, and God shall be with thee: Be thou for the people to Godward, that thou mayest bring the causes unto God: And thou shalt teach them ordinances and laws, and shalt shew them the way wherein they must walk, and the work that they must do. Moreover thou shalt provide out of all the people able men, such as fear God, men of truth, hating covetousness; and place such over them, to be rulers of thousands, and rulers of hundreds, rulers of fifties, and rulers of tens: And let them judge the people at all seasons: and it shall be, that every great matter they shall bring unto thee, but every small matter they shall judge: so shall it be easier for thyself, and they shall bear the burden with thee. If thou shalt do this thing, and God command thee so, then thou shalt be able to endure, and all this people shall also go to their place in peace.

> *So Moses hearkened to the voice of his father in law, and did all that he had said. And Moses chose able men out of all Israel, and made them heads over the people, rulers of thousands, rulers of hundreds, rulers of fifties, and rulers of tens. And they judged the people at all seasons: the hard causes they brought unto Moses, but every small matter they judged themselves.*
>
> (Exodus 18:13-26)

Image Two - Stage Three

Later, things started to turn. In time of trouble, rather than turning to the LORD, they accepted the pressure of their alliance with Moab, to incite themselves against the children of Israel, which they knew to be God's chosen people.

> *And Moab was sore afraid of the people, because they were many: and Moab was distressed because of the children of Israel. And Moab said unto the elders of Midian, Now shall this company lick up all that are round about us, as the ox licketh up the grass of the field. And Balak the son of Zippor was king of the Moabites at that time. He sent messengers therefore unto Balaam the son of Beor to Pethor, which is by the river of the land of the children of his people, to call him, saying, Behold, there is a people come out from Egypt: behold, they cover the face of the earth, and they abide over against me: Come now therefore, I pray thee, curse me this people; for they are too mighty for me: peradventure I shall prevail, that we may smite them, and that I may drive them out of the land: for I wot that he whom thou blessest is blessed, and he whom thou cursest is cursed.*
>
> *And the elders of Moab and the elders of Midian departed with the rewards of divination in their hand; and they came unto Balaam, and spake unto him the words of Balak.*
>
> (Numbers 22:3-7)

They attempted to ensnare other nations, and bring them down to their level.

*And, behold, one of the children of Israel came and brought unto his brethren a **Midianitish** woman in the sight of Moses, and in the sight of all the congregation of the children of Israel, who were weeping before the door of the tabernacle of the congregation.*

(Numbers 25:6)

And the LORD spake unto Moses, saying, Vex the Midianites, and smite them: For they vex you with their wiles, wherewith they have beguiled you in the matter of Peor, and in the matter of Cozbi, the daughter of a prince of Midian, their sister, which was slain in the day of the plague for Peor's sake.

(Numbers 25:16-18)

Image Two - Stage Four

They became an abomination to God. God commanded that they receive the recompense of their actions against His will.

And the LORD spake unto Moses, saying, Avenge the children of Israel of the Midianites: afterward shalt thou be gathered unto thy people.

And Moses spake unto the people, saying, Arm some of yourselves unto the war, and let them go against the Midianites, and avenge the LORD of Midian. Of every tribe a thousand, throughout all the tribes of Israel, shall ye send to the war. So there were delivered out of the thousands of Israel, a thousand of every tribe, twelve thousand armed for war. And Moses sent them to the war, a thousand of every tribe, them and Phinehas the son of Eleazar the priest, to the war, with the holy instruments, and the trumpets to blow in his hand. And they warred against the Midianites, as the LORD commanded Moses; and they slew all the males. And they slew the kings of Midian, beside the rest of them that were slain; namely, Evi, and Rekem, and Zur, and Hur, and Reba, five kings of Midian: Balaam also the son of Beor they slew with the sword.

And the children of Israel took all the women of Midian captives, and their little ones, and took the spoil of all their cattle, and all their flocks, and all their goods. And they burnt all their cities wherein they dwelt, and all their goodly castles, with fire. And they took all the spoil, and all the prey, both of men and of beasts. And they brought the captives, and the prey, and the spoil, unto Moses, and Eleazar the priest, and unto the congregation of the children of Israel, unto the camp at the plains of Moab, which are by Jordan near Jericho.

And Moses, and Eleazar the priest, and all the princes of the congregation, went forth to meet them without the camp. And Moses was wroth with the officers of the host, with the captains over thousands, and captains over hundreds, which came from the battle. And Moses said unto them, Have ye saved all the women alive? Behold, these caused the children of Israel, through the counsel of Balaam, to commit trespass against the LORD in the matter of Peor, and there was a plague among the congregation of the LORD. Now therefore kill every male among the little ones, and kill every woman that hath known man by lying with him. But all the women children, that have not known a man by lying with him, keep alive for yourselves.

And do ye abide without the camp seven days: whosoever hath killed any person, and whosoever hath touched any slain, purify both yourselves and your captives on the third day, and on the seventh day. And purify all your raiment, and all that is made of skins, and all work of goats' hair, and all things made of wood.

(Numbers 31:1-20)

+=+=+=+=+=+=+=+=+=+=+=+=+=+=+=+=+=+=+

Structure of Nations - Image Three

Image Three - Stage One

And some fell among thorns; and the thorns sprung up, and choked them:

This type of nation started out with an ear to God, but somewhere along its line, things just go really wrong. The nation prospers and is blessed by God, but attributes this only to things of the world. Recorded in Scripture are two national leaders (kings) and one nation that fit the image of this type of nation. It is appropriate to mention the two men because they were kings over their nations; therefore, they were, effectively, the national character, within themselves.

Saul

> *And Samuel said, When thou wast little in thine own sight, wast thou not made the head of the tribes of Israel, and the LORD anointed thee king over Israel? And the LORD sent thee on a journey, and said, Go and utterly destroy the sinners the Amalekites, and fight against them until they be consumed. Wherefore then didst thou not obey the voice of the LORD, but didst fly upon the spoil, and didst evil in the sight of the LORD?*
>
> *And Saul said unto Samuel, Yea, I have obeyed the voice of the LORD, and have gone the way which the LORD sent me, and have brought Agag the king of Amalek, and have utterly destroyed the Amalekites. But the people took of the spoil, sheep and oxen, the chief of the things which should have been utterly destroyed, to sacrifice unto the LORD thy God in Gilgal.*
>
> *And Samuel said, Hath the LORD as great delight in burnt offerings and sacrifices, as in obeying the voice of the LORD? Behold, to obey is better than sacrifice, and to hearken than the fat of rams. For rebellion is as the sin of witchcraft, and stubbornness is as iniquity and idolatry. Because thou hast rejected the word of the LORD, he hath also rejected thee from being king.*
>
> *And Saul said unto Samuel, I have sinned: for I have transgressed the commandment of the LORD, and thy words: because I feared the people, and obeyed their voice.*
>
> (1 Samuel 15:17-24)

Nebuchadnezzar

> *This is the interpretation, O king, and this is the decree of the most High, which is come upon my lord the king: That they shall drive thee from men, and thy dwelling shall be with the beasts of the field, and they shall make thee to eat grass as oxen, and they shall wet thee with the dew of heaven, and seven times shall pass over thee, till thou know that the most High ruleth in the kingdom of men, and giveth it to whomsoever he will. And whereas they commanded to leave the stump of the tree roots; thy kingdom shall be sure unto thee, after that thou shalt have known that the heavens do rule. Wherefore, O king, let my counsel be acceptable unto thee, and break off thy sins by righteousness, and thine iniquities by showing mercy to the poor; if it may be a lengthening of thy tranquillity.*
>
> (Daniel 4:24-27)

Moab

First they were protected by God because of the promise made to their righteous father, Lot.

> *And when we passed by from our brethren the children of Esau, which dwelt in Seir, through the way of the plain from Elath, and from Eziongaber, we turned and passed by the way of the wilderness of Moab. And the LORD said unto me, Distress not the Moabites, neither contend with them in battle: for I will not give thee of their land for a possession; because I have given Ar unto the children of Lot for a possession.*
>
> (Deuteronomy 2:8-9)

We have already seen how Moab, as a result of its grip on things of the world, attempted to destroy the forward progress of the nation of Israel. God does not, in any way, lose sight of an offense against Him.

> *An Ammonite or Moabite shall not enter into the congregation of the LORD; even to their tenth generation shall they not enter into the congregation of the LORD for ever: Because they met you not with bread and with water in the way, when ye came forth out of Egypt; and because*

they hired against thee Balaam the son of Beor of Pethor of Mesopotamia, to curse thee. Nevertheless the LORD thy God would not hearken unto Balaam; but the LORD thy God turned the curse into a blessing unto thee, because the LORD thy God loved thee. Thou shalt not seek their peace nor their prosperity all thy days for ever.

(Deuteronomy 23:3-6)

Image Three - Stage Two

Such national leaders and nations will be corrected by God. Sometimes the correction will be fatal. For an unfruitful nation, God will invoke His established protocol for their handling.

I am the true vine, and my Father is the husbandman. Every branch in me that beareth not fruit he taketh away: and every branch that beareth fruit, he purgeth it, that it may bring forth more fruit.

(John 15:1-2)

Saul

Now Samuel was dead, and all Israel had lamented him, and buried him in Ramah, even in his own city. And Saul had put away those that had familiar spirits, and the wizards, out of the land. And the Philistines gathered themselves together, and came and pitched in Shunem: and Saul gathered all Israel together, and they pitched in Gilboa. And when Saul saw the host of the Philistines, he was afraid, and his heart greatly trembled. And when Saul inquired of the LORD, the LORD answered him not, neither by dreams, nor by Urim, nor by prophets. Then said Saul unto his servants, Seek me a woman that hath a familiar spirit, that I may go to her, and inquire of her.

And his servants said to him, Behold, there is a woman that hath a familiar spirit at Endor.

And Saul disguised himself, and put on other raiment, and he went, and two men with him, and they came to the woman by night: and he said, I pray thee, divine unto me by the familiar spirit, and bring me him up, whom I shall name unto thee.

And the woman said unto him, Behold, thou knowest what Saul hath done, how he hath cut off those that have familiar spirits, and the wizards, out of the land: wherefore then layest thou a snare for my life, to cause me to die?

And Saul sware to her by the LORD, saying, As the LORD liveth, there shall no punishment happen to thee for this thing.

Then said the woman, Whom shall I bring up unto thee?

And he said, Bring me up Samuel.

And when the woman saw Samuel, she cried with a loud voice: and the woman spake to Saul, saying, Why hast thou deceived me? for thou art Saul.

And the king said unto her, Be not afraid: for what sawest thou?

And the woman said unto Saul, I saw gods ascending out of the earth.

And he said unto her, What form is he of?

And she said, An old man cometh up; and he is covered with a mantle.

And Saul perceived that it was Samuel, and he stooped with his face to the ground, and bowed himself.

And Samuel said to Saul, Why hast thou disquieted me, to bring me up?

And Saul answered, I am sore distressed; for the Philistines make war against me, and God is departed from me, and answereth me no more, neither by prophets, nor by dreams: therefore I have called thee, that thou mayest make known unto me what I shall do.

Then said Samuel, Wherefore then dost thou ask of me, seeing the LORD is departed from thee, and is become thine enemy? And the LORD hath done to him, as he spake by me: for the LORD hath rent the kingdom out of thine hand, and given it to thy neighbour, even to David: Because thou obeyedst not the voice of the LORD, nor executedst his fierce wrath upon Amalek, therefore hath the LORD done this thing unto thee this day. Moreover the LORD will also deliver Israel with thee into the hand of the Philistines: and to morrow shalt thou and thy sons be with me: the LORD also shall deliver the host of Israel into the hand of the Philistines.

Then Saul fell straightway all along on the earth, and was sore afraid, because of the words of Samuel: and there was no strength in him; for he had eaten no bread all the day, nor all the night.

(1 Samuel 28:3-20)

Nebuchadnezzar

At the end of twelve months he walked in the palace of the kingdom of Babylon. The king spake, and said, Is not this great Babylon, that I have built for the house of the kingdom by the might of my power, and for the honour of my majesty?

While the word was in the king's mouth, there fell a voice from heaven, saying, O king Nebuchadnezzar, to thee it is spoken; The kingdom is departed from thee. And they shall drive thee from men, and thy dwelling shall be with the beasts of the field: they shall make thee to eat grass as oxen, and seven times shall pass over thee, until thou know that the most High ruleth in the kingdom of men, and giveth it to whomsoever he will.

The same hour was the thing fulfilled upon Nebuchadnezzar: and he was driven from men, and did eat grass as oxen, and his body was wet with the dew of heaven, till his hairs were grown like eagles' feathers, and his nails like birds' claws.

(Daniel 4:29-33)

But God allowed Nebuchadnezzar to see deliverance.

And at the end of the days I Nebuchadnezzar lifted up mine eyes unto heaven, and mine understanding returned unto

> me, and I blessed the most High, and I praised and honoured him that liveth for ever, whose dominion is an everlasting dominion, and his kingdom is from generation to generation: And all the inhabitants of the earth are reputed as nothing: and he doeth according to his will in the army of heaven, and among the inhabitants of the earth: and none can stay his hand, or say unto him, What doest thou? At the same time my reason returned unto me; and for the glory of my kingdom, mine honour and brightness returned unto me; and my counsellors and my lords sought unto me; and I was established in my kingdom, and excellent majesty was added unto me.
>
> Now I Nebuchadnezzar praise and extol and honour the King of heaven, all whose works are truth, and his ways judgment: and those that walk in pride he is able to abase.
>
> (Daniel 4:34-37)

Moab

> But now the LORD hath spoken, saying, Within three years, as the years of an hireling, and the glory of Moab shall be contemned, with all that great multitude; and the remnant shall be very small and feeble.
>
> (Isaiah 16:14)

In my day, there is a very great nation that sits on this precipice. This nation, and any similar nation, might want to review the actions of the king and the people of Nineveh. It may be that God will perform the same forgiveness that He did with them.

> And Jonah began to enter into the city a day's journey, and he cried, and said, Yet forty days, and Nineveh shall be overthrown.
>
> So the people of Nineveh believed God, and proclaimed a fast, and put on sackcloth, from the greatest of them even to the least of them. For word came unto the king of Nineveh, and he arose from his throne, and he laid his robe from him, and covered him with sackcloth, and sat in ashes. And he caused it to be proclaimed and published through Nineveh by the decree of the king and his nobles, saying, Let neither man nor

beast, herd nor flock, taste any thing: let them not feed, nor drink water: But let man and beast be covered with sackcloth, and cry mightily unto God: yea, let them turn every one from his evil way, and from the violence that is in their hands. Who can tell if God will turn and repent, and turn away from his fierce anger, that we perish not?

And God saw their works, that they turned from their evil way; and God repented of the evil, that he had said that he would do unto them; and he did it not.

(Jonah 3:4-10)

+=+=+=+=+=+=+=+=+=+=+=+=+=+=+=+=+=+=+=+

Structure of Nations - Image Four

Image Four - Phase One

But other fell into good ground, and brought forth fruit, some an hundredfold, some sixtyfold, some thirtyfold.

This leads us to another type of nation that is in existence on this earth. This type of nation was presented in the blessing of Noah to Shem. *And he said, Blessed be the LORD God of Shem.* Note in this blessing that he did not directly bless Shem, but instead gave his blessing upon the God of Shem. This is not an oversight on Noah's part. In this statement, Noah was saying that the Lord God would have a special relationship with Shem. The Lord God would be the God of Shem. Through this relationship, Shem would be blessed, surely. Therefore, it is unnecessary to give the blessing directly to Shem, for he will receive it many fold from the God of Shem.

According to the Bible, God often refers to Himself as the God of Abraham, Isaac and Jacob. The lineage starts from Shem . . .

These are the generations of Shem: Shem was an hundred years old, and begat Arphaxad two years after the flood:

(Genesis 11:10)

. . . and reaches Abraham

Now these are the generations of Terah: Terah begat Abram, Nahor, and Haran; and Haran begat Lot.

(Genesis 11:27)

For us, it is of special note that He is the God of Abraham. For, in being the God of Abraham, He becomes the God of all the descendants of Abraham; as they hold to the principles that Abraham followed. It is the set of principles of Abraham that God recognized in saying that He is the God of Abraham. The core principle is briefly summarized as, having faith in the God of the Universe, Who created heaven and earth and all that therein is.

The nations that serve God are called to have a special relationship with the other nations of the world. In olden times it was necessary for them to separate themselves from those around them. The reasons that this was done was because of the immaturity of the leaders of those nations relative to the things of the world, and a weakness of connection of these leaders with God. There was not yet a constancy of interaction between the leaders of the nations and the God that made these nations. Additionally, there were not many nations that willingly held to the principles of God, at that time. As recorded in the Bible, the one that was selected by God to carry His message forward to the world is the nation of Israel.

Image Four - Phase Two

Rules of conduct were directly presented to the children of Israel. They were given strict instructions about how to deal with the nations around them.

> *When the LORD thy God shall bring thee into the land whither thou goest to possess it, and hath cast out many nations before thee, the Hittites, and the Girgashites, and the Amorites, and the Canaanites, and the Perizzites, and the Hivites, and the Jebusites, seven nations greater and mightier than thou; And when the LORD thy God shall deliver them before thee; thou shalt smite them, and utterly destroy them; thou shalt make no covenant with them, nor show mercy unto them: Neither shalt thou make marriages with them; thy daughter thou shalt not give unto his son, nor his daughter shalt thou take unto thy son.*

(Deuteronomy 7:1-3)

The people of Israel were also given the reasons why such rigorous measures had to be invoked in their dealings with the other nations.

> *For they will turn away thy son from following me, that they may serve other gods: so will the anger of the LORD be kindled against you, and destroy thee suddenly.*
>
> (Deuteronomy 7:4)

Furthermore, the people of Israel were told the price that would have to be paid if they chose to relax, even moderately, these strict rules of engagement.

> *Take heed to yourselves, that your heart be not deceived, and ye turn aside, and serve other gods, and worship them; And then the LORD'S wrath be kindled against you, and he shut up the heaven, that there be no rain, and that the land yield not her fruit; and lest ye perish quickly from off the good land which the LORD giveth you.*
>
> (Deuteronomy 11:16-17)

The people of Israel were told how to accomplish this form of worship within their nation.

> *Therefore shall ye lay up these my words in your heart and in your soul, and bind them for a sign upon your hand, that they may be as frontlets between your eyes. And ye shall teach them your children, speaking of them when thou sittest in thine house, and when thou walkest by the way, when thou liest down, and when thou risest up. And thou shalt write them upon the door posts of thine house, and upon thy gates:*
>
> (Deuteronomy 11:18-20)

And finally the people of Israel were told what was *in it for them*; that ever present question among we who are, oh so, human.

> *That your days may be multiplied, and the days of your children, in the land which the LORD sware unto your fathers to give them, as the days of heaven upon the earth. For if ye shall diligently keep all these commandments which I command you, to do them, to love the LORD your*

> *God, to walk in all his ways, and to cleave unto him; Then will the LORD drive out all these nations from before you, and ye shall possess greater nations and mightier than yourselves. Every place whereon the soles of your feet shall tread shall be yours: from the wilderness and Lebanon, from the river, the river Euphrates, even unto the uttermost sea shall your coast be. There shall no man be able to stand before you: for the LORD your God shall lay the fear of you and the dread of you upon all the land that ye shall tread upon, as he hath said unto you.*

(Deuteronomy 11:21-25)

So, there are nations that have emerged from Noah, in the mold of Shem, nations that understand that their existence is by an act of God. Furthermore, in this world of many nations, they knew that their sustenance depends on receiving blessings from God, on a constant basis. One of the most important things that they seek from God is an understanding of their neighbor nations. The strongest ones among this type of nation know that adoption of the ways of their fellow nations is not necessary. What is necessary is: a constant communication with God, through prayer, in all matters of interaction; especially, those matters that involve nations other than their own.

When such a nation stays in touch with God, they will be given the information that they require about the other nations. They will then be able to determine who and what to accept, and what to reject; for, they will be doing neither by their own will, but solely by the will of the LORD.

+=+

Tools for the Nations

Thus, through our progressive review of *The Parable of the Sower*, we have explored more deeply the nature of man. This is the same nature that is revealed to us in the nations of the world. Let us as nations learn from this, and apply the tools that God provided for the development of all the nations of the world; among which are the following tools, described by type of nation.

Tools for the Nations of Images One

When any one heareth the word of the kingdom, and understandeth it not, then cometh the wicked one, and catcheth away that which was sown in his heart. This is he which received seed by the way side.

Your answer is found in Jesus Christ, the Son of God.

At that time Jesus answered and said, I thank thee, O Father, Lord of heaven and earth, because thou hast hid these things from the wise and prudent, and hast revealed them unto babes. Even so, Father: for so it seemed good in thy sight.

All things are delivered unto me of my Father: and no man knoweth the Son, but the Father; neither knoweth any man the Father, save the Son, and he to whomsoever the Son will reveal him.

Come unto me, all ye that labour and are heavy laden, and I will give you rest. Take my yoke upon you, and learn of me; for I am meek and lowly in heart: and ye shall find rest unto your souls. For my yoke is easy, and my burden is light.

(Matthew 11:25-30)

Tools for the Nations of Images Two

But he that received the seed into stony places, the same is he that heareth the word, and anon with joy receiveth it; Yet hath he not root in himself, but dureth for a while: for when tribulation or persecution ariseth because of the word, by and by he is offended.

If, after serious evaluation of your national operations, you discover that you are a part of this branch of the nations, quickly petition God; asking Him to crush the stones into powder and mix with them some good dirt, so that you can have a place to take root. Then, ask Him for some fertilizer, and Godly cultivation techniques, to treat the spiritual soil in which you lay. Seek the blessing of God on your nation and on its growth. Not that you are asking God to remove you from the ground in which He planted you. Rather you are asking God to give you the equipment necessary to excel in what He has delivered unto you.

> *Then came the word of the LORD unto Jeremiah, saying, Behold, I am the LORD, the God of all flesh: is there any thing too hard for me?*
>
> (Jeremiah 32:26-27)

Tools for the Nations of Images Three

> *He also that received seed among the thorns is he that heareth the word; and the care of this world, and the deceitfulness of riches, choke the word, and he becometh unfruitful.*

If you are this type of nation, then quickly petition God; asking Him to provide the herbicide of the Spirit that is able to remove the thorns without killing the good fruit. Seek the blessing of God on your nation and on its growth. Not that you are asking God to remove you from the ground in which He planted you. Rather you are asking God to give you the equipment necessary to excel in what he has delivered unto you.

> *Finally, brethren, whatsoever things are true, whatsoever things are honest, whatsoever things are just, whatsoever things are pure, whatsoever things are lovely, whatsoever things are of good report; if there be any virtue, and if there be any praise, think on these things. Those things, which ye have both learned, and received, and heard, and seen in me, do: and the God of peace shall be with you.*
>
> *But I rejoiced in the Lord greatly, that now at the last your care of me hath flourished again; wherein ye were also careful, but ye lacked opportunity. Not that I speak in respect of want: for I have learned, in whatsoever state I am, therewith to be content. I know both how to be abased, and I know how to abound: every where and in all things I am instructed both to be full and to be hungry, both to abound and to suffer need. I can do all things through Christ which strengtheneth me.*
>
> (Philippians 4:8-13)

Tools for the Nations of Image Four

But he that received seed into the good ground is he that heareth the word, and understandeth it; which also beareth fruit, and bringeth forth, some an hundredfold, some sixty, some thirty.

If, however, you are blessed to be a part of a nation that is of this branch of the nations, give all glory and honor to God.

And he showed me a pure river of water of life, clear as crystal, proceeding out of the throne of God and of the Lamb. In the midst of the street of it, and on either side of the river, was there the tree of life, which bare twelve manner of fruits, and yielded her fruit every month: and the leaves of the tree were for the healing of the nations.

And there shall be no more curse: but the throne of God and of the Lamb shall be in it; and his servants shall serve him: And they shall see his face; and his name shall be in their foreheads. And there shall be no night there; and they need no candle, neither light of the sun; for the Lord God giveth them light: and they shall reign for ever and ever.

And he said unto me, These sayings are faithful and true: and the Lord God of the holy prophets sent his angel to show unto his servants the things which must shortly be done. Behold, I come quickly: blessed is he that keepeth the sayings of the prophecy of this book.

And I John saw these things, and heard them. And when I had heard and seen, I fell down to worship before the feet of the angel which showed me these things.

Then saith he unto me, See thou do it not: for I am thy fellowservant, and of thy brethren the prophets, and of them which keep the sayings of this book: worship God.

(Revelation 22:1-9)

+=+=+=+=+=+=+=+=+=+=+=+=+=+=+=+=+=+=+=+

Development of Nations - ALL

And above all things have fervent charity among yourselves: for charity shall cover the multitude of sins. Use hospitality one to another without grudging. As every man hath received the gift, even so minister the same one to another, as good stewards of the manifold grace of God. If any man speak, let him speak as the oracles of God; if any man minister, let him do it as of the ability which God giveth: that God in all things may be glorified through Jesus Christ, to whom be praise and dominion for ever and ever. Amen.

(1 Peter 4:8-11)

Since mankind developed
From just one name,
Biologically speaking
We are all the same.

But God in His wisdom,
The Most Majestic LORD,
Gave us a gift,
So we will not be bored.

The gift is the ability
To change our course;
To live in pleasure,
Or wallow in remorse.

Riding with this gift
Is a, will to survive:
So, we collect together
In order to thrive;

Forming nations,
As flocks of men,
Who build lifestyles,
Which they, then, defend.

Thinking we must separate,
And establish our own way,
To prevent others
From causing our decay.

But among these groups,
God still sees only a few;
Nations relate to Him
In what they choose to do.

One way is, the nations
That deny His name,
Striving for separation,
Seeking personal fame.

The next are two types
That go with the flow;

*Whatever the powerful do,
This must be the way to go.*

*Then, there are the nations
That serve God Most High:
These are the nations
That will never die.*

Chapter 7a

Before the Foundation
(A Human Thought)

We will have to start this explanation with a statement of some of the restrictions that we face. The first one is that we must write to you in the manner of mankind. This is obvious to most folk; however, it is said for the benefit of those who speak with the tongues of angels, in the language of God. Even if I did speak with the tongue of angels, there would have to be an interpreter to translate it back to the tongue of man.

"What," you say, "*is* he talking about?"

I am talking about this. The limitation of the language--which is the means of communication--is important to bring out because of the period at which we will be looking. Before the foundation of the earth there were no people, and thus human languages were unnecessary as a means of communication. During this time the most likely means of communication that was used was the language of love.

As we who have been smitten by another, know; the language of love is a heart-to-heart thing. Even when words are used, the real message still flows from somewhere around the words. It can bypass the restrictive mechanisms of the brain. In true love it only lightly touches on the spirit: for the most part it goes directly to the soul. Those who have been there know what I mean.

Unfortunately, I cannot use the language of love, here. Unless one knows the other, who has established the communication, it is very hard, if not impossible, to transfer a message on the medium of love. And this is particularly true about attempting to deliver it in writing. I am, therefore, restricted to the tool of, logical discourse.

To begin, I would like to ask a favor. As you think of God, picture Him for this moment as a super human, beyond all of the superheroes you have ever heard tell of, combined. For those who do not wish to acknowledge a belief in God, think about a being that is more logical and intelligent than all the earth's intellects combined. And for those of us, who really love the LORD, and the Lord, think about a Being beyond the combination of both of the other two patterns of thought. I will think about a Being that is beyond the combination, to the power of the combination, with this cubed. (You mathematicians will understand.)

With this in mind, let us go back to a reality before there was time. As we push into it, we see a being of the austerity we have just envisioned. It is alone; it is the first being (such a small word *being*; oh well) of existence. It is by definition omnipresent, for there is none who can track its start, and as yet nothing has started. Since it is of this nature, we will say that it is omnipotent; since there is no one and nothing able to hold power, besides it.

And naturally, it is omniscient; because anything that happens will be because this being does it, and it will always remember what it does. Furthermore, it will know when anything is done by anything else that it creates because it will provide the authorization for the others doing whatever it is that they are authorized by the being to do. And, oh, need I mention that it will always have these attributes; because everything that will ever be must be sustained by it. Poof! Without it there is nothing.

Since I'm getting kind of lost in the "its," let us say that the first thing it does is to give itself a personality, a frame of reference. This will allow it to distinguish itself from anything that it does. Skipping political correctness, I will refer to it using masculine pronouns from this point on: He, His, Him, etc. Furthermore, because of His power, I will capitalize the pronouns; wherever I remember to do so. Please forgive me if there are a few slips in my capitalization. You will perceive the reference to Him from the context.

To reduce confusion even further I acknowledge that He has given Himself a title. Since I am willing to be accused of religious bias, I will use the title God. Again, it is capital G to differentiate it from any small g designee or pretender.

So what does God do, now that He has established Himself for the sake of what is to follow? Why not design some stuff? This is where it gets sticky, however. He cannot just go on a brainstorming session; this would have wild results. You see; because of the nature of God, when he thinks it, it is: no drawing board or construction necessary. Not just by His word, but also in His mind, is the reality.

In the beginning God created the heaven and the earth. And the earth was without form, and void; and darkness was upon the face of the deep. And the Spirit of God moved upon the face of the waters.

And God said, Let there be light: and there was light. And God saw the light, that it was good: and God divided the light from the darkness. And God called the light Day, and the darkness he called Night. And the evening and the morning were the first day.

(Genesis 1:1-5)

And God said, Let there be a firmament in the midst of the waters, and let it divide the waters from the waters. And God made the firmament, and divided the waters which were under the firmament from the waters which were above the firmament: and it was so. And God called the firmament Heaven. And the evening and the morning were the second day.

(Genesis 1:6-8)

And God said, Let there be lights in the firmament of the heaven to divide the day from the night; and let them be for signs, and for seasons, and for days, and years: And let them be for lights in the firmament of the heaven to give light upon the earth: and it was so. And God made two great lights; the greater light to rule the day, and the lesser light to rule the night: he made the stars also. And God set them in the firmament of the heaven to give light upon the earth, And to rule over the day and over the night, and to divide the light from the darkness: and God saw that it was good.

(Genesis 1:14-18)

He also cannot do things top down or bottom up. Since what He designs is immediately operative, all pieces that come from Him have to be in place at the moment of the start of the total project. Did I mention that He has the benefit that He does not change?

For I am the LORD, I change not; therefore ye sons of Jacob are not consumed.

(Malachi 3:6)

> *Do not err, my beloved brethren. Every good gift and every perfect gift is from above, and cometh down from the Father of lights, with whom is no variableness, neither shadow of turning.*
>
> (James 1:16-17)

There is a term that is gaining some measure of popularity. It is the expression "intelligent design". This is elevated to the status of describing God, by calling Him the Intelligent Designer. The purpose of this expression is to fight against those who abuse the theory of evolution; or, it is said to be the purpose. This fighting, however, does not honor an apostolic admonition.

> *O Timothy, keep that which is committed to thy trust, avoiding profane and vain babblings, and oppositions of science falsely so called: Which some professing have erred concerning the faith.*
>
> *Grace be with thee.*
>
> *Amen.*
>
> (1 Timothy 6:20-21)

It is also not wise.

> *He that reproveth a scorner getteth to himself shame: and he that rebuketh a wicked man getteth himself a blot. Reprove not a scorner, lest he hate thee: rebuke a wise man, and he will love thee. Give instruction to a wise man, and he will be yet wiser: teach a just man, and he will increase in learning.*
>
> (Proverbs 9:7-9)

The misuse of evolution is addressed quite simply. What seems apparent to man in hindsight is not what is true, except where there is true visible hindsight. Probably the most difficult part of evolution, as it is sometimes abused, is that man comes from other species, such as the ape. This is not the theory of evolution. Briefly, the theory says that all creatures came about along their own evolutionary paths. Man has his path; apes have theirs.

It should be no surprise to anyone that mankind has evolved. We see greater intellect, delivered faster and at younger ages than before.

However, man is still man. Modern man did not change his nature when he became modern; at least not yet. Throughout his recognized timeline man is homo-*something*. It is only during the unrecognized and invisible pre-timeline of homo-*something* that it becomes dicey. This is the so-called time of the missing link and other evolutionary intermediaries.

It is easy for me to believe that the missing link is a direct product of God, at an instant in time. It is just as easy for me to say that the missing link is a development of God across time. It is equally as easy for me to believe that God created man just as he is now, without any intermediate stages; He does have this power, after all. It is sufficient for me to say that man started at a time. All is done by God.

> *In the beginning was the Word, and the Word was with God, and the Word was God. The same was in the beginning with God. All things were made by him; and without him was not any thing made that was made.*
>
> (John 1:1-3)

No matter how far we choose to go back, we will eventually reach a point where the process starts. It is at this point that we have to say that God, He who AM before the foundation of the earth, said and there was. Whatever that "was" is, which existed before man rose to become man, is totally in the hands of God. Once we pass from the time before the foundation of the earth, to the time at and after the foundation of the earth, we are in the era of the evident works of God. Man is only one of these evident works. Man still required, and requires, God for his establishment and continuation. What was done, then, is done multiple times a second every day today.

> *And the LORD God formed man of the dust of the ground, and breathed into his nostrils the breath of life; and man became a living soul.*
>
> *(Genesis 2:7)*

It is more appropriate to say of Him that He is The Instant Activator. He does not spend time on design and He does not waste time on establishing an explanation, or a path of understanding the works that He does, or has done. The arrival of understanding, as with the creation, once it happens will be instant. There is no process that man has, or that man can establish, that will lead to this understanding. It either is, or it is not; and when it is, it is of God. This is no less true in religion than it is in science. God said it, it is, and that is that.

> *For I am not ashamed of the gospel of Christ: for it is the power of God unto salvation to every one that believeth; to the Jew first, and also to the Greek. For therein is the righteousness of God revealed from faith to faith: as it is written, The just shall live by faith.*

> *For the wrath of God is revealed from heaven against all ungodliness and unrighteousness of men, who hold the truth in unrighteousness; Because that which may be known of God is manifest in them; for God hath showed it unto them. For the invisible things of him from the creation of the world are clearly seen, being understood by the things that are made, even his eternal power and Godhead; so that they are without excuse: Because that, when they knew God, they glorified him not as God, neither were thankful; but became vain in their imaginations, and their foolish heart was darkened. Professing themselves to be wise, they became fools, And changed the glory of the uncorruptible God into an image made like to corruptible man, and to birds, and fourfooted beasts, and creeping things. Wherefore God also gave them up to uncleanness through the lusts of their own hearts, to dishonour their own bodies between themselves: Who changed the truth of God into a lie, and worshipped and served the creature more than the Creator, who is blessed for ever. Amen.*

> *For this cause God gave them up unto vile affections: for even their women did change the natural use into that which is against nature: And likewise also the men, leaving the natural use of the woman, burned in their lust one toward another; men with men working that which is unseemly, and receiving in themselves that recompense of their error which was meet.*

> *And even as they did not like to retain God in their knowledge, God gave them over to a reprobate mind, to do those things which are not convenient; Being filled with all unrighteousness, fornication, wickedness, covetousness,*

maliciousness; full of envy, murder, debate, deceit, malignity; whisperers, Backbiters, haters of God, despiteful, proud, boasters, inventors of evil things, disobedient to parents, Without understanding, covenantbreakers, without natural affection, implacable, unmerciful: Who knowing the judgment of God, that they which commit such things are worthy of death, not only do the same, but have pleasure in them that do them.

(Romans 1:16-32)

The Word from the Bible

Exodus 32:1-6

And when the people saw that Moses delayed to come down out of the mount, the people gathered themselves together unto Aaron, and said unto him, Up, make us gods, which shall go before us; for as for this Moses, the man that brought us up out of the land of Egypt, we wot not what is become of him.

And Aaron said unto them, Break off the golden earrings, which are in the ears of your wives, of your sons, and of your daughters, and bring them unto me. And all the people brake off the golden earrings which were in their ears, and brought them unto Aaron. And he received them at their hand, and fashioned it with a graving tool, after he had made it a molten calf: and they said, These be thy gods, O Israel, which brought thee up out of the land of Egypt. And when Aaron saw it, he built an altar before it; and Aaron made proclamation, and said, To morrow is a feast to the LORD. And they rose up early on the morrow, and offered burnt offerings, and brought peace offerings; and the people sat down to eat and to drink, and rose up to play.

Exodus 17:1-7

And all the congregation of the children of Israel journeyed from the wilderness of Sin, after their journeys, according to the commandment of the LORD, and pitched in Rephidim: and there was no water for the people to drink. Wherefore the people did chide with Moses, and said, Give us water that we may drink. And Moses said unto them, Why chide ye with me? wherefore do ye tempt the LORD? And the people thirsted there for water; and the people murmured against Moses, and said, Wherefore is this that thou hast brought us up out of Egypt, to kill us and our children and our cattle with thirst?

And Moses cried unto the LORD, saying, What shall I do unto this people? they be almost ready to stone me.

And the LORD said unto Moses, Go on before the people, and take with thee of the elders of Israel; and thy rod, wherewith thou smotest the river, take in thine hand, and go. Behold, I will stand before thee there upon the rock in Horeb; and thou shalt smite the rock, and there shall come water out of it, that the people may drink. And Moses did so in the sight of the elders of Israel.

And he called the name of the place Massah, and Meribah, because of the chiding of the children of Israel, and because they tempted the LORD, saying, Is the LORD among us, or not?

Numbers 20:1-13

Then came the children of Israel, even the whole congregation, into the desert of Zin in the first month: and the people abode in Kadesh; and Miriam died there, and was buried there. And there was no water for the congregation: and they gathered themselves together against Moses and against Aaron. And the people chided with Moses, and spake, saying, Would God that we had died when our brethren died before the LORD! And why have ye brought up the congregation of the LORD into this wilderness, that we and our cattle should die there? And wherefore have ye made us to come up out of Egypt, to bring us in unto this evil place? it is no place of seed, or of figs, or of vines, or of pomegranates; neither is there any water to drink.

And Moses and Aaron went from the presence of the assembly unto the door of the tabernacle of the congregation, and they fell upon their faces: and the glory of the LORD appeared unto them. And the LORD spake unto Moses, saying, Take the rod, and gather thou the assembly together, thou, and Aaron thy brother, and speak ye unto the rock before their eyes; and it shall give forth his water, and thou shalt bring forth to them water out of the rock: so thou shalt give the congregation and their beasts drink.

And Moses took the rod from before the LORD, as he commanded him. And Moses and Aaron gathered the congregation together before the rock, and he said unto them, Hear now, ye rebels; must we fetch you water out of this rock?

And Moses lifted up his hand, and with his rod he smote the rock twice: and the water came out abundantly, and the congregation drank, and their beasts also.

And the LORD spake unto Moses and Aaron, Because ye believed me not, to sanctify me in the eyes of the children of Israel, therefore ye shall not bring this congregation into the land which I have given them. This is the water of Meribah, because the children of Israel strove with the LORD, and he was sanctified in them.

Numbers 20:23-29

And the LORD spake unto Moses and Aaron in mount Hor, by the coast of the land of Edom, saying, Aaron shall be gathered unto his people: for he shall not enter into the land which I have given unto the children of Israel, because ye rebelled against my word at the water of Meribah. Take Aaron and Eleazar his son, and bring them up unto mount Hor: And strip Aaron of his garments, and put them upon Eleazar his son: and Aaron shall be gathered unto his people, and shall die there.

And Moses did as the LORD commanded: and they went up into mount Hor in the sight of all the congregation. And Moses stripped Aaron of his garments, and put them upon Eleazar his son; and Aaron died there in the top of the mount: and Moses and Eleazar came down from the mount.

And when all the congregation saw that Aaron was dead, they mourned for Aaron thirty days, even all the house of Israel.

Deuteronomy 3:23-26

And I besought the LORD at that time, saying, O Lord GOD, thou hast begun to show thy servant thy greatness, and thy mighty hand: for what God is there in heaven or in earth, that can do according to thy works, and according to thy might? I pray thee, let me go over, and see the good land that is beyond Jordan, that goodly mountain, and Lebanon.

But the LORD was wroth with me for your sakes, and would not hear me: and the LORD said unto me, Let it suffice thee; speak no more unto me of this matter.

Deuteronomy 34:1-8

And Moses went up from the plains of Moab unto the mountain of Nebo, to the top of Pisgah, that is over against Jericho. And the LORD showed him all the land of Gilead, unto Dan, And all Naphtali, and the land of Ephraim, and Manasseh, and all the land of Judah, unto the utmost sea, And the south, and the plain of the valley of Jericho, the city of palm trees, unto Zoar.

And the LORD said unto him, This is the land which I sware unto Abraham, unto Isaac, and unto Jacob, saying, I will give it unto thy seed: I have caused thee to see it with thine eyes, but thou shalt not go over thither.

So Moses the servant of the LORD died there in the land of Moab, according to the word of the LORD. And he buried him in a valley in the land of Moab, over against Bethpeor: but no man knoweth of his sepulchre unto this day. And Moses was an hundred and twenty years old when he died: his eye was not dim, nor his natural force abated.

And the children of Israel wept for Moses in the plains of Moab thirty days: so the days of weeping and mourning for Moses were ended.

Chapter Eight

No Respect of Persons

It has been written that God's ways are above our ways.

> *Seek ye the LORD while he may be found, call ye upon him while he is near: Let the wicked forsake his way, and the unrighteous man his thoughts: and let him return unto the LORD, and he will have mercy upon him; and to our God, for he will abundantly pardon. For my thoughts are not your thoughts, neither are your ways my ways, saith the LORD. For as the heavens are higher than the earth, so are my ways higher than your ways, and my thoughts than your thoughts.*
>
> *For as the rain cometh down, and the snow from heaven, and returneth not thither, but watereth the earth, and maketh it bring forth and bud, that it may give seed to the sower, and bread to the eater: So shall my word be that goeth forth out of my mouth: it shall not return unto me void, but it shall accomplish that which I please, and it shall prosper in the thing whereto I sent it.*
>
> *For ye shall go out with joy, and be led forth with peace: the mountains and the hills shall break forth before you into singing, and all the trees of the field shall clap their hands. Instead of the thorn shall come up the fir tree, and instead of the brier shall come up the myrtle tree: and it shall be to the LORD for a name, for an everlasting sign that shall not be cut off.*
>
> (Isaiah 55:6-13)

Most of the time, this Scripture is used to justify the creation of nebulous concepts. We like to call these mysteries. But Scripture also tells us that His work is clearly understood.

> *For the wrath of God is revealed from heaven against all ungodliness and unrighteousness of men, who hold the truth in unrighteousness; Because that which may be known of God is manifest in them; for God hath showed it unto them. For the invisible things of him from the creation of the world are clearly seen, being understood by the things that are made, even his eternal power and Godhead; so that they are without excuse:*
>
> (Romans 1:18-20)

Furthermore, it is the lesson of the New Testament writers that this revelation of God is even more apparent now. Whereas there were once these things known as mysteries, they have been revealed.

> *Now to him that is of power to stablish you according to my gospel, and the preaching of Jesus Christ, according to the revelation of the mystery, which was kept secret since the world began, But now is made manifest, and by the scriptures of the prophets, according to the commandment of the everlasting God, made known to all nations for the obedience of faith: To God only wise, be glory through Jesus Christ for ever. Amen.*
>
> (Romans 16:25-27)

Therefore, do we say that Scripture fights against Scripture? Is it another New Testament against Old Testament thing? Are we in the situation where the New Testament brings an end to the Old Covenant? There have been occasions where this seems to have been stated.

> *Brethren, my heart's desire and prayer to God for Israel is, that they might be saved. For I bear them record that they have a zeal of God, but not according to knowledge. For they being ignorant of God's righteousness, and going about to establish their own righteousness, have not submitted themselves unto the righteousness of God.*
>
> *For Christ is the end of the law for righteousness to every one that believeth.*
>
> (Romans 10:1-4)

But no, the answer is: none of the above. Scripture, in declaring that God's ways are above our ways, means that His motives are pure and just; where ours, typically, are not. Well, He *is* Holy; and we are not. Thus, by definition, and by fact, His actions are the greater ones. Still, Scripture does not indicate that God ways are totally beyond our understanding.

I like to think that there will come times when God will give me understanding of His way. I know that because of my limitation, the LORD will have to do so slowly. His word to the nation of Israel, in Exodus 23:30, has a special significance for me, in waiting for God to move in my life. I apply it to my life by reminding myself that he moves me to success and peace in Him *By little and little*, lest the beasts of pride, arrogance and selfishness overwhelm the ground God has established in me through the Holy Ghost.

> *And ye shall serve the LORD your God, and he shall bless thy bread, and thy water; and I will take sickness away from the midst of thee. There shall nothing cast their young, nor be barren, in thy land: the number of thy days I will fulfil.*
>
> *I will send my fear before thee, and will destroy all the people to whom thou shalt come, and I will make all thine enemies turn their backs unto thee. And I will send hornets before thee, which shall drive out the Hivite, the Canaanite, and the Hittite, from before thee. I will not drive them out from before thee in one year; lest the land become desolate, and the beast of the field multiply against thee.*
>
> (Exodus 23:25-29)
>
> *By little and little I will drive them out from before thee, until thou be increased, and inherit the land.*
>
> (Exodus 23:30)

It is my prayer that the LORD continues to manifest Himself slowly, by little and little, in this writing; from cover to cover. Let us therefore, go forth to expand our understanding of what is meant by one other of God's marvelous ways toward man. This is the concept of having "respect of persons".

> *And whatsoever ye do, do it heartily, as to the Lord, and not unto men; Knowing that of the Lord ye shall receive the*

> *reward of the inheritance: for ye serve the Lord Christ. But he that doeth wrong shall receive for the wrong which he hath done: and there is no respect of persons.*

(Colossians 3:23-25)

But before I proceed to the meat of the concept, I must share a little milk. There might be an attempt to read this as somehow fragmenting the bounds that God placed on the responsibility given to male and female. Sorry ladies, and some men, the author still holds to the bounds set in Scripture for these two types of human creations. To briefly tell you on what basis I say this, I will reference one of the most widely used passages that seemingly explode these bounds.

> *For ye are all the children of God by faith in Christ Jesus. For as many of you as have been baptized into Christ have put on Christ. There is neither Jew nor Greek, there is neither bond nor free, there is neither male nor female: for ye are all one in Christ Jesus. And if ye be Christ's, then are ye Abraham's seed, and heirs according to the promise.*

(Galatians 3:26-29)

To dissolve the boundaries placed on the church, there is a need for a few more words: words that are not there, either in fact or in context. The words that must be added are, "in the offices of service to and for God."

We know that the following is true: during the time of this Scripture, the slave was still the slave. In the Bible, the slave is called upon to worship God as the slave; without a need for any change in condition before doing so. The Jew is still the Jew, and is similarly called upon to worship God in that station.

All who are in the positions mentioned in the Scripture are in the same state when they start to serve God as they were before they started to serve Him. Indeed, each one, in whatever station, must honor their designation as that which is ordained by God as what is best for them, at the time. Trust God in this. And though there is much more to be said about this, I will not attempt to cover it all. Let God establish you in your position; but I would not have you be ignorant of my belief about this matter. Having thus established this ground of understanding, we will proceed to the topic at hand.

"Finally," you say.

Well, to continue, God deals with the leaders of the nations.

And it came to pass on the morrow, that Moses sat to judge the people: and the people stood by Moses from the morning unto the evening.

And when Moses' father in law saw all that he did to the people, he said, What is this thing that thou doest to the people? why sittest thou thyself alone, and all the people stand by thee from morning unto even?

And Moses said unto his father in law, Because the people come unto me to enquire of God: When they have a matter, they come unto me; and I judge between one and another, and I do make them know the statutes of God, and his laws.

And Moses' father in law said unto him, The thing that thou doest is not good. Thou wilt surely wear away, both thou, and this people that is with thee: for this thing is too heavy for thee; thou art not able to perform it thyself alone. Hearken now unto my voice, I will give thee counsel, and God shall be with thee: Be thou for the people to Godward, that thou mayest bring the causes unto God:

(Exodus 18:13-19)

In this way the leaders can delegate, to others, the matters that do not need the intervention of God directly. These are the ones that are made captains over thousands, captains over hundreds, and so on. The matters that they hear are those that can be decided based on the Law of God, already given to the people; in writing, and in their hearts. The following instructions that Moses relayed to the children of Israel can be extended a few steps further to all nations in their service to God. This is tailor-made for the leaders of the nations.

And thou shalt teach them ordinances and laws, and shalt shew them the way wherein they must walk, and the work that they must do.

Moreover thou shalt provide out of all the people able men, such as fear God, men of truth, hating covetousness; and place such over them, to be rulers of thousands, and rulers of hundreds, rulers of fifties, and rulers of tens: And let them judge the people at all seasons: and it shall be, that every great matter they shall bring unto thee, but every small matter they shall judge: so shall it be easier for

> *thyself, and they shall bear the burden with thee. If thou shalt do this thing, and God command thee so, then thou shalt be able to endure, and all this people shall also go to their place in peace.*
>
> *So Moses hearkened to the voice of his father in law, and did all that he had said. And Moses chose able men out of all Israel, and made them heads over the people, rulers of thousands, rulers of hundreds, rulers of fifties, and rulers of tens. And they judged the people at all seasons: the hard causes they brought unto Moses, but every small matter they judged themselves.*
>
> (Exodus 18:20-26)

As humans we like to be able to drop names. This is our way of acquiring the power of the person whose name we drop, as if it were our own. There is a difference in the impact when one says that "the President said ..." than when one says "President Lastname said . . .". There is even more power implied in saying "Presfirstname Preslastname told me . . .". And, possibly, ultimate power is acquired when one can say "Presfirstname told me . . ."; that is, when our intended listeners know who we are talking about.

The power for us is derived from our attachment to the person with the title. This is understandable because each person carries the same title in a different way. Thus, by specifying the person we are saying what *kind* of power we have acquired. This is why we have the phrase "Law of Moses".

Though this may be helpful, and sometimes necessary; we should not extend it to our worship of God. At the level of the Spirit, God does not do that. Throughout Scripture the LORD refers to the title. God, who knew Moses by name, based Moses' authority on his title: servant of God. It was only when the children needed a human reminder of who currently held the title that the LORD added the name to the title.

> *(Now the man Moses was very meek, above all the men which were upon the face of the earth.) And the LORD spake suddenly unto Moses, and unto Aaron, and unto Miriam, Come out ye three unto the tabernacle of the congregation.*
>
> *And they three came out.*

> *And the LORD came down in the pillar of the cloud, and stood in the door of the tabernacle, and called Aaron and Miriam: and they both came forth.*
>
> *And he said, Hear now my words: If there be a prophet among you, I the LORD will make myself known unto him in a vision, and will speak unto him in a dream. My servant Moses is not so, who is faithful in all mine house. With him will I speak mouth to mouth, even apparently, and not in dark speeches; and the similitude of the LORD shall he behold: wherefore then were ye not afraid to speak against my servant Moses?*
>
> (Numbers 12:3-8)

God does not give authority to a name; because He does not change. Therefore, whoever holds a title given to them for service to God, must serve in this title as it is framed by Him. There is no need to know the nature of the authority, or the means by which it is wielded through the name of a human. God made this clear when he told us that His chosen people could as easily be called the children of Moses as they are now called the children of Israel.

> *And the LORD said unto Moses, How long will this people provoke me? and how long will it be ere they believe me, for all the signs which I have showed among them? I will smite them with the pestilence, and disinherit them, and will make of thee a greater nation and mightier than they.*
>
> *And Moses said unto the LORD, Then the Egyptians shall hear it, (for thou broughtest up this people in thy might from among them;) And they will tell it to the inhabitants of this land: for they have heard that thou LORD art among this people, that thou LORD art seen face to face, and that thy cloud standeth over them, and that thou goest before them, by day time in a pillar of a cloud, and in a pillar of fire by night.*
>
> *Now if thou shalt kill all this people as one man, then the nations which have heard the fame of thee will speak, saying, Because the LORD was not able to bring this people into the land which he sware unto them, therefore he hath slain them in the wilderness.*

> *And now, I beseech thee, let the power of my LORD be great, according as thou hast spoken, saying, The LORD is longsuffering, and of great mercy, forgiving iniquity and transgression, and by no means clearing the guilty, visiting the iniquity of the fathers upon the children unto the third and fourth generation. Pardon, I beseech thee, the iniquity of this people according unto the greatness of thy mercy, and as thou hast forgiven this people, from Egypt even until now.*
>
> *And the LORD said, I have pardoned according to thy word:*
>
> (Numbers 14:11-20)

The name is fluid, the title is solid; and the offices are unchanging. God has no respect of the person who is chosen by Him to hold the title and fill the office. To highlight this, let us look at some unique officeholders in the service of God. You will have to open your spirit and yield to the Spirit of Truth to follow me with these. Above all, do not use these examples in order to castigate any current officeholders; they are still God's anointed.

+=+=+=+=+=+=+=+=+=+=+=+=+=+=+=+=+=+=+=+

Various kinds of angels

> *And Moses took the bones of Joseph with him: for he had straitly sworn the children of Israel, saying, God will surely visit you; and ye shall carry up my bones away hence with you. And they took their journey from Succoth, and encamped in Etham, in the edge of the wilderness.*
>
> *And the LORD went before them by day in a pillar of a cloud, to lead them the way; and by night in a pillar of fire, to give them light; to go by day and night: He took not away the pillar of the cloud by day, nor the pillar of fire by night, from before the people.*
>
> (Exodus 13:19-22)
>
> *And Moses said unto the people, Fear ye not, stand still, and see the salvation of the LORD, which he will shew to you to day: for the Egyptians whom ye have seen to day, ye*

shall see them again no more for ever. The LORD shall fight for you, and ye shall hold your peace.

And the LORD said unto Moses, Wherefore criest thou unto me? speak unto the children of Israel, that they go forward: But lift thou up thy rod, and stretch out thine hand over the sea, and divide it: and the children of Israel shall go on dry ground through the midst of the sea. And I, behold, I will harden the hearts of the Egyptians, and they shall follow them: and I will get me honour upon Pharaoh, and upon all his host, upon his chariots, and upon his horsemen. And the Egyptians shall know that I am the LORD, when I have gotten me honour upon Pharaoh, upon his chariots, and upon his horsemen.

And the angel of God, which went before the camp of Israel, removed and went behind them; and the pillar of the cloud went from before their face, and stood behind them: And it came between the camp of the Egyptians and the camp of Israel; and it was a cloud and darkness to them, but it gave light by night to these: so that the one came not near the other all the night.

And Moses stretched out his hand over the sea; and the LORD caused the sea to go back by a strong east wind all that night, and made the sea dry land, and the waters were divided. And the children of Israel went into the midst of the sea upon the dry ground: and the waters were a wall unto them on their right hand, and on their left. And the Egyptians pursued, and went in after them to the midst of the sea, even all Pharaoh's horses, his chariots, and his horsemen. And it came to pass, that in the morning watch the LORD looked unto the host of the Egyptians through the pillar of fire and of the cloud, and troubled the host of the Egyptians, And took off their chariot wheels, that they drave them heavily: so that the Egyptians said, Let us flee from the face of Israel; for the LORD fighteth for them against the Egyptians.

And the LORD said unto Moses, Stretch out thine hand over the sea, that the waters may come again upon the Egyptians, upon their chariots, and upon their horsemen.

And Moses stretched forth his hand over the sea, and the sea returned to his strength when the morning appeared; and the Egyptians fled against it; and the LORD overthrew the Egyptians in the midst of the sea. And the waters returned, and covered the chariots, and the horsemen, and all the host of Pharaoh that came into the sea after them; there remained not so much as one of them.

(Exodus 14:13-28)

Unique witnesses of God's glory

And Balaam rose up in the morning, and saddled his ass, and went with the princes of Moab.

And God's anger was kindled because he went: and the angel of the LORD stood in the way for an adversary against him. Now he was riding upon his ass, and his two servants were with him. And the ass saw the angel of the LORD standing in the way, and his sword drawn in his hand: and the ass turned aside out of the way, and went into the field: and Balaam smote the ass, to turn her into the way. But the angel of the LORD stood in a path of the vineyards, a wall being on this side, and a wall on that side. And when the ass saw the angel of the LORD, she thrust herself unto the wall, and crushed Balaam's foot against the wall: and he smote her again.

And the angel of the LORD went further, and stood in a narrow place, where was no way to turn either to the right hand or to the left. And when the ass saw the angel of the LORD, she fell down under Balaam: and Balaam's anger was kindled, and he smote the ass with a staff.

And the LORD opened the mouth of the ass, and she said unto Balaam, What have I done unto thee, that thou hast smitten me these three times?

And Balaam said unto the ass, Because thou hast mocked me: I would there were a sword in mine hand, for now would I kill thee.

And the ass said unto Balaam, Am not I thine ass, upon which thou hast ridden ever since I was thine unto this day? was I ever wont to do so unto thee?

And he said, Nay. Then the LORD opened the eyes of Balaam, and he saw the angel of the LORD standing in the way, and his sword drawn in his hand: and he bowed down his head, and fell flat on his face.

(Numbers 22:21-31)

And the angel said unto them, Fear not: for, behold, I bring you good tidings of great joy, which shall be to all people. For unto you is born this day in the city of David a Saviour, which is Christ the Lord. And this shall be a sign unto you; Ye shall find the babe wrapped in swaddling clothes, lying in a manger. And suddenly there was with the angel a multitude of the heavenly host praising God, and saying, Glory to God in the highest, and on earth peace, good will toward men.

(Luke 2:10-14)

+=+

For me, the most potent lessons that I received pertaining to respect of persons, comes from my study of John the Baptist. When I consider John the Baptist and what was said about him, I gain a renewed appreciation of the power of the office, as opposed to that of the person.

And as they departed, Jesus began to say unto the multitudes concerning John, What went ye out into the wilderness to see? A reed shaken with the wind? But what went ye out for to see? A man clothed in soft raiment? behold, they that wear soft clothing are in kings' houses. But what went ye out for to see? A prophet? yea, I say unto you, and more than a prophet. For this is he, of whom it is written, Behold, I send my messenger before thy face, which shall prepare thy way before thee. Verily I say unto you, Among them that are born of women there hath not risen a greater than John the Baptist: notwithstanding he that is least in the kingdom of heaven is greater than he.

(Matthew 11:7-11)

Of even greater potency to me is the office of Son of God, who also holds the titles of Christ, the Messiah and the Son of man. The prophet stated that this is the highest position given to anyone.

> *For unto us a child is born, unto us a son is given: and the government shall be upon his shoulder: and his name shall be called Wonderful, Counsellor, The mighty God, The everlasting Father, The Prince of Peace. Of the increase of his government and peace there shall be no end, upon the throne of David, and upon his kingdom, to order it, and to establish it with judgment and with justice from henceforth even for ever. The zeal of the LORD of hosts will perform this.*
>
> (Isaiah 9:6-7)

The apostle Paul tells us that it is the highest position given to anything that is a product of God.

> *Let this mind be in you, which was also in Christ Jesus: Who, being in the form of God, thought it not robbery to be equal with God: But made himself of no reputation, and took upon him the form of a servant, and was made in the likeness of men: And being found in fashion as a man, he humbled himself, and became obedient unto death, even the death of the cross. Wherefore God also hath highly exalted him, and given him a name which is above every name:*
>
> (Philippians 2:5-9)

Even so, the position has limits: this name has bounds.

"Uh, oh, brother," I hear someone saying, "you're stepping on dangerous ground. This might lead to blasphemy."

Well, to eliminate that possibility, let me once again *write in tongues*, by quoting Scripture. Afterward, to fulfill the requirement of Scripture, I will listen to the Comforter in me for an interpretation.

> *That at the name of Jesus every knee should bow, of things in heaven, and things in earth, and things under the earth; And that every tongue should confess that Jesus Christ is Lord, to the glory of God the Father.*
>
> (Philippians 2:10-11)

The interpretation is this: the *name* of Jesus will signal to everyone to bow. That which will cause them to honor the name is "the glory of God the Father." We all will bow. However, it is not to the name of Jesus that we bow; we will bow to God the Father. Then, everyone will admit that Jesus Christ is authorized by God the Father to hold all power in heaven and in earth. And in doing this, we will glorify God the Father. The focus is on God the Father; and this is in agreement with the will of the Son. This is the direction in which all honor must flow from the servants of the LORD, without respect of persons.

> *Look unto me, and be ye saved, all the ends of the earth: for I am God, and there is none else. I have sworn by myself, the word is gone out of my mouth in righteousness, and shall not return, That unto me every knee shall bow, every tongue shall swear. Surely, shall one say, in the LORD have I righteousness and strength: even to him shall men come; and all that are incensed against him shall be ashamed.*

(Isaiah 45:22-25)

*Who we know,
Dropping the name;
This is surely
Our claim to fame.*

*Who it is,
Not what we know;
This often determines
How far we go.*

*We need not measure
Up to their worth,
In order to borrow
Their power on earth.*

*We can obtain
Unrestricted success,
When we let all know
We have **access**.*

*But in God's service
This is not the way
To order our lives
From day to day.*

*A position of service
Is what we must seek,
To live a life that
Fulfills our week*

*Of decades on the earth,
From toil to rest;
In this way serving
God, and man, best.*

*Not looking for power,
Not even from Heaven above;
Just God's smile,
As we show His love.*

*The Son of man, is our example
Of the way we must serve*

*To receive from God
Much more than we deserve.*

*Serve God in truth;
Faithfully be the one
Of which He says,
"This is my beloved son".*

Chapter 8a

The First Sending Forth
(The being, Christ)

Let us resume our exploration into the concept of a Design. This is, for us, a weak thing to say when referring to the Instant Activator; it is necessary, however, for our understanding. In our design frame, at this point of continuation, the *physical plan* is complete. Now, if you were He, what would be the next step in this design? Might He not want to have a clone, almost? This is the process of giving birth, or, for you men, causing the process leading to birth. So, God has a Son: the begotten Son of God

> *I will declare the decree: the LORD hath said unto me, Thou art my Son; this day have I begotten thee. Ask of me, and I shall give thee the heathen for thine inheritance, and the uttermost parts of the earth for thy possession.*
>
> (Psalm 2:7-8)

In this phase, God does not have to set forth an example for anything. Therefore, He does not have to use the process of creation; the process that serves as instruction for all that He will call into being to make things. At this level, God says, **Let there be**; and there is: and the Son of God Am.

Furthermore, there is no need to have any more than one Son: one will do. The key function of the Son will be mediation. God is not preparing a scenario of negotiation where two or more might be needed. He is only preparing for mediation, where one being moves between Him and one or more others. Therefore, there is only one Son. Okay, so that no one will get too jealous, there are many sons (not all human), which will have duties that are directed by the Son.

For God the Father to only have one Son makes sense. The Father of the Son would not want to cause others to envy someone who is only looking out for their best interest. However, even though

He has only one Son, for mediation; it does make sense for God the Father to have many sons. One important reason is that this will give the Son someone else to talk to, and to share himself with. It will allow the Son to have other friends, as we see in the Scripture.

> *Likewise the Spirit also helpeth our infirmities: for we know not what we should pray for as we ought: but the Spirit itself maketh intercession for us with groanings which cannot be uttered. And he that searcheth the hearts knoweth what is the mind of the Spirit, because he maketh intercession for the saints according to the will of God.*
>
> *And we know that all things work together for good to them that love God, to them who are the called according to his purpose. For whom he did foreknow, he also did predestinate to be conformed to the image of his Son, that he might be the firstborn among many brethren. Moreover whom he did predestinate, them he also called: and whom he called, them he also justified: and whom he justified, them he also glorified.*
>
> *What shall we then say to these things? If God be for us, who can be against us?*
>
> (Romans 8:26-31)

Having called forth a Son, it seems reasonable that God would show His Son the part of the Design that is the responsibility of the Son. Leafing quickly through reality, God finds it; that thing known as mankind. A new title which has a nice ring and a new crown which fits the Son well: Son of man. This is the responsibility ordained for the Son of God.

Then to add some depth to reality, God invoked the task to call forth other workers. These are the ones we call angels. Some will be good workers, and some will be rebellious (must have variety, to keep the Son growing in all wisdom). For clarity we will call the rebellious angels, *demons*. God even provided a leader for the rebels: we call him Satan.

Now as God stretches and sits down, He looks at the Son.

"Well," the Son projects (words are not necessary in this domain), "guess its time to go to work. The foundation will not build itself. Besides, someday they will be writing about me and my work."

"Yes, they will," says God. "That is, when I finish creating them by My Word." There is a brief pause in pre-human existence, and then the Father continues. "Pause for a moment, Son. Let me take care of this first. Let me read something to you from the Design," says the Father.

And the Father reads:

> *"In the beginning God created the heaven and the earth. And the earth was without form, and void; and darkness was upon the face of the deep. And the Spirit of God moved upon the face of the waters. And God said, Let there be light: and there was light. And God saw the light, that it was good: and God divided the light from the darkness. And God called the light Day, and the darkness he called Night. And the evening and the morning were the first day."*

"Well Son," sends forth the Father, "now that you have light and a place to call your own, you can really begin your studies. Call on Me when you need Me."

"Love you, Dad," says the Son.

"Love you too, Son," says Dad.

And all present, in this place they call Heaven, smile. And all the "to be's", and the "created's", and the "let there be's" that are in the Plan--even those that have not yet been seen--are fired up with expectation of their discovery.

+=+=+=+=+=+=+=+=+=+=+=+=+=+=+=+=+=+=+=+

Benefits of Being the Son

The concept of inheritance is introduced, and the Son is designated as inheritor of all that he has created for the Father, and of all that the Father has created for him. The first and most precious of these, is to be able to learn from the Father. We have listed some of the many benefits starting with this one. This is, of course, only a partial list. The Bible clearly states the limitation of our viewpoint on this matter.

> *This is the disciple which testifieth of these things, and wrote these things: and we know that his testimony is true. And there are also many other things which Jesus did, the which, if they should be written every one, I suppose that*

even the world itself could not contain the books that should be written. Amen.

(John 21:24-25)

~~~~~~~~~~~~~~~~~~~~~~~~~~~~~~~~~~

Full and exclusive access to the Father

These words spake Jesus, and lifted up his eyes to heaven, and said, Father, the hour is come; glorify thy Son, that thy Son also may glorify thee: As thou hast given him power over all flesh, that he should give eternal life to as many as thou hast given him. And this is life eternal, that they might know thee the only true God, and Jesus Christ, whom thou hast sent. I have glorified thee on the earth: I have finished the work which thou gavest me to do.

And now, O Father, glorify thou me with thine own self with the glory which I had with thee before the world was. I have manifested thy name unto the men which thou gavest me out of the world: thine they were, and thou gavest them me; and they have kept thy word. Now they have known that all things whatsoever thou hast given me are of thee. For I have given unto them the words which thou gavest me; and they have received them, and have known surely that I came out from thee, and they have believed that thou didst send me.

(John 17:1-8)

At that time Jesus answered and said, I thank thee, O Father, Lord of heaven and earth, because thou hast hid these things from the wise and prudent, and hast revealed them unto babes. Even so, Father: for so it seemed good in thy sight. All things are delivered unto me of my Father: and no man knoweth the Son, but the Father; neither knoweth any man the Father, save the Son, and he to whomsoever the Son will reveal him.

(Matthew 11:25)

It is written in the prophets, And they shall be all taught of God. Every man therefore that hath heard, and hath learned of the Father, cometh unto me. Not that any man hath seen the Father, save he which is of God, he hath seen the Father.

(John 6:45-46)

Ownership of all things in common with the Father

I have yet many things to say unto you, but ye cannot bear them now. Howbeit when he, the Spirit of truth, is come, he will guide you into all truth: for he shall not speak of himself; but whatsoever he shall hear, that shall he speak: and he will shew you things to come. He shall glorify me: for he shall receive of mine, and shall shew it unto you. All things that the Father hath are mine: therefore said I, that he shall take of mine, and shall shew it unto you.

(John 16:12-15)

Being allowed to be a full representative of the Father

Jesus answered them, I told you, and ye believed not: the works that I do in my Father's name, they bear witness of me. But ye believe not, because ye are not of my sheep, as I said unto you. My sheep hear my voice, and I know them, and they follow me: And I give unto them eternal life; and they shall never perish, neither shall any man pluck them out of my hand. My Father, which gave them me, is greater than all; and no man is able to pluck them out of my Father's hand. I and my Father are one.

(John 10:25-30)

Given access to the complete set of tools and abilities of the Father

Let this mind be in you, which was also in Christ Jesus: Who, being in the form of God, thought it not robbery to be equal with God: But made himself of no reputation, and took upon him the form of a servant, and was made in the likeness of men:

(Philippians 2:5-7)

Having the full confidence of the Father

And Jesus, when he was baptized, went up straightway out of the water: and, lo, the heavens were opened unto him, and he saw the Spirit of God descending like a dove, and lighting upon him: And lo a voice from heaven, saying, This is my beloved Son, in whom I am well pleased.

(Matthew 3:16-17)

Having revealed to him the positive patterns of behavior in the Father

In that day shall there be a highway out of Egypt to Assyria, and the Assyrian shall come into Egypt, and the Egyptian into Assyria, and the Egyptians shall serve with the Assyrians. In that day shall Israel be the third with Egypt and with Assyria, even a blessing in the midst of the land: Whom the LORD of hosts shall bless, saying, Blessed be Egypt my people, and Assyria the work of my hands, and Israel mine inheritance.

(Isaiah 19:23-25)

Being set loose to emulate and glorify the Father

I will declare the decree: the LORD hath said unto me, Thou art my Son; this day have I begotten thee. Ask of me, and I shall give thee the heathen for thine inheritance, and the uttermost parts of the earth for thy possession. Thou shalt break them with a rod of iron; thou shalt dash them in pieces like a potter's vessel.

Be wise now therefore, O ye kings: be instructed, ye judges of the earth. Serve the LORD with fear, and rejoice with trembling. Kiss the Son, lest he be angry, and ye perish from the way, when his wrath is kindled but a little. Blessed are all they that put their trust in him.

(Psalm 2:7-12)

Receiving the everlasting seal of the Father

But to which of the angels said he at any time, Sit on my right hand, until I make thine enemies thy footstool? Are they not all ministering spirits, sent forth to minister for them who shall be heirs of salvation?

(Hebrews 1:13-14)

Obtaining the respect of all, by the word of the Father

And being found in fashion as a man, he humbled himself, and became obedient unto death, even the death of the cross. Wherefore God also hath highly exalted him, and given him a name which is above every name:

(Philippians 2:8-9)

Binding all existence to the will of the Father and for His glory

That at the name of Jesus every knee should bow, of things in heaven, and things in earth, and things under the earth; And that every tongue should confess that Jesus Christ is Lord, to the glory of God the Father.

(Philippians 2:10-11)

+=+=+=+=+=+=+=+=+=+=+=+=+=+=+=+=+=+=+=+

Wouldn't it be nice if we could obtain this kind of relationship with God?

What, you say that we can?

Where does it say that?

Here:

> *There is therefore now no condemnation to them which are in Christ Jesus, who walk not after the flesh, but after the Spirit. For the law of the Spirit of life in Christ Jesus hath made me free from the law of sin and death. For what the law could not do, in that it was weak through the flesh, God sending his own Son in the likeness of sinful flesh, and for sin, condemned sin in the flesh: That the righteousness of the law might be fulfilled in us, who walk not after the flesh, but after the Spirit. For they that are after the flesh do mind the things of the flesh; but they that are after the Spirit the things of the Spirit.*
>
> *For to be carnally minded is death; but to be spiritually minded is life and peace. Because the carnal mind is enmity*

against God: for it is not subject to the law of God, neither indeed can be. So then they that are in the flesh cannot please God. But ye are not in the flesh, but in the Spirit, if so be that the Spirit of God dwell in you. Now if any man have not the Spirit of Christ, he is none of his. And if Christ be in you, the body is dead because of sin; but the Spirit is life because of righteousness. But if the Spirit of him that raised up Jesus from the dead dwell in you, he that raised up Christ from the dead shall also quicken your mortal bodies by his Spirit that dwelleth in you. Therefore, brethren, we are debtors, not to the flesh, to live after the flesh. For if ye live after the flesh, ye shall die: but if ye through the Spirit do mortify the deeds of the body, ye shall live.

For as many as are led by the Spirit of God, they are the sons of God. For ye have not received the spirit of bondage again to fear; but ye have received the Spirit of adoption, whereby we cry, Abba, Father. The Spirit itself beareth witness with our spirit, that we are the children of God: And if children, then heirs; heirs of God, and joint-heirs with Christ; if so be that we suffer with him, that we may be also glorified together.

(Romans 8:1-17)

Very good! And so I shall become: and so I am.

The Word from the Bible

Numbers 11:24-29

And Moses went out, and told the people the words of the LORD, and gathered the seventy men of the elders of the people, and set them round about the tabernacle. And the LORD came down in a cloud, and spake unto him, and took of the spirit that was upon him, and gave it unto the seventy elders: and it came to pass, that, when the spirit rested upon them, they prophesied, and did not cease.

But there remained two of the men in the camp, the name of the one was Eldad, and the name of the other Medad: and the spirit rested upon them; and they were of them that were written, but went not out unto the tabernacle: and they prophesied in the camp. And there ran a young man, and told Moses, and said, Eldad and Medad do prophesy in the camp. And Joshua the son of Nun, the servant of Moses, one of his young men, answered and said, My lord Moses, forbid them.

And Moses said unto him, Enviest thou for my sake? would God that all the LORD'S people were prophets, and that the LORD would put his spirit upon them!

Joel 2:28-32

And it shall come to pass afterward, that I will pour out my spirit upon all flesh; and your sons and your daughters shall prophesy, your old men shall dream dreams, your young men shall see visions: And also upon the servants and upon the handmaids in those days will I pour out my spirit. And I will show wonders in the heavens and in the earth, blood, and fire, and pillars of smoke. The sun shall be turned into darkness, and the moon into blood, before the great and the terrible day of the LORD come. And it shall come to pass, that whosoever shall call on the name of the LORD shall be delivered: for in mount Zion and in Jerusalem shall be deliverance, as the LORD hath said, and in the remnant whom the LORD shall call.

1 Corinthians 14:1-5

Follow after charity, and desire spiritual gifts, but rather that ye may prophesy. For he that speaketh in an unknown tongue speaketh not unto men, but unto God: for no man understandeth him; howbeit in the spirit he speaketh mysteries. But he that prophesieth speaketh unto men to edification, and exhortation, and comfort. He that speaketh in an unknown tongue edifieth himself; but he that prophesieth edifieth the church. I would that ye all spake with tongues, but rather that ye prophesied: for greater is he that prophesieth than he that speaketh with tongues, except he interpret, that the church may receive edifying.

1 Corinthians 14:18-19

I thank my God, I speak with tongues more than ye all: Yet in the church I had rather speak five words with my understanding, that by my voice I might teach others also, than ten thousand words in an unknown tongue.

1 Corinthians 14:23-25

If therefore the whole church be come together into one place, and all speak with tongues, and there come in those that are unlearned, or unbelievers, will they not say that ye are mad? But if all prophesy, and there come in one that believeth not, or one unlearned, he is convinced of all, he is judged of all: And thus are the secrets of his heart made manifest; and so falling down on his face he will worship God, and report that God is in you of a truth.

Chapter Nine

The Power of Prophecy

Let me introduce you to the most powerful prophet of all time; past, present and future.

> *The woman saith unto him, Sir, I perceive that thou art a prophet. Our fathers worshipped in this mountain; and ye say, that in Jerusalem is the place where men ought to worship.*
>
> *Jesus saith unto her, Woman, believe me, the hour cometh, when ye shall neither in this mountain, nor yet at Jerusalem, worship the Father. Ye worship ye know not what: we know what we worship: for salvation is of the Jews. But the hour cometh, and now is, when the true worshippers shall worship the Father in spirit and in truth: for the Father seeketh such to worship him. God is a Spirit: and they that worship him must worship him in spirit and in truth.*
>
> *The woman saith unto him, I know that Messias cometh, which is called Christ: when he is come, he will tell us all things.*
>
> *Jesus saith unto her, I that speak unto thee am he.*
>
> (John 4:19-26)

The work of a prophet of God in the days of old is described in Scripture.

> *Since the day that your fathers came forth out of the land of Egypt unto this day I have even sent unto you all my servants the prophets, daily rising up early and sending them: Yet they hearkened not unto me, nor inclined their ear, but hardened their neck: they did worse than their fathers.*
>
> (Jeremiah 7:25-26)

The challenge of a prophet of God in the days of old is described in Scripture.

> *And the LORD came down in the pillar of the cloud, and stood in the door of the tabernacle, and called Aaron and Miriam: and they both came forth. And he said, Hear now my words: If there be a prophet among you, I the LORD will make myself known unto him in a vision, and will speak unto him in a dream. My servant Moses is not so, who is faithful in all mine house. With him will I speak mouth to mouth, even apparently, and not in dark speeches; and the similitude of the LORD shall he behold: wherefore then were ye not afraid to speak against my servant Moses?*
>
> (Numbers 12:5-8)

Prophecy, in our time, however, is probably the simplest thing that God requires of the man who would serve Him. It is something that every one who believes in God can do. Other than having a desire to honor God, there are no special requirements. There isn't even any training necessary, speaking of things of this earth. God no longer uses *dark speeches* to convey His message. His message has been fully revealed by His Son, the Lord Jesus Christ, and the apostles and disciples given to His Son by the Father.

Yes, there may be times when the prophet will be called upon to go forth *daily rising up early*. This is very useful for the *early bird*, to *catch* the attention of *the worms*, and other slithering creatures, pressing forth in defiance of the will of God.

The callings--such as pastor, teacher, preacher, and other workers mentioned in Scripture--require some form of structural preparation. The structure is this: they are only done by the direct election of God to serve in what is called an *office*.

> *Now ye are the body of Christ, and members in particular. And God hath set some in the church, first apostles, secondarily prophets, thirdly teachers, after that miracles, then gifts of healings, helps, governments, diversities of tongues.*
>
> (1 Corinthians 12:27-28)

Prophecy, on the other hand, is open to all who believe in God: this is because of the nature of prophecy. Prophecy is simply saying what God tells us to say. As such, we do not have to prepare a message.

Prophecy is saying things in the way that God tells us to say them. We do not have to be worried about putting things in a proper context to catch anyone's attention. We just have to say it.

But why do I say that this is so simple?

It is simple because God has prepared the script and written it down beforehand. He just has to stir it up when it is needed.

> *And it shall come to pass afterward, that I will pour out my spirit upon all flesh; and your sons and your daughters shall prophesy, your old men shall dream dreams, your young men shall see visions: And also upon the servants and upon the handmaids in those days will I pour out my spirit.*
>
> (Joel 2:28-29)

> *Behold, the days come, saith the LORD, that I will make a new covenant with the house of Israel, and with the house of Judah: Not according to the covenant that I made with their fathers in the day that I took them by the hand to bring them out of the land of Egypt; which my covenant they brake, although I was an husband unto them, saith the LORD: But this shall be the covenant that I will make with the house of Israel; After those days, saith the LORD, I will put my law in their inward parts, and write it in their hearts; and will be their God, and they shall be my people. And they shall teach no more every man his neighbour, and every man his brother, saying, Know the LORD: for they shall all know me, from the least of them unto the greatest of them, saith the LORD: for I will forgive their iniquity, and I will remember their sin no more.*
>
> (Jeremiah 31:31-34)

The apostles did not have it so easy. They had to wait for the message; and sometimes this was at the most stressful of times for them.

And Jesus answered and said unto them, Take heed that no man deceive you. For many shall come in my name, saying, I am Christ; and shall deceive many.

And ye shall hear of wars and rumours of wars: see that ye be not troubled: for all these things must come to pass, but the end is not yet. For nation shall rise against nation, and kingdom against kingdom: and there shall be famines, and pestilences, and earthquakes, in divers places. All these are the beginning of sorrows. Then shall they deliver you up to be afflicted, and shall kill you: and ye shall be hated of all nations for my name's sake.

(Matthew 24:4-9)

Be careful when you think about prophecy, however. There is old prophecy, and there is new prophecy. The old prophecy was heavily entwined with God's judgment. The prophets were sent to deliver message of condemnation and reproof. This, in many cases, cost them their lives. The old prophecy has been replaced.

The law and the prophets were until John: since that time the kingdom of God is preached, and every man presseth into it.

(Luke 16:16)

The Gospel, as presented in the Bible, is now available to perform the functions of the old prophecy.

All scripture is given by inspiration of God, and is profitable for doctrine, for reproof, for correction, for instruction in righteousness: That the man of God may be perfect, thoroughly furnished unto all good works.

(2 Timothy 3:16-17)

The power of the old covenant prophets is contained in the Bible. We see an affirmation of this in the words that Jesus delivered to his followers about the division that his message would bring between individuals. This is the sword of the word that he is describing. It is activated by his words, which are recorded in the Bible. It is revealed through the steering of the Holy Ghost.

Think not that I am come to send peace on earth: I came not to send peace, but a sword. For I am come to set a man at variance against his father, and the daughter against her mother, and the daughter in law against her mother in law. And a man's foes shall be they of his own household.

(Matthew 10:34-36)

This is the same sword that is expressed to all people, on that day when the Lord displays his power.

Repent; or else I will come unto thee quickly, and will fight against them with the sword of my mouth.

(Revelation 2:16)

This is why God has elected individuals to certain offices; so that they can be as active with the written word of God as the prophets in the olden times were with the spoken word of God. Back then, the prophets *were* the Bible: they were the Bible in development. And yes, sometimes the life of an elect individual will be the cost of transformation in society. We who are so called must be ready. However, we also must not be reckless. We must not sacrifice our lives where it is not necessary, and where a greater good can be served by our continuing to live. We have no points to prove in this regard.

For to me to live is Christ, and to die is gain. But if I live in the flesh, this is the fruit of my labour: yet what I shall choose I wot not. For I am in a strait betwixt two, having a desire to depart, and to be with Christ; which is far better: Nevertheless to abide in the flesh is more needful for you.

(Philippians 1:21-24)

A note here: we are all called to give our life to God. However, we are not all called to be ready to lose our life for God. Some of us are allowed to continue in service in hiding. To lose ones life for the LORD is preparation that must be a part of the life of the selected few; among which are, the disciples of Jesus, and apostles, or other ones specifically called thereto among the elect. But even though the selected ones must be ready to lose their life for the word of God, they are not called to throw it away.

There are many who are saved by Jesus' death and resurrection. There are, however, few who are chosen to go the full distance for him. God understands our weaknesses and our capabilities; and yes, He does assign us responsibilities based on these things. One example from Scripture involves the subject of marriage and divorce. Yes, this too is subject to the direction of God in our lives.

> *They say unto him, Why did Moses then command to give a writing of divorcement, and to put her away?*
>
> *He saith unto them, Moses because of the hardness of your hearts suffered you to put away your wives: but from the beginning it was not so. And I say unto you, Whosoever shall put away his wife, except it be for fornication, and shall marry another, committeth adultery: and whoso marrieth her which is put away doth commit adultery.*
>
> *His disciples say unto him, If the case of the man be so with his wife, it is not good to marry.*
>
> *But he said unto them, All men cannot receive this saying, save they to whom it is given. For there are some eunuchs, which were so born from their mother's womb: and there are some eunuchs, which were made eunuchs of men: and there be eunuchs, which have made themselves eunuchs for the kingdom of heaven's sake. He that is able to receive it, let him receive it.*
>
> (Matthew 19:7-12)

Now, let us get back to prophecy. What is new prophecy? It is summarized by the apostle Peter.

> *But sanctify the Lord God in your hearts: and be ready always to give an answer to every man that asketh you a reason of the hope that is in you with meekness and fear: Having a good conscience; that, whereas they speak evil of you, as of evildoers, they may be ashamed that falsely accuse your good conversation in Christ.*
>
> (1 Peter 3:15-16)

This is why it is so simple. We are really just answering a question about ourselves. And as we know, there are very few people that are unwilling to talk about themselves; especially about their strengths. Or is that really so straightforwardly true?

Actually, it is a little bit more complex than it seems. Yes, it is simple to acquire this means of service to God; but there are many complexities involved in its activation. I will cover only two.

First is the matter of popularity. To the general public, it seems that having Godly ideals are not very entertaining. There aren't many movies or publications with the title, "Christians gone wild." This should be true of all religions, but unfortunately, it is not. Christians are under some rather strict directives relative to this type of behavior. It is not just that we cannot *do* things like the world does them; we cannot even talk about things in the same fashion.

> *Be ye therefore followers of God, as dear children; And walk in love, as Christ also hath loved us, and hath given himself for us an offering and a sacrifice to God for a sweetsmelling savour. But fornication, and all uncleanness, or covetousness, let it not be once named among you, as becometh saints; Neither filthiness, nor foolish talking, nor jesting, which are not convenient: but rather giving of thanks.*
>
> (Ephesians 5:1-4)

Please note: the word *Christian*, when used in this context, is not just a title. It is used in reference to a way of life. This way of life is one in which people have committed themselves to following the message of Jesus Christ. It is not just someone who goes to church, or even someone who says that they are a follower. This is not to say that Christians don't forget who they serve, sometimes. At these times they can and do *go wild*.

Some of the times in history where this happened would have headlines such as "Inquisitors gone wild", "Hitler gone wild", "Radical popes gone wild", "Protestants gone wild", Reformers gone wild" and "Political activists gone wild". Yes, titles such as these, but not "Christians gone wild"; at least, not while they are in *uniform*. A true follower of Christ just does not do that. A true follower of Christ does not have to. One does not have to go wild to give an answer of hope-- highly expressive, sometimes, but never wild.

The second reason it is difficult, sometimes, for us to prophesy, is best seen in the change that is coming about in the United States of America (USA). The laws of the land are being re-formed to take the slogan of the flag one step further. The statement made on behalf of the flag is "don't tread on me". The USA is now at a point where organizations and collections of people have adopted this slogan, *with a vengeance*. In somewhat simplistic legalize it is expressed as:

"I will of course sue you if you step on me, but I will also sue you if I think you are thinking about stepping on me. And this I will define as, doing or saying anything that might cause me any pressure about the nature or impact of any of my actions. And this is especially true when what you do may hurt my, oh so delicate, conscience. This is, as you may know, the same conscience which I will not use for moral issues, anymore; but only to make myself feel good. And I will modify all laws, and other appearances of reality, to fit my renewed sense of the importance of self, over society. And I will win!"

In a nutshell, as they say, it is becoming illegal to be religious; or more specifically, it is becoming illegal to be truly Christian in the USA. And this is occurring in the "land of the free" and in the "home(s) of the brave". Woe unto the rest of the world if this is viewed as the ideal or even optimal society.

Mankind seems to be moving toward a renewed condemnation of itself by engaging in actions that were condemned by the prophets of old. Soon everyone will be too busy with self, to spend any time preserving the benefit of others; at least, this seems to be the trend in law and in the courts. But God will not accept it. Whoever follows this path will answer to Him. In this regard it is very wise to remember the caution of Scripture.

> *For we know him that hath said, Vengeance belongeth unto me, I will recompense, saith the Lord. And again, The Lord shall judge his people. It is a fearful thing to fall into the hands of the living God.*
>
> (Hebrews 10:30-31)

We need to get much more into the sharing character of the Gospel of Jesus Christ. But first, we need to concentrate, first, on our own reformation before we look to others.

> *Judge not, that ye be not judged. For with what judgment ye judge, ye shall be judged: and with what measure ye mete, it shall be measured to you again.*
>
> *And why beholdest thou the mote that is in thy brother's eye, but considerest not the beam that is in thine own eye? Or how wilt thou say to thy brother, Let me pull out the*

> *mote out of thine eye; and, behold, a beam is in thine own eye? Thou hypocrite, first cast out the beam out of thine own eye; and then shalt thou see clearly to cast out the mote out of thy brother's eye.*
>
> (Matthew 7:1-5)

The lure of popularity and the unrighteous over-reaching of the laws of the land are two of the pitfalls of modern society for which prophecy of today was tailor-made. This is the power of prophecy. Its power is in the peace it gives to the prophet who rests in God. Its power is also in the peace it gives to the one receiving the prophecy, as sent by God.

> *And as Moses lifted up the serpent in the wilderness, even so must the Son of man be lifted up: That whosoever believeth in him should not perish, but have eternal life. For God so loved the world, that he gave his only begotten Son, that whosoever believeth in him should not perish, but have everlasting life. For God sent not his Son into the world to condemn the world; but that the world through him might be saved.*
>
> (John 3:14-17)

All those of us who would honor God, grab hold of this gift. Then hang on for the most enchanting ride of your life. It is marvelous.

> *Jesus answered and said unto him, If a man love me, he will keep my words: and my Father will love him, and we will come unto him, and make our abode with him. He that loveth me not keepeth not my sayings: and the word which ye hear is not mine, but the Father's which sent me. These things have I spoken unto you, being yet present with you. But the Comforter, which is the Holy Ghost, whom the Father will send in my name, he shall teach you all things, and bring all things to your remembrance, whatsoever I have said unto you.*
>
> *Peace I leave with you, my peace I give unto you: not as the world giveth, give I unto you. Let not your heart be troubled, neither let it be afraid.*
>
> (John 14:23-27)

*Sometimes, the thing
That is most grand
Is that which is easiest
To understand.*

*There is such a thing,
Which God gives
To every soul
That lives:*

*It is the gift of prophecy,
With its power sublime;
Powered by God in man,
Across all our time.*

*It is that which
Causes us to say
The word of God,
With little delay.*

*Not a lot of thought,
No need for a plan;
Just speak the Word
To your fellow man.*

*No need to scheme
Or even plot,
Or cross each 't',
Or '.' each dot.*

*The word is given
Within your heart,
Merged with the soul,
Forever a part*

*Of what you may
Share with anyone
Wanting to know
Why you have such fun:*

*What is the hope
That lives in you,*

*Shining forth
In all you do?*

*Ah, the power of prophecy,
Given by God's own hand,
To be shared with others
At your instant command.*

Chapter 9a

The Pattern of the First

We must always strive to improve ourselves. One way this can be done is by modeling the behavior of successful others. However, this must be done with great care by a child of God. Really, this should be done with the same amount of care by everyone. Attention must be given to whether the means used to achieve self improvement is edifying to the whole of God's family. It is still true that the means do not necessarily justify the ends.

To gain insight into the replication of ones self by modeling from another, I studied the first success of all. This is that one which Christians call the Word.

> *In the beginning was the Word, and the Word was with God, and the Word was God. The same was in the beginning with God.*
>
> (John 1:1-2)

The Word is that aspect of God which we think of as being His authority. To understand this better, think about the fact that a person may have many titles. The words, female, student, teacher, mother, wife and several more, can all refer to the same person. God is differentiated from humans only in that all His titles are MAJOR. As such they all begin with a capital letter, and at least one of them is fully capitalized (AM). Furthermore, each action that God performs is so important that it has its own nature, or, character. Such is the nature of the Word.

Consider now what the Word did (and this is just one event in the Word).

> *All things were made by him; and without him was not any thing made that was made.*
>
> (John 1:3)

I pray that you will believe this; and by doing so, that you will, thereby, understand why I persuade everyone to obtain knowledge from the Word. I hope that you now understand why I feel that this is the best model for success. Well, I do. Therefore, I'll explain what is in the model.

The Word is very careful about providing for human understanding. This is no less true now than it was before there were any humans in existence. The Word provides for what will be, as well as what is. To provide a truly working system for our understanding, there are some key functions that are required. The first is to build the platform for what is to come. This includes the vision of the workers, as well as of the structures. The Word did this prior to the beginning, by the establishment of the Kingdom of Heaven. This is the pattern that is also set forth for His workers on the earth.

> *After this manner therefore pray ye: Our Father which art in heaven, Hallowed be thy name. Thy kingdom come, Thy will be done in earth, as it is in heaven. Give us this day our daily bread. And forgive us our debts, as we forgive our debtors. And lead us not into temptation, but deliver us from evil: For thine is the kingdom, and the power, and the glory, for ever. Amen.*

(Matthew 6:9-13)

Once the pattern is set, it is time to build an environment in which the enterprise can exist. For earthly endeavors, this involves site selection and inspection. For the Word, it involved site creation and visitation.

> *In the beginning God created the heaven and the earth. And the earth was without form, and void; and darkness was upon the face of the deep. And the Spirit of God moved upon the face of the waters.*

(Genesis 1:1-2)

Then, we must discover or create support structures for the components that are to be established on the site. For us, this might involve favorable laws, relationships with suppliers, authorization to modify an existing location to fit our needs, and so on. In general, these are the things that will allow our workers to concentrate on building the product. The Word established the natural laws to govern the universe enterprise, and the associated items controlled thereby.

> *And God said, Let there be light: and there was light. And God saw the light, that it was good: and God divided the light from the darkness. And God called the light Day, and the darkness he called Night. And the evening and the morning were the first day.*
>
> *And God said, Let there be a firmament in the midst of the waters, and let it divide the waters from the waters. And God made the firmament, and divided the waters which were under the firmament from the waters which were above the firmament: and it was so. And God called the firmament Heaven. And the evening and the morning were the second day.*
>
> *And God said, Let the waters under the heaven be gathered together unto one place, and let the dry land appear: and it was so. And God called the dry land Earth; and the gathering together of the waters called he Seas: and God saw that it was good.*
>
> (Genesis 1:3-10)

God also did some site modification after the universe enterprise was created.

> *And God said, Let there be lights in the firmament of the heaven to divide the day from the night; and let them be for signs, and for seasons, and for days, and years: And let them be for lights in the firmament of the heaven to give light upon the earth: and it was so. And God made two great lights; the greater light to rule the day, and the lesser light to rule the night: he made the stars also. And God set them in the firmament of the heaven to give light upon the earth, And to rule over the day and over the night, and to divide the light from the darkness: and God saw that it was good.*
>
> (Genesis 1:14-18)

Once the site is ready, we need a strong and deep support layer. This is comparable to the foundations we dig for buildings. In addition to being strong, they must be set on a firm layer of earth: the bedrock. The Word did this by filling the site with a unique kind of foundation: the animals, fish and plants. And the Word did all this, using the workers in the environment that had been established. These *workers* are the earth and the waters.

> *And God said, Let the earth bring forth grass, the herb yielding seed, and the fruit tree yielding fruit after his kind, whose seed is in itself, upon the earth: and it was so. And the earth brought forth grass, and herb yielding seed after his kind, and the tree yielding fruit, whose seed was in itself, after his kind: and God saw that it was good.*
>
> (Genesis 1:11-12)
>
> *And God said, Let the waters bring forth abundantly the moving creature that hath life, and fowl that may fly above the earth in the open firmament of heaven. And God created great whales, and every living creature that moveth, which the waters brought forth abundantly, after their kind, and every winged fowl after his kind: and God saw that it was good. And God blessed them, saying, Be fruitful, and multiply, and fill the waters in the seas, and let fowl multiply in the earth.*
>
> (Genesis 1:20-22)
>
> *And God said, Let the earth bring forth the living creature after his kind, cattle, and creeping thing, and beast of the earth after his kind: and it was so. And God made the beast of the earth after his kind, and cattle after their kind, and every thing that creepeth upon the earth after his kind: and God saw that it was good.*
>
> (Genesis 1:24-25)

Next on the list of tasks for establishing a successful enterprise is to obtain a staff of workers. This, the Word did in two stages. The first stage is to provide a place for the officer of the enterprise. However, before creating the office, God reviewed with His associates the nature of the staff that would be *employed* by Him in the *company* He made; called earth. He also wrote the job description for the first worker. (And of course, He presented the benefits package, too.)

> *And God said, Let us make man in our image, after our likeness: and let them have dominion over the fish of the sea, and over the fowl of the air, and over the cattle, and*

over all the earth, and over every creeping thing that creepeth upon the earth. So God created man in his own image, in the image of God created he him; male and female created he them.

(Genesis 1:26-27)

And God said, Behold, I have given you every herb bearing seed, which is upon the face of all the earth, and every tree, in the which is the fruit of a tree yielding seed; to you it shall be for meat. And to every beast of the earth, and to every fowl of the air, and to every thing that creepeth upon the earth, wherein there is life, I have given every green herb for meat: and it was so.

(Genesis 1:29-30)

Then, God gave a review--call it a flashback for His creation--of the work that He had done, in building an office for His staff. It is, of course, a very spacious office; therefore, it will need very special care.

And the LORD God planted a garden eastward in Eden; and there he put the man whom he had formed. And out of the ground made the LORD God to grow every tree that is pleasant to the sight, and good for food; the tree of life also in the midst of the garden, and the tree of knowledge of good and evil.

(Genesis 2:8-9)

And the LORD God took the man, and put him into the garden of Eden to dress it and to keep it. And the LORD God commanded the man, saying, Of every tree of the garden thou mayest freely eat: But of the tree of the knowledge of good and evil, thou shalt not eat of it: for in the day that thou eatest thereof thou shalt surely die.

(Genesis 2:15-17)

Well, if we are to have a fully functioning office, we cannot expect one person to do everything. Somebody has to, as they say, *watch his back*. The first assistance that was given to God's officer on earth came from the foundation, the creatures. These could be instrumental in bearing burdens, providing sustenance and sometimes for companionship; as well as other things that pertain to assistance with the work of maintaining the enterprise. This is much like the machines that a company places in the building to perform the work of manufacturing the product, or provision of the service of the business.

> *And the LORD God said, It is not good that the man should be alone; I will make him an help meet for him. And out of the ground the LORD God formed every beast of the field, and every fowl of the air; and brought them unto Adam to see what he would call them: and whatsoever Adam called every living creature, that was the name thereof. And Adam gave names to all cattle, and to the fowl of the air, and to every beast of the field; but for Adam there was not found an help meet for him.*
>
> (Genesis 2:18-20)

But neither foundations nor machines are sufficient as companions for humans, in the long run. Yes, my computer provides me with some company, but not the kind that I can really appreciate; for this I need someone of my own kind, someone to talk to and share with. The Word understands this, now, as the Word did then. So, then, the Word created an assistant. Furthermore, the Word was very thorough in presenting and confirming that the man and his assistant both understood their assignments. The man had now been given a *promotion* to the rank of supervisor. Now he had help, to which he could delegate functions.

> *And the LORD God caused a deep sleep to fall upon Adam, and he slept: and he took one of his ribs, and closed up the flesh instead thereof; And the rib, which the LORD God had taken from man, made he a woman, and brought her unto the man. And Adam said, This is now bone of my bones, and flesh of my flesh: she shall be called Woman, because she was taken out of Man. Therefore shall a man leave his father and his mother, and shall cleave unto his wife: and they shall be one flesh.*
>
> (Genesis 2:21-24)

But the supervisor, Adam, was not the only one who would delegate to the executive assistant. The Word, being the *owner* of the *corporation*, did not feel that it was unjust to delegate some function to both of them; this, he did when he gave them the responsibility and authority to create more workers for the LORD. Undoubtedly, He had already put the functionality to do so within them, at some time before God gave them the responsibility to do so.

> *And God blessed them, and God said unto them, Be fruitful, and multiply, and replenish the earth, and subdue it: and have dominion over the fish of the sea, and over the fowl of the air, and over every living thing that moveth upon the earth.*
>
> (Genesis 1:28)

Policies and procedures were delivered to the supervisor. These included safety concerns, as well.

> *And the LORD God commanded the man, saying, Of every tree of the garden thou mayest freely eat: But of the tree of the knowledge of good and evil, thou shalt not eat of it: for in the day that thou eatest thereof thou shalt surely die.*
>
> (Genesis 2:16-17)

Then the enterprise is ready to establish itself in the universe.

+=+=+=+=+=+=+=+=+=+=+=+=+=+=+=+=+=+=+

Up to this point we have only covered the creation of the enterprise, and the start of the example of success. There are many more points that need to be covered in the ongoing enterprise. Among these points are the following:

- codify the mission

> *And unto Adam he said, Because thou hast hearkened unto the voice of thy wife, and hast eaten of the tree, of which I commanded thee, saying, Thou shalt not eat of it: cursed is the ground for thy sake; in sorrow shalt thou eat of it all the days of thy life; Thorns also and thistles shall it bring forth to thee; and thou shalt eat the herb of the field; In the sweat of thy face shalt thou eat bread, till thou return unto the ground; for out of it wast thou taken: for dust thou art, and unto dust shalt thou return.*
>
> (Genesis 3:17-19)

- office relocation

> *Unto Adam also and to his wife did the LORD God make coats of skins, and clothed them. And the LORD God*

said, Behold, the man is become as one of us, to know good and evil: and now, lest he put forth his hand, and take also of the tree of life, and eat, and live for ever: Therefore the LORD God sent him forth from the garden of Eden, to till the ground from whence he was taken. So he drove out the man; and he placed at the east of the garden of Eden Cherubims, and a flaming sword which turned every way, to keep the way of the tree of life.

(Genesis 3:21-24)

- product enhancement and staff education

And God spake unto Noah, and to his sons with him, saying, And I, behold, I establish my covenant with you, and with your seed after you; And with every living creature that is with you, of the fowl, of the cattle, and of every beast of the earth with you; from all that go out of the ark, to every beast of the earth. And I will establish my covenant with you; neither shall all flesh be cut off any more by the waters of a flood; neither shall there any more be a flood to destroy the earth.

(Genesis 9:8-11)

- rules to meet changing regulatory environments

And the LORD said unto Moses, Come up to me into the mount, and be there: and I will give thee tables of stone, and a law, and commandments which I have written; that thou mayest teach them.

(Exodus 24:12)

- governmental lobbying

For there is one God, and one mediator between God and men, the man Christ Jesus; Who gave himself a ransom for all, to be testified in due time. Whereunto I am ordained a preacher, and an apostle, (I speak the truth in Christ, and lie not;) a teacher of the Gentiles in faith and verity.

(1 Timothy 2:5-7)

- establishing a durable mission statement, and other policies

And the Pharisees also, who were covetous, heard all these things: and they derided him. And he said unto them, Ye are they which justify yourselves before men; but God knoweth your hearts: for that which is highly esteemed among men is abomination in the sight of God. The law and the prophets were until John: since that time the kingdom of God is preached, and every man presseth into it. And it is easier for heaven and earth to pass, than one tittle of the law to fail.

(Luke 16:14-17)

- perpetuation of the enterprise

Jesus said unto her, I am the resurrection, and the life: he that believeth in me, though he were dead, yet shall he live: And whosoever liveth and believeth in me shall never die. Believest thou this?

(John 11:25-26)

- conflict resolution

At the same time came the disciples unto Jesus, saying, Who is the greatest in the kingdom of heaven? And Jesus called a little child unto him, and set him in the midst of them, And said, Verily I say unto you, Except ye be converted, and become as little children, ye shall not enter into the kingdom of heaven. Whosoever therefore shall humble himself as this little child, the same is greatest in the kingdom of heaven.

(Matthew 18:1-4)

These are all covered in the *divine corporate manual* for the body of mankind; which body is the human building of God. This *manual* is also for the establishment of the church of Christ. The body of the church of Christ is the product of the body of mankind, through the work of the Christ in the building process.

+=+=+=+=+=+=+=+=+=+=+=+=+=+=+=+=+=+=+=+

During the original creation and the product enhancement, the mission has been the same. There has been no wavering of the Word in managing the enterprise, and the mission statement has been forever in focus.

> *In the beginning was the Word, and the Word was with God, and the Word was God. The same was in the beginning with God. All things were made by him; and without him was not any thing made that was made. In him was life; and the life was the light of men. And the light shineth in darkness; and the darkness comprehended it not.*
>
> *There was a man sent from God, whose name was John. The same came for a witness, to bear witness of the Light, that all men through him might believe. He was not that Light, but was sent to bear witness of that Light.*
>
> *That was the true Light, which lighteth every man that cometh into the world. He was in the world, and the world was made by him, and the world knew him not. He came unto his own, and his own received him not.*
>
> *But as many as received him, to them gave he power to become the sons of God, even to them that believe on his name: Which were born, not of blood, nor of the will of the flesh, nor of the will of man, but of God.*
>
> *And the Word was made flesh, and dwelt among us, (and we beheld his glory, the glory as of the only begotten of the Father,) full of grace and truth. John bare witness of him, and cried, saying, This was he of whom I spake, He that cometh after me is preferred before me: for he was before me. And of his fulness have all we received, and grace for grace. For the law was given by Moses, but grace and truth came by Jesus Christ.*
>
> (John 1:1-17)

This is the mark of a truly successful enterprise: no matter what comes its way, the mission is kept in focus and keeps going forward. This is what the Word gives to us. This is why I study the Word, to know how to build any enterprise with which I become involved. My mission statement will always be the same as the one that God gave to Noah.

> *And God spake unto Noah, saying, Go forth of the ark, thou, and thy wife, and thy sons, and thy sons' wives with*

thee. Bring forth with thee every living thing that is with thee, of all flesh, both of fowl, and of cattle, and of every creeping thing that creepeth upon the earth; that they may breed abundantly in the earth, and be fruitful, and multiply upon the earth.

(Genesis 8:15-17)

However, do not think this just means making human babies. The total mission also includes the work of those who do not or cannot make babies. Not just babies; it is the act of replicating the best that is placed in each of us by God. This may be done through intervention with friends, students, parishioners, brothers, sisters, constituents, and others; as well as any other form of human development for which we are charged by God. This is the full scope of being fruitful and multiplying.

In order to do this, we must be sure that God has prepared in us a thing that is worthy of replication. This is another reason for study of the Word; so that we will have something worth building anew in others. It is this sharing of ourselves, in righteousness, which makes the human enterprise so rich. It is this sharing of ourselves, in righteousness, which we should all seek to do; of course, with the help of God, and according to the directive of the Holy Ghost sent from God. I fully intend to enlist God's assistance to equip me to do so. Hopefully you will, too.

Whether therefore ye eat, or drink, or whatsoever ye do, do all to the glory of God. Give none offence, neither to the Jews, nor to the Gentiles, nor to the church of God:

(1 Corinthians 10:31-32)

The Word from the Bible

Genesis 18:16-19

And the men rose up from thence, and looked toward Sodom: and Abraham went with them to bring them on the way.

And the LORD said, Shall I hide from Abraham that thing which I do; Seeing that Abraham shall surely become a great and mighty nation, and all the nations of the earth shall be blessed in him? For I know him, that he will command his children and his household after him, and they shall keep the way of the LORD, to do justice and judgment; that the LORD may bring upon Abraham that which he hath spoken of him.

Acts 17:22-31

Then Paul stood in the midst of Mars' hill, and said, Ye men of Athens, I perceive that in all things ye are too superstitious. For as I passed by, and beheld your devotions, I found an altar with this inscription, TO THE UNKNOWN GOD. Whom therefore ye ignorantly worship, him declare I unto you.

God that made the world and all things therein, seeing that he is Lord of heaven and earth, dwelleth not in temples made with hands; Neither is worshipped with men's hands, as though he needed any thing, seeing he giveth to all life, and breath, and all things; And hath made of one blood all nations of men for to dwell on all the face of the earth, and hath determined the times before appointed, and the bounds of their habitation; That they should seek the Lord, if haply they might feel after him, and find him, though he be not far from every one of us: For in him we live, and move, and have our being; as certain also of your own poets have said, For we are also his offspring.

Forasmuch then as we are the offspring of God, we ought not to think that the Godhead is like unto gold, or silver, or stone, graven by art and man's device. And the times of this ignorance God winked at; but now commandeth all men every where to repent: Because he hath appointed a day, in the which he will judge the world in righteousness by that man whom he hath ordained; whereof he hath given assurance unto all men, in that he hath raised him from the dead.

Exodus 3:1-10

Now Moses kept the flock of Jethro his father in law, the priest of Midian: and he led the flock to the backside of the desert, and came to the mountain of God, even to Horeb. And the angel of the LORD appeared unto him in a flame of fire out of the midst of a bush: and he looked, and, behold, the bush burned with fire, and the bush was not consumed.

And Moses said, I will now turn aside, and see this great sight, why the bush is not burnt.

And when the LORD saw that he turned aside to see, God called unto him out of the midst of the bush, and said, Moses, Moses.

And he said, Here am I.

And he said, Draw not nigh hither: put off thy shoes from off thy feet, for the place whereon thou standest is holy ground. Moreover he said, I am the God of thy father, the God of Abraham, the God of Isaac, and the God of Jacob.

And Moses hid his face; for he was afraid to look upon God.

And the LORD said, I have surely seen the affliction of my people which are in Egypt, and have heard their cry by reason of their taskmasters; for I know their sorrows; And I am come down to deliver them out of the hand of the Egyptians, and to bring them up out of that land unto a good land and a large, unto a land flowing with milk and honey; unto the place of the Canaanites, and the Hittites, and the Amorites, and the Perizzites, and the Hivites, and the Jebusites. Now therefore, behold, the cry of the children of Israel is come unto me: and I have also seen the oppression wherewith the Egyptians oppress them. Come now therefore, and I will send thee unto Pharaoh, that thou mayest bring forth my people the children of Israel out of Egypt.

Deuteronomy 6:20-25

And when thy son asketh thee in time to come, saying, What mean the testimonies, and the statutes, and the judgments, which the LORD our God hath commanded you? Then thou shalt say unto thy son, We were Pharaoh's bondmen in Egypt; and the LORD brought us out of Egypt with a mighty hand: And the LORD showed signs and wonders, great and sore, upon Egypt, upon Pharaoh, and upon all his household, before our eyes: And he brought us out from thence, that he might bring us in, to give us the land which he sware unto our fathers. And the LORD commanded us to do all these statutes, to fear the LORD our God, for our good always, that he might preserve us alive, as it is at this day. And it shall be our righteousness, if we observe to do all these commandments before the LORD our God, as he hath commanded us.

Deuteronomy 11:26-29

Behold, I set before you this day a blessing and a curse; A blessing, if ye obey the commandments of the LORD your God, which I command you this day: And a curse, if ye will not obey the commandments of the LORD your God, but turn aside out of the way which I command you this day, to go after other gods, which ye have not known.

And it shall come to pass, when the LORD thy God hath brought thee in unto the land whither thou goest to possess it, that thou shalt put the blessing upon mount Gerizim, and the curse upon mount Ebal.

Deuteronomy 27:11-13

And Moses charged the people the same day, saying, These shall stand upon mount Gerizim to bless the people, when ye are come over Jordan; Simeon, and Levi, and Judah, and Issachar, and Joseph, and Benjamin: And these shall stand upon mount Ebal to curse; Reuben, Gad, and Asher, and Zebulun, Dan, and Naphtali.

Deuteronomy 27:14-26

And the Levites shall speak, and say unto all the men of Israel with a loud voice, Cursed be the man that maketh any graven or molten image, an abomination unto the LORD, the work of the hands of the craftsman, and putteth it in a secret place. And all the people shall answer and say, Amen.

Cursed be he that setteth light by his father or his mother. And all the people shall say, Amen.

Cursed be he that removeth his neighbour's landmark. And all the people shall say, Amen.

Cursed be he that maketh the blind to wander out of the way. And all the people shall say, Amen.

Cursed be he that perverteth the judgment of the stranger, fatherless, and widow. And all the people shall say, Amen.

Cursed be he that lieth with his father's wife; because he uncovereth his father's skirt. And all the people shall say, Amen.

Cursed be he that lieth with any manner of beast. And all the people shall say, Amen.

Cursed be he that lieth with his sister, the daughter of his father, or the daughter of his mother. And all the people shall say, Amen.

Cursed be he that lieth with his mother in law. And all the people shall say, Amen.

Cursed be he that smiteth his neighbour secretly. And all the people shall say, Amen.

Cursed be he that taketh reward to slay an innocent person. And all the people shall say, Amen.

Cursed be he that confirmeth not all the words of this law to do them. And all the people shall say, Amen.

Deuteronomy 28:1-14

And it shall come to pass, if thou shalt hearken diligently unto the voice of the LORD thy God, to observe and to do all his commandments which I command thee this day, that the LORD thy God will set thee on high above all nations of the earth: And all these blessings shall come on thee, and overtake thee, if thou shalt hearken unto the voice of the LORD thy God.

Blessed shalt thou be in the city, and blessed shalt thou be in the field.

Blessed shall be the fruit of thy body, and the fruit of thy ground, and the fruit of thy cattle, the increase of thy kine, and the flocks of thy sheep.

Blessed shall be thy basket and thy store.

Blessed shalt thou be when thou comest in, and blessed shalt thou be when thou goest out.

The LORD shall cause thine enemies that rise up against thee to be smitten before thy face: they shall come out against thee one way, and flee before thee seven ways.

The LORD shall command the blessing upon thee in thy storehouses, and in all that thou settest thine hand unto; and he shall bless thee in the land which the LORD thy God giveth thee.

The LORD shall establish thee an holy people unto himself, as he hath sworn unto thee, if thou shalt keep the commandments of the LORD thy God, and walk in his ways. And all people of the earth shall see that thou art called by the name of the LORD; and they shall be afraid of thee. And the LORD shall make thee plenteous in goods, in the fruit of thy body, and in the fruit of thy cattle, and in the fruit of thy ground, in the land which the LORD sware unto thy fathers to give thee.

The LORD shall open unto thee his good treasure, the heaven to give the rain unto thy land in his season, and to bless all the work of thine hand: and thou shalt lend unto many nations, and thou shalt not borrow. And the LORD shall make thee the head, and not the tail; and thou shalt be above only, and thou shalt not be beneath; if that thou hearken unto the commandments of the LORD thy God, which I command thee this day, to observe and to do them: And thou shalt not go aside from any of the words which I command thee this day, to the right hand, or to the left, to go after other gods to serve them.

Chapter Ten

Separation of a People

I sometimes wonder if God shared with Abraham the full weight of what would happen to a portion of his descendants. It would seem from Scripture that God did not fully load Abraham's mind with the weight of what was to happen. It was not until Moses' time that God presented the full understanding of His total mission for mankind.

> *And the LORD descended in the cloud, and stood with him there, and proclaimed the name of the LORD. And the LORD passed by before him, and proclaimed, The LORD, The LORD God, merciful and gracious, longsuffering, and abundant in goodness and truth, Keeping mercy for thousands, forgiving iniquity and transgression and sin, and that will by no means clear the guilty; visiting the iniquity of the fathers upon the children, and upon the children's children, unto the third and to the fourth generation.*
>
> *And Moses made haste, and bowed his head toward the earth, and worshipped. And he said, If now I have found grace in thy sight, O LORD, let my LORD, I pray thee, go among us; for it is a stiffnecked people; and pardon our iniquity and our sin, and take us for thine inheritance.*
>
> *And he said, Behold, I make a covenant: before all thy people I will do marvels, such as have not been done in all the earth, nor in any nation: and all the people among which thou art shall see the work of the LORD: for it is a terrible thing that I will do with thee. Observe thou that which I command thee this day: behold, I drive out before thee the Amorite, and the Canaanite, and the Hittite, and the Perizzite, and the Hivite, and the Jebusite.*

(Exodus 34:5-11)

For a little while I struggled with the question of why God put forth the effort that He did with these children of Abraham. Looking from there, I connected it to the question of why God selected Noah and invoked the flood. Noah's event in history is similar to the selection of Abram. It was done by God to give mankind a fresh start toward a right relationship with Him. Is the selection of Israel the next phase in that process? It seems to be.

As God did with Noah, the LORD established a unique relationship between Himself and the children of Israel. By selecting Abram, God was preparing for an increase in the size of the example. This is not the same as the size of the result: the descendants of Noah include those of Abram and many more. The lesser size of the example is contained in the fact that with Noah, it was the example of a relationship between God and a righteous man. The Bible has another example on this order, in the life of Job. On the other hand, with the children of Israel, God presented the example of how He relates to a righteous nation.

> *In that day shall there be a highway out of Egypt to Assyria, and the Assyrian shall come into Egypt, and the Egyptian into Assyria, and the Egyptians shall serve with the Assyrians. In that day shall Israel be the third with Egypt and with Assyria, even a blessing in the midst of the land: Whom the LORD of hosts shall bless, saying, Blessed be Egypt my people, and Assyria the work of my hands, and Israel mine inheritance.*

(Isaiah 19:23-25)

Looking ahead, might the next major example be that of God and a righteous world; that is, a righteous mankind? We will not make that leap, at this time; for now, let us concentrate on the national level.

When I read Isaiah 19:23-25, I asked myself, "Isn't the entire world God's? Don't all the nations belong to God?"

Of course, the answer is, yes.

A Psalm of David.

> *The earth is the LORD'S, and the fulness thereof; the world, and they that dwell therein. For he hath founded it upon the seas, and established it upon the floods.*

(Psalm 24:1-2)

Therefore, since all is the LORD'S, He has a stewardship over it all. Just like the Father, which God is; it falls to Him to prepare the world for His presence: or more precisely to prepare the world to crawl in His presence; then to walk in His presence; then to stand in His presence. But why not just command the world to walk, immediately? Dads, you know why. Explain it to those who God has given you to love.

Okay, I cannot keep this sealed. It is because this would not be very Dad-like. The LORD knew that man could not endure His hand, even at its gentlest, if He chose to issue this edict.

A Song of degrees.

> *Out of the depths have I cried unto thee, O LORD. Lord, hear my voice: let thine ears be attentive to the voice of my supplications. If thou, LORD, shouldest mark iniquities, O Lord, who shall stand? But there is forgiveness with thee, that thou mayest be feared.*

(Psalm 130:1-4)

I am also reminded of a certain episode God had with the children of Israel, once they had been identified as the vessel He was preparing. It was, for God, a normal visit, and a simple conversation. It was, for the people, such a terrifying event, such that they pleaded with God never again to visit it upon them.

> *And all the people saw the thunderings, and the lightnings, and the noise of the trumpet, and the mountain smoking: and when the people saw it, they removed, and stood afar off. And they said unto Moses, Speak thou with us, and we will hear: but let not God speak with us, lest we die.*

> *And Moses said unto the people, Fear not: for God is come to prove you, and that his fear may be before your faces, that ye sin not.*

> *And the people stood afar off, and Moses drew near unto the thick darkness where God was.*

(Exodus 20:18-21)

Such would have been the world's reaction if God had issued a global edict, directly from His mouth.

The level at which mankind sits, relative to God, is such that we will always need a mediator between us and God. Besides that, we were not really equipped for instantaneous absorption of massively complex procedures--from a human point of view. This is why we instituted schools. This is why God works in a process of unfolding, for us humans: a very, very slow process, of unfolding; by little and little. It is by this method that the inheritance to the children of Israel is given to the tribes.

> *I will not drive them out from before thee in one year; lest the land become desolate, and the beast of the field multiply against thee. By little and little I will drive them out from before thee, until thou be increased, and inherit the land.*
>
> (Exodus 23:29-30)

So to transform the world, God selected a starting point. But why not start with an established nation?

The answer is clearly revealed later in the history of mankind. In due time, we are introduced to a king named Nebuchadnezzar; a king who shows us why this is not the way to establish the rule of God with man. Nebuchadnezzar shows us our human limitations, which cause our successes to get in the way of us accepting the ways of God. For, even after having been told what he should do, Nebuchadnezzar was still limited by his past accomplishments.

> *This is the interpretation, O king, and this is the decree of the most High, which is come upon my lord the king: That they shall drive thee from men, and thy dwelling shall be with the beasts of the field, and they shall make thee to eat grass as oxen, and they shall wet thee with the dew of heaven, and seven times shall pass over thee, till thou know that the most High ruleth in the kingdom of men, and giveth it to whomsoever he will. And whereas they commanded to leave the stump of the tree roots; thy kingdom shall be sure unto thee, after that thou shalt have known that the heavens do rule. Wherefore, O king, let my counsel be acceptable unto thee, and break off thy sins by righteousness, and thine iniquities by showing mercy to the poor; if it may be a lengthening of thy tranquillity.*

> *All this came upon the king Nebuchadnezzar. At the end of twelve months he walked in the palace of the kingdom of Babylon. The king spake, and said, Is not this great Babylon, that I have built for the house of the kingdom by the might of my power, and for the honour of my majesty?*
>
> *While the word was in the king's mouth, there fell a voice from heaven, saying, O king Nebuchadnezzar, to thee it is spoken; The kingdom is departed from thee. And they shall drive thee from men, and thy dwelling shall be with the beasts of the field: they shall make thee to eat grass as oxen, and seven times shall pass over thee, until thou know that the most High ruleth in the kingdom of men, and giveth it to whomsoever he will. The same hour was the thing fulfilled upon Nebuchadnezzar: and he was driven from men, and did eat grass as oxen, and his body was wet with the dew of heaven, till his hairs were grown like eagles' feathers, and his nails like birds' claws.*

(Daniel 4:24-33)

No, God knew, that to make a way to Him required a structuring from the bottom up. He knew that the nation would have to be built from raw materials. The nation must come from a people that *is no nation*. The nation would have to be new; a nation born like a baby.

> *And thou shalt say unto Pharaoh, Thus saith the LORD, Israel is my son, even my firstborn:*

(Exodus 4:22)

And as all infants are born, so this one must be, in the womb of the world. The world would have to experience the labor pains associated with the birth. This started in Egypt with the delivery to freedom of the children of Israel. It continued with their journey through the wilderness. The nations around them came to know that the birth of this nation was by the overshadowing of the Holy Ghost.

Furthermore, just as a child struggles to be born; this nation must also struggle to be established. As it is the *to-be-born's* task, to start the process through the unknown places to present itself outside the womb; so it was with Israel. This nation had to go through the unknown places outside of Egypt. Sometimes they murmured about returning to the womb; but this is not to be.

> *And when Pharaoh drew nigh, the children of Israel lifted up their eyes, and, behold, the Egyptians marched after them; and they were sore afraid: and the children of Israel cried out unto the LORD. And they said unto Moses, Because there were no graves in Egypt, hast thou taken us away to die in the wilderness? wherefore hast thou dealt thus with us, to carry us forth out of Egypt? Is not this the word that we did tell thee in Egypt, saying, Let us alone, that we may serve the Egyptians? For it had been better for us to serve the Egyptians, than that we should die in the wilderness.*
>
> (Exodus 14:10-12)
>
> *And the mixed multitude that was among them fell a lusting: and the children of Israel also wept again, and said, Who shall give us flesh to eat? We remember the fish, which we did eat in Egypt freely; the cucumbers, and the melons, and the leeks, and the onions, and the garlic: But now our soul is dried away: there is nothing at all, beside this manna, before our eyes.*
>
> (Numbers 11:4-6)

As the child's crown is shaped by the passage through the birth canal, so is it also with Israel. The shape of the house for the human brain of the nation that was being formed was established by the pressure placed on it by the trials of the nation. Moses emerged and was put in place as the first prophet of the nation of Israel. In that office, he became the house of the human brain of the nation. Indeed, Moses was originally the first god representing God to Pharaoh--he could not be so for Israel, since God reserves this place for Himself.

> *And the LORD said unto Moses, See, I have made thee a god to Pharaoh: and Aaron thy brother shall be thy prophet. Thou shalt speak all that I command thee: and Aaron thy brother shall speak unto Pharaoh, that he send the children of Israel out of his land.*
>
> (Exodus 7:1-2)

All this was done so that the entire world of nations would have a righteous example for its start. It is this presentation of a righteous example that is at the heart of the Law of Moses. These words were not written to encumber the nation of Israel, but to cause them to fulfill their calling.

> *And Moses went up unto God, and the LORD called unto him out of the mountain, saying, Thus shalt thou say to the house of Jacob, and tell the children of Israel; Ye have seen what I did unto the Egyptians, and how I bare you on eagles' wings, and brought you unto myself. Now therefore, if ye will obey my voice indeed, and keep my covenant, then ye shall be a peculiar treasure unto me above all people: for all the earth is mine: And ye shall be unto me a kingdom of priests, and an holy nation. These are the words which thou shalt speak unto the children of Israel.*

(Exodus 19:3-6)

A perfect God is taking an imperfect vessel, and transforming it into His image of perfection. This image of perfection is then to be presented to the world, as a pointer to God. Such an image can endure no imperfections if it is to truly persuade the world that it is from the LORD. Such is the reason for the heavy burden on Israel--from a human point of view. But God does not forget that we are humans, even within the nation of Israel.

> *Wherefore let him that thinketh he standeth take heed lest he fall. There hath no temptation taken you but such as is common to man: but God is faithful, who will not suffer you to be tempted above that ye are able; but will with the temptation also make a way to escape, that ye may be able to bear it.*

(1 Corinthians 10:12-13)

This is where the sacrifices and offerings made the difference. This is the difference that prepared the way for the presentation of the message of God, to the world. The Law of Moses could never have been satisfied by humans without sacrifices and offerings. The Law of Moses unfolded the compensatory mechanism for being human and subject to failure; but with a divine calling.

> *Bring ye all the tithes into the storehouse, that there may be meat in mine house, and prove me now herewith, saith the LORD of hosts, if I will not open you the windows of heaven, and pour you out a blessing, that there shall not be*

> room enough to receive it. And I will rebuke the devourer for your sakes, and he shall not destroy the fruits of your ground; neither shall your vine cast her fruit before the time in the field, saith the LORD of hosts. And all nations shall call you blessed: for ye shall be a delightsome land, saith the LORD of hosts.
>
> (Malachi 3:10-12)

Now the nation was ready to serve as an example to the world. They were now in place to proclaim the Kingdom of God to mankind.

> *Now therefore hearken, O Israel, unto the statutes and unto the judgments, which I teach you, for to do them, that ye may live, and go in and possess the land which the LORD God of your fathers giveth you. Ye shall not add unto the word which I command you, neither shall ye diminish ought from it, that ye may keep the commandments of the LORD your God which I command you.*
>
> *Your eyes have seen what the LORD did because of Baalpeor: for all the men that followed Baalpeor, the LORD thy God hath destroyed them from among you. But ye that did cleave unto the LORD your God are alive every one of you this day. Behold, I have taught you statutes and judgments, even as the LORD my God commanded me, that ye should do so in the land whither ye go to possess it. Keep therefore and do them; for this is your wisdom and your understanding in the sight of the nations, which shall hear all these statutes, and say, Surely this great nation is a wise and understanding people. For what nation is there so great, who hath God so nigh unto them, as the LORD our God is in all things that we call upon him for? And what nation is there so great, that hath statutes and judgments so righteous as all this law, which I set before you this day?*
>
> *Only take heed to thyself, and keep thy soul diligently, lest thou forget the things which thine eyes have seen, and lest they depart from thy heart all the days of thy life: but teach them thy sons, and thy sons' sons; Specially the day that thou stoodest before the LORD thy God in Horeb, when the LORD said unto me, Gather me the people together, and I will make them hear my words, that they may learn to fear*

me all the days that they shall live upon the earth, and that they may teach their children.

(Deuteronomy 4:1-10)

In the matter of sacrifices and offerings, and, indeed, in all things, we must remember that God is not shortsighted. The sacrifices were instituted to prove, and improve, the congregation's devotion to God. They did so by causing each man to give to God some part of his own life and livelihood. Somewhat like children, livestock and other domestic animals require some part of our life to survive. Unlike plants that you place in the right ground, water, and then leave to God to prosper; animals cannot be treated that way.

Consider this; it is a rare man that says he loves his apple tree--maybe the fruit of the tree, but not the tree itself. It is, however, not uncommon for people to say they love their pets. This is because, if we truly honor them, we place a part of ourselves in them. This God knows, and it is for this reason that He instituted animal sacrifices. It is my belief that it is for this reason that Abel's offering was acceptable and Cain's was not. Abel gave of his love; Cain gave of his human achievement. There is a lesson there, for us all.

And in process of time it came to pass, that Cain brought of the fruit of the ground an offering unto the LORD. And Abel, he also brought of the firstlings of his flock and of the fat thereof. And the LORD had respect unto Abel and to his offering: But unto Cain and to his offering he had not respect. And Cain was very wroth, and his countenance fell.

And the LORD said unto Cain, Why art thou wroth? and why is thy countenance fallen? If thou doest well, shalt thou not be accepted? and if thou doest not well, sin lieth at the door. And unto thee shall be his desire, and thou shalt rule over him.

(Genesis 4:3-7)

But, as they say, "Wait, there's more." God knew that mankind would eventually reach a point where this procedure would become odious for man to do (think animal rights here). Therefore, the LORD published a better way.

> *And Samuel said, When thou wast little in thine own sight, wast thou not made the head of the tribes of Israel, and the LORD anointed thee king over Israel? And the LORD sent thee on a journey, and said, Go and utterly destroy the sinners the Amalekites, and fight against them until they be consumed. Wherefore then didst thou not obey the voice of the LORD, but didst fly upon the spoil, and didst evil in the sight of the LORD?*
>
> *And Saul said unto Samuel, Yea, I have obeyed the voice of the LORD, and have gone the way which the LORD sent me, and have brought Agag the king of Amalek, and have utterly destroyed the Amalekites. But the people took of the spoil, sheep and oxen, the chief of the things which should have been utterly destroyed, to sacrifice unto the LORD thy God in Gilgal.*
>
> *And Samuel said, Hath the LORD as great delight in burnt offerings and sacrifices, as in obeying the voice of the LORD? Behold, to obey is better than sacrifice, and to hearken than the fat of rams. For rebellion is as the sin of witchcraft, and stubbornness is as iniquity and idolatry.*
>
> *Because thou hast rejected the word of the LORD, he hath also rejected thee from being king.*
>
> (1 Samuel 15:17-23)

Then God presented the ultimate way. Remember that God said of Abraham that *all the nations of the earth shall be blessed in him.* This God has done by sending to us the Messiah, Jesus of Nazareth, who is, the Christ. This was done through the seed of king David, the son of Jesse; who is of the seed of Abraham.

> *And in that day there shall be a root of Jesse, which shall stand for an ensign of the people; to it shall the Gentiles seek: and his rest shall be glorious.*
>
> (Isaiah 11:10)

So, now the greatest act of obedience that we can do is to accept this gift of the Messiah. This will shine forth as our highest devotion to God.

And at midnight Paul and Silas prayed, and sang praises unto God: and the prisoners heard them. And suddenly there was a great earthquake, so that the foundations of the prison were shaken: and immediately all the doors were opened, and every one's bands were loosed. And the keeper of the prison awaking out of his sleep, and seeing the prison doors open, he drew out his sword, and would have killed himself, supposing that the prisoners had been fled.

But Paul cried with a loud voice, saying, Do thyself no harm: for we are all here.

Then he called for a light, and sprang in, and came trembling, and fell down before Paul and Silas, And brought them out, and said, Sirs, what must I do to be saved?

And they said, Believe on the Lord Jesus Christ, and thou shalt be saved, and thy house. And they spake unto him the word of the Lord, and to all that were in his house.

And he took them the same hour of the night, and washed their stripes; and was baptized, he and all his, straightway. And when he had brought them into his house, he set meat before them, and rejoiced, believing in God with all his house.

(Acts 16:25-34)

The LORD had refreshed
The path for all mankind,
By removing those
Who were spiritually blind.

In the days of Noah
And the magnificent ark,
God established a road
On which all must embark.

But man so quickly forgets
What he is told,
Choosing not to retain
What the LORD doth unfold.

So, an example was revealed
From the people of the land;
A nation was called forth
To meet His demand

To set before mankind
An example true,
One that gives God
What is surely to Him due.

Through trials and pains
They were molded by Him;
Through times that were bright
And times that were dim.

You say, "Those trials
I could surely endure;"
But you just might not
Be so self-sufficiently sure

If you were among nations
That knew your fame,
And collected together
To wipe out your name.

God knows what to do
To prepare the course,

Which the entire world
Must surely endorse.

So honor the work
That He has done,
And come together
In God, as one.

Chapter 10a

The Godhead Complete

The word Godhead appears in the Bible, but has no direct definition given therein. The closest we come to defining the Godhead is by our understanding of a statement made by the apostle Paul.

> *God that made the world and all things therein, seeing that he is Lord of heaven and earth, dwelleth not in temples made with hands; Neither is worshipped with men's hands, as though he needed any thing, seeing he giveth to all life, and breath, and all things; And hath made of one blood all nations of men for to dwell on all the face of the earth, and hath determined the times before appointed, and the bounds of their habitation; That they should seek the Lord, if haply they might feel after him, and find him, though he be not far from every one of us: For in him we live, and move, and have our being; as certain also of your own poets have said, For we are also his offspring. Forasmuch then as we are the offspring of God, we ought not to think that the Godhead is like unto gold, or silver, or stone, graven by art and man's device.*

(Acts 17:24-29)

Further information on the Godhead is contained in the following passage.

> *For the wrath of God is revealed from heaven against all ungodliness and unrighteousness of men, who hold the truth in unrighteousness; Because that which may be known of God is manifest in them; for God hath showed it unto them. For the invisible things of him from the creation of the world are clearly seen, being understood by the things that are made, even his eternal power and Godhead;*

> *so that they are without excuse: Because that, when they knew God, they glorified him not as God, neither were thankful; but became vain in their imaginations, and their foolish heart was darkened.*

(Romans 1:18-21)

But what is the working of the Godhead? It must be more than just a Heavenly set of beings. This particular presence has a definite function and a definite sphere of authority. To start the thought rolling, consider this description: the Godhead is the means by which God represents His purposes in the kingdom of man.

It is through the work of the Godhead that the kingdom of man is being transformed into the Kingdom of God on this earth. Wherefore as Jesus Christ told us to do, so we must do.

> *After this manner therefore pray ye: Our Father which art in heaven, Hallowed be thy name. Thy kingdom come, Thy will be done in earth, as it is in heaven. Give us this day our daily bread. And forgive us our debts, as we forgive our debtors. And lead us not into temptation, but deliver us from evil: For thine is the kingdom, and the power, and the glory, for ever. Amen.*

(Matthew 6:9-13)

Let us take a look at some of the specifics of the Godhead relative to mankind. We will only look at a few: this is by no means an exhaustive list. It is, however, the list that will lead the lost to salvation. These are the principles of the Gospel.

Herein is the will of God, which is fulfilled in Jesus of Nazareth. This is the favor of God that came with the law of Love, which the Law of Moses could not complete. This is why it is no longer up to man to secure his salvation. Freedom from the penalty of sin is presented to mankind from God as a free gift: a gift delivered by his servant and Son, the Lord Jesus Christ. For this reason, the Law unto righteousness saw an end in Christ.

> *Brethren, my heart's desire and prayer to God for Israel is, that they might be saved. For I bear them record that they have a zeal of God, but not according to knowledge. For they being ignorant of God's righteousness, and going about to establish their own righteousness, have not*

> submitted themselves unto the righteousness of God. For Christ is the end of the law for righteousness to every one that believeth.
>
> For Moses describeth the righteousness which is of the law, That the man which doeth those things shall live by them. But the righteousness which is of faith speaketh on this wise, Say not in thine heart, Who shall ascend into heaven? (that is, to bring Christ down from above:) Or, Who shall descend into the deep? (that is, to bring up Christ again from the dead.)
>
> But what saith it? The word is nigh thee, even in thy mouth, and in thy heart: that is, the word of faith, which we preach; That if thou shalt confess with thy mouth the Lord Jesus, and shalt believe in thine heart that God hath raised him from the dead, thou shalt be saved. For with the heart man believeth unto righteousness; and with the mouth confession is made unto salvation.
>
> (Romans 10:1-10)

Cancellation vs. Remission

The Israelites often had their sins cancelled. This was done through the sacrifices, of which the following are examples.

> If the priest that is anointed do sin according to the sin of the people; then let him bring for his sin, which he hath sinned, a young bullock without blemish unto the LORD for a sin offering. And he shall bring the bullock unto the door of the tabernacle of the congregation before the LORD; and shall lay his hand upon the bullock's head, and kill the bullock before the LORD.
>
> (Leviticus 4:3-4)
>
> And if the whole congregation of Israel sin through ignorance, and the thing be hid from the eyes of the assembly, and they have done somewhat against any of the commandments of the LORD concerning things which should not be done, and are guilty; When the sin, which they have sinned against it, is known, then the congregation

> shall offer a young bullock for the sin, and bring him before the tabernacle of the congregation.
>
> (Leviticus 4:13-14)

> When a ruler hath sinned, and done somewhat through ignorance against any of the commandments of the LORD his God concerning things which should not be done, and is guilty; Or if his sin, wherein he hath sinned, come to his knowledge; he shall bring his offering, a kid of the goats, a male without blemish:
>
> (Leviticus 4:22-23)

> And if any one of the common people sin through ignorance, while he doeth somewhat against any of the commandments of the LORD concerning things which ought not to be done, and be guilty; Or if his sin, which he hath sinned, come to his knowledge: then he shall bring his offering, a kid of the goats, a female without blemish, for his sin which he hath sinned.
>
> (Leviticus 4:27-28)

> And if he bring a lamb for a sin offering, he shall bring it a female without blemish.
>
> (Leviticus 4:32)

However, as the apostles shared with us, this is a temporary solution for management of sin. It is, though, still a very good solution for the welfare of the ministers of God; the priests and apostles.

> For the law having a shadow of good things to come, and not the very image of the things, can never with those sacrifices which they offered year by year continually make the comers thereunto perfect. For then would they not have ceased to be offered? because that the worshippers once purged should have had no more conscience of sins. But in those sacrifices there is a remembrance again made of sins every year. For it is not possible that the blood of bulls and of goats should take away sins.
>
> (Hebrews 10:1-4)

In the time stated in Scripture, Jesus Christ paid the permanent price for the remission of sins. With remission it is no longer necessary to constantly remove. Remission removes the power of a dangerous thing.

Consider the case of a cancer in a vital organ that keeps returning after being removed surgically. There will only be so many times that the invasive procedure of removal can be done without weakening the body. However, even if the cancer stays; once it goes into remission, the doctors feel that the patient's life is no longer in danger. This is what The Lord Jesus Christ did for us.

> *And as they were eating, Jesus took bread, and blessed it, and brake it, and gave it to the disciples, and said, Take, eat; this is my body. And he took the cup, and gave thanks, and gave it to them, saying, Drink ye all of it; For this is my blood of the new testament, which is shed for many for the remission of sins.*

(Matthew 26:26-28)

Absorbing vs. Payment

The children of Israel had been, for a long time, absorbing the penalty for their sins. God tells them precisely how this would happen, in five layers.

Layer One:

> *I am the LORD your God, which brought you forth out of the land of Egypt, that ye should not be their bondmen; and I have broken the bands of your yoke, and made you go upright.*

> *But if ye will not hearken unto me, and will not do all these commandments; And if ye shall despise my statutes, or if your soul abhor my judgments, so that ye will not do all my commandments, but that ye break my covenant: I also will do this unto you; I will even appoint over you terror, consumption, and the burning ague, that shall consume the eyes, and cause sorrow of heart: and ye shall sow your seed in vain, for your enemies shall eat it. And I will set my face against you, and ye shall be slain before your enemies: they that hate you shall reign over you; and ye shall flee when none pursueth you.*

Layer Two:

And if ye will not yet for all this hearken unto me, then I will punish you seven times more for your sins. And I will break the pride of your power; and I will make your heaven as iron, and your earth as brass: And your strength shall be spent in vain: for your land shall not yield her increase, neither shall the trees of the land yield their fruits.

Layer Three:

And if ye walk contrary unto me, and will not hearken unto me; I will bring seven times more plagues upon you according to your sins. I will also send wild beasts among you, which shall rob you of your children, and destroy your cattle, and make you few in number; and your high ways shall be desolate.

Layer Four:

And if ye will not be reformed by me by these things, but will walk contrary unto me; Then will I also walk contrary unto you, and will punish you yet seven times for your sins. And I will bring a sword upon you, that shall avenge the quarrel of my covenant: and when ye are gathered together within your cities, I will send the pestilence among you; and ye shall be delivered into the hand of the enemy. And when I have broken the staff of your bread, ten women shall bake your bread in one oven, and they shall deliver you your bread again by weight: and ye shall eat, and not be satisfied.

Layer Five:

And if ye will not for all this hearken unto me, but walk contrary unto me; Then I will walk contrary unto you also in fury; and I, even I, will chastise you seven times for your sins. And ye shall eat the flesh of your sons, and the flesh of your daughters shall ye eat. And I will destroy your high places, and cut down your images, and cast your carcases upon the carcases of your idols, and my soul shall abhor you. And I will make your cities waste, and bring your sanctuaries unto desolation, and I will not smell the savour of your sweet odours. And I will bring the land into desolation: and your enemies which dwell therein shall be astonished at it.

And I will scatter you among the heathen, and will draw out a sword after you: and your land shall be desolate, and your cities waste. Then shall the land enjoy her sabbaths, as long as it lieth desolate, and ye be in your enemies' land; even then shall the land rest, and enjoy her sabbaths. As long as it lieth desolate it shall rest; because it did not rest in your sabbaths, when ye dwelt upon it.

And upon them that are left alive of you I will send a faintness into their hearts in the lands of their enemies; and the sound of a shaken leaf shall chase them; and they shall flee, as fleeing from a sword; and they shall fall when none pursueth. And they shall fall one upon another, as it were before a sword, when none pursueth: and ye shall have no power to stand before your enemies. And ye shall perish among the heathen, and the land of your enemies shall eat you up. And they that are left of you shall pine away in their iniquity in your enemies' lands; and also in the iniquities of their fathers shall they pine away with them.

(Leviticus 26:13-39)

Of course, the LORD provided a way to escape from this layered judgment, and recompense for the sins that were committed by the people of Israel. The LORD provided a means of removing the sins that the people of Israel were, layer by layer, absorbing into their account of judgment. However, this, too, is a temporary solution. It is temporary not because of God, but because of the weak state of the spirit and soul of individual humans. Nonetheless, it was a means of extracting the weighty sin from the soul of the individual, until the cycle repeated itself again.

If they shall confess their iniquity, and the iniquity of their fathers, with their trespass which they trespassed against me, and that also they have walked contrary unto me; And that I also have walked contrary unto them, and have brought them into the land of their enemies; if then their uncircumcised hearts be humbled, and they then accept of the punishment of their iniquity: Then will I remember my covenant with Jacob, and also my covenant with Isaac, and

> *also my covenant with Abraham will I remember; and I will remember the land. The land also shall be left of them, and shall enjoy her sabbaths, while she lieth desolate without them: and they shall accept of the punishment of their iniquity: because, even because they despised my judgments, and because their soul abhorred my statutes. And yet for all that, when they be in the land of their enemies, I will not cast them away, neither will I abhor them, to destroy them utterly, and to break my covenant with them: for I am the LORD their God. But I will for their sakes remember the covenant of their ancestors, whom I brought forth out of the land of Egypt in the sight of the heathen, that I might be their God: I am the LORD. These are the statutes and judgments and laws, which the LORD made between him and the children of Israel in mount Sinai by the hand of Moses.*
>
> (Leviticus 26:40-46)

The Lord Jesus Christ absorbed all penalties for the sin of all persons, for all time: permanently. When he did this, the penalty was paid in full, and the debt was cancelled by God.

> *Behold, the days come, saith the LORD, that I will make a new covenant with the house of Israel, and with the house of Judah: Not according to the covenant that I made with their fathers in the day that I took them by the hand to bring them out of the land of Egypt; which my covenant they brake, although I was an husband unto them, saith the LORD: But this shall be the covenant that I will make with the house of Israel; After those days, saith the LORD, I will put my law in their inward parts, and write it in their hearts; and will be their God, and they shall be my people. And they shall teach no more every man his neighbour, and every man his brother, saying, Know the LORD: for they shall all know me, from the least of them unto the greatest of them, saith the LORD: for I will forgive their iniquity, and I will remember their sin no more.*
>
> (Jeremiah 31:31-34)

> *Now we know that what things soever the law saith, it saith to them who are under the law: that every mouth may be*

> *stopped, and all the world may become guilty before God. Therefore by the deeds of the law there shall no flesh be justified in his sight: for by the law is the knowledge of sin. But now the righteousness of God without the law is manifested, being witnessed by the law and the prophets; Even the righteousness of God which is by faith of Jesus Christ unto all and upon all them that believe: for there is no difference: For all have sinned, and come short of the glory of God; Being justified freely by his grace through the redemption that is in Christ Jesus: Whom God hath set forth to be a propitiation through faith in his blood, to declare his righteousness for the remission of sins that are past, through the forbearance of God; To declare, I say, at this time his righteousness: that he might be just, and the justifier of him which believeth in Jesus.*
>
> (Romans 3:19-26)

Penalty vs. Consequence

The *propitiation through faith in his blood* does not mean that we can now live any way we want to. Yes, the penalty of sin has been paid in full, but the consequences can linger. When we have lived a reckless life, and subjected our physical body to abuse, we cannot expect it to rebound immediately once we change our ways. Though we have no additional physical deterioration, we still have to reverse the damage that has been done. This is why there is the Comforter.

> *If ye love me, keep my commandments. And I will pray the Father, and he shall give you another Comforter, that he may abide with you for ever; Even the Spirit of truth; whom the world cannot receive, because it seeth him not, neither knoweth him: but ye know him; for he dwelleth with you, and shall be in you. I will not leave you comfortless: I will come to you.*
>
> (John 14:15-18)

Father (Soul of God) and Holy Ghost (Spirit of God)

> *For the word of God is quick, and powerful, and sharper than any twoedged sword, piercing even to the dividing asunder of soul and spirit, and of the joints and marrow,*

> *and is a discerner of the thoughts and intents of the heart. Neither is there any creature that is not manifest in his sight: but all things are naked and opened unto the eyes of him with whom we have to do.*
>
> (Hebrews 4:12-13)

One of the thought procedures that I use to understand the Father is to consider God's statement at Creation.

> *And God said, Let us make man in our image, after our likeness: and let them have dominion over the fish of the sea, and over the fowl of the air, and over the cattle, and over all the earth, and over every creeping thing that creepeth upon the earth. So God created man in his own image, in the image of God created he him; male and female created he them.*
>
> (Genesis 1:26-27)

I apply a reverse kind of logic, to arrive at a way of visualizing the Father. The image draws upon the fact that God created us with a soul and a spirit. Therefore, it seems reasonable to think that God would manifest His Self with a Soul and a Spirit. This is confirmed by a reference to God's soul, in the Bible.

> *And now therefore thus saith the LORD, the God of Israel, concerning this city, whereof ye say, It shall be delivered into the hand of the king of Babylon by the sword, and by the famine, and by the pestilence; Behold, I will gather them out of all countries, whither I have driven them in mine anger, and in my fury, and in great wrath; and I will bring them again unto this place, and I will cause them to dwell safely: And they shall be my people, and I will be their God: And I will give them one heart, and one way, that they may fear me for ever, for the good of them, and of their children after them: And I will make an everlasting covenant with them, that I will not turn away from them, to do them good; but I will put my fear in their hearts, that they shall not depart from me. Yea, I will rejoice over them to do them good, and I will plant them in this land assuredly with my whole heart and with my whole soul.*
>
> (Jeremiah 32:36-41)

The spirit of man is that which contains the essence of man's motivations: consciousness. Those of us who believe in the Lord Jesus Christ know that God is a Spirit, for Jesus told us so.

> *Jesus saith unto her, Woman, believe me, the hour cometh, when ye shall neither in this mountain, nor yet at Jerusalem, worship the Father. Ye worship ye know not what: we know what we worship: for salvation is of the Jews. But the hour cometh, and now is, when the true worshippers shall worship the Father in spirit and in truth: for the Father seeketh such to worship him. God is a Spirit: and they that worship him must worship him in spirit and in truth.*
>
> (John 4:21-24)

We know that God indeed has a Spirit component, which He expresses to mankind as multiple Spirits. The Bible tells us that there are seven Spirits of God. These may, too, be sets of seven Spirits; I will have to wait for further enlightenment from God before trying to edify you on this matter. For now, I give you the Scripture that mentions these Spirits.

> *John to the seven churches which are in Asia: Grace be unto you, and peace, from him which is, and which was, and which is to come; and from the seven Spirits which are before his throne;*
>
> (Revelation 1:4)
>
> *And unto the angel of the church in Sardis write; These things saith he that hath the seven Spirits of God, and the seven stars; I know thy works, that thou hast a name that thou livest, and art dead.*
>
> (Revelation 3:1)
>
> *And out of the throne proceeded lightnings and thunderings and voices: and there were seven lamps of fire burning before the throne, which are the seven Spirits of God.*
>
> (Revelation 4:5)
>
> *And I beheld, and, lo, in the midst of the throne and of the four beasts, and in the midst of the elders, stood a Lamb*

> *as it had been slain, having seven horns and seven eyes, which are the seven Spirits of God sent forth into all the earth.*

(Revelation 5:6)

God may have presented these Spirits for the purpose of providing understanding to mankind, without overloading our minds. It may be that the LORD introduces us to each of the individual Spirits as our spirit is ready for the understanding. One of the Spirits of God is described in Scripture by name. Jesus told us this name.

> *And I will pray the Father, and he shall give you another Comforter, that he may abide with you for ever; Even the Spirit of truth; whom the world cannot receive, because it seeth him not, neither knoweth him: but ye know him; for he dwelleth with you, and shall be in you.*

(John 14:16-17)

> *But the Comforter, which is the Holy Ghost, whom the Father will send in my name, he shall teach you all things, and bring all things to your remembrance, whatsoever I have said unto you.*

(John 14:26)

> *But when the Comforter is come, whom I will send unto you from the Father, even the Spirit of truth, which proceedeth from the Father, he shall testify of me:*

(John 15:26)

But, what then might be the Soul of God?

To begin answering that question, let us explore the soul of man. The soul of man is that which contains the essence of man's understanding. To give us a glimpse into the LORD'S soul, God revealed the essence of His understanding, to mankind. This is clearly seen in the interactions of God with Moses. God not only shared His understanding with Moses, but He also sealed His understanding in Moses. For this reason Moses referred to God as *father* (*is not he thy father that hath bought thee*). We capitalize the word, when we write Father, so that it is clear that we are referring to this manifestation of God, and not to man.

> *Give ear, O ye heavens, and I will speak; and hear, O earth, the words of my mouth. My doctrine shall drop as the rain, my speech shall distil as the dew, as the small rain upon the tender herb, and as the showers upon the grass: Because I will publish the name of the LORD: ascribe ye greatness unto our God. He is the Rock, his work is perfect: for all his ways are judgment: a God of truth and without iniquity, just and right is he. They have corrupted themselves, their spot is not the spot of his children: they are a perverse and crooked generation. Do ye thus requite the LORD, O foolish people and unwise? is not he thy father that hath bought thee? hath he not made thee, and established thee? Remember the days of old, consider the years of many generations: ask thy father, and he will show thee; thy elders, and they will tell thee.*

(Deuteronomy 32:1-7)

This, then, is the Soul of God: the Father.

There is one other humanly perceived manifestation of the working of God that He revealed to mankind; and that is His Word. God's Word is the Authority of God. It is this, revealed attribute of God, which said, "Let there be"; and after having thus given that command, "There was".

> *In the beginning was the Word, and the Word was with God, and the Word was God. The same was in the beginning with God. All things were made by him; and without him was not any thing made that was made.*

(John 1:1-3)

The Word is the bridge between God and man, which He presented to us in His Son, Jesus Christ.

> *And the Word was made flesh, and dwelt among us, (and we beheld his glory, the glory as of the only begotten of the Father,) full of grace and truth. John bare witness of him, and cried, saying, This was he of whom I spake, He that cometh after me is preferred before me: for he was before me. And of his fulness have all we received, and grace for grace. For the law was given by Moses, but grace and truth came by Jesus Christ.*

(John 1:14-17)

Son = servant of God

Contrary to popular opinion, the Son is not the Father, and the Son of God is not Almighty God; nowhere in Scripture does he state that he is, in either rendition. Take a good look at the last thing revealed in Scripture that Jesus said about his self.

Revelation 22:6-15

And he said unto me, These sayings are faithful and true: and the Lord God of the holy prophets sent his angel to show unto his servants the things which must shortly be done. Behold, I come quickly: blessed is he that keepeth the sayings of the prophecy of this book.

And I John saw these things, and heard them. And when I had heard and seen, I fell down to worship before the feet of the angel which showed me these things. Then saith he unto me, See thou do it not: for I am thy fellowservant, and of thy brethren the prophets, and of them which keep the sayings of this book: worship God.

And he saith unto me, Seal not the sayings of the prophecy of this book: for the time is at hand. He that is unjust, let him be unjust still: and he which is filthy, let him be filthy still: and he that is righteous, let him be righteous still: and he that is holy, let him be holy still. And, behold, I come quickly; and my reward is with me, to give every man according as his work shall be. I am Alpha and Omega, the beginning and the end, the first and the last.

Blessed are they that do his commandments, that they may have right to the tree of life, and may enter in through the gates into the city. For without are dogs, and sorcerers, and whoremongers, and murderers, and idolaters, and whosoever loveth and maketh a lie.

Revelation 22:16-17

I Jesus have sent mine angel to testify unto you these things in the churches. I am the root and the offspring of David, and the bright and morning star. And the Spirit and the bride say, Come. And let him that heareth say, Come. And let him that is athirst come. And whosoever will, let him take the water of life freely.

If this is as it is written, then it is a direct statement by Jesus that he is not God. In fact, he reveals precisely who he is: ***I am thy fellowservant, and of thy brethren the prophets.*** Furthermore, Jesus admonishes us not to worship him, but to worship God.

The only somewhat *sticky* point is the reference in 22:16 to the angel. This is not the angel that is delivering the message to John, but it is a different angel, which was sent to testify to the churches. In fact, this reference to an angel seems to be directed to those who are called to *do his commandments*. As such it fits the mission that was given to John. He was told not to seal up the words, or keep them to himself. Instead, he is to go to the churches and deliver the message from Jesus, saying that he will return, under the authority of the Father, to make all things right. John the Revelator is the angel of 22:16, and he has done what he was told to do: we have these commandments from Jesus.

The Godhead Complete

When the Lord Jesus Christ was revealed to us, our knowledge of the Godhead was, then, completed. Now we could fully see the working of God with man. In Jesus is revealed to us the fullness of the love of God.

In times before, God used a stern rod to move his people to excellence. With the Revelation of Jesus Christ, He showed forth the *carrot and stick* method of persuasion that He had prepared from the foundation of the world. The Godhead of the love of God for man was complete with the revelation to mankind of his Son, Jesus Christ.

> *As ye have therefore received Christ Jesus the Lord, so walk ye in him: Rooted and built up in him, and stablished in the faith, as ye have been taught, abounding therein with thanksgiving. Beware lest any man spoil you through philosophy and vain deceit, after the tradition of men, after the rudiments of the world, and not after Christ. For in him dwelleth all the fulness of the Godhead bodily. And ye are complete in him, which is the head of all principality and power: In whom also ye are circumcised with the circumcision made without hands, in putting off the body of the sins of the flesh by the circumcision of Christ: Buried with him in baptism, wherein also ye are risen with him*

through the faith of the operation of God, who hath raised him from the dead.

(Colossians 2:6-12)

Strong Delusion

There seems to be some very strong delusions circulating in the church, and in other Christian institutions. It seems that many of our pastors, ministers and other religious spokespersons are in a rush to give Jesus a status that he himself never sought. I pray that they are doing so out of ignorance; which God forgives. I pray there is no one doing so by design; for which God will hold them accountable. If it is ignorance, then their education is found in this set of messages.

This type of behavior was foretold in the Bible.

Now we beseech you, brethren, by the coming of our Lord Jesus Christ, and by our gathering together unto him, That ye be not soon shaken in mind, or be troubled, neither by spirit, nor by word, nor by letter as from us, as that the day of Christ is at hand. Let no man deceive you by any means: for that day shall not come, except there come a falling away first, and that man of sin be revealed, the son of perdition; Who opposeth and exalteth himself above all that is called God, or that is worshipped; so that he as God sitteth in the temple of God, showing himself that he is God. Remember ye not, that, when I was yet with you, I told you these things? And now ye know what withholdeth that he might be revealed in his time. For the mystery of iniquity doth already work: only he who now letteth will let, until he be taken out of the way.

And then shall that Wicked be revealed, whom the Lord shall consume with the spirit of his mouth, and shall destroy with the brightness of his coming: Even him, whose coming is after the working of Satan with all power and signs and lying wonders, And with all deceivableness of unrighteousness in them that perish; because they received not the love of the truth, that they might be saved.

And for this cause God shall send them strong delusion, that they should believe a lie: That they all might be damned who believed not the truth, but had pleasure in unrighteousness.

But we are bound to give thanks alway to God for you, brethren beloved of the Lord, because God hath from the beginning chosen you to salvation through sanctification of the Spirit and belief of the truth:

(2 Thessalonians 2:1-13)

By stating that Jesus is God, when Jesus clearly differentiates himself from God, they are adding to the words of this book, and thus the closing verses refer directly to them.

For I testify unto every man that heareth the words of the prophecy of this book, If any man shall add unto these things, God shall add unto him the plagues that are written in this book: And if any man shall take away from the words of the book of this prophecy, God shall take away his part out of the book of life, and out of the holy city, and from the things which are written in this book.

He which testifieth these things saith, Surely I come quickly. Amen. Even so, come, Lord Jesus.

(Revelation 22:18-20)

Lord, please correct me if I have misinterpreted: Lord, if I have not misinterpreted, please enlighten those who stand in service to you in the churches. This I ask in Jesus name, and most definitely for his sake. Amen.

The Word from the Bible

Exodus 15:13-18

Thou in thy mercy hast led forth the people which thou hast redeemed: thou hast guided them in thy strength unto thy holy habitation. The people shall hear, and be afraid: sorrow shall take hold on the inhabitants of Palestina. Then the dukes of Edom shall be amazed; the mighty men of Moab, trembling shall take hold upon them; all the inhabitants of Canaan shall melt away. Fear and dread shall fall upon them; by the greatness of thine arm they shall be as still as a stone; till thy people pass over, O LORD, till the people pass over, which thou hast purchased. Thou shalt bring them in, and plant them in the mountain of thine inheritance, in the place, O LORD, which thou hast made for thee to dwell in, in the Sanctuary, O LORD, which thy hands have established. The LORD shall reign for ever and ever.

Exodus 34:5-11

And the LORD descended in the cloud, and stood with him there, and proclaimed the name of the LORD. And the LORD passed by before him, and proclaimed, The LORD, The LORD God, merciful and gracious, longsuffering, and abundant in goodness and truth, Keeping mercy for thousands, forgiving iniquity and transgression and sin, and that will by no means clear the guilty; visiting the iniquity of the fathers upon the children, and upon the children's children, unto the third and to the fourth generation.

And Moses made haste, and bowed his head toward the earth, and worshipped. And he said, If now I have found grace in thy sight, O LORD, let my LORD, I pray thee, go among us; for it is a stiffnecked people; and pardon our iniquity and our sin, and take us for thine inheritance.

And he said, Behold, I make a covenant: before all thy people I will do marvels, such as have not been done in all the earth, nor in any nation: and all the people among which thou art shall see the work of the LORD: for it is a terrible thing that I will do with thee. Observe thou that which I command thee this day: behold, I drive out before thee the Amorite, and the Canaanite, and the Hittite, and the Perizzite, and the Hivite, and the Jebusite.

Psalm 2:7-12

I will declare the decree: the LORD hath said unto me, Thou art my Son; this day have I begotten thee. Ask of me, and I shall give thee the heathen for thine inheritance, and the uttermost parts of the earth for thy possession. Thou shalt break them with a rod of iron; thou shalt dash them in pieces like a potter's vessel.

Be wise now therefore, O ye kings: be instructed, ye judges of the earth. Serve the LORD with fear, and rejoice with trembling. Kiss the Son, lest he be angry, and ye perish from the way, when his wrath is kindled but a little. Blessed are all they that put their trust in him.

Deuteronomy 32:16-21

They provoked him to jealousy with strange gods, with abominations provoked they him to anger. They sacrificed unto devils, not to God; to gods whom they knew not, to new gods that came newly up, whom your fathers feared not. Of the Rock that begat thee thou art unmindful, and hast forgotten God that formed thee. And when the LORD saw it, he abhorred them, because of the provoking of his sons, and of his daughters. And he said, I will hide my face from them, I will see what their end shall be: for they are a very froward generation, children in whom is no faith. They have moved me to jealousy with that which is not God; they have provoked me to anger with their vanities: and I will move them to jealousy with those which are not a people; I will provoke them to anger with a foolish nation.

Romans 10:17-21

So then faith cometh by hearing, and hearing by the word of God.

But I say, Have they not heard? Yes verily, their sound went into all the earth, and their words unto the ends of the world.

But I say, Did not Israel know? First Moses saith, I will provoke you to jealousy by them that are no people, and by a foolish nation I will anger you. But Esaias is very bold, and saith, I was found of them that sought me not; I was made manifest unto them that asked not after me. But to Israel he saith, All day long I have stretched forth my hands unto a disobedient and gainsaying people.

Chapter 11

Provision for the Others

God made a covenant with Abraham, and bound Himself to it as an eternal covenant. Let us look at one of the pieces of this covenant, and discover why all the children of Abraham participate. In fact, the part of the covenant that we will explore now gives benefit to all peoples of the earth.

> *And the men rose up from thence, and looked toward Sodom: and Abraham went with them to bring them on the way. And the LORD said, Shall I hide from Abraham that thing which I do; Seeing that Abraham shall surely become a great and mighty nation, and all the nations of the earth shall be blessed in him?*
>
> (Genesis 18:16)

This is an awesome statement about a man, as well as an awesome responsibility given to man, in general. God did not say this about Abraham to indicate that regardless of what he did, this would occur. God said this to indicate that because of what Abraham had already been seen by God to do, God was revealing this about him. God is not limited by either the past or the present; all time is visible to Him. He had already seen that Abraham would stand before Him as a righteous servant.

> *For I know him, that he will command his children and his household after him, and they shall keep the way of the LORD, to do justice and judgment; that the LORD may bring upon Abraham that which he hath spoken of him.*
>
> (Genesis 18:19)

Such is not a light responsibility. This is not just a responsibility to the nation to which it is given; nor to the individual and his family to which it is given. This is a responsibility to the world. In all this discussion of the relationship of the children of Abraham, let us not forget that there is a larger world. Abraham held responsibility for it all; not just for his own immediate family.

Furthermore, God did not say that all nations *might* be blessed. God said that all nations *shall* be blessed. This is absolute and unchangeable.

> *For I am the LORD, I change not; therefore ye sons of Jacob are not consumed.*
>
> (Malachi 3:6)
>
> *Every good gift and every perfect gift is from above, and cometh down from the Father of lights, with whom is no variableness, neither shadow of turning.*
>
> (James 1:17)

But, just how will this happen?

Let us study Scripture, through some of the historical episodes.

We begin at the point where the word of the LORD declares that God will raise up a nation that will represent Him before all the other nations. This will be a nation of example.

> *Now therefore hearken, O Israel, unto the statutes and unto the judgments, which I teach you, for to do them, that ye may live, and go in and possess the land which the LORD God of your fathers giveth you. Ye shall not add unto the word which I command you, neither shall ye diminish ought from it, that ye may keep the commandments of the LORD your God which I command you.*
>
> *Your eyes have seen what the LORD did because of Baalpeor: for all the men that followed Baalpeor, the LORD thy God hath destroyed them from among you. But ye that did cleave unto the LORD your God are alive every one of you this day. Behold, I have taught you statutes and judgments, even as the LORD my God commanded me, that ye should do so in the land whither ye go to possess it. Keep therefore and do them; for this is your wisdom and your understanding in the sight of the nations, which shall hear all these statutes, and say, Surely this great nation is a wise and understanding people.*
>
> (Deuteronomy 4:1-6)

The nation will not just be spiritually blessed; it will also be materially blessed. It will be so blessed that it will be able to take of its surplus and assist other nations.

> *For the LORD thy God blesseth thee, as he promised thee: and thou shalt lend unto many nations, but thou shalt not borrow; and thou shalt reign over many nations, but they shall not reign over thee.*
>
> *If there be among you a poor man of one of thy brethren within any of thy gates in thy land which the LORD thy God giveth thee, thou shalt not harden thine heart, nor shut thine hand from thy poor brother: But thou shalt open thine hand wide unto him, and shalt surely lend him sufficient for his need, in that which he wanteth.*
>
> (Deuteronomy 15:6-8)

This nation of Abraham will be the bearer of the covenant between God and Abraham. As the nation stays in line with the things of God it will receive an overflowing blessing.

> *And it shall come to pass, if thou shalt hearken diligently unto the voice of the LORD thy God, to observe and to do all his commandments which I command thee this day, that the LORD thy God will set thee on high above all nations of the earth: And all these blessings shall come on thee, and overtake thee, if thou shalt hearken unto the voice of the LORD thy God.*
>
> *Blessed shalt thou be in the city, and blessed shalt thou be in the field.*
>
> *Blessed shall be the fruit of thy body, and the fruit of thy ground, and the fruit of thy cattle, the increase of thy kine, and the flocks of thy sheep.*
>
> *Blessed shall be thy basket and thy store.*
>
> *Blessed shalt thou be when thou comest in, and blessed shalt thou be when thou goest out.*
>
> *The LORD shall cause thine enemies that rise up against thee to be smitten before thy face: they shall come out against thee one way, and flee before thee seven ways.*

> *The LORD shall command the blessing upon thee in thy storehouses, and in all that thou settest thine hand unto; and he shall bless thee in the land which the LORD thy God giveth thee.*
>
> *The LORD shall establish thee an holy people unto himself, as he hath sworn unto thee, if thou shalt keep the commandments of the LORD thy God, and walk in his ways.*
>
> *And all people of the earth shall see that thou art called by the name of the LORD; and they shall be afraid of thee.*
>
> *And the LORD shall make thee plenteous in goods, in the fruit of thy body, and in the fruit of thy cattle, and in the fruit of thy ground, in the land which the LORD sware unto thy fathers to give thee. The LORD shall open unto thee his good treasure, the heaven to give the rain unto thy land in his season, and to bless all the work of thine hand: and thou shalt lend unto many nations, and thou shalt not borrow. And the LORD shall make thee the head, and not the tail; and thou shalt be above only, and thou shalt not be beneath; if that thou hearken unto the commandments of the LORD thy God, which I command thee this day, to observe and to do them: And thou shalt not go aside from any of the words which I command thee this day, to the right hand, or to the left, to go after other gods to serve them.*
>
> (Deuteronomy 28:1-14)

Also, as the nation moves away from God, it will serve as an example of the seriousness of the LORD, about His name being honored in all the earth. This is revealed in Scripture through the curse that is written of in Deuteronomy 28:15-88. It is not included here, so as not to disrupt the flow of the blessing.

Deuteronomy 28:1-14, above, is the blessed possibility of the nation. But God does not stop here. This nation can be an example of righteousness to the world. However, whether this nation obeys or not, God will still be exalted among all men.

> *For from the rising of the sun even unto the going down of the same my name shall be great among the Gentiles; and*

> *in every place incense shall be offered unto my name, and a pure offering: for my name shall be great among the heathen, saith the LORD of hosts.*

(Malachi 1:11)

God has made a place for all nations. None is too small. None is insignificant. None is too large. None is too important. If there is no nation that will represent Him, then He will raise up a person to establish a nation that will. As the priest of Israel understood, God will always have a mediator between Himself and mankind. No one will be summarily denied access.

> *Come, behold the works of the LORD, what desolations he hath made in the earth. He maketh wars to cease unto the end of the earth; he breaketh the bow, and cutteth the spear in sunder; he burneth the chariot in the fire.*
>
> *Be still, and know that I am God: I will be exalted among the heathen, I will be exalted in the earth.*
>
> *The LORD of hosts is with us; the God of Jacob is our refuge. Selah.*

(Psalm 46:8-11)

Please do not ever
Think that the LORD
Would, at any time,
Neglect so great a hoard

Of humans outside of
God's selected part
That carries the word
From His own heart.

I'd like you to know
That God is not remiss;
Your needs, the LORD
Will never dismiss.

God is love,
With unlimited bounds;
Throughout the earth
His word resounds.

He poured the love
Into a vessel of man,
And sent it forth
To show His plan;

Revealing to all
His blessed face;
By little and little,
At His own pace.

No hurry for God,
Eternity is His frame
To teach mankind
To honor His name.

Surely, the LORD has
Spread God's word:
In all nations
His voice is heard.

His name is flowing
Throughout the earth;

*A very real witness
To mankind's worth.*

*All, to God's wisdom,
Will one day bow.
Please do not wait;
You can do it now.*

Chapter 11a

The Child is Born
(only a child)

My world is now seeing an emergence of a preoccupation with the personal life of the man known as Jesus of Nazareth. There are books being written about what he may have done, and with whom he may have done it. Of course, none of these are considered authoritative sources, but rather conjecture. However, some are from writings that are accepted by certain religious groups; but, not all. We will discuss the futility of this preoccupation.

God has established Himself among us in a fashion similar to a family. Putting it more correctly, from a human perspective; God has illustrated Himself as the head of a single parent family. God, through the Scripture, is presented as a Father with sons. Among these sons there is one who is called the Son. This is because this Son was the first of the family of God, and he will be the culmination of the family of God. How, you say is this possible?

+=+=+=+=+=+=+=+=+=+=+=+=+=+=+=+=+=+=+=+

God delivers to man the example of what a family of God should be

Before the foundation of the world, the Son was presented by God. It is believed that he was instrumental, along with the Father, in the creation of existence as we now know it. From the Father, the Son learned all that he needed to know about the mission that he has, to the world of men. We know this Son by many titles. Among these titles are Christ, Messiah, the Son of man and the Son of God.

From the time of his presentation, until sometime around the turn of the timescale, the Son resided in Heaven. Around the turn of the timescale, from BC to AD, events started that would allow him to present himself to the people of the earth. The prophet Isaiah describes these events.

> *For unto us a child is born, unto us a son is given: and the government shall be upon his shoulder: and his name shall be called Wonderful, Counsellor, The mighty God, The everlasting Father, The Prince of Peace. Of the increase of his government and peace there shall be no end, upon the throne of David, and upon his kingdom, to order it, and to establish it with judgment and with justice from henceforth even for ever. The zeal of the LORD of hosts will perform this.*
>
> (Isaiah 9:6-7)

+=+

Unto us a child is born

The preparation for the arrival of the spirit of the Son of God begins with a young lady named Mary.

> *Then said Mary unto the angel, How shall this be, seeing I know not a man?*
>
> *And the angel answered and said unto her, The Holy Ghost shall come upon thee, and the power of the Highest shall overshadow thee: therefore also that holy thing which shall be born of thee shall be called the Son of God. And, behold, thy cousin Elisabeth, she hath also conceived a son in her old age: and this is the sixth month with her, who was called barren. For with God nothing shall be impossible.*
>
> (Luke 1:34-37)

Further Understanding:

- The importance of the virgin birth
- A vessel crafted in purity, as were the temple vessels

The importance of the virgin birth

The virgin birth is not a nice touch for God to do in creating the house for the Son of God; it is a necessity. Throughout the

Scripture; in the biblical configuration of human families, it is the father who is the one to set the pattern for the development of the spirit of the son. This is so important that even though they are two distinct persons, the father and the son, the actions of the father set the pattern for the actions of the son. This is noted most dramatically in God's pronouncement of the weight of the sins of the father.

> *Thou shalt not make unto thee any graven image, or any likeness of any thing that is in heaven above, or that is in the earth beneath, or that is in the water under the earth. Thou shalt not bow down thyself to them, nor serve them: for I the LORD thy God am a jealous God, visiting the iniquity of the fathers upon the children unto the third and fourth generation of them that hate me; And shewing mercy unto thousands of them that love me, and keep my commandments.*
>
> (Exodus 20:4-6)

A vessel crafted in purity as the temple vessels

So, it is only fitting that the pattern for the soul, of he who is to be the house of the Son of God, be crafted in purity. The only way for this to be done is for God to provide the means by which the Son begins his time as a human on this earth. It is for this reason that Jesus is called the only begotten Son of God.

> *And as Moses lifted up the serpent in the wilderness, even so must the Son of man be lifted up: That whosoever believeth in him should not perish, but have eternal life. For God so loved the world, that he gave his only begotten Son, that whosoever believeth in him should not perish, but have everlasting life. For God sent not his Son into the world to condemn the world; but that the world through him might be saved.*
>
> (John 3:14-17)

There are other sons of God, but only one begotten Son of God. Thus, the child starts life with a clean slate, as man goes, and is a fitting vessel for residence by the Spirit of the Son of God.

+=+=+=+=+=+=+=+=+=+=+=+=+=+=+=+=+=+

Only a child at birth, but with a mighty destiny

The child starts life with a mighty destiny. This was foretold by the angel that appeared unto Mary and told her about the birth to come . . .

> *And the angel said unto her, Fear not, Mary: for thou hast found favour with God. And, behold, thou shalt conceive in thy womb, and bring forth a son, and shalt call his name JESUS. He shall be great, and shall be called the Son of the Highest: and the Lord God shall give unto him the throne of his father David: And he shall reign over the house of Jacob for ever; and of his kingdom there shall be no end.*
>
> (Luke 1:30-33)

. . . and that visited Joseph, as he pondered what to do about the pregnancy of his espoused, which was not of his doing.

> *Then Joseph her husband, being a just man, and not willing to make her a publick example, was minded to put her away privily. But while he thought on these things, behold, the angel of the LORD appeared unto him in a dream, saying, Joseph, thou son of David, fear not to take unto thee Mary thy wife: for that which is conceived in her is of the Holy Ghost. And she shall bring forth a son, and thou shalt call his name JESUS: for he shall save his people from their sins.*
>
> (Matthew 1:19-21)

+=+

Qualification for the titles which he received

Jesus came to demonstrate to the world that God has high regard for mankind. Jesus showed us that a man can achieve honor and righteousness with God even while living in a fallen world, starting with "fallen" father and mother figures.

Further Understanding:

- Jesus' Father is God throughout his life

- The fatherly responsibility for, and authority over, the family are held by Joseph
- A normal husband-wife relationship, to give the child a place in the community
- Special instruction given by the Father to the designated earthly mother and father and through them to the child

Jesus' Father is God throughout his life

This child begins life under the tutelage of the Holy Ghost. The child of Mary was not the only one under the direct tutelage of the Holy Ghost. This honor was also given to John the Baptist. John, too, had a unique, though not virgin, birth.

> *But the angel said unto him, Fear not, Zacharias: for thy prayer is heard; and thy wife Elisabeth shall bear thee a son, and thou shalt call his name John. And thou shalt have joy and gladness; and many shall rejoice at his birth. For he shall be great in the sight of the Lord, and shall drink neither wine nor strong drink; and he shall be filled with the Holy Ghost, even from his mother's womb.*
>
> (Luke 1:13-15)

The fatherly responsibility for, and authority over, the family are held by Joseph

The mother of the child was selected according to the promise to Abraham. She, along with her husband, was of the line of David; who is of the line of Abraham. It is important that the father be of the line of David, even though the birth was directed by the Holy Ghost. This is required to establish the place of the child in the society. Also, it was kind of dangerous in that day for a woman to have no visible male progenitor for a child. This designation Joseph willingly took upon himself, to protect both the mother and the child.

> *Now the birth of Jesus Christ was on this wise: When as his mother Mary was espoused to Joseph, before they came together, she was found with child of the Holy Ghost. Then Joseph her husband, being a just man, and not willing to*

> *make her a publick example, was minded to put her away privily.*
>
> (Matthew 1:18-19)

A normal husband-wife relationship to give the child place in the community

There is no need to look for anything special about the child that was born to Mary. It is not necessary to see anything miraculous about Mary: there is no need for her to have been the product of a virgin birth; which she is not. There is no need for her to experience a pain-free delivery. There is no need for Jesus to have never cried as a baby. And, of course, there is no need for him to have come out of the womb walking.

Jesus' birth was, by the will of God, a normal one. This established Jesus of Nazareth as a human like unto us. If there had been such dramatics, Scripture could never have described Jesus as a man who experienced the same things that we experienced. If there had been such dramatics, Jesus would have had an edge that we can never experience. No, it is *very* important that he be as normal as any other human infant.

> *But we see Jesus, who was made a little lower than the angels for the suffering of death, crowned with glory and honour; that he by the grace of God should taste death for every man. For it became him, for whom are all things, and by whom are all things, in bringing many sons unto glory, to make the captain of their salvation perfect through sufferings. For both he that sanctifieth and they who are sanctified are all of one: for which cause he is not ashamed to call them brethren, Saying, I will declare thy name unto my brethren, in the midst of the church will I sing praise unto thee. And again, I will put my trust in him. And again, Behold I and the children which God hath given me.*
>
> *Forasmuch then as the children are partakers of flesh and blood, he also himself likewise took part of the same; that through death he might destroy him that had the power of death, that is, the devil; And deliver them who through fear of death were all their lifetime subject to bondage. For verily he took not on him the nature of angels; but he took*

on him the seed of Abraham. Wherefore in all things it behoved him to be made like unto his brethren, that he might be a merciful and faithful high priest in things pertaining to God, to make reconciliation for the sins of the people. For in that he himself hath suffered being tempted, he is able to succour them that are tempted.

(Hebrews 2:9-18)

Special instruction given by the Father to the designated earthly mother and father; and through them, to the child

However, it is not unfair to think of God providing unique training for a vessel that will serve Him. This is common among mankind for human father-son relationships. This was also done with the prophets and priests, in their relationship with the LORD. This was done with Moses, and with Noah. This will be done with all who are selected by God for a special work in His Kingdom. Indeed, this is done by God for all who seek Him. We can all have the assurance of the prophet Jeremiah, about our place with the Father.

The words of Jeremiah the son of Hilkiah, of the priests that were in Anathoth in the land of Benjamin: To whom the word of the LORD came in the days of Josiah the son of Amon king of Judah, in the thirteenth year of his reign. It came also in the days of Jehoiakim the son of Josiah king of Judah, unto the end of the eleventh year of Zedekiah the son of Josiah king of Judah, unto the carrying away of Jerusalem captive in the fifth month.

Then the word of the LORD came unto me, saying, Before I formed thee in the belly I knew thee; and before thou camest forth out of the womb I sanctified thee, and I ordained thee a prophet unto the nations.

(Jeremiah 1:1-5)

+=+=+=+=+=+=+=+=+=+=+=+=+=+=+=+=+=+

Reaching into manhood

The glimpses into Jesus' childhood are fragmentary and normal. The boy Jesus had the child's curiosity about things, and a desire to stretch himself beyond *normal* limitations. This came through, as it does in many highly intelligent children, in his being drawn to discuss matters with his elders.

Some of us have been around many children who preferred talking to adults more than to their peers. Sometimes, these children feel that the adults are their peers; and in some cases, unfortunately, the adults are. I am not implying that these children have in any way near the glory of the child born by the overshadowing of the Holy Ghost.

Jesus experienced this feeling when he entered the temple and was captured by the drive within him to share in his Father's teachings.

> *Now his parents went to Jerusalem every year at the feast of the passover. And when he was twelve years old, they went up to Jerusalem after the custom of the feast. And when they had fulfilled the days, as they returned, the child Jesus tarried behind in Jerusalem; and Joseph and his mother knew not of it. But they, supposing him to have been in the company, went a day's journey; and they sought him among their kinsfolk and acquaintance. And when they found him not, they turned back again to Jerusalem, seeking him. And it came to pass, that after three days they found him in the temple, sitting in the midst of the doctors, both hearing them, and asking them questions. And all that heard him were astonished at his understanding and answers.*
>
> (Luke 2:41-47)

Further Understanding:
- A child subject to, and subservient to, the God-selected parents
- Pretty much a normal Hebrew child of devoted parents
- Like the Nazarites
- Knowledge of the birth Father is given

A child subject to, and subservient to, the God-selected parents

The boy Jesus also explained to his parents why he felt compelled to do what he was doing. However, since God does not raise any brats, he submitted to his parents in this matter. The boy understood that they were still his parents, and that, for a time, he still had to follow their guidance.

> *And he said unto them, How is it that ye sought me? wist ye not that I must be about my Father's business?*
>
> *And they understood not the saying which he spake unto them.*
>
> *And he went down with them, and came to Nazareth, and was subject unto them: but his mother kept all these sayings in her heart. And Jesus increased in wisdom and stature, and in favour with God and man.*
>
> (Luke 2:49-52)

Pretty much a normal Hebrew child of devoted parents

The reason there is very little said about the years after the experience in the temple is that there is very little to say. Jesus was, as we have said, just a normal child. This was according to the design of God. God has shown throughout history that he uses ordinary people to do extraordinary things. Why should the LORD veer from this course in the presentation to the world of God's only begotten Son? The child will have enough to weigh upon him when he is a man; there is no need to inflict these burdens on him before it is time.

Like the Nazarites

Often when I think of Jesus, I think of the Nazarites; theirs was a similar dedication to God. This is seen in the birth and dedication to the LORD of Samson. The difference between the baby Jesus and the Nazarites is in the birth, as was mentioned before. Samson did not have the benefit of being born of a virgin, by the Holy Ghost. Samson was conceived in the old fashioned and still generally and widely accepted way.

> *And the children of Israel did evil again in the sight of the LORD; and the LORD delivered them into the hand of the Philistines forty years.*
>
> *And there was a certain man of Zorah, of the family of the Danites, whose name was Manoah; and his wife was barren, and bare not. And the angel of the LORD appeared*

unto the woman, and said unto her, Behold now, thou art barren, and bearest not: but thou shalt conceive, and bear a son. Now therefore beware, I pray thee, and drink not wine nor strong drink, and eat not any unclean thing: For, lo, thou shalt conceive, and bear a son; and no razor shall come on his head: for the child shall be a Nazarite unto God from the womb: and he shall begin to deliver Israel out of the hand of the Philistines.

Then the woman came and told her husband, saying, A man of God came unto me, and his countenance was like the countenance of an angel of God, very terrible: but I asked him not whence he was, neither told he me his name: But he said unto me, Behold, thou shalt conceive, and bear a son; and now drink no wine nor strong drink, neither eat any unclean thing: for the child shall be a Nazarite to God from the womb to the day of his death.

Then Manoah entreated the LORD, and said, O my Lord, let the man of God which thou didst send come again unto us, and teach us what we shall do unto the child that shall be born. And God hearkened to the voice of Manoah; and the angel of God came again unto the woman as she sat in the field: but Manoah her husband was not with her. And the woman made haste, and ran, and showed her husband, and said unto him, Behold, the man hath appeared unto me, that came unto me the other day. And Manoah arose, and went after his wife, and came to the man, and said unto him, Art thou the man that spakest unto the woman?

And he said, I am.

And Manoah said, Now let thy words come to pass. How shall we order the child, and how shall we do unto him?

And the angel of the LORD said unto Manoah, Of all that I said unto the woman let her beware. She may not eat of any thing that cometh of the vine, neither let her drink wine or strong drink, nor eat any unclean thing: all that I commanded her let her observe.

And Manoah said unto the angel of the LORD, I pray thee, let us detain thee, until we shall have made ready a kid for thee.

And the angel of the LORD said unto Manoah, Though thou detain me, I will not eat of thy bread: and if thou wilt offer a burnt offering, thou must offer it unto the LORD. For Manoah knew not that he was an angel of the LORD.

And Manoah said unto the angel of the LORD, What is thy name, that when thy sayings come to pass we may do thee honour?

And the angel of the LORD said unto him, Why askest thou thus after my name, seeing it is secret?

So Manoah took a kid with a meat offering, and offered it upon a rock unto the LORD: and the angel did wonderously; and Manoah and his wife looked on. For it came to pass, when the flame went up toward heaven from off the altar, that the angel of the LORD ascended in the flame of the altar. And Manoah and his wife looked on it, and fell on their faces to the ground. But the angel of the LORD did no more appear to Manoah and to his wife. Then Manoah knew that he was an angel of the LORD.

And Manoah said unto his wife, We shall surely die, because we have seen God.

But his wife said unto him, If the LORD were pleased to kill us, he would not have received a burnt offering and a meat offering at our hands, neither would he have showed us all these things, nor would as at this time have told us such things as these.

And the woman bare a son, and called his name Samson: and the child grew, and the LORD blessed him. And the spirit of the LORD began to move him at times in the camp of Dan between Zorah and Eshtaol.

(Judges 13:1-25)

Knowledge of the birth Father is given

About the most child-like thing done by Jesus that is recorded in the Bible is found in his response to his parents. He knew that he had a special calling, and I am sure that his parents knew that, too, by this time. For, it is not every day that two people experience a virgin birth--

and at that time they were the only two who actually knew that it had happened. There were several others who believed that it was true; but only Mary and Joseph knew, for sure. However, Jesus felt that he had to remind them of what they already knew.

> *And all that heard him were astonished at his understanding and answers. And when they saw him, they were amazed: and his mother said unto him, Son, why hast thou thus dealt with us? behold, thy father and I have sought thee sorrowing.*
>
> *And he said unto them, How is it that ye sought me? wist ye not that I must be about my Father's business?*
>
> (Luke 2:47-49)

This is so much like a child with a new toy. Sorry all you folks out there, who think that there is something sacrilegious about thinking of Jesus as a normal child; but, he was. And as a child, he had a child's temperament and reactions. Yes, he was a very smart child, and highly motivated; but a child nonetheless. Besides, he was a slight bit premature in this assessment. There was a little more time for him to be a child, before he really **had to be** about his Father's business. There was a little more he had to learn about the structure of the Family Business, before he could take it on full steam. Jesus was being given a glimpse of what he must do. Jesus, the boy, was also allowed to remind his parents that they were a part of a great destiny for mankind.

+=+=+=+=+=+=+=+=+=+=+=+=+=+=+=+=+=+=+=+

A young man who was steeped in the word of God through the Law of Moses

Indications are that his parents did a very good job of either directly instructing him or in staying out of the way of the Spirit in instructing him in the Law of Moses. This must have been a marvelous thing to watch, as he was growing up. Sometimes I wonder at what age God changed the lesson plan to include the things of a weightier nature that Jesus would have to experience. Among these are such things as having disciples, and being disliked by almost the entire nation of which he was a part.

Maybe it was unnecessary for the Spirit to share any of this with the young man Jesus. Maybe it all came as a part of the package that came to him from above. Maybe all he had to learn was to trust God, no matter what; as he evidenced even at the end.

> *And he came out, and went, as he was wont, to the mount of Olives; and his disciples also followed him. And when he was at the place, he said unto them, Pray that ye enter not into temptation. And he was withdrawn from them about a stone's cast, and kneeled down, and prayed, Saying, Father, if thou be willing, remove this cup from me: nevertheless not my will, but thine, be done.*
>
> *And there appeared an angel unto him from heaven, strengthening him.*
>
> *And being in an agony he prayed more earnestly: and his sweat was as it were great drops of blood falling down to the ground.*
>
> (Luke 22:39-44)

Further Understanding:

- Man's vain search for a record of the years
- Not yet called forth to contain, or exhibit, the full power of the Son of man
- A normal spirit of inquiry, as any other man
- No special place for siblings of Jesus

Man's vain search for a record of the years

Man's search for a record of the early years of Jesus is all vanity. The only reason that this search is being done is to find some way of categorizing the things that we might do, alongside the things that Jesus did. There is a very good reason that Moses burial place was not revealed by God. This was so that the nation of Israel could not make an idol of the location. There is a very good reason that the early years of Jesus' life are shrouded. This is so that no parent will try to create in their child a carbon copy of Christ; which is impossible. This is futile and dangerous to even ponder as a parental response to the life of a child. It is my prayer that his early years stay forever shrouded, until such time as we have new bodies and an eternal perspective on existence.

> *For we know in part, and we prophesy in part. But when that which is perfect is come, then that which is in part shall be done away. When I was a child, I spake as a child, I understood as a child, I thought as a child: but when I became a man, I put away childish things. For now we see through a glass, darkly; but then face to face: now I know in part; but then shall I know even as also I am known.*
>
> (1 Corinthians 13:9-12)

Not yet called forth to contain, or exhibit, the full power of the Son of man

Because Jesus as a young man was not yet called forth to contain the full power of the Son of man, this allowed him to listen to God without worry about what was coming. It directly fulfills the Scripture that he later gave to us about our own behavior in time.

> *Therefore I say unto you, Take no thought for your life, what ye shall eat, or what ye shall drink; nor yet for your body, what ye shall put on. Is not the life more than meat, and the body than raiment? Behold the fowls of the air: for they sow not, neither do they reap, nor gather into barns; yet your heavenly Father feedeth them. Are ye not much better than they?*
>
> *Which of you by taking thought can add one cubit unto his stature? And why take ye thought for raiment? Consider the lilies of the field, how they grow; they toil not, neither do they spin: And yet I say unto you, That even Solomon in all his glory was not arrayed like one of these. Wherefore, if God so clothe the grass of the field, which to day is, and to morrow is cast into the oven, shall he not much more clothe you, O ye of little faith?*
>
> *Therefore take no thought, saying, What shall we eat? or, What shall we drink? or, Wherewithal shall we be clothed? (For after all these things do the Gentiles seek:) for your heavenly Father knoweth that ye have need of all these things. But seek ye first the kingdom of God, and his*

righteousness; and all these things shall be added unto you. Take therefore no thought for the morrow: for the morrow shall take thought for the things of itself. Sufficient unto the day is the evil thereof.

(Matthew 6:25-34)

A normal spirit of inquiry, as any other man

Irrelevances: whether he married

whether he had children

Reason: Up to this point, the body of Jesus is normal humanity, created by direct intervention of God the Father.

Thus, from all that we understand of the way God works, Jesus was allowed to live a normal life until he was called forth to fulfill the mission for which God had given him life. He had a normal spirit, as every man is given a spirit.

The reason that it is irrelevant whether Jesus married, or whether he had children is that there would be nothing unique about either his wife, if there is one, nor about his children, if such exist. His body before the transfiguration was a normal body. His spirit was a human spirit, with the one edge of not having an earthly father who instilled the baggage of a past-ill-spent.

No special place for siblings of Jesus

Since there is no need to give any special place to the sibling of Jesus, we need not look for uniqueness in either the mother, or in the consummation of the union of Mary and Joseph. The fact that children were born of the union of Mary and Joseph, does not make them different from anyone else. Mary was not deemed by God to be a special woman before her selection by God. It is presumptuous of us, and totally unnecessary, to make the addition to Scripture that the Virgin Mary is born of a virgin.

It is also a violation of the commandment of God, which says not to add anything to the Bible. We are told in the words of the Bible, most notably in the book of Revelation, of the evil of adding anything to the words of the Bible. This addition falls within that condemnation, along with any other addition. The marvel of the birth of Jesus is that the single-source birth of a female is a scientifically explainable phenomenon, while the birth of a male is not. By trying to change the Bible in this fashion, the offenders of God's word are attempting to dilute the importance of Mary's overshadowing by the Holy Ghost.

Mary's own words tell us as much as we need to know about her status with God.

> *And Mary said, Behold the handmaid of the Lord; be it unto me according to thy word.*
>
> *And the angel departed from her.*
>
> (Luke 1:38)

+=+=+=+=+=+=+=+=+=+=+=+=+=+=+=+=+=+=+

Bottom Line

Jesus was begotten by the overshadowing of the Holy Ghost for a special mission. The baby Jesus was as normal as a virgin born individual can be, up to the point of the activation of his mission. But when the mission was revealed, the world saw a majesty that it had never seen before in a man . . .

> *Then cometh Jesus from Galilee to Jordan unto John, to be baptized of him. But John forbad him, saying, I have need to be baptized of thee, and comest thou to me?*
>
> *And Jesus answering said unto him, Suffer it to be so now: for thus it becometh us to fulfil all righteousness.*
>
> *Then he suffered him.*
>
> *And Jesus, when he was baptized, went up straightway out of the water: and, lo, the heavens were opened unto him, and he saw the Spirit of God descending like a dove, and lighting upon him: And lo a voice from heaven, saying, This is my beloved Son, in whom I am well pleased.*
>
> (Matthew 3:13-17)

. . . And a majesty that the world would not see after a little while; until after a little while more.

> *If ye love me, keep my commandments. And I will pray the Father, and he shall give you another Comforter, that he may abide with you for ever; Even the Spirit of truth; whom*

the world cannot receive, because it seeth him not, neither knoweth him: but ye know him; for he dwelleth with you, and shall be in you.

I will not leave you comfortless: I will come to you.

Yet a little while, and the world seeth me no more; but ye see me: because I live, ye shall live also. At that day ye shall know that I am in my Father, and ye in me, and I in you. He that hath my commandments, and keepeth them, he it is that loveth me: and he that loveth me shall be loved of my Father, and I will love him, and will manifest myself to him.

Judas saith unto him, not Iscariot, Lord, how is it that thou wilt manifest thyself unto us, and not unto the world?

Jesus answered and said unto him, If a man love me, he will keep my words: and my Father will love him, and we will come unto him, and make our abode with him. He that loveth me not keepeth not my sayings: and the word which ye hear is not mine, but the Father's which sent me.

These things have I spoken unto you, being yet present with you. But the Comforter, which is the Holy Ghost, whom the Father will send in my name, he shall teach you all things, and bring all things to your remembrance, whatsoever I have said unto you. Peace I leave with you, my peace I give unto you: not as the world giveth, give I unto you. Let not your heart be troubled, neither let it be afraid.

Ye have heard how I said unto you, I go away, and come again unto you. If ye loved me, ye would rejoice, because I said, I go unto the Father: for my Father is greater than I. And now I have told you before it come to pass, that, when it is come to pass, ye might believe.

(John 14:15-29)

The Word from the Bible

Psalm 46:4-11

There is a river, the streams whereof shall make glad the city of God, the holy place of the tabernacles of the most High. God is in the midst of her; she shall not be moved: God shall help her, and that right early. The heathen raged, the kingdoms were moved: he uttered his voice, the earth melted. The LORD of hosts is with us; the God of Jacob is our refuge. Selah.

Come, behold the works of the LORD, what desolations he hath made in the earth. He maketh wars to cease unto the end of the earth; he breaketh the bow, and cutteth the spear in sunder; he burneth the chariot in the fire. Be still, and know that I am God: I will be exalted among the heathen, I will be exalted in the earth. The LORD of hosts is with us; the God of Jacob is our refuge. Selah.

Deuteronomy 28:15-68

But it shall come to pass, if thou wilt not hearken unto the voice of the LORD thy God, to observe to do all his commandments and his statutes which I command thee this day; that all these curses shall come upon thee, and overtake thee: Cursed shalt thou be in the city, and cursed shalt thou be in the field.

Cursed shall be thy basket and thy store.

Cursed shall be the fruit of thy body, and the fruit of thy land, the increase of thy kine, and the flocks of thy sheep.

Cursed shalt thou be when thou comest in, and cursed shalt thou be when thou goest out.

The LORD shall send upon thee cursing, vexation, and rebuke, in all that thou settest thine hand unto for to do, until thou be destroyed, and until thou perish quickly; because of the wickedness of thy doings, whereby thou hast forsaken me. The LORD shall make the pestilence cleave unto thee, until he have consumed thee from off the land, whither thou goest to possess it. The LORD shall smite thee with a consumption, and with a fever, and with an inflammation, and with an extreme burning, and with the sword, and with blasting, and with mildew; and they shall pursue thee until thou perish. And thy heaven that is over thy head shall be brass, and the earth that is under thee shall be iron.

The LORD shall make the rain of thy land powder and dust: from heaven shall it come down upon thee, until thou be destroyed. The LORD shall cause thee to be smitten before thine enemies: thou shalt go out one way against them, and flee seven ways before them: and shalt be removed into all the kingdoms of the earth. And thy carcase shall be meat unto all fowls of the air, and unto the beasts of the earth, and no man shall fray them away.

The LORD will smite thee with the botch of Egypt, and with the emerods, and with the scab, and with the itch, whereof thou canst not be healed. The LORD shall smite thee with madness, and blindness, and astonishment of heart: And thou shalt grope at noonday, as the blind gropeth in darkness, and thou shalt not prosper in thy ways: and thou shalt be only oppressed and spoiled evermore, and no man shall save thee.

Thou shalt betroth a wife, and another man shall lie with her: thou shalt build an house, and thou shalt not dwell therein: thou shalt plant a vineyard, and shalt not gather the grapes thereof. Thine ox shall be slain before thine eyes, and thou shalt not eat thereof: thine ass shall be violently taken away from before thy face, and shall not be restored to thee: thy sheep shall be given unto thine enemies, and thou shalt have none to rescue them. Thy sons and thy daughters shall be given unto another people, and thine eyes shall look, and fail with longing for them all the day long: and there shall be no might in thine hand. The fruit of thy land, and all thy labours, shall a nation which thou knowest not eat up; and thou shalt be only oppressed and crushed alway: So that thou shalt be mad for the sight of thine eyes which thou shalt see.

The LORD shall smite thee in the knees, and in the legs, with a sore botch that cannot be healed, from the sole of thy foot unto the top of thy head. The LORD shall bring thee, and thy king which thou shalt set over thee, unto a nation which neither thou nor thy fathers have known; and there shalt thou serve other gods, wood and stone. And thou shalt become an astonishment, a proverb, and a byword, among all nations whither the LORD shall lead thee.

Thou shalt carry much seed out into the field, and shalt gather but little in; for the locust shall consume it. Thou shalt plant vineyards, and dress them, but shalt neither drink of the wine, nor gather the grapes; for the worms shall eat them. Thou shalt have olive trees throughout all thy coasts, but thou shalt not anoint thyself with the oil; for thine olive shall cast his fruit. Thou shalt beget sons and daughters, but thou shalt not enjoy them; for they shall go into captivity. All thy trees and fruit of thy land shall the locust consume.

The stranger that is within thee shall get up above thee very high; and thou shalt come down very low. He shall lend to thee, and thou shalt not lend to him: he shall be the head, and thou shalt be the tail.

Moreover all these curses shall come upon thee, and shall pursue thee, and overtake thee, till thou be destroyed; because thou hearkenedst not unto the voice of the LORD thy God, to keep his commandments and his statutes which he commanded thee: And they shall be upon thee for a sign and for a wonder, and upon thy seed for ever. Because thou servedst not the LORD thy God with joyfulness, and with gladness of heart, for the abundance of all things; Therefore shalt thou serve thine enemies which the LORD shall send against thee, in hunger, and in thirst, and in nakedness, and in want of all things: and he shall put a yoke of iron upon thy neck, until he have destroyed thee.

The LORD shall bring a nation against thee from far, from the end of the earth, as swift as the eagle flieth; a nation whose tongue thou shalt not understand; A nation of fierce countenance, which shall not regard the person of the old, nor show favour to the young: And he shall eat the fruit of thy cattle, and the fruit of thy land, until thou be destroyed: which also shall not leave thee either corn, wine, or oil, or the increase of thy kine, or flocks of thy sheep, until he have destroyed thee. And he shall besiege thee in all thy gates, until thy high and fenced walls come down, wherein thou trustedst, throughout all thy land: and he shall besiege thee in all thy gates throughout all thy land, which the LORD thy God hath given thee. And thou shalt eat the fruit of thine own body, the flesh of thy sons and of thy daughters, which the LORD thy God hath given thee, in the siege, and in the straitness, wherewith thine enemies shall distress thee: So that the man that is tender among you, and very delicate, his eye shall be evil toward his brother, and toward the wife of his bosom, and toward the remnant of his children which he shall leave: So that he will not give to any of them of the flesh of his children whom he shall eat: because he hath nothing left him in the siege, and in the straitness, wherewith thine enemies shall distress thee in all thy gates.

The tender and delicate woman among you, which would not adventure to set the sole of her foot upon the ground for delicateness and tenderness, her eye shall be evil toward the husband of her bosom, and toward her son, and toward her daughter, And toward her young one that cometh out from between her feet, and toward her children which she shall bear: for she shall eat them for want of all things secretly in the siege and straitness, wherewith thine enemy shall distress thee in thy gates.

If thou wilt not observe to do all the words of this law that are written in this book, that thou mayest fear this glorious and fearful name, THE LORD THY GOD; Then the LORD will make thy plagues wonderful, and the plagues of thy seed, even great plagues, and of long continuance, and sore sicknesses, and of long continuance. Moreover he will bring upon thee all the diseases of Egypt, which thou wast afraid of; and they shall cleave unto thee. Also every sickness, and every plague, which is not written in the book of this law, them will the LORD bring upon thee, until thou be destroyed. And ye shall be left few in number, whereas ye were as the stars of heaven for multitude; because thou wouldest not obey the voice of the LORD thy God.

And it shall come to pass, that as the LORD rejoiced over you to do you good, and to multiply you; so the LORD will rejoice over you to destroy you, and to bring you to nought; and ye shall be plucked from off the land whither thou goest to possess it. And the LORD shall scatter thee among all people, from the one end of the earth even unto the other; and there thou shalt serve other gods, which neither thou nor thy fathers have known, even wood and stone. And among these nations shalt thou find no ease, neither shall the sole of thy foot have rest: but the LORD shall give thee there a trembling heart, and failing of eyes, and sorrow of mind: And thy life shall hang in doubt before thee; and thou shalt fear day and night, and shalt have none assurance of thy life: In the morning thou shalt say, Would God it were even! and at even thou shalt say, Would God it were morning! for the fear of thine heart wherewith thou shalt fear, and for the sight of thine eyes which thou shalt see.

And the LORD shall bring thee into Egypt again with ships, by the way whereof I spake unto thee, Thou shalt see it no more again: and there ye shall be sold unto your enemies for bondmen and bondwomen, and no man shall buy you.

Chapter 12

Laying Out the Journey

We have read how things can proceed when we choose to follow the path of righteousness, in the LORD. This does not mean that we must be infallible; God knows that we are human. For this reason, God has established, in Scripture, some other, more indirect, ways His will is done. For, directly or indirectly, God's will is always done: this is the *definition* of God.

> *For as the rain cometh down, and the snow from heaven, and returneth not thither, but watereth the earth, and maketh it bring forth and bud, that it may give seed to the sower, and bread to the eater: So shall my word be that goeth forth out of my mouth: it shall not return unto me void, but it shall accomplish that which I please, and it shall prosper in the thing whereto I sent it.*
> (Isaiah 55:10-11)

The children of Israel had unlimited access to the wisdom of God, through Moses and the prophets; even so, they traveled another route. This *choice* of theirs did not surprise God! The LORD had already said that they would do this; sending it through a message from Moses, and in a message to Moses.

> *And the LORD said unto Moses, Behold, thou shalt sleep with thy fathers; and this people will rise up, and go a whoring after the gods of the strangers of the land, whither they go to be among them, and will forsake me, and break my covenant which I have made with them. Then my anger shall be kindled against them in that day, and I will forsake them, and I will hide my face from them, and they shall be devoured, and many evils and troubles shall befall them; so that they will say in that day, Are not these evils come upon*

us, because our God is not among us? And I will surely hide my face in that day for all the evils which they shall have wrought, in that they are turned unto other gods.

Now therefore write ye this song for you, and teach it the children of Israel: put it in their mouths, that this song may be a witness for me against the children of Israel. For when I shall have brought them into the land which I sware unto their fathers, that floweth with milk and honey; and they shall have eaten and filled themselves, and waxen fat; then will they turn unto other gods, and serve them, and provoke me, and break my covenant. And it shall come to pass, when many evils and troubles are befallen them, that this song shall testify against them as a witness; for it shall not be forgotten out of the mouths of their seed: for I know their imagination which they go about, even now, before I have brought them into the land which I sware.

(Deuteronomy 31:16-21)

And Moses spake in the ears of all the congregation of Israel the words of this song, until they were ended.

(Deuteronomy 31:30)

For the LORD'S portion is his people; Jacob is the lot of his inheritance. He found him in a desert land, and in the waste howling wilderness; he led him about, he instructed him, he kept him as the apple of his eye. As an eagle stirreth up her nest, fluttereth over her young, spreadeth abroad her wings, taketh them, beareth them on her wings: So the LORD alone did lead him, and there was no strange god with him. He made him ride on the high places of the earth, that he might eat the increase of the fields; and he made him to suck honey out of the rock, and oil out of the flinty rock; Butter of kine, and milk of sheep, with fat of lambs, and rams of the breed of Bashan, and goats, with the fat of kidneys of wheat; and thou didst drink the pure blood of the grape.

But Jeshurun waxed fat, and kicked: thou art waxen fat, thou art grown thick, thou art covered with fatness; then he forsook God which made him, and lightly esteemed the

Rock of his salvation. They provoked him to jealousy with strange gods, with abominations provoked they him to anger. They sacrificed unto devils, not to God; to gods whom they knew not, to new gods that came newly up, whom your fathers feared not. Of the Rock that begat thee thou art unmindful, and hast forgotten God that formed thee.

(Deuteronomy 32:9-18)

Wherefore God used another method. This method is called, captivity. Their ancestor Joseph had shown them the power of captivity, when he was sold into Egypt. Though it is most often used by man for evil purposes; God used Joseph's captivity to promote His will, and to spread His blessings upon the people of Israel; and through them, upon the world. Let us quickly review the chain of events in Joseph's life.

- The path of blessing began when Joseph's brothers left him in a pit to die
- Travelers passed by and took him out
- God allowed some of the children of Ishmael to transport Joseph to his position of service
- In that place of service, Joseph was sold into servitude

And Joseph was brought down to Egypt; and Potiphar, an officer of Pharaoh, captain of the guard, an Egyptian, bought him of the hands of the Ishmeelites, which had brought him down thither.

(Genesis 39:1)

Always believe that God can use many nations to perform His work; furthermore, what seems to be destructive to man is sometimes a part of the plan of God. Through his position of servitude in Egypt, Joseph produced benefits for his brethren. Joseph knew that it was of God; eventually.

And Joseph said unto his brethren, I am Joseph; doth my father yet live? And his brethren could not answer him; for they were troubled at his presence.

And Joseph said unto his brethren, Come near to me, I pray you. And they came near. And he said, I am Joseph your

> brother, whom ye sold into Egypt. Now therefore be not grieved, nor angry with yourselves, that ye sold me hither: for God did send me before you to preserve life. For these two years hath the famine been in the land: and yet there are five years, in the which there shall neither be earing nor harvest. And God sent me before you to preserve you a posterity in the earth, and to save your lives by a great deliverance. So now it was not you that sent me hither, but God: and he hath made me a father to Pharaoh, and lord of all his house, and a ruler throughout all the land of Egypt. Haste ye, and go up to my father, and say unto him, Thus saith thy son Joseph, God hath made me lord of all Egypt: come down unto me, tarry not: And thou shalt dwell in the land of Goshen, and thou shalt be near unto me, thou, and thy children, and thy children's children, and thy flocks, and thy herds, and all that thou hast: And there will I nourish thee; for yet there are five years of famine; lest thou, and thy household, and all that thou hast, come to poverty.
>
> (Genesis 45:3-11)

The nation to which Joseph went felt the blessings flowing to them as well. Surely, Pharaoh appreciated these blessings, and he showed his appreciation by his actions.

> Now therefore let Pharaoh look out a man discreet and wise, and set him over the land of Egypt. Let Pharaoh do this, and let him appoint officers over the land, and take up the fifth part of the land of Egypt in the seven plenteous years. And let them gather all the food of those good years that come, and lay up corn under the hand of Pharaoh, and let them keep food in the cities. And that food shall be for store to the land against the seven years of famine, which shall be in the land of Egypt; that the land perish not through the famine.
>
> And the thing was good in the eyes of Pharaoh, and in the eyes of all his servants. And Pharaoh said unto his servants, Can we find such a one as this is, a man in whom the Spirit of God is? And Pharaoh said unto Joseph, Forasmuch as God hath shewed thee all this, there is none so discreet and wise as thou art: Thou shalt be over my

> *house, and according unto thy word shall all my people be ruled: only in the throne will I be greater than thou. And Pharaoh said unto Joseph, See, I have set thee over all the land of Egypt. And Pharaoh took off his ring from his hand, and put it upon Joseph's hand, and arrayed him in vestures of fine linen, and put a gold chain about his neck; And he made him to ride in the second chariot which he had; and they cried before him, Bow the knee: and he made him ruler over all the land of Egypt.*
>
> *And Pharaoh said unto Joseph, I am Pharaoh, and without thee shall no man lift up his hand or foot in all the land of Egypt. And Pharaoh called Joseph's name Zaphnathpaaneah; and he gave him to wife Asenath the daughter of Potipherah priest of On.*
>
> *And Joseph went out over all the land of Egypt. And Joseph was thirty years old when he stood before Pharaoh king of Egypt. And Joseph went out from the presence of Pharaoh, and went throughout all the land of Egypt.*
>
> (Genesis 41:33-46)

The world outside of Egypt appreciated the blessing of Joseph's captivity.

> *And the seven years of dearth began to come, according as Joseph had said: and the dearth was in all lands; but in all the land of Egypt there was bread. And when all the land of Egypt was famished, the people cried to Pharaoh for bread: and Pharaoh said unto all the Egyptians, Go unto Joseph; what he saith to you, do. And the famine was over all the face of the earth: and Joseph opened all the storehouses, and sold unto the Egyptians; and the famine waxed sore in the land of Egypt. And all countries came into Egypt to Joseph for to buy corn; because that the famine was so sore in all lands.*
>
> (Genesis 41:54-57)

Then, all the children of Israel were moved to Egypt.

> *All the souls that came with Jacob into Egypt, which came out of his loins, besides Jacob's sons' wives, all the souls*

> *were threescore and six; And the sons of Joseph, which were born him in Egypt, were two souls: all the souls of the house of Jacob, which came into Egypt, were threescore and ten. And he sent Judah before him unto Joseph, to direct his face unto Goshen; and they came into the land of Goshen.*
>
> (Genesis 46:26-28)

At that time, things went on quite well for the nation of Egypt and for the children of Israel. The blessings were flowing from God to Egypt because of their presence, and the children of Israel were prospering as well. Joseph lived to an old age and died:

> *And Joseph dwelt in Egypt, he, and his father's house: and Joseph lived an hundred and ten years. And Joseph saw Ephraim's children of the third generation: the children also of Machir the son of Manasseh were brought up upon Joseph's knees. And Joseph said unto his brethren, I die: and God will surely visit you, and bring you out of this land unto the land which he sware to Abraham, to Isaac, and to Jacob. And Joseph took an oath of the children of Israel, saying, God will surely visit you, and ye shall carry up my bones from hence. So Joseph died, being an hundred and ten years old: and they embalmed him, and he was put in a coffin in Egypt.*
>
> (Genesis 50:22-26)

Unfortunately, both Joseph and his service to Pharaoh were eventually forgotten by the other rulers of Egypt. The children of Israel still provided blessings to Egypt, but they were treated as slaves, instead of guests. The time of Joseph was over and the time of burden had begun.

> *Now there arose up a new king over Egypt, which knew not Joseph. And he said unto his people, Behold, the people of the children of Israel are more and mightier than we: Come on, let us deal wisely with them; lest they multiply, and it come to pass, that, when there falleth out any war, they join also unto our enemies, and fight against us, and so get them up out of the land.*
>
> *Therefore they did set over them taskmasters to afflict them with their burdens. And they built for Pharaoh*

treasure cities, Pithom and Raamses. But the more they afflicted them, the more they multiplied and grew. And they were grieved because of the children of Israel. And the Egyptians made the children of Israel to serve with rigour: And they made their lives bitter with hard bondage, in morter, and in brick, and in all manner of service in the field: all their service, wherein they made them serve, was with rigour.

(Exodus 1:8-14)

But this was not the end of the story. The time came for the nation of Israel to be spawned from the children of Israel. The children of Israel had passed through the time of servitude that had been revealed to Abram, by God.

After these things the word of the LORD came unto Abram in a vision, saying, Fear not, Abram: I am thy shield, and thy exceeding great reward.

And Abram said, Lord GOD, what wilt thou give me, seeing I go childless, and the steward of my house is this Eliezer of Damascus? And Abram said, Behold, to me thou hast given no seed: and, lo, one born in my house is mine heir.

And, behold, the word of the LORD came unto him, saying, This shall not be thine heir; but he that shall come forth out of thine own bowels shall be thine heir. And he brought him forth abroad, and said, Look now toward heaven, and tell the stars, if thou be able to number them: and he said unto him, So shall thy seed be.

And he believed in the LORD; and he counted it to him for righteousness.

And he said unto him, I am the LORD that brought thee out of Ur of the Chaldees, to give thee this land to inherit it.

And he said, Lord GOD, whereby shall I know that I shall inherit it?

And he said unto him, Take me an heifer of three years old, and a she goat of three years old, and a ram of three years old, and a turtledove, and a young pigeon.

And he took unto him all these, and divided them in the midst, and laid each piece one against another: but the birds divided he not. And when the fowls came down upon the carcases, Abram drove them away. And when the sun was going down, a deep sleep fell upon Abram; and, lo, an horror of great darkness fell upon him.

And he said unto Abram, Know of a surety that thy seed shall be a stranger in a land that is not theirs, and shall serve them; and they shall afflict them four hundred years; And also that nation, whom they shall serve, will I judge: and afterward shall they come out with great substance.

(Genesis 15:1-14)

The first lesson of captivity was mainly centered on an individual, Joseph, and an *accident* of the children of Israel being in "the right place at the wrong time", from a human point of view. Let us skip ahead a bit. The children of Israel leave Egypt and become the nation of Israel in a substantial portion, but not all, of the lands that the LORD delivered them to the land of Canaan to acquire. Progress was stopped because some of the Israelites just did not believe in the power of God, to deliver the land. So, the final acquisition is delayed.

Though the first of the lessons of captivity are ended, there are more to come. The remaining captivities would involve intentional, "eyes wide open" misdeeds of larger parts of the nation of Israel; sometimes, all of it. One more of God's blessing to the nations of the world, through the medium of captivity, is revealed in Daniel. Daniel was taken as a captive to Babylon.

"Wait a minute! I thought that the next captivities would involve the entire nation. Daniel is only an individual. What do you mean the entire nation?"

Okay, let me explain how God works. The nation of Israel, in the time of Daniel, was in captivity to the Babylonians. However, God still chooses to send His message through individuals: sometimes they are referred to as prophets; sometimes simply as servants. Remember, the message was going out to the entire world; particularly, the world outside of the nation of Israel. As a result of the nation of Israel's captivity, other nations were able to capitalize on the wealth of blessings from God that flowed through righteous individuals of the nation: Daniel is one of them.

> *The word of the LORD came again to me, saying, Son of man, when the land sinneth against me by trespassing grievously, then will I stretch out mine hand upon it, and will break the staff of the bread thereof, and will send famine upon it, and will cut off man and beast from it: Though these three men, Noah, Daniel, and Job, were in it, they should deliver but their own souls by their righteousness, saith the Lord GOD.*
>
> *If I cause noisome beasts to pass through the land, and they spoil it, so that it be desolate, that no man may pass through because of the beasts: Though these three men were in it, as I live, saith the Lord GOD, they shall deliver neither sons nor daughters; they only shall be delivered, but the land shall be desolate.*
>
> *Or if I bring a sword upon that land, and say, Sword, go through the land; so that I cut off man and beast from it: Though these three men were in it, as I live, saith the Lord GOD, they shall deliver neither sons nor daughters, but they only shall be delivered themselves.*
>
> *Or if I send a pestilence into that land, and pour out my fury upon it in blood, to cut off from it man and beast: Though Noah, Daniel, and Job, were in it, as I live, saith the Lord GOD, they shall deliver neither son nor daughter; they shall but deliver their own souls by their righteousness*

(Ezekiel 14:12-20)

It should not be surprising that God directs his message at the individuals of the nation, in order to reach the soul of nation. Additionally, if one of those individuals happens to be the leader of the nation, then the message takes flight much faster. Furthermore, when the leader is, shall we say, not democratic enough as to allow for choice; the message takes hold much surer; at least over the short-term. This is the position that the Babylonians were in, at the time of the capture of the nation of Israel. This is the scenario that occurs when Daniel is activated to do the will of God. Once activated, Daniel will reach the king, and sparks will fly. Now, let us get back to the flow.

Daniel describes his purpose, quite simply.

> *Now among these were of the children of Judah, Daniel, Hananiah, Mishael, and Azariah: Unto whom the prince of the eunuchs gave names: for he gave unto Daniel the name of Belteshazzar; and to Hananiah, of Shadrach; and to Mishael, of Meshach; and to Azariah, of Abednego. But Daniel purposed in his heart that he would not defile himself with the portion of the king's meat, nor with the wine which he drank: therefore he requested of the prince of the eunuchs that he might not defile himself. Now God had brought Daniel into favour and tender love with the prince of the eunuchs.*
>
> (Daniel 1:6-9)

The blessings to the nations that flowed through its ruler, king Nebuchadnezzar, are indicated by the king's own statement.

> *Then Nebuchadnezzar came near to the mouth of the burning fiery furnace, and spake, and said, Shadrach, Meshach, and Abednego, ye servants of the most high God, come forth, and come hither. Then Shadrach, Meshach, and Abednego, came forth of the midst of the fire. And the princes, governors, and captains, and the king's counsellors, being gathered together, saw these men, upon whose bodies the fire had no power, nor was an hair of their head singed, neither were their coats changed, nor the smell of fire had passed on them.*
>
> *Then Nebuchadnezzar spake, and said, Blessed be the God of Shadrach, Meshach, and Abednego, who hath sent his angel, and delivered his servants that trusted in him, and have changed the king's word, and yielded their bodies, that they might not serve nor worship any god, except their own God. Therefore I make a decree, That every people, nation, and language, which speak any thing amiss against the God of Shadrach, Meshach, and Abednego, shall be cut in pieces, and their houses shall be made a dunghill: because there is no other God that can deliver after this sort.*
>
> (Daniel 3:26-29)

However, as we have seen before; messages from God have a limited memory-span among humans. This is no less true for messages delivered by the servants of God, to the people; we saw this with Joseph in Israel. Well, it happened again with Babylon. "No problem," as they say; since the nation of Israel is still captive. As a captive people, the LORD provides the opportunity for the Israelites to continue to perform their function of being God priests and prophets. God even calls forth other messengers from the nation of their captors to reinforce His Word.

Daniel is still in active service when King Cyrus of Persia takes over the lead position of political dominion, in the world. However, the effect of Abraham's children in the world of king Cyrus does not reach fruition until the deeds of Nehemiah. It is through the work of the Spirit of God in king Cyrus, and its continuation in the good will of Artaxerxes the king, that the visible example for service to God on earth is re-established. This example is God's son, the nation of Israel; redeemed again.

> *And it came to pass in the month Nisan, in the twentieth year of Artaxerxes the king, that wine was before him: and I took up the wine, and gave it unto the king. Now I had not been beforetime sad in his presence. Wherefore the king said unto me, Why is thy countenance sad, seeing thou art not sick? this is nothing else but sorrow of heart.*
>
> *Then I was very sore afraid, And said unto the king, Let the king live for ever: why should not my countenance be sad, when the city, the place of my fathers' sepulchres, lieth waste, and the gates thereof are consumed with fire?*
>
> *Then the king said unto me, For what dost thou make request?*
>
> *So I prayed to the God of heaven. And I said unto the king, If it please the king, and if thy servant have found favour in thy sight, that thou wouldest send me unto Judah, unto the city of my fathers' sepulchres, that I may build it.*
>
> *And the king said unto me, (the queen also sitting by him,) For how long shall thy journey be? and when wilt thou return?*
>
> *So it pleased the king to send me; and I set him a time. Moreover I said unto the king, If it please the king, let letters be given me to the governors beyond the river, that they may convey me over till I come into Judah; And a*

> *letter unto Asaph the keeper of the king's forest, that he may give me timber to make beams for the gates of the palace which appertained to the house, and for the wall of the city, and for the house that I shall enter into.*
>
> *And the king granted me, according to the good hand of my God upon me.*
>
> (Nehemiah 2:1-8)

There are many more examples of the Godly effect of the children of Abraham on the world; these are just a few selected ones. Through these examples, we see that God has in no way forgotten about the other nations; in the flow of His design God has shown that He will transform them unto righteousness. The tool for the transformation is not more important in God's sight than that which is being transformed. Indeed, God has no respect of persons.

In these examples, we see where God used His son, the nation of Israel, to deliver blessings to the nations of the world. It should, therefore, come as no surprise that God has also used His Son, the Messiah, to bring blessings to all nations. If you do not already know His Son, stay tuned; we will present more detail in other places. However, the following is an introduction to the Messiah.

+=+=+=+=+=+=+=+=+=+=+=+=+=+=+=+=+=+

By way of fulfillment of the statement to Abraham--that all nations of the earth would be blessed by his seed--God arranged matters so that His Son is born of the seed of Abraham. The following is a glimpse at the flow of the introduction of the Son of God to the waiting world of the Roman Empire, through the channel of the son of God, Israel.

The world receives a son, described as being *The Prince of Peace*, as one of his majestic qualifications:

> *For unto us a child is born, unto us a son is given: and the government shall be upon his shoulder: and his name shall be called Wonderful, Counsellor, The mighty God, The everlasting Father, The Prince of Peace. Of the increase of his government and peace there shall be no end, upon the*

throne of David, and upon his kingdom, to order it, and to establish it with judgment and with justice from henceforth even for ever. The zeal of the LORD of hosts will perform this.

(Isaiah 9:6-7)

The world experienced the fulfillment of the prophecy that *Behold, a virgin shall conceive, and bear a son*:

Moreover the LORD spake again unto Ahaz, saying, Ask thee a sign of the LORD thy God; ask it either in the depth, or in the height above.

But Ahaz said, I will not ask, neither will I tempt the LORD.

And he said, Hear ye now, O house of David; Is it a small thing for you to weary men, but will ye weary my God also? Therefore the Lord himself shall give you a sign; Behold, a virgin shall conceive, and bear a son, and shall call his name Immanuel. Butter and honey shall he eat, that he may know to refuse the evil, and choose the good. For before the child shall know to refuse the evil, and choose the good, the land that thou abhorrest shall be forsaken of both her kings.

(Isaiah 7:10-16)

A virgin is chosen to fulfill prophecy; it being by the will of God that *before they came together, she was found with child of the Holy Ghost*:

Now the birth of Jesus Christ was on this wise: When as his mother Mary was espoused to Joseph, before they came together, she was found with child of the Holy Ghost. Then Joseph her husband, being a just man, and not willing to make her a publick example, was minded to put her away privily.

But while he thought on these things, behold, the angel of the LORD appeared unto him in a dream, saying, Joseph, thou son of David, fear not to take unto thee Mary thy wife: for that which is conceived in her is of the Holy

Ghost. And she shall bring forth a son, and thou shalt call his name JESUS: for he shall save his people from their sins.

Now all this was done, that it might be fulfilled which was spoken of the Lord by the prophet, saying, Behold, a virgin shall be with child, and shall bring forth a son, and they shall call his name Emmanuel, which being interpreted is, God with us.

(Matthew 1:18-23)

The mission begins, *unto the lost sheep of the house of Israel*:

Then Jesus went thence, and departed into the coasts of Tyre and Sidon. And, behold, a woman of Canaan came out of the same coasts, and cried unto him, saying, Have mercy on me, O Lord, thou son of David; my daughter is grievously vexed with a devil.

But he answered her not a word.

And his disciples came and besought him, saying, Send her away; for she crieth after us.

But he answered and said, I am not sent but unto the lost sheep of the house of Israel.

Then came she and worshipped him, saying, Lord, help me.

But he answered and said, It is not meet to take the children's bread, and to cast it to dogs.

And she said, Truth, Lord: yet the dogs eat of the crumbs which fall from their masters' table.

Then Jesus answered and said unto her, O woman, great is thy faith: be it unto thee even as thou wilt. And her daughter was made whole from that very hour.

(Matthew 15:21-28)

The voice of divine power is heard, saying, *I lay down my life, that I might take it again*:

> *I am the good shepherd, and know my sheep, and am known of mine. As the Father knoweth me, even so know I the Father: and I lay down my life for the sheep.*
>
> *And other sheep I have, which are not of this fold: them also I must bring, and they shall hear my voice; and there shall be one fold, and one shepherd.*
>
> *Therefore doth my Father love me, because I lay down my life, that I might take it again. No man taketh it from me, but I lay it down of myself. I have power to lay it down, and I have power to take it again. This commandment have I received of my Father.*
>
> (John 10:14-18)

Introducing the Gospel, that you may *Believe on the Lord Jesus Christ, and thou shalt be saved, and thy house*:

> *And at midnight Paul and Silas prayed, and sang praises unto God: and the prisoners heard them. And suddenly there was a great earthquake, so that the foundations of the prison were shaken: and immediately all the doors were opened, and every one's bands were loosed. And the keeper of the prison awaking out of his sleep, and seeing the prison doors open, he drew out his sword, and would have killed himself, supposing that the prisoners had been fled.*
>
> *But Paul cried with a loud voice, saying, Do thyself no harm: for we are all here.*
>
> *Then he called for a light, and sprang in, and came trembling, and fell down before Paul and Silas, And brought them out, and said, Sirs, what must I do to be saved?*
>
> *And they said, Believe on the Lord Jesus Christ, and thou shalt be saved, and thy house. And they spake unto him the word of the Lord, and to all that were in his house.*

And he took them the same hour of the night, and washed their stripes; and was baptized, he and all his, straightway. And when he had brought them into his house, he set meat before them, and rejoiced, believing in God with all his house.

(Acts 16:25-34)

+=+=+=+=+=+=+=+=+=+=+=+=+=+=+=+=+=+=+=+

The heathen forgotten,
Or so it was thought;
But a miracle for them
God has wrought:

A people prepared
To carry His name,
To the forgotten ones
They deliver the same.

The nation of Israel,
The chosen one,
Called by God,
His stiffnecked son.

Sometimes up,
And often down;
Still, the world's peace
In them was found.

A message prepared
According to a Holy plan,
To deliver the redemption
Of every man.

Redemption from sin's grip,
A burden on mankind,
Which expresses itself
In all that we find

In the world around us,
And in all that we do;
Even in sharing
Between me and you.

A journey most glorious,
Sometimes causing grief;
Yet, it moves to a place of
Blessed, sweet relief.

The burden is not heavy,
As delivered by the LORD;

*He accomplishes His purpose
By the power of His Word.*

*The heathen remembered,
By God above;
In a people sent forth
To show His love.*

Chapter 12a

If They Will Not Hear

What I write now is not meant to condone anyone's evil action. It is also not written to justify those who take aggressive actions today because these actions were allowed by God in times past. These actions were allowed then because of the newness of the nations that were in existence: people need to understand that mankind has progressed in the last thousand, or so, years. I, personally, would like to think that mankind has progressed to a level of confidence that does not fear any form of disagreement among us, especially not about the logic of our religious stance before God.

I would like to think that in each religion that exists, those who truly participate have been able to tap into the power of God. Furthermore, it is my prayer that this power will be raised, through the actions of those who love God, to stand against any adversary; without having to destroy the adversary. This I would like to think. However, beyond my thoughts; surely, this is the power of the Word.

But when I take myself back to the time of the Old Testament, I begin to understand where those nations that are stuck in that period could experience a different world from the one in which I live. Furthermore, I understand that there are nations that have not accepted the message of Christ. I would like it very much if all men were followers of God through the message of Jesus Christ. However, I am constrained by God to work with what is, in anticipation of what will be.

I pray to my Father in Heaven that by this message we can accomplish two things: to give wisdom to the nations, and to send a reminder to the saints of God.

All nations, including those that are not in agreement with Christian principles, have the ability to remove those who are offensive to them; rather than destroying them by murder or government sanctioned executions. The wisdom of God tells you to proceed in a milder manner for those who are basically ignorant of what the nation's religious leaders hold to be the truth of God about good and evil. I believe that by applying the rules of a child to those who have entered your midst, you can best serve God in this matter. God declared to the nation of Israel that he did not punish the children for not knowing what is good and evil.

> *Also the LORD was angry with me for your sakes, saying, Thou also shalt not go in thither. But Joshua the son of Nun, which standeth before thee, he shall go in thither: encourage him: for he shall cause Israel to inherit it. Moreover your little ones, which ye said should be a prey, and your children, which in that day had no knowledge between good and evil, they shall go in thither, and unto them will I give it, and they shall possess it. But as for you, turn you, and take your journey into the wilderness by the way of the Red sea.*
>
> (Deuteronomy 1:37-40)

To my sibling in the Christian faith, and any others who believe in the message of Jesus Christ (even if they only see him as a prophet of God), I say: study his manner of personal behavior, and his interactions with his followers. Of particular interest for our purposes here, are the instructions he gave to these seventy that he sent forth to do missionary work.

> *After these things the Lord appointed other seventy also, and sent them two and two before his face into every city and place, whither he himself would come.*
>
> *Therefore said he unto them, The harvest truly is great, but the labourers are few: pray ye therefore the Lord of the harvest, that he would send forth labourers into his harvest. Go your ways: behold, I send you forth as lambs among wolves. Carry neither purse, nor scrip, nor shoes: and salute no man by the way.*
>
> *And into whatsoever house ye enter, first say, Peace be to this house. And if the son of peace be there, your peace shall rest upon it: if not, it shall turn to you again. And in the same house remain, eating and drinking such things as*

> *they give: for the labourer is worthy of his hire. Go not from house to house.*
>
> *And into whatsoever city ye enter, and they receive you, eat such things as are set before you: And heal the sick that are therein, and say unto them, The kingdom of God is come nigh unto you. But into whatsoever city ye enter, and they receive you not, go your ways out into the streets of the same, and say, Even the very dust of your city, which cleaveth on us, we do wipe off against you: notwithstanding be ye sure of this, that the kingdom of God is come nigh unto you.*
>
> *But I say unto you, that it shall be more tolerable in that day for Sodom, than for that city.*
>
> (Luke 10:1-12)

Do not add to the message; do not add any measure of flavor; do not add any requirement for unnecessary sacrifice; in an attempt to prove your devotion to God. God knows who is and who is not truly devoted to Him. No amount of work, and no amount of sacrifice, can compensate for a lack of faith.

> *Not every one that saith unto me, Lord, Lord, shall enter into the kingdom of heaven; but he that doeth the will of my Father which is in heaven. Many will say to me in that day, Lord, Lord, have we not prophesied in thy name? and in thy name have cast out devils? and in thy name done many wonderful works? And then will I profess unto them, I never knew you: depart from me, ye that work iniquity.*
>
> (Matthew 7:21-23)

Furthermore, only the burdens placed upon you by God, are to be carried forward. It is only through the yokes placed by God that eternal benefit is achieved. Regardless of what any man says; regardless of what any man writes, including these writings; follow God. Additionally, do not lose track of the pronouncement of Christ that tells of his yoke.

> *All things are delivered unto me of my Father: and no man knoweth the Son, but the Father; neither knoweth any man*

> *the Father, save the Son, and he to whomsoever the Son will reveal him.*
>
> *Come unto me, all ye that labour and are heavy laden, and I will give you rest. Take my yoke upon you, and learn of me; for I am meek and lowly in heart: and ye shall find rest unto your souls. For my yoke is easy, and my burden is light.*

(Matthew 11:27-30)

Also remember; some of the old ways are still followed among those nations of the world that have not received the witness of Christ (yet). These nations may not know the fullness of the law of Love. They might still follow the law of judgment and fear. In such nations, the religious leaders only partially hear the word of the LORD, and they strictly follow this incomplete message. Be sure that you personally know the, already fulfilled, rules of law that they may be using to execute judgment, rather than extending mercy. We need to pay attention to their motivations.

The following may be one starting point for the aggressive treatment of those thought to be religiously different from the mainstream. The following Scripture may be used as justification for malicious actions by the ruling religious order, against anyone professing a relationship with God that is different from the ruling religious order.

> *When the LORD thy God shall cut off the nations from before thee, whither thou goest to possess them, and thou succeedest them, and dwellest in their land; Take heed to thyself that thou be not snared by following them, after that they be destroyed from before thee; and that thou inquire not after their gods, saying, How did these nations serve their gods? even so will I do likewise. Thou shalt not do so unto the LORD thy God: for every abomination to the LORD, which he hateth, have they done unto their gods; for even their sons and their daughters they have burnt in the fire to their gods. What thing soever I command you, observe to do it: thou shalt not add thereto, nor diminish from it.*

(Deuteronomy 12:29-32)

In some nations, any augmentation, diminution or transformation of the written text of old to fit the new dispensation, given by God through the Messiah, has its dangers; **real dangers**. This is perceived as the practice of making other gods, which can be either physical objects or mental images for the mind of man. The new dispensation, given by God through the Messiah, is perceived by some nations as not being the true presence with man of the power of the Living God, encased in the frame of a man.

This aggressive logic does not allow God to give grace to mankind. This greatly limit's the ability of ministers to present the message of the Gospel. For, it is this grace of God, allowing us to move in the power of God, which adds the responsibility for us to present the blessing of conversion to others. Our participation in conversion is limited to the process of communing with someone who does not believe as we do, and sharing with him the message that we have received from God. The objective of conversion is to change the life of the person being converted; its purpose is not, to take the life of anyone. The sanctity of the life of the hearer, also applies to those who do not listen to what we say. God wants converts; not corpses.

Fear and destruction was mainly what early man understood, when relating to different nations. God allowed us to proceed in this primitive fashion until we had achieved maturity in Him. God has advanced mankind beyond this point, but there are some who still have not accepted this advancement. They are still following their interpretation of the proper application of the correction to society that is described in the Scripture that follows.

> *If thy brother, the son of thy mother, or thy son, or thy daughter, or the wife of thy bosom, or thy friend, which is as thine own soul, entice thee secretly, saying, Let us go and serve other gods, which thou hast not known, thou, nor thy fathers; Namely, of the gods of the people which are round about you, nigh unto thee, or far off from thee, from the one end of the earth even unto the other end of the earth; Thou shalt not consent unto him, nor hearken unto him; neither shall thine eye pity him, neither shalt thou spare, neither shalt thou conceal him: But thou shalt surely kill him; thine hand shall be first upon him to put him to death, and afterwards the hand of all the people. And thou shalt stone him with stones, that he die; because he hath*

sought to thrust thee away from the LORD thy God, which brought thee out of the land of Egypt, from the house of bondage.

(Deuteronomy 13:6-10)

Under the former rule of law, even the prophets were subject to strict discipline. God has advanced mankind beyond this point, but there are some who have still not accepted this advancement. The former behavior was God's behavioral allowance that was given to somewhat primitive man, to assist him in his intellectual pursuit of understanding of God and the world around him.

If there arise among you a prophet, or a dreamer of dreams, and giveth thee a sign or a wonder, And the sign or the wonder come to pass, whereof he spake unto thee, saying, Let us go after other gods, which thou hast not known, and let us serve them; Thou shalt not hearken unto the words of that prophet, or that dreamer of dreams: for the LORD your God proveth you, to know whether ye love the LORD your God with all your heart and with all your soul. Ye shall walk after the LORD your God, and fear him, and keep his commandments, and obey his voice, and ye shall serve him, and cleave unto him. And that prophet, or that dreamer of dreams, shall be put to death; because he hath spoken to turn you away from the LORD your God, which brought you out of the land of Egypt, and redeemed you out of the house of bondage, to thrust thee out of the way which the LORD thy God commanded thee to walk in. So shalt thou put the evil away from the midst of thee.

(Deuteronomy 13:1-5)

And yes, the former behavior was even applied to those who followed the sayings and practices of such prophecies and prophets. God has advanced mankind beyond this point, but there are some who have still not accepted this advancement. This was a behavioral allowance for somewhat primitive man, to assist him in his intellectual pursuit of understanding of God and the world around him.

If thou shalt hear say in one of thy cities, which the LORD thy God hath given thee to dwell there, saying, Certain men, the children of Belial, are gone out from among you, and have withdrawn the inhabitants of their city, saying, Let us go and serve other gods, which ye have not known; Then shalt thou inquire, and make search, and ask diligently; and, behold, if it be truth, and the thing certain, that such abomination is wrought among you; Thou shalt surely smite the inhabitants of that city with the edge of the sword, destroying it utterly, and all that is therein, and the cattle thereof, with the edge of the sword. And thou shalt gather all the spoil of it into the midst of the street thereof, and shalt burn with fire the city, and all the spoil thereof every whit, for the LORD thy God: and it shall be an heap for ever; it shall not be built again. And there shall cleave nought of the cursed thing to thine hand: that the LORD may turn from the fierceness of his anger, and show thee mercy, and have compassion upon thee, and multiply thee, as he hath sworn unto thy fathers;

(Deuteronomy 13:12-17)

    These early rules of law are no longer applicable to the people of God, according to the word of God, delivered by the prophets; as we will see in a moment

    The continued practice of the early rules, in some nations, makes it very difficult for missionaries to proclaim the word of the LORD through the message of Christ. This is especially true when the message includes the notion that Jesus is God. This would be perceived by these nations as being equivalent to causing the people to go after other gods. Thus, they might feel justified in putting the person producing the message to death. However, even if such claims are made, God no longer allows them any such excuse under the law of Love and obedience--which is better than sacrifice--especially, not the sacrifice of a human life. But not all have accepted this; yet.

    God modified the stern requirements, as mankind became more and more mature. In times past, we were just a shade above the animals in our behavior; and some of us are still there. God, however, has pressed us forth to a higher calling. This calling is to express His message to the world. God is moving us toward the higher messages of peace among men. The LORD, through the prophets, told us the better way of serving God: this is active now.

And there shall come forth a rod out of the stem of Jesse, and a Branch shall grow out of his roots: And the spirit of the LORD shall rest upon him, the spirit of wisdom and understanding, the spirit of counsel and might, the spirit of knowledge and of the fear of the LORD; And shall make him of quick understanding in the fear of the LORD: and he shall not judge after the sight of his eyes, neither reprove after the hearing of his ears: But with righteousness shall he judge the poor, and reprove with equity for the meek of the earth: and he shall smite the earth with the rod of his mouth, and with the breath of his lips shall he slay the wicked.

And righteousness shall be the girdle of his loins, and faithfulness the girdle of his reins. The wolf also shall dwell with the lamb, and the leopard shall lie down with the kid; and the calf and the young lion and the fatling together; and a little child shall lead them. And the cow and the bear shall feed; their young ones shall lie down together: and the lion shall eat straw like the ox. And the sucking child shall play on the hole of the asp, and the weaned child shall put his hand on the cockatrice' den.

They shall not hurt nor destroy in all my holy mountain: for the earth shall be full of the knowledge of the LORD, as the waters cover the sea.

(Isaiah 11:1-9)

And it shall come to pass afterward, that I will pour out my spirit upon all flesh; and your sons and your daughters shall prophesy, your old men shall dream dreams, your young men shall see visions: And also upon the servants and upon the handmaids in those days will I pour out my spirit.

And I will show wonders in the heavens and in the earth, blood, and fire, and pillars of smoke. The sun shall be turned into darkness, and the moon into blood, before the great and the terrible day of the LORD come.

And it shall come to pass, that whosoever shall call on the name of the LORD shall be delivered: for in mount Zion and in Jerusalem shall be deliverance, as the LORD hath said, and in the remnant whom the LORD shall call.

(Joel 2:28-32)

Furthermore, if you still accept instruction under the former rules, I will show you another way that is contained in these Scriptures.

God, in His wisdom, proclaimed a better way for us to use. We have briefly touched on the change that God has proclaimed in the kingdom of man. For you to start taking hold of the power of that change, I send this petition, by the grace of God, to you, O nations that are not in agreement with Christian principles. In full agreement with your religious beliefs, go to God and ask Him to further reveal to you the milder manner that must be used with those who are considered to be ignorant of that which you hold to be true about Him. Ask the LORD for full understanding of His intentions in the action He performed in the time of Moses. Ask Him to open up your understanding of the concept of children.

Moreover your little ones, which ye said should be a prey, and your children, which in that day had no knowledge between good and evil, they shall go in thither, and unto them will I give it, and they shall possess it.

(Deuteronomy 1:39)

I believe that He will show you that a child may be anyone who truly does not understand the good and evil of a particular situation. God does not work as man's courts operate. The LORD does not punish an individual for being ignorant. Thank you, God, that You do not punish us when we are ignorant. For, if You did, then no man would stand in Your presence, ever.

You must clearly understand that God will hold you accountable for judging your brother: and that every man is your brother.

Judge not, that ye be not judged. For with what judgment ye judge, ye shall be judged: and with what measure ye mete, it shall be measured to you again.

And why beholdest thou the mote that is in thy brother's eye, but considerest not the beam that is in thine own eye? Or how wilt thou say to thy brother, Let me pull out the mote out of thine eye; and, behold, a beam is in thine own eye? Thou hypocrite, first cast out the beam out of thine own eye; and then shalt thou see clearly to cast out the mote out of thy brother's eye.

(Matthew 7:1-5)

For if ye forgive men their trespasses, your heavenly Father will also forgive you: But if ye forgive not men their trespasses, neither will your Father forgive your trespasses.

(Matthew 6:14-15)

I believe that by applying the rule of the childlike state to those who have entered your midst, you can best serve God in this matter. God in His judgment of the nation of Israel did not punish the children for not knowing what is good and evil. Each nation has the responsibility to apply this grace of God to those among them who are basically children as pertains to matters involving the worship of God in the nation.

The way to do this as a nation is to invoke your right to remove those who are offensive to your culture. This is the righteous way; as opposed to the unrighteous action of destroying them by murder or government sanctioned execution. The removal, if done in a public fashion, will surely fulfill the requirement to set an example. By a definite removal you have done what is required even under the old rules. You have, thereby, reacted, before God in such a way that all the listening people of your nation *shall hear, and fear, and shall do no more any such wickedness as this is among you.*

If, however, you decide to show grace, as God has shown you grace; and you allow them to stay; then, remember your obligation. The government and the religious leaders have the responsibility from God, and the accountability to God, to protect those that they have allowed into the nation. This responsibility must be carried out in a fashion like unto that of the treatment of a native born inhabitant of the country. This too, is a part of the Law of God, as given to Moses.

And if a stranger sojourn with thee in your land, ye shall not vex him. But the stranger that dwelleth with you shall be unto you as one born among you, and thou shalt love him as thyself; for ye were strangers in the land of Egypt: I am the LORD your God.

(Leviticus 19:33-34)

Also, for those Christians who have an extreme desire to be martyrs; understand that this is not necessary. Furthermore, it may be in violation of the principles of Christ. Remember the charge that Jesus gave to the twelve he sent out.

> *And he called unto him the twelve, and began to send them forth by two and two; and gave them power over unclean spirits; And commanded them that they should take nothing for their journey, save a staff only; no scrip, no bread, no money in their purse: But be shod with sandals; and not put on two coats. And he said unto them, In what place soever ye enter into an house, there abide till ye depart from that place. And whosoever shall not receive you, nor hear you, when ye depart thence, shake off the dust under your feet for a testimony against them. Verily I say unto you, It shall be more tolerable for Sodom and Gomorrha in the day of judgment, than for that city.*

(Mark 6:7-11)

Sometimes, it shows greater love for God, and for those to whom we witness, to leave them alone and pray for them; than it does to persist in attempting to modify their behavior. After all, it is not by our words that we can convert anyone, but by the moving of the Spirit of God. This can be done from near or from afar, as Jesus Christ demonstrated.

> *And when Jesus was entered into Capernaum, there came unto him a centurion, beseeching him, And saying, Lord, my servant lieth at home sick of the palsy, grievously tormented.*
>
> *And Jesus saith unto him, I will come and heal him.*
>
> *The centurion answered and said, Lord, I am not worthy that thou shouldest come under my roof: but speak the word only, and my servant shall be healed. For I am a man under authority, having soldiers under me: and I say to this man, Go, and he goeth; and to another, Come, and he cometh; and to my servant, Do this, and he doeth it.*
>
> *When Jesus heard it, he marvelled, and said to them that followed, Verily I say unto you, I have not found so great faith, no, not in Israel. And I say unto you, That many shall*

> *come from the east and west, and shall sit down with Abraham, and Isaac, and Jacob, in the kingdom of heaven. But the children of the kingdom shall be cast out into outer darkness: there shall be weeping and gnashing of teeth.*
>
> *And Jesus said unto the centurion, Go thy way; and as thou hast believed, so be it done unto thee. And his servant was healed in the selfsame hour.*
>
> (Matthew 8:5-13)

Finally, remember the words of the apostle who told us how to love others. Be sure that we are not placing ourselves in a position to be seen for a public display, for our sacrifice: not even to be seen by the LORD and the Lord for this. The favor of man does not fulfill the requirement of God.

However, we must all do what we feel God requires of us; even if this means that we sacrifice our life in the doing. But be very sure that this is a requirement of God for you, and not goading of man. Be very sure that it is the price that God has called you to pay; for, if it is not of God, then ---

> *Though I speak with the tongues of men and of angels, and have not charity, I am become as sounding brass, or a tinkling cymbal. And though I have the gift of prophecy, and understand all mysteries, and all knowledge; and though I have all faith, so that I could remove mountains, and have not charity, I am nothing. And though I bestow all my goods to feed the poor, and though I give my body to be burned, and have not charity, it profiteth me nothing.*
>
> (1 Corinthians 13:1-3)

The Word from the Bible

Deuteronomy 4:12-19

And the LORD spake unto you out of the midst of the fire: ye heard the voice of the words, but saw no similitude; only ye heard a voice. And he declared unto you his covenant, which he commanded you to perform, even ten commandments; and he wrote them upon two tables of stone.

And the LORD commanded me at that time to teach you statutes and judgments, that ye might do them in the land whither ye go over to possess it. Take ye therefore good heed unto yourselves; for ye saw no manner of similitude on the day that the LORD spake unto you in Horeb out of the midst of the fire: Lest ye corrupt yourselves, and make you a graven image, the similitude of any figure, the likeness of male or female, The likeness of any beast that is on the earth, the likeness of any winged fowl that flieth in the air, The likeness of any thing that creepeth on the ground, the likeness of any fish that is in the waters beneath the earth: And lest thou lift up thine eyes unto heaven, and when thou seest the sun, and the moon, and the stars, even all the host of heaven, shouldest be driven to worship them, and serve them, which the LORD thy God hath divided unto all nations under the whole heaven.

1 Chronicles 16:23-35

Sing unto the LORD, all the earth; show forth from day to day his salvation. Declare his glory among the heathen; his marvellous works among all nations. For great is the LORD, and greatly to be praised: he also is to be feared above all gods. For all the gods of the people are idols: but the LORD made the heavens. Glory and honour are in his presence; strength and gladness are in his place.

Give unto the LORD, ye kindreds of the people, give unto the LORD glory and strength. Give unto the LORD the glory due unto his name: bring an offering, and come before him: worship the LORD in the beauty of holiness.

Fear before him, all the earth: the world also shall be stable, that it be not moved. Let the heavens be glad, and let the earth rejoice: and let men say among the nations, The LORD reigneth. Let the sea roar, and the fulness thereof: let the fields rejoice, and all that is therein. Then shall the trees of the wood sing out at the presence of the LORD, because he cometh to judge the earth.

O give thanks unto the LORD; for he is good; for his mercy endureth for ever. And say ye, Save us, O God of our salvation, and gather us together, and deliver us from the heathen, that we may give thanks to thy holy name, and glory in thy praise.

Psalm 86:8-10

Among the gods there is none like unto thee, O Lord; neither are there any works like unto thy works. All nations whom thou hast made shall come and worship before thee, O Lord; and shall glorify thy name. For thou art great, and doest wondrous things: thou art God alone.

Acts 17:24-29

God that made the world and all things therein, seeing that he is Lord of heaven and earth, dwelleth not in temples made with hands; Neither is worshipped with men's hands, as though he needed any thing, seeing he giveth to all life, and breath, and all things; And hath made of one blood all nations of men for to dwell on all the face of the earth, and hath determined the times before appointed, and the bounds of their habitation; That they should seek the Lord, if haply they might feel after him, and find him, though he be not far from every one of us: For in him we live, and move, and have our being; as certain also of your own poets have said, For we are also his offspring. Forasmuch then as we are the offspring of God, we ought not to think that the Godhead is like unto gold, or silver, or stone, graven by art and man's device.

Psalm 100:1-5

A Psalm of praise.

Make a joyful noise unto the LORD, all ye lands. Serve the LORD with gladness: come before his presence with singing. Know ye that the LORD he is God: it is he that hath made us, and not we ourselves; we are his people, and the sheep of his pasture. Enter into his gates with thanksgiving, and into his courts with praise: be thankful unto him, and bless his name. For the LORD is good; his mercy is everlasting; and his truth endureth to all generations.

Chapter 13

The Great Consolidation

This part of our journey of understanding is almost complete. We have only two steps remaining. Let us in this phase put the finishing touches on where we are heading.

Our explanations to this point have been designed to provoke you to want to join in an ongoing enterprise of Godly living. We have laid out where we came from, as a world. We have shown the requirement for living in a right relationship with the LORD that God places on mankind. We will now tell you, if you do not already know, what is in it for you.

The Great Consolidation: This sounds like a myth that is unachievable with the current state of mankind. Each nation has its own view of how reality must be shaped; there is little room among nations for compromise. Furthermore, where there is compromise, it generally follows some carefully mapped out political script for each nation. These scripts are designed to promote the best interest of the nation that developed them; naturally. There is, however, a best way of obtaining unity.

The Great Consolidation: This is the time when mankind understands that many of the slogans that have arisen from nations, like the United States of America, for example, are in fact directions from God. Those who have lived in the United States of America, as well as those who have observed the actions of this country, know of the preoccupation with Human Rights. This is a most noble thing to attempt to achieve; however, it is incomplete. Even so, let us start with this notion of Human Rights.

Human rights are said to be inalienable rights, which were endowed by our Creator. The ones that are listed are life, liberty and the pursuit of happiness. Well, all those who are reading this can agree with one of these; that is life. Since you are reading this, it is a real STRONG probability that you have life. This life was endowed by the

Creator. Yes, the vessels that were used are called mom and dad, by some, and mother and father, by almost all others. Some, however, in this day, have fathers that are little more than a test-tube. Yes, there was a human behind the contents of the test-tube, but this human has been rendered unnecessary by the modern processes of science. So far, however, mothers have not been rendered unnecessary; at least not at the time of this writing.

There are still two other rights to ponder, if you believe in this minimalist view of the endowments of the Creator. What about this thing known as liberty. Well this one becomes sticky when dealing with God. You see, God never promised us liberty. Oh, he did say that we would be able to enjoy the fruits of the land; however, with this enjoyment comes responsibility. This is the standard maxim: with authority comes responsibility. This is, furthermore, not a responsibility directly man to man, but only tangentially.

"Whoa! What do you mean that we only have a tangential responsibility to one another?"

Consider the children of Israel. God gave them a really big set of things to do, on a daily basis. He covered everything that can be thought of in human interactions. There are laws for major crimes; there are laws for minor incidents. There are rules of conduct for interaction with one another; there are edicts for interactions with the servants of God, known as priests in that day.

God declared who was included, and who was excluded. He told the children of Israel how to behave with their neighbors, as well as how to behave with foreigners. God covered all that one can imagine that man can do with man, and with the land. There is, for the follower of the Law of Moses, no liberty. They are bound to the Law, and can do nothing but what it says if righteousness is their goal.

The penalties for violations of the Law of Moses can be as easy as saying, "I'm sorry". They can be as comprehensive as the loss of life by stoning. They can even be as catastrophic as to cause entire nations to be removed from the face of the earth: this one is ONLY at God's bidding, or by His direct action. Liberty is not mentioned in the Law of Moses.

What then is mentioned? The word that best describes this is *obligation*. The children of Israel have an obligation to obey God. They have an obligation to seek after God. And when they are wrong they have an obligation to make things right with God. How they will do this is also described in the Law. Written below is a relevant extract from the Law.

> *And the LORD spake unto Moses, saying, Speak unto the children of Israel, saying, If a soul shall sin through ignorance against any of the commandments of the LORD concerning things which ought not to be done, and shall do against any of them:*
>
> (Leviticus 4:1-2)
>
> *If the priest that is anointed do sin according to the sin of the people; then let him bring for his sin, which he hath sinned, a young bullock without blemish unto the LORD for a sin offering. And he shall bring the bullock unto the door of the tabernacle of the congregation before the LORD; and shall lay his hand upon the bullock's head, and kill the bullock before the LORD.*
>
> (Leviticus 4:3-4)
>
> *And if the whole congregation of Israel sin through ignorance, and the thing be hid from the eyes of the assembly, and they have done somewhat against any of the commandments of the LORD concerning things which should not be done, and are guilty; When the sin, which they have sinned against it, is known, then the congregation shall offer a young bullock for the sin, and bring him before the tabernacle of the congregation.*
>
> (Leviticus 4:13-14)
>
> *When a ruler hath sinned, and done somewhat through ignorance against any of the commandments of the LORD his God concerning things which should not be done, and is guilty; Or if his sin, wherein he hath sinned, come to his knowledge; he shall bring his offering, a kid of the goats, a male without blemish:*
>
> (Leviticus 4:22-23)
>
> *And if any one of the common people sin through ignorance, while he doeth somewhat against any of the commandments of the LORD concerning things which ought not to be done, and be guilty; Or if his sin, which he*

hath sinned, come to his knowledge: then he shall bring his offering, a kid of the goats, a female without blemish, for his sin which he hath sinned.

(Leviticus 4:27-28)

And if he bring a lamb for a sin offering, he shall bring it a female without blemish.

(Leviticus 4:32)

"But," you say, "This was all modified starting in some of the writing of the prophets. They mention a different type of world. They tell of a world that is ordained by God to include peace and well-being of humans."

And there shall come forth a rod out of the stem of Jesse, and a Branch shall grow out of his roots: And the spirit of the LORD shall rest upon him, the spirit of wisdom and understanding, the spirit of counsel and might, the spirit of knowledge and of the fear of the LORD; And shall make him of quick understanding in the fear of the LORD: and he shall not judge after the sight of his eyes, neither reprove after the hearing of his ears: But with righteousness shall he judge the poor, and reprove with equity for the meek of the earth: and he shall smite the earth with the rod of his mouth, and with the breath of his lips shall he slay the wicked. And righteousness shall be the girdle of his loins, and faithfulness the girdle of his reins.

The wolf also shall dwell with the lamb, and the leopard shall lie down with the kid; and the calf and the young lion and the fatling together; and a little child shall lead them. And the cow and the bear shall feed; their young ones shall lie down together: and the lion shall eat straw like the ox. And the sucking child shall play on the hole of the asp, and the weaned child shall put his hand on the cockatrice' den.

(Isaiah 11:1-8)

This starts with the nation of Israel.

Behold, the days come, saith the LORD, that I will make a new covenant with the house of Israel, and with the house of Judah: Not according to the covenant that I made with

> *their fathers in the day that I took them by the hand to bring them out of the land of Egypt; which my covenant they brake, although I was an husband unto them, saith the LORD: But this shall be the covenant that I will make with the house of Israel; After those days, saith the LORD, I will put my law in their inward parts, and write it in their hearts; and will be their God, and they shall be my people. And they shall teach no more every man his neighbour, and every man his brother, saying, Know the LORD: for they shall all know me, from the least of them unto the greatest of them, saith the LORD: for I will forgive their iniquity, and I will remember their sin no more.*
>
> (Jeremiah 31:31-34)

In the meantime, and as preparation for that time spreading throughout the world, Scripture admonishes us to voluntarily surrender ourselves to God.

> *I beseech you therefore, brethren, by the mercies of God, that ye present your bodies a living sacrifice, holy, acceptable unto God, which is your reasonable service. And be not conformed to this world: but be ye transformed by the renewing of your mind, that ye may prove what is that good, and acceptable, and perfect, will of God.*
>
> (Romans 12:1-2)

Again, we have this thing of obligation. Let us go a step further and discover how this obligation is to be carried out. As we stated above, God will not force His way upon you. However, those who are wise will clearly understand that we have only one of two choices. We can either submit to God as a willing instrument, or we can be called into the service of God as an unwilling tool. God will have all mankind to promote **His** agenda; not the agenda created by any power of man solely for the benefit of a select group of men.

> *Look unto me, and be ye saved, all the ends of the earth: for I am God, and there is none else. I have sworn by myself, the word is gone out of my mouth in righteousness, and shall not return, That unto me every knee shall bow, every tongue shall swear. Surely, shall one say, in the LORD have I righteousness and strength: even to him shall*

men come; and all that are incensed against him shall be ashamed.

(Isaiah 45:22-24)

God would prefer that we give him this service in a voluntary fashion; as a cheerful giver.

But this I say, He which soweth sparingly shall reap also sparingly; and he which soweth bountifully shall reap also bountifully. Every man according as he purposeth in his heart, so let him give; not grudgingly, or of necessity: for God loveth a cheerful giver. And God is able to make all grace abound toward you; that ye, always having all sufficiency in all things, may abound to every good work: (As it is written, He hath dispersed abroad; he hath given to the poor: his righteousness remaineth for ever.

(2 Corinthians 9:6-9)

You already do this? You freely give your offerings when you go to church? You freely give your offerings when you donate to charities? That's really good! However, it's not enough.

Your offerings are not just money and substance; they are also, talents. It has always been interesting to me that there is a parable of the talents. It is of interest to me because in this context talents are monetary units. How fitting it is that they are called talents, and that we now view talents as those intangible things which we possess as a part of our soul. For us, the term talent has become our abilities to serve: it does not matter whether this service is only for ourselves, or is truly given to others. As you read the following, think of equating them with the talents of the souls of man.

For the kingdom of heaven is as a man travelling into a far country, who called his own servants, and delivered unto them his goods. And unto one he gave five talents, to another two, and to another one; to every man according to his several ability; and straightway took his journey. Then he that had received the five talents went and traded with the same, and made them other five talents. And likewise he that had received two, he also gained other two. But he that had received one went and digged in the earth, and hid his lord's money.

> *After a long time the lord of those servants cometh, and reckoneth with them. And so he that had received five talents came and brought other five talents, saying, Lord, thou deliveredst unto me five talents: behold, I have gained beside them five talents more.*
>
> *His lord said unto him, Well done, thou good and faithful servant: thou hast been faithful over a few things, I will make thee ruler over many things: enter thou into the joy of thy lord.*
>
> *He also that had received two talents came and said, Lord, thou deliveredst unto me two talents: behold, I have gained two other talents beside them.*
>
> *His lord said unto him, Well done, good and faithful servant; thou hast been faithful over a few things, I will make thee ruler over many things: enter thou into the joy of thy lord.*
>
> *Then he which had received the one talent came and said, Lord, I knew thee that thou art an hard man, reaping where thou hast not sown, and gathering where thou hast not strawed: And I was afraid, and went and hid thy talent in the earth: lo, there thou hast that is thine.*
>
> *His lord answered and said unto him, Thou wicked and slothful servant, thou knewest that I reap where I sowed not, and gather where I have not strawed: Thou oughtest therefore to have put my money to the exchangers, and then at my coming I should have received mine own with usury. Take therefore the talent from him, and give it unto him which hath ten talents.*
>
> *For unto every one that hath shall be given, and he shall have abundance: but from him that hath not shall be taken away even that which he hath.*

(Matthew 25:14-29)

This parable, translated into modern times, indicates that we are to use our skills for the Kingdom of God. However, we are not just to utilize those skills; we must improve them, to make them multiply. This is an ability that God gives to us, which can be activated by the spirit that God placed in us. Furthermore, even more talents of the soul can be activated by the Holy Ghost. This is the Holy Ghost, the Spirit of truth, which God has said is available to touch us. By this touch, the Holy Ghost can ignite those parts of us that lie dormant. The Holy Ghost can bring us to our full potential. This is the ten talent solution.

> *But the Comforter, which is the Holy Ghost, whom the Father will send in my name, he shall teach you all things, and bring all things to your remembrance, whatsoever I have said unto you.*
>
> (John 14:26)

So, it can be said that God did give us liberty, of a sort. However, this gift of God is not liberty as we understand liberty. The liberty which God gave us is to take what He has given and multiply it. Note that the ten talent solution was achieved by one who knew what the Master required of him. In fact, all three knew what was required, but one decided that he would interpret the requirement for his own benefit. In this interpretation, he missed the true meaning of the message of the Master; and, you see the result. This is the one talent solution.

Liberty is the ability to recognize that God made us with worth. It is the responsibility to take that worth and increase it. Then it is the wisdom that calls us to take that which we have increased and return it to God. When we do this, God will be able to give us other assignments of a greater level of service for His kingdom. This is liberty.

Finally, there is that matter of the pursuit of happiness. We have to be very careful about this one. It is not the same pursuit of happiness that the children of Israel went after when they thought that they could do what pleased them. That was the way that the people in the day of Noah behaved.

> *And it came to pass, when men began to multiply on the face of the earth, and daughters were born unto them, That the sons of God saw the daughters of men that they were fair; and they took them wives of all which they chose. And the LORD said, My spirit shall not always strive with man, for that he also is flesh: yet his days shall be an hundred and twenty years.*
>
> (Genesis 6:1-3)

It was for this reason that God delivered a fresh start for mankind: called, the flood.

And God saw that the wickedness of man was great in the earth, and that every imagination of the thoughts of his heart was only evil continually.

(Genesis 6:5)

Later, Moses delivered the new rules that must govern the interactions of man with man, and man with God.

These are the statutes and judgments, which ye shall observe to do in the land, which the LORD God of thy fathers giveth thee to possess it, all the days that ye live upon the earth. Ye shall utterly destroy all the places, wherein the nations which ye shall possess served their gods, upon the high mountains, and upon the hills, and under every green tree: And ye shall overthrow their altars, and break their pillars, and burn their groves with fire; and ye shall hew down the graven images of their gods, and destroy the names of them out of that place. Ye shall not do so unto the LORD your God.

But unto the place which the LORD your God shall choose out of all your tribes to put his name there, even unto his habitation shall ye seek, and thither thou shalt come: And thither ye shall bring your burnt offerings, and your sacrifices, and your tithes, and heave offerings of your hand, and your vows, and your freewill offerings, and the firstlings of your herds and of your flocks: And there ye shall eat before the LORD your God, and ye shall rejoice in all that ye put your hand unto, ye and your households, wherein the LORD thy God hath blessed thee. Ye shall not do after all the things that we do here this day, every man whatsoever is right in his own eyes.

(Deuteronomy 12:1-8)

The pursuit of happiness is not the acquisition of substance; that is only a temporary pleasure. Look a little deeper at the creation that God made in man. God put a lot of emphasis on the internal when he created man. There is little mention about how Adam actually looked. We do not know if Adam was handsome or ugly. We do not know whether Eve was comely or homely. We do not know if their children were beautiful babies or just *healthy*.

The focus of God, when He started mankind, was on the internal nature of man: this is the same focus that the LORD has for each of us. This became obvious to Cain when he presented his sacrifice; and through Cain it is obvious to us all.

> *And the LORD said unto Cain, Why art thou wroth? and why is thy countenance fallen? If thou doest well, shalt thou not be accepted? and if thou doest not well, sin lieth at the door. And unto thee shall be his desire, and thou shalt rule over him.*

(Genesis 4:6-7)

The pursuit of happiness for man, is the quest for the right relationship with God. No matter how much substance we acquire, we will not find happiness in it. Substance is too tenuous. Consider the following:

> *And he spake a parable unto them, saying, The ground of a certain rich man brought forth plentifully: And he thought within himself, saying, What shall I do, because I have no room where to bestow my fruits? And he said, This will I do: I will pull down my barns, and build greater; and there will I bestow all my fruits and my goods. And I will say to my soul, Soul, thou hast much goods laid up for many years; take thine ease, eat, drink, and be merry.*

> *But God said unto him, Thou fool, this night thy soul shall be required of thee: then whose shall those things be, which thou hast provided?*

> *So is he that layeth up treasure for himself, and is not rich toward God.*

(Luke 12:16-21)

But even those who store up in barns, yet keep their concentration on God, do not mind so much when they come to die. They will lose the substance of earth, but gain the peace of Heaven. I guarantee you that the peace of God, whether on earth or after this life, is to be preferred over anything else that we may acquire. This was the anguish of Jesus Christ when he was on the earth. He had been a part of the pursuit of happiness that is bound in the relationship with God. He had to leave it to come to ***this*** earth. What a downer, as they used to say.

> *As thou hast sent me into the world, even so have I also sent them into the world. And for their sakes I sanctify myself, that they also might be sanctified through the truth.*
>
> *Neither pray I for these alone, but for them also which shall believe on me through their word; That they all may be one; as thou, Father, art in me, and I in thee, that they also may be one in us: that the world may believe that thou hast sent me. And the glory which thou gavest me I have given them; that they may be one, even as we are one: I in them, and thou in me, that they may be made perfect in one; and that the world may know that thou hast sent me, and hast loved them, as thou hast loved me.*
>
> *Father, I will that they also, whom thou hast given me, be with me where I am; that they may behold my glory, which thou hast given me: for thou lovedst me before the foundation of the world. O righteous Father, the world hath not known thee: but I have known thee, and these have known that thou hast sent me. And I have declared unto them thy name, and will declare it: that the love wherewith thou hast loved me may be in them, and I in them.*

(John 17:18-26)

This is the pursuit of happiness: to be glorified by God because of a right relationship with Him.

This is The Great Consolidation: When all people have come to understand that they will only achieve true happiness as they enter the glory of God. Notice that in *John 17:18-26*, written above, Jesus did not ask for glory because he deserved it; which he truly did. Jesus' request was because he had glorified God. Moreover, Jesus asked for this gift from God not to hoard it for himself, but to share it.

Not in fear, but for righteousness sake, Jesus boldly presented his request to God the Father. For *The wicked flee when no man pursueth: but the righteous are bold as a lion.* (Proverbs 28:1) And this is the boldness he had: knowing that he had done what God required. He knew, therefore, that God would honor him, even in the darkest of days. The boldness was freely shared by the apostle Paul, in his personal life and in his ministry; which are actually the same thing. Paul drew freely on the glory given to him by God through Jesus Christ.

> *Be not thou therefore ashamed of the testimony of our Lord, nor of me his prisoner: but be thou partaker of the afflictions of the gospel according to the power of God; Who hath saved us, and called us with an holy calling, not according to our works, but according to his own purpose and grace, which was given us in Christ Jesus before the world began, But is now made manifest by the appearing of our Saviour Jesus Christ, who hath abolished death, and hath brought life and immortality to light through the gospel: Whereunto I am appointed a preacher, and an apostle, and a teacher of the Gentiles.*
>
> *For the which cause I also suffer these things: nevertheless I am not ashamed: for I know whom I have believed, and am persuaded that he is able to keep that which I have committed unto him against that day.*
>
> (2 Timothy 1:8-12)

The correct attitude for the servant of God to achieve, and project, is summed up in the Scripture:

> *No man can serve two masters: for either he will hate the one, and love the other; or else he will hold to the one, and despise the other. Ye cannot serve God and mammon.*
>
> *Therefore I say unto you, Take no thought for your life, what ye shall eat, or what ye shall drink; nor yet for your body, what ye shall put on. Is not the life more than meat, and the body than raiment? Behold the fowls of the air: for they sow not, neither do they reap, nor gather into barns; yet your heavenly Father feedeth them. Are ye not much better than they?*
>
> *Which of you by taking thought can add one cubit unto his stature? And why take ye thought for raiment? Consider the lilies of the field, how they grow; they toil not, neither do they spin: And yet I say unto you, That even Solomon in all his glory was not arrayed like one of these. Wherefore, if God so clothe the grass of the field, which to day is, and*

to morrow is cast into the oven, shall he not much more clothe you, O ye of little faith?

Therefore take no thought, saying, What shall we eat? or, What shall we drink? or, Wherewithal shall we be clothed? (For after all these things do the Gentiles seek:) for your heavenly Father knoweth that ye have need of all these things. But seek ye first the kingdom of God, and his righteousness; and all these things shall be added unto you.

Take therefore no thought for the morrow: for the morrow shall take thought for the things of itself. Sufficient unto the day is the evil thereof.

(Matthew 6:24-34)

When all mankind does this, we will achieve the Great Consolidation.

Running to and
Running fro,
Chasing things,
Man doth go;

In a frantic attempt
To make a name,
To gain a prize
Of earthly fame.

In pursuit of this,
Trying that;
Too often, simply
Falling flat.

We think that
Achieving true worth
Is being special
To folks on earth.

Mankind is surely
Paying the price
For this continuous
Roll of the dice.

Men destroy one another
With no reason or rhyme;
Sometimes, simply
To pass the time.

God's voice is not heard,
Though loud and clear;
We let other, so-called,
Important, things interfere.

Our hearing is blocked
By our quest for the now;
This world is our god,
To it we bow.

But it's really very simple,
The thing to be done;

*The answer is clear
And there's only one.*

*Of all the actions you do,
This must be the start:
Seek God's presence
With all your heart.*

Chapter 13a

The Spirit Descends Like a Dove

Many are aware of the presence of the Spirit of God with man. There are many instances of God's presence erupting within mankind in the Old Testament of the Bible. This was the way that God empowered the prophets, and manifested Himself through them.

> *And it was so, that when he had turned his back to go from Samuel, God gave him another heart: and all those signs came to pass that day. And when they came thither to the hill, behold, a company of prophets met him; and the spirit of God came upon him, and he prophesied among them.*
>
> *And it came to pass, when all that knew him beforetime saw that, behold, he prophesied among the prophets, then the people said one to another, What is this that is come unto the son of Kish? Is Saul also among the prophets? And one of the same place answered and said, But who is their father? Therefore it became a proverb, Is Saul also among the prophets?*
>
> (1 Samuel 10:9-12)

After a time, there is a special time in history in which God changed His interaction with mankind. This time is the time between the Old Testament and the New Testament. The prophets of the Old Testament heralded the coming of the change.

> *And it shall come to pass afterward, that I will pour out my spirit upon all flesh; and your sons and your daughters shall prophesy, your old men shall dream dreams, your young men shall see visions: And also upon the servants and upon the handmaids in those days will I pour out my spirit.*
>
> (Joel 2:28-29)

So that you may understand it clearly, we briefly restate God's manifestation to the prophets, in the time prior to the unfolding. In that day, the Spirit came upon certain men, to move them to action. However, once the task was done, the Spirit seemed to dissipate. The prophets were subject to continual refilling, with new instructions, when the next challenge came. Of course, there are some exceptions to this method; such as seems to be the case for Moses and Elijah, with whom the Spirit seemed to have an almost continual abiding presence.

The first record of a new form of indwelling of the Spirit, specifically, the Holy Ghost, occurs in John the Baptist. In John the Baptist, there is a different interaction of the Spirit with man.

> *But the angel said unto him, Fear not, Zacharias: for thy prayer is heard; and thy wife Elisabeth shall bear thee a son, and thou shalt call his name John. And thou shalt have joy and gladness; and many shall rejoice at his birth. For he shall be great in the sight of the Lord, and shall drink neither wine nor strong drink; and he shall be filled with the Holy Ghost, even from his mother's womb. And many of the children of Israel shall he turn to the Lord their God. And he shall go before him in the spirit and power of Elias, to turn the hearts of the fathers to the children, and the disobedient to the wisdom of the just; to make ready a people prepared for the Lord.*
>
> (Luke 1:13-17)

The mission of John the Baptist ushered in the age when God sends His Spirit in a *residential* fashion to man. No longer is the Spirit just a guest in the nature of man; now the Spirit comes to inhabit the elected person. This is a critical part of the fulfillment of John's mission, as it was revealed to us through the prophet Isaiah.

> *Comfort ye, comfort ye my people, saith your God. Speak ye comfortably to Jerusalem, and cry unto her, that her warfare is accomplished, that her iniquity is pardoned: for she hath received of the Lord's hand double for all her sins. The voice of him that crieth in the wilderness, Prepare ye the way of the LORD, make straight in the desert a highway for our God. Every valley shall be exalted, and every mountain and hill shall be made low: and the crooked shall be made straight, and the rough places plain: And the glory*

of the LORD shall be revealed, and all flesh shall see it together: for the mouth of the LORD hath spoken it.

(Isaiah 40:1-5)

John the Baptist is the one elected to prepare the world for the introduction of the Gospel of the Kingdom of God. This is confirmed by the words of Jesus, in which he tells us that we no longer have to depend on the prophets for the seal of our commitment to God.

And the Pharisees also, who were covetous, heard all these things: and they derided him.

And he said unto them, Ye are they which justify yourselves before men; but God knoweth your hearts: for that which is highly esteemed among men is abomination in the sight of God. The law and the prophets were until John: since that time the kingdom of God is preached, and every man presseth into it.

(Luke 16:14-16)

Now we will receive the words that direct us in forming our commitment to God, directly through the indwelling Holy Ghost. With this new empowerment, by God, a new unfolding has been accomplished. A new way is now before us. John is only the beginning of the example. There is another, whose name is Jesus of Nazareth. The prophets spoke of him as well.

For unto us a child is born, unto us a son is given: and the government shall be upon his shoulder: and his name shall be called Wonderful, Counsellor, The mighty God, The everlasting Father, The Prince of Peace. Of the increase of his government and peace there shall be no end, upon the throne of David, and upon his kingdom, to order it, and to establish it with judgment and with justice from henceforth even for ever. The zeal of the LORD of hosts will perform this.

(Isaiah 9:6-7)

The story of the unfolding into the world of the Prince of Peace begins with a virgin birth, recorded in several books of the Bible. This child is named Jesus, and we know him as Jesus of Nazareth; plus some other names that we will encounter, later. The unfolding reaches a major turning point with the meeting between Jesus of Nazareth and John the Baptist.

> *Then cometh Jesus from Galilee to Jordan unto John, to be baptized of him. But John forbad him, saying, I have need to be baptized of thee, and comest thou to me?*
>
> *And Jesus answering said unto him, Suffer it to be so now: for thus it becometh us to fulfil all righteousness.*
>
> *Then he suffered him.*
>
> *And Jesus, when he was baptized, went up straightway out of the water: and, lo, the heavens were opened unto him, and he saw the Spirit of God descending like a dove, and lighting upon him: And lo a voice from heaven, saying, This is my beloved Son, in whom I am well pleased.*
>
> (Matthew 3:13-17)

Of particular significance for all who love God, is the descending of the Spirit. This is the example for all mankind; a preview of what is to follow. It is the example that all mankind would now be able to accomplish. But why did we need another example? Wasn't John the Baptist enough of an example of the way we are to be in the LORD?

Well, yes and no. If we can start a child from birth in commitment to God, it would be ideal. However, it is not possible since an infant has no knowledge of right and wrong. A young child, therefore, cannot make a choice relative to God; and it is the choice that is critical to the equation. Therefore, for another child like John the Baptist to arise, it can only happen where God directly intervenes with a special miracle in the life of the infant. There is, however, no Scripture that foretells any other such occurrence. We must also remember the power of the Holy Ghost. Only where God has specially prepared the child for service, will the child be able to withstand the presence of the Holy Ghost at such a tender age.

Also, a great part of the child's interaction with the Spirit of God depends on the parents. They, too, must be made ready by God to raise a human vessel such as John the Baptist. And this will not be done by force; it requires prior dedication to God.

> *There was in the days of Herod, the king of Judaea, a certain priest named Zacharias, of the course of Abia: and his wife was of the daughters of Aaron, and her name was*

> *Elisabeth. And they were both righteous before God, walking in all the commandments and ordinances of the Lord blameless. And they had no child, because that Elisabeth was barren, and they both were now well stricken in years. And it came to pass, that while he executed the priest's office before God in the order of his course, According to the custom of the priest's office, his lot was to burn incense when he went into the temple of the Lord.*

(Luke 1:5-9)

The ministry of John the Baptist was necessary to start the Israelites on the path to understanding the new way of the Father, in the Son. This uniqueness is not needed now. What we need is a normal man, living an extraordinary life, in consistent service to God. The Scripture describes the mold of the modern man of God, as declared by Jesus Christ.

> *Ye sent unto John, and he bare witness unto the truth. But I receive not testimony from man: but these things I say, that ye might be saved. He was a burning and a shining light: and ye were willing for a season to rejoice in his light. But I have greater witness than that of John: for the works which the Father hath given me to finish, the same works that I do, bear witness of me, that the Father hath sent me. And the Father himself, which hath sent me, hath borne witness of me. Ye have neither heard his voice at any time, nor seen his shape. And ye have not his word abiding in you: for whom he hath sent, him ye believe not.*
>
> *Search the scriptures; for in them ye think ye have eternal life: and they are they which testify of me.*

(John 5:33-39)

Furthermore, as in all matters of understanding, in the way of the LORD; God provides us with a second witness of the installation of that type of spirit in history; which Spirit is contained in Christ Jesus.

> *But we see Jesus, who was made a little lower than the angels for the suffering of death, crowned with glory and honour; that he by the grace of God should taste death for every man. For it became him, for whom are all things, and by whom are all things, in bringing many sons unto glory,*

> *to make the captain of their salvation perfect through sufferings. For both he that sanctifieth and they who are sanctified are all of one: for which cause he is not ashamed to call them brethren, Saying, I will declare thy name unto my brethren, in the midst of the church will I sing praise unto thee. And again, I will put my trust in him. And again, Behold I and the children which God hath given me.*
>
> *Forasmuch then as the children are partakers of flesh and blood, he also himself likewise took part of the same; that through death he might destroy him that had the power of death, that is, the devil; And deliver them who through fear of death were all their lifetime subject to bondage. For verily he took not on him the nature of angels; but he took on him the seed of Abraham.*
>
> *Wherefore in all things it behoved him to be made like unto his brethren, that he might be a merciful and faithful high priest in things pertaining to God, to make reconciliation for the sins of the people. For in that he himself hath suffered being tempted, he is able to succour them that are tempted.*
>
> (Hebrews 2:9-18)

Jesus of Nazareth is the example of a man who lived that ordinary life, until God pulled him forward to do extraordinary things. His birth was visibly that of ***a*** son of man. However, inside the casing of humanity, God had delivered the soul and the Spirit of ***the*** Son of man. God spawned in this flesh of Jesus the fullness of His glory, as of the Son of God. No human restrictions in morals, ethics or learning. Jesus has the full compliment of God, as designated for containment in humanity, as poured into him by the Word of God, according to the will of God.

> *And the Word was made flesh, and dwelt among us, (and we beheld his glory, the glory as of the only begotten of the Father,) full of grace and truth. John bare witness of him, and cried, saying, This was he of whom I spake, He that cometh after me is preferred before me: for he was before me. And of his fulness have all we received, and grace for grace. For the law was given by Moses, but grace and truth came by Jesus Christ.*
>
> (John 1:14-17)

Jesus Christ is the highest example of the power of God.

> *Let this mind be in you, which was also in Christ Jesus: Who, being in the form of God, thought it not robbery to be equal with God: But made himself of no reputation, and took upon him the form of a servant, and was made in the likeness of men: And being found in fashion as a man, he humbled himself, and became obedient unto death, even the death of the cross. Wherefore God also hath highly exalted him, and given him a name which is above every name: That at the name of Jesus every knee should bow, of things in heaven, and things in earth, and things under the earth; And that every tongue should confess that Jesus Christ is Lord, to the glory of God the Father.*

(Philippians 2:5-11)

The Lord Jesus Christ is the highest example of the full potential of mankind.

> *And we know that all things work together for good to them that love God, to them who are the called according to his purpose. For whom he did foreknow, he also did predestinate to be conformed to the image of his Son, that he might be the firstborn among many brethren.*

(Romans 8:28-29)

This was done when the Spirit descended upon him. At that time, a man was activated who had the permanent indwelling of the Spirit of God. This permanent indwelling gave man an agent of God, working in cooperation with the Spirit of God. This agent operates to unfold a soul with full access to the total knowledge and power of God. This is the spirit and soul of man, fired to the highest heat of accomplishment, by the working of the Spirit of God. Where John was under authority, the Lord Jesus Christ is in possession of complete authority.

> *And Jesus came and spake unto them, saying, All power is given unto me in heaven and in earth.*

(Matthew 28:18)

This is only possible because Jesus Christ fully accepted God as his Father. In fact, Jesus had no other father. To add to the majestic example, Jesus did precisely what his Father told him to. Furthermore, Jesus Christ accomplished all that his Father set before him to do.

> *These words spake Jesus, and lifted up his eyes to heaven, and said, Father, the hour is come; glorify thy Son, that thy Son also may glorify thee: As thou hast given him power over all flesh, that he should give eternal life to as many as thou hast given him. And this is life eternal, that they might know thee the only true God, and Jesus Christ, whom thou hast sent. I have glorified thee on the earth: I have finished the work which thou gavest me to do.*
>
> *And now, O Father, glorify thou me with thine own self with the glory which I had with thee before the world was. I have manifested thy name unto the men which thou gavest me out of the world: thine they were, and thou gavest them me; and they have kept thy word. Now they have known that all things whatsoever thou hast given me are of thee. For I have given unto them the words which thou gavest me; and they have received them, and have known surely that I came out from thee, and they have believed that thou didst send me.*
>
> (John 17:1-8)

The descending of the Spirit at the baptism of Jesus is the signal of a new benefit allowed to all mankind. The veil, which caused restricted access to God, is being removed. Man has reached the turning point; the point where mankind is able, each one of us, to speak directly to God. In case I have slipped somewhere in this writing, and stressed that this manifestation was solely *new*, let me correct that error. This is not a new thing; it is an unfolding of a thing that is from before the foundation of the world.

> *When the Son of man shall come in his glory, and all the holy angels with him, then shall he sit upon the throne of his glory: And before him shall be gathered all nations: and he shall separate them one from another, as a shepherd divideth his sheep from the goats: And he shall set the sheep on his right hand, but the goats on the left. Then shall the King say unto them on his right hand, Come, ye blessed of my Father, inherit the kingdom prepared for you from the foundation of the world: For I was an hungred, and ye gave me meat: I was thirsty, and ye gave*

me drink: I was a stranger, and ye took me in: Naked, and ye clothed me: I was sick, and ye visited me: I was in prison, and ye came unto me.

(Matthew 25:31-36)

Jesus Christ is the revelation of the mystery that was there before our eyes, all along. Jesus Christ is the embodiment of the proclamation of many prophecies. Jesus Christ is the full representation of the Everlasting Father.

And therefore did the Jews persecute Jesus, and sought to slay him, because he had done these things on the sabbath day. But Jesus answered them, My Father worketh hitherto, and I work.

Therefore the Jews sought the more to kill him, because he not only had broken the sabbath, but said also that God was his Father, making himself equal with God.

(John 5:16-18)

As the Son of God, he has full right to consider himself of the same nature as his Father. Wherefore Scripture tells us:

Let this mind be in you, which was also in Christ Jesus: Who, being in the form of God, thought it not robbery to be equal with God:

(Philippians 2:5)

As the first heir of the Father, the only begotten Son of God, the Son of man, in Jesus Christ is the full Authority of God. Ownership of all that belongs to the Father has been given to the Son of man by His Father.

All things are delivered unto me of my Father: and no man knoweth the Son, but the Father; neither knoweth any man the Father, save the Son, and he to whomsoever the Son will reveal him.

(Matthew 11:27)

Though the Son holds all that is the Father's, there is no possessiveness about the ownership that the Father has given to the Son.

> *For he whom God hath sent speaketh the words of God: for God giveth not the Spirit by measure unto him. The Father loveth the Son, and hath given all things into his hand. He that believeth on the Son hath everlasting life: and he that believeth not the Son shall not see life; but the wrath of God abideth on him.*
>
> (John 3:34-36)

For, Jesus turned over, as a good Son will, all that was given to him by the Father, back to the Father. Jesus employs all that he is, in the service of the Father; this includes all of his life's works. And the most blessed of all the service of Jesus Christ, to the Father, is the sacrifice of his life to satisfy God's requirement for the redemption of mankind. This includes all who come to him for salvation, redemption, and reconciliation with God.

> *I pray for them: I pray not for the world, but for them which thou hast given me; for they are thine. And all mine are thine, and thine are mine; and I am glorified in them.*
>
> (John 17:9-10)

As the Ultimate Student of God, he becomes the greatest Teacher of man. His example is the one that empowers mankind to please God. The word of the Son, to the Father on behalf of mankind, is all that will make a difference to the present of mankind and the future of every human; and beyond. There are no more excuses. God is not distant from the world, anymore. God has presented His mediator, the Son of God, who is, the Son of man. The Son of man is the way between man and God. Jesus' own proclamation states it best.

> *Jesus saith unto him, I am the way, the truth, and the life: no man cometh unto the Father, but by me.*
>
> (John 14:6)

The confirmation of the apostles, fulfills the requirement of two or three witnesses.

> *For there is one God, and one mediator between God and men, the man Christ Jesus; Who gave himself a ransom for all, to be testified in due time.*
>
> (1 Timothy 2:5-6)

> *My little children, these things write I unto you, that ye sin not. And if any man sin, we have an advocate with the Father, Jesus Christ the righteous: And he is the propitiation for our sins: and not for ours only, but also for the sins of the whole world. And hereby we do know that we know him, if we keep his commandments.*

(1 John 2:1-3)

Let me stress this one more time: ***We are without excuse***.

> *God that made the world and all things therein, seeing that he is Lord of heaven and earth, dwelleth not in temples made with hands; Neither is worshipped with men's hands, as though he needed any thing, seeing he giveth to all life, and breath, and all things; And hath made of one blood all nations of men for to dwell on all the face of the earth, and hath determined the times before appointed, and the bounds of their habitation; That they should seek the Lord, if haply they might feel after him, and find him, though he be not far from every one of us: For in him we live, and move, and have our being; as certain also of your own poets have said, For we are also his offspring.*

> *Forasmuch then as we are the offspring of God, we ought not to think that the Godhead is like unto gold, or silver, or stone, graven by art and man's device. And the times of this ignorance God winked at; but now commandeth all men every where to repent: Because he hath appointed a day, in the which he will judge the world in righteousness by that man whom he hath ordained; whereof he hath given assurance unto all men, in that he hath raised him from the dead.*

(Acts 17:24-31)

The, power of the example, is the greatest gift given to mankind. By the unswerving devotion of Jesus Christ to God, he showed us what we can be. Jesus Christ both lived his life in God and gave his life for God. And God received His Son's offering of himself with great pleasure.

> *And Jesus, when he was baptized, went up straightway out of the water: and, lo, the heavens were opened unto him,*

> *and he saw the Spirit of God descending like a dove, and lighting upon him: And lo a voice from heaven, saying, This is my beloved Son, in whom I am well pleased.*

(Matthew 3:17)

Jesus' work on earth is not the end of the example; there is one other lesson that we must learn. Jesus, though he rose from the earth to Heaven, did not stop serving. Jesus continues to serve by defying the ease of death (eternal rest); returning to enter the fight. In the day before Jesus' resurrection, death was the end of the struggle. Jesus Christ, however, continues to serve after his resurrection in the biggest, most eternal, job of all.

> *I will declare the decree: the LORD hath said unto me, Thou art my Son; this day have I begotten thee. Ask of me, and I shall give thee the heathen for thine inheritance, and the uttermost parts of the earth for thy possession. Thou shalt break them with a rod of iron; thou shalt dash them in pieces like a potter's vessel.*
>
> *Be wise now therefore, O ye kings: be instructed, ye judges of the earth. Serve the LORD with fear, and rejoice with trembling. Kiss the Son, lest he be angry, and ye perish from the way, when his wrath is kindled but a little. Blessed are all they that put their trust in him.*

(Psalm 2:7-12)

Jesus also carries the burden of our human reality in himself. This is currently done in the spiritual realm, as the mediator. At a time announced by the Father, Jesus' rule is also done among all mankind; in the fullness of time.

> *For unto us a child is born, unto us a son is given: and the government shall be upon his shoulder: and his name shall be called Wonderful, Counsellor, The mighty God, The everlasting Father, The Prince of Peace. Of the increase of his government and peace there shall be no end, upon the throne of David, and upon his kingdom, to order it, and to establish it with judgment and with justice from henceforth even for ever. The zeal of the LORD of hosts will perform this.*

(Isaiah 9:6-7)

No, the work will not be done until all nations go beyond just knowing of God; the work will continue until all nations know God, even any new ones that may emerge. This is our driving force in the world. This is why we continue to move toward understanding God and His Son. Every nation will bow. Every nation must understand why they should bow. It is sufficient for God that every nation knows this; for with that, the Father will have accomplished the transfer of responsibility for mankind, to mankind.

> *A new commandment I give unto you, That ye love one another; as I have loved you, that ye also love one another. By this shall all men know that ye are my disciples, if ye have love one to another.*
>
> (John 13:34-35)

The Word from the Bible

Luke 9:23-26

And he said to them all, If any man will come after me, let him deny himself, and take up his cross daily, and follow me. For whosoever will save his life shall lose it: but whosoever will lose his life for my sake, the same shall save it. For what is a man advantaged, if he gain the whole world, and lose himself, or be cast away? For whosoever shall be ashamed of me and of my words, of him shall the Son of man be ashamed, when he shall come in his own glory, and in his Father's, and of the holy angels.

Ephesians 4:11-16

And he gave some, apostles; and some, prophets; and some, evangelists; and some, pastors and teachers; For the perfecting of the saints, for the work of the ministry, for the edifying of the body of Christ: Till we all come in the unity of the faith, and of the knowledge of the Son of God, unto a perfect man, unto the measure of the stature of the fulness of Christ: That we henceforth be no more children, tossed to and fro, and carried about with every wind of doctrine, by the sleight of men, and cunning craftiness, whereby they lie in wait to deceive; But speaking the truth in love, may grow up into him in all things, which is the head, even Christ: From whom the whole body fitly joined together and compacted by that which every joint supplieth, according to the effectual working in the measure of every part, maketh increase of the body unto the edifying of itself in love.

Numbers 11:23-30

And the LORD said unto Moses, Is the LORD'S hand waxed short? thou shalt see now whether my word shall come to pass unto thee or not.

And Moses went out, and told the people the words of the LORD, and gathered the seventy men of the elders of the people, and set them round about the tabernacle. And the LORD came down in a cloud, and spake unto him, and took of the spirit that was upon him, and gave it unto the seventy elders: and it came to pass, that, when the spirit rested upon them, they prophesied, and did not cease.

But there remained two of the men in the camp, the name of the one was Eldad, and the name of the other Medad: and the spirit rested upon them; and they were of them that were written, but went not out unto the tabernacle: and they prophesied in the camp. And there ran a young man, and told Moses, and said, Eldad and Medad do prophesy in the camp. And Joshua the son of Nun, the servant of Moses, one of his young men, answered and said, My lord Moses, forbid them.

And Moses said unto him, Enviest thou for my sake? would God that all the LORD'S people were prophets, and that the LORD would put his spirit upon them!

And Moses gat him into the camp, he and the elders of Israel.

1 Corinthians 14:1-5

Follow after charity, and desire spiritual gifts, but rather that ye may prophesy. For he that speaketh in an unknown tongue speaketh not unto men, but unto God: for no man understandeth him; howbeit in the spirit he speaketh mysteries. But he that prophesieth speaketh unto men to edification, and exhortation, and comfort. He that speaketh in an unknown tongue edifieth himself; but he that prophesieth edifieth the church. I would that ye all spake with tongues, but rather that ye prophesied: for greater is he that prophesieth than he that speaketh with tongues, except he interpret, that the church may receive edifying.

Ephesians 1:3-12

Blessed be the God and Father of our Lord Jesus Christ, who hath blessed us with all spiritual blessings in heavenly places in Christ: According as he hath chosen us in him before the foundation of the world, that we should be holy and without blame before him in love: Having predestinated us unto the adoption of children by Jesus Christ to himself, according to the good pleasure of his will, To the praise of the glory of his grace, wherein he hath made us accepted in the beloved.

In whom we have redemption through his blood, the forgiveness of sins, according to the riches of his grace; Wherein he hath abounded toward us in all wisdom and prudence; Having made known unto us the mystery of his will, according to his good pleasure which he hath purposed in himself: That in the dispensation of the fulness of times he might gather together in one all things in Christ, both which are in heaven, and which are on earth; even in him: In whom also we have obtained an inheritance, being predestinated according to the purpose of him who worketh all things after the counsel of his own will: That we should be to the praise of his glory, who first trusted in Christ.

Chapter 14

The Pedal to the Metal

What do you think would happen if everyone searched for God? What do you think would happen if everyone sought to know from God what their purpose is for being here? What do you think would happen if God started to reveal to each person their mission in life? What do you think would happen if it turns out that the mission of every man is to use the abilities that he or she currently has, to the best of their abilities? What do you think would happen if everyone started to apply themselves wholeheartedly to the tasks that they know how to do? Do you think that the world would be a better place?

What? You say that you do not believe in God? Well, why not? Have you searched for God, and not found Him? Is this why you say that you do not believe in God?

You say that you do not want to search for God; because you know that He does not exist?

How can you be sure, unless you've searched?

On a trivial level: when I was young, I did not believe that good tasting pizza existed. Then, one day, when I was older, I went on a search for good tasting pizza; and I found it. I found out that not only do I consider it to be good, but I consider it to be very good. Turns out that I was wrong; and a large number of other people were right. Might this be something that could happen to you if you were to embark on a sincere search for God? Maybe you will find that He does, in fact, exist. Maybe you will find that He is in fact good; huh?

Or, did you once find God, only to watch as He slowly died?

On another trivial note: I still do not believe that good tasting oatmeal exists. I will not even search for this. You see, sometime in my youth there was a bowl of oatmeal in front of me, and a terrible thing happened. Just as I was about to take a big spoonful, a bug invaded my oatmeal. It just dropped in it from the sky. I determined then and there that oatmeal could never taste good. Does this mean that I'm right and that good tasting oatmeal truly does not exist? Or, does it simply mean that this experience in my life has caused me to create a separate reality for myself, relative to oatmeal; different from the reality in which a large part of the rest of humanity abides? I think no one would find it difficult to answer that question. And in case you wonder, "Yes, indeed, if my life depends on it, I will eat oatmeal!"

Or, have your friends and acquaintances--or, at least, the significant ones--told you that it is stupid, or foolish, or even wrong to search for God? Did they tell you that He just **does not** exist?

Again, I share with you an episode from my younger days. For a long time, my buddies told me what girls were useful for. They mentioned the things that **the boys** are always saying about girls. So, as many other young men do, I started on a search for ways to exploit girls, as my friends directed me to do. Fortunately for me, my mother was a stronger influence in my life than my friends. I never told her what I had learned, nor did she ever sit me down to tell me the facts of life from a woman's perspective; she simply lived a life before me that made me want to honor women. She revealed the girl in her to me that engendered respect of all girls. Boy did I turn out to be a square. But I did find the truth about what a male-female relationship should be; especially one that is rooted in the things that promote the best interest of mankind. (Thought I was gonna say God here, huh? Well you get the idea anyway.)

The things and the people that come into our lives have a major affect on how we view reality. This does not mean that reality changes to fit the way we think it is. It does say, however, that we live our reality according to those things that we are willing to accept. In some cases, this can be a powerful thing. In other cases, this can be a very crippling thing. If you think about the number of people who said they *could not* and so they *did not*, it could cause you to become very sad. If only they had stopped to understand that by just a little application of imagination and foresight, miracles can happen. Most of the great inventors know that what they invented was once something that *could not be made*, or, *could not be done*. They searched, and they found; and they prospered. God says that if we seek Him, the same thing will happen.

> *Ask, and it shall be given you; seek, and ye shall find; knock, and it shall be opened unto you: For every one that asketh receiveth; and he that seeketh findeth; and to him that knocketh it shall be opened.*

> *Or what man is there of you, whom if his son ask bread, will he give him a stone? Or if he ask a fish, will he give him a serpent? If ye then, being evil, know how to give good gifts unto your children, how much more shall your Father which is in heaven give good things to them that ask him?*

(Matthew 7:7-11)

So let me ask a favor of you who do not believe that there is a God, and yet for some reason has made it this far into this book. Let me ask you to imagine that there is a God, for the sake of this reading. Then imagine that the entire world is actively searching for their place in the reality that He spawned for existence. Then, walk with me as we explore what this would mean to mankind, the earth, and--since man has now ventured into space--the entire universe.

Now that you have made it this far, let us ponder what it will be like when God starts unfolding the mission of each individual to them. I say unfolding because God works in the way that is best for a person. Most of us, when we get too much to do, become overwhelmed at the work ahead of us. This is another reason that some of us have moved away from an active belief in God, and the things of God. We were once active, but we were told that we had to do so much; that we had to be so much more than we were; and that we had to do it **NOW!** Trust me, please; this is not God's way. Well, you do not actually have to trust me, just trust the Bible. In it is a record of the way God worked to provide excellence to the nation of Israel: *By little and little.*

> *And I will send hornets before thee, which shall drive out the Hivite, the Canaanite, and the Hittite, from before thee. I will not drive them out from before thee in one year; lest the land become desolate, and the beast of the field multiply against thee. By little and little I will drive them out from before thee, until thou be increased, and inherit the land.*

(Exodus 23:28-30)

The Bible also contains a promise for those who will follow God. The promise is that even when we think that we are far from being in the center of God's purpose for our lives, there is an answer. This is the time when we think that we are yucky because all these negative thoughts are going through our head. We might even be thinking that if we could we would do harm to someone. Or, we might be plotting revenge against someone for slighting us. Since we have previously agreed to, at a minimum, imagine that there is a God, and that we will go on a search for our purpose in His plan, therefore, we know that these things are not supportive of this agreement. The official term for these is temptation.

Probably for the entire span of our remaining life, at least for those who are able to comprehend this book, we will be subject to temptation. Remember, God does not, as they say, "throw the baby out with the bath water"; God has made a way for this too.

> *Wherefore let him that thinketh he standeth take heed lest he fall. There hath no temptation taken you but such as is common to man: but God is faithful, who will not suffer you to be tempted above that ye are able; but will with the temptation also make a way to escape, that ye may be able to bear it.*

(1 Corinthians 10:12-13)

We do not need to, and we cannot afford to, sit down and succumb to the depression that can come from a revealed lack of ability to perform this or that thing, or in this or that way. Actually, when we are in this state, this is the best time to seek out God. We need to seek God, asking Him to return us to the light of His presence. We need to ask Him to give us a renewed sense of His presence in the world. We need to once again ask Him to reveal to us that He indeed has a purpose in this creation which we call the universe. We must get back into the light of His presence; we cannot afford to stay in the darkness of depression and despair; our forward motion depends on it. Jesus of Nazareth, one of the most persecuted of all humans, applied this to his life, in spite of the forces around him.

> *And as Jesus passed by, he saw a man which was blind from his birth. And his disciples asked him, saying, Master, who did sin, this man, or his parents, that he was born blind?*
>
> *Jesus answered, Neither hath this man sinned, nor his parents: but that the works of God should be made manifest in him.*
>
> *I must work the works of him that sent me, while it is day: the night cometh, when no man can work. As long as I am in the world, I am the light of the world.*

(John 9:1-5)

However, there is a major obstacle to the knowledge of God. This obstacle is, others and what they want to see come of the world. Each person seems to have a circuit in them that causes their finger to point, as they say, at the drop of a hat. There will always be someone who will tell you what you should be doing, and when you should be doing it. When this is between a parent and their child, it is appropriate. When it is between any others among the human race, it must be listened to with caution, and validated for accuracy. The Scripture tells us of a people who understood this quite well.

> *And the brethren immediately sent away Paul and Silas by night unto Berea: who coming thither went into the synagogue of the Jews. These were more noble than those in Thessalonica, in that they received the word with all readiness of mind, and searched the scriptures daily, whether those things were so. Therefore many of them believed; also of honourable women which were Greeks, and of men, not a few.*
>
> (Acts 17:10-12)

Yes, we have embarked on a search for our purpose in God. No, we have not given anyone else license to tell us what this purpose should, or must, be. The search that we are undertaking is a joint venture between "me and God", or one of God's <u>divine</u> representatives. We may receive advice from others, but the final statement must come from God. This applies to the height, as well as the depth. When we are told that we have such overwhelming capabilities, or that everyone should be performing at what some human perceives is the highest level of service, WALK AWAY.

God, and God alone, has set the bounds of our service. God, and God alone, knows the worth of our service. We who are doing the service may not fully understand our bounds, but we can trust that God understands, and that He will keep us operating within our bounds. Furthermore, in relation to what we do understand, we must not allow other to *puff it up* beyond what it should be.

> *For I say, through the grace given unto me, to every man that is among you, not to think of himself more highly than he ought to think; but to think soberly, according as God hath dealt to every man the measure of faith. For as we*

> *have many members in one body, and all members have not the same office: ...*

(Romans 12:3-4)

Sometimes, I listen to religious folk talking, particularly, folks who are in a leadership position; and I hear them say that everyone must become a *disciple* of Christ, to fully understand God. I, too, believe that this is true, but I do so with one modification. I believe that first everyone should be a *follower* of Christ. In the days of his life Christ had many followers, but only a few disciples, comparatively speaking. I believe that everyone should strive to be a disciple of Christ; but not in a hurry.

You see, those of us who believe in the Gospel, as preached by Christ, do not get in any needless hurries. We believe that our eternity has already begun. We are willing to believe that God will progress us to true discipleship in Christ; indeed, we believe that God will conform us to the very image of His Son Jesus Christ. We are just not willing to say whether the Father will accomplish that on this side of life, on earth part one; or on the other side. Some of us may have to wait until we are absent from the body and present with the Lord, before we will finish that transformation. This is perfectly alright with God. God accepts us just as we are; and works with us to accomplish our transformation into what we will be in Him.

> *Beloved, now are we the sons of God, and it doth not yet appear what we shall be: but we know that, when he shall appear, we shall be like him; for we shall see him as he is. And every man that hath this hope in him purifieth himself, even as he is pure.*

(1 John 3:2-3)

A place of service in discipleship, world evangelism, the pastorate, the deaconate, ministry of this, or ministry of that, is not for everyone. God will have various flavors of humans present in the church on this earth. It is absolutely definite that God will have various flavors of people in the Kingdom that He is bringing, according to the Gospel that is preached.

> *After this I beheld, and, lo, a great multitude, which no man could number, of all nations, and kindreds, and people, and*

tongues, stood before the throne, and before the Lamb, clothed with white robes, and palms in their hands;

(Revelation 7:9)

The pedal to the metal: Start where you are and, if you have not already done so, begin the search for your purpose in God. For some this may mean beginning a search for God Himself. For others, it means tapping into the commitments that have already been made. If you think about it, and since you have agreed to at least imagine that there is a God, you will also see that in this environment, this is the only thing to do. Mankind has repeatedly shown that there is no force of man that can transform and unify all mankind. Many empires and countries have tried and failed. God, alone, holds the knowledge of how each piece of the human conglomerate fits together. God, alone, knows how the people must interact, and He knows how the nations must interact.

The knowledge of God is available for the asking; He is not stingy with His information, as some people are. It does not change the LORD one iota if you know even as much as He knows. He will always be the ancient of days, and it is in the application of the knowledge that He will forever surpass us.

When I was very little I thought that as I got older, one day I would catch up with my brothers in age. I thought that as the years passed, I would be one year closer to catching them. Well, I hope you believe me when I say that I have grown out of that. No matter how long I live, I will not catch up in age to that of either my older brothers or my earthly father.

But you say that if we consider death to be a stopping point for age and experience then I can indeed catch up.

Even if we allow this, we will not catch up with God; for, God cannot die. Besides that, all that is, was created by God; and there are possibly many other things that He created that are not a part of this realm that we call the universe. In fact, there is an easily understood piece of reality that is outside of our universe; this is the realm of the spirits, and of the Spirit of God. So no matter how much we know, we can never reach the grandeur of God. We should never want to.

Again I recall a youthful thought. (Flashback time again!) Sometime, when I got angry at someone, I would say, "If I were God, I'd . . .". Then, as I became older, I would say, "If I could persuade God to, I'd . . .". Finally, as God revealed to me the nature of His presence, I said, "Thank you God that there is no way for me to be God. For if there were, there would be no way for there to even be a way."

Seek God. Seek to understand God. Seek to please God. Do it for a selfish reason, if you must. Do it because God holds a Priceless (small word for a huge benefit, but it will have to do) treasure of--well--everything. Begin the process of tapping into the wealth that is available, from God to man. God proved Himself by creating us, and allowing us to continue existing. He has earned the title of Father.

It is now time for us to earn the title of, child of God. Jesus showed us how the Son of God manifests himself before the Father. Let us start to accept this example, and ask God to seal it into our lives. And let us ask God to do this for us **JUST AS WE ARE**. When all mankind is working at this level then we will have achieved The Great Consolidation.

> *Now faith is the substance of things hoped for, the evidence of things not seen. For by it the elders obtained a good report.*
>
> *Through faith we understand that the worlds were framed by the word of God, so that things which are seen were not made of things which do appear.*
>
> *By faith Abel offered unto God a more excellent sacrifice than Cain, by which he obtained witness that he was righteous, God testifying of his gifts: and by it he being dead yet speaketh. By faith Enoch was translated that he should not see death; and was not found, because God had translated him: for before his translation he had this testimony, that he pleased God.*
>
> *But without faith it is impossible to please him: for he that cometh to God must believe that he is, and that he is a rewarder of them that diligently seek him.*
>
> *By faith Noah, being warned of God of things not seen as yet, moved with fear, prepared an ark to the saving of his house; by the which he condemned the world, and became heir of the righteousness which is by faith. By faith Abraham, when he was called to go out into a place which he should after receive for an inheritance, obeyed; and he went out, not knowing whither he went. By faith he*

sojourned in the land of promise, as in a strange country, dwelling in tabernacles with Isaac and Jacob, the heirs with him of the same promise: For he looked for a city which hath foundations, whose builder and maker is God.

Through faith also Sara herself received strength to conceive seed, and was delivered of a child when she was past age, because she judged him faithful who had promised. Therefore sprang there even of one, and him as good as dead, so many as the stars of the sky in multitude, and as the sand which is by the sea shore innumerable.

(Hebrews 11:1-12)

Each one has a destiny,
A uniqueness, which God planned;
Not by the will of man,
Or, even, parental demand.

A place in existence,
Uniquely their own;
This does not mean
We must go it alone.

We start as a unit,
Standing before the LORD;
A being most precious,
And, by God, adored.

We struggle, with His help,
To find our place
In this mass of creation
Called, the human race.

Sometimes we are up,
Sometimes we are down,
But with God's help
We always rebound;

Staying in His hands
As life's game we play,
To have another try
At another day.

Then we join with others,
Standing side by side,
Our mission in God's design
To in Him abide.

Together we approach Him,
Still in His perfect plan
For the revelation of reality
To the mind of man.

Then, as He ordained,
We collect into nations,

*Filling the earth
With sweet incarnations.*

*But never forget
Our infant start:
Raised hands to God,
To reach His heart.*

Chapter 14a

My Bewildered Prayer

LORD,

I know that You are, and that You are the rewarder of them that diligently seek You.

I have felt Your presence in my life, and thank you for Your indwelling Spirit, and for Your anointing to present these works to the world, which You have created.

I thank You for my parents, who early in my life presented me to You, and allowed me to cling to You as an actual babe in the Word.

I thank You for accepting this offering of my parents and for Your work in my life to manifest Yourself as the God of the universe.

I thank You for the introduction of Your Son, Jesus Christ, into my life, and for the indwelling presence of the Holy Ghost, which he caused you to send to me on his behalf and at his behest.

I thank You for your Son, Jesus Christ, and that I shall see him in eternity when I pass from this life into the next; as he announced to the thief on the cross, and caused to be recorded in the book of John.

However (and I know You knew that there would be a rejoinder attached to this prayer), there are others who did not have the benefits that I enjoyed. They did not have a parent that delivered them to You. They did not have a place with You at an age when You can make the greatest impact on the fresh mind. They did not receive a specific calling and election from You to serve You in Your ministry (or at least they have not received it yet). And it is this, not yet, that I would like to discuss further with You in this prayer.

Please LORD, manifest Yourself and Your Son, Jesus Christ, in a most powerful way in their lives. The logic of this world can greatly overwhelm the mind, and allow an individual to be subject to strong delusions. I know that You have indicated that those who choose not to follow You will succumb to these delusions. It is not because You chose them to suffer, but that they have removed Your hand of protection from them, and as a result of that action on their part, they make themselves subject to the germs of unrighteousness that are ever present in the air. Then, as a man who goes out in the cold without proper protection and succumbs to illness; in like fashion they have made themselves subject to the delusions of the world that are always around and being pushed upon mankind by the remaining forces of the prince of the powers of the air.

I pray for those who have not made a choice against You. These are they who just do not understand Who You Are; or more appropriately, they do not understand who I AM Is. Give them some reason to acknowledge your existence. Allow them to understand that You are ever present and available to each of us. I do not pray for signs and wonders of an external nature, but I do pray for signs and wonders of an internal nature. Maybe, You can let them experience your peace for just a moment, and then release them to their former state. In this way, You will be able to set up a yearning for the things of Your Kingdom. And in this way, You will cause them to seek Your hand of protection; which, when You are asked to give, You will do so liberally to any man who asks. I freely admit that the most difficult part of this prayer is my request that if there is any part I can play in this, opening up of the world to you, transform me to the image of he who will demonstrate the full love and power of God; which love allows anyone to persevere in all matters pertaining to the kingdom of man. He is your Son, Jesus Christ.

Additionally, I pray for those who feel that they have discovered a reason to reject you. Maybe they have a religion that they feel is appropriate for their existence; even if this religion is the logic of man. Please forgive me if I sound impertinent; but sometimes the things that You have done, and the requirements that You set forth for mankind under the Old Dispensation, may seem to be illogical from the natural perspective; to those who do not know You. You said it best, "*The wisdom of God is foolish to the wise*". And, this world pushes every man to be wise in his or her own self, and not to depend on anyone or anything for the final wisdom that governs their lives. I do not have any idea what to ask You to do in this regard; but I do want You to do something, to show even the wise of this world the supremacy of Your wisdom. This, I believe, is why you directed the creation of these works of literature (if they can be seen to rise to that standard). But even though I have no idea what to ask, I know that You know how to reach them.

But in all things, Your will be done. On this note, I pray that I can take as being an absolute action of Yours, the words that "*God would have none to perish, but that all should come to repentance*". It is my prayer that this is not just a matter of desire, but is a *fate accompli* in this Universe of Yours.

Give me increased understanding and acceptance of Your way in spite of my preferences; and beyond that, I pray that you transform my preferences into conformity with Your preferences. Only in this way will I be able to live at peace with myself in Christ. I do not want to enter eternity with the tremendous burden that I did not, at least, ask you to intervene on behalf of all mankind, no matter how stubborn they may be.

I live with the passage from Jonah in which you state, "*And should not I spare Nineveh, that great city, wherein are more than sixscore thousand persons that cannot discern between their right hand and their left hand; and also much cattle?*" With that passage of Scripture in mind, I ask You to apply it to the earth in total. And I echo the words of my Lord and Savior Jesus Christ, your only begotten Son, when he said "*Father, forgive them; for they know not what they do*". I send this to You by way of prayer, on behalf of all those who have not come to know You.

This is my prayer in the name of Jesus of Nazareth, the Christ, who is the Son of the Living God; and for his sake I pray.

Amen.

In My Conclusion (Almost)

Malachi 4

For, behold, the day cometh, that shall burn as an oven; and all the proud, yea, and all that do wickedly, shall be stubble: and the day that cometh shall burn them up, saith the LORD of hosts, that it shall leave them neither root nor branch. But unto you that fear my name shall the Sun of righteousness arise with healing in his wings; and ye shall go forth, and grow up as calves of the stall. And ye shall tread down the wicked; for they shall be ashes under the soles of your feet in the day that I shall do this, saith the LORD of hosts.

Remember ye the law of Moses my servant, which I commanded unto him in Horeb for all Israel, with the statutes and judgments.

Behold, I will send you Elijah the prophet before the coming of the great and dreadful day of the LORD: And he shall turn the heart of the fathers to the children, and the heart of the children to their fathers, lest I come and smite the earth with a curse.

Matthew 1:18-25

Now the birth of Jesus Christ was on this wise: When as his mother Mary was espoused to Joseph, before they came together, she was found with child of the Holy Ghost.

Then Joseph her husband, being a just man, and not willing to make her a publick example, was minded to put her away privily. But while he thought on these things, behold, the angel of the LORD appeared unto him in a dream, saying, Joseph, thou son of David, fear not to take unto thee Mary thy wife: for that which is conceived in her is of the Holy Ghost. And she shall bring forth a son, and thou shalt call his name JESUS: for he shall save his people from their sins.

Now all this was done, that it might be fulfilled which was spoken of the Lord by the prophet, saying, Behold, a virgin shall be with child, and shall bring forth a son, and they shall call his name Emmanuel, which being interpreted is, God with us.

Then Joseph being raised from sleep did as the angel of the Lord had bidden him, and took unto him his wife: And knew her not till she had brought forth her firstborn son: and he called his name JESUS.

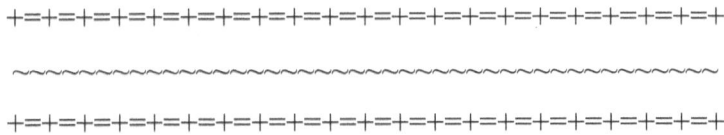

How does one end a discussion about the future of the world? What presumptuousness would allow a person to think that they could have enough information or intelligence to diagnose the situation of the world?

The title of this work is The Great Consolidation, but I have not forcefully declared what needs to be consolidated. The *best* is saved for last. The consolidation that must be done is that of the entire world of man; that which is sometimes called the kingdom of man. This is a call for the understanding of God by all mankind. This is an understanding that will teach us that destruction will not solve the problem.

Some might think that when a nation proclaims that it has caused the destruction of another nation, or national system, this is the end of the matter. No, when a nation makes such a proclamation, this is only the beginning of the matter. It is a different story when God makes such a proclamation. Indeed when He does, this is the end of any revisions to the story for that nation; no improvements in the status of that nation are possible. However, some of the people may still live on.

Any attempt by a nation to destroy another will draw the attention of God. The LORD will look to see who is trying to usurp His authority. Nation building and dissolution is strictly held in the hands of God; only God can authorize or directly accomplish their creation and their destruction.

> *Be not afraid of their faces: for I am with thee to deliver thee, saith the LORD.*
>
> *Then the LORD put forth his hand, and touched my mouth. And the LORD said unto me, Behold, I have put my words in thy mouth. See, I have this day set thee over the nations and over the kingdoms, to root out, and to pull down, and to destroy, and to throw down, to build, and to plant.*

Moreover the word of the LORD came unto me, saying, Jeremiah, what seest thou?

And I said, I see a rod of an almond tree.

Then said the LORD unto me, Thou hast well seen: for I will hasten my word to perform it.

(Jeremiah 1:8-12)

For man to attempt to destroy a nation is to attempt to nullify a work of God. To say such a thing should not be done, is too mild: it cannot be done. Whenever one nation attempts to destroy another, they will have no assurance of success. A nation is not just a regional thing; a nation is a worldwide creation.

Think about the number of place to which the children of Israel were dispersed, under the judgment of God. Any attempt by man to destroy them, in all the places that they were sent, would have caused a war on a global scale. No other nation that is not involved in your conflict will willingly allow you to enter their nation, to destroy someone you say is your *enemy-in-hiding*. They will invoke national sovereignty. The nation might attack anyway. However, should they prevail; unless they are willing to stay eternally involved with that nation, their victory is not sure. God is always and eternally involved with every nation

Furthermore, you never know when God has chosen a nation for a mission of the LORD. There were many *undeserving* nations that were chosen by God to advance mankind. Look at what happened during the various captivities of Israel. Some of the nations chosen from the *undeserving* set included Babylon, Persia and ancient Rome. History has shown, however, that these nations had a significant contribution to the betterment of mankind. No, they did not do everything right before God; but they left a legacy that is still being enjoyed today.

An isolationist view of nations is totally counterproductive. The economic structures of the world, along with the dispersal among the nations of the products that are needed for a full life, have made friends out of military enemies. Do you think this might be what God intended? After all, it is God who placed the various resources where they are located on the earth. Do you think the LORD might have ordained, by this means, a need for nations to have a reason to tolerate one another?

No nation can take it upon itself to do God's work for Him. God needs no other nation of people to perform His wonders: especially not when it comes to the affairs of nations. The LORD has an *army* in nature that can easily dwarf any that is on the earth, in both size and might. Consider the power of a hurricane, compared to the most sophisticated of bombs that man has invented. Consider the power of a sunspot, compared to the most sophisticated energy generating apparatus that provides power to mankind. In nature, God has limitless power, and powers, which He can call forth to perform His works among the nations.

God also has unlimited power in the hosts of angels. The LORD showed the children of Israel this when He introduced Joshua to the captain of the hosts of God.

> *And it came to pass, when Joshua was by Jericho, that he lifted up his eyes and looked, and, behold, there stood a man over against him with his sword drawn in his hand: and Joshua went unto him, and said unto him, Art thou for us, or for our adversaries?*
>
> *And he said, Nay; but as captain of the host of the LORD am I now come.*
>
> *And Joshua fell on his face to the earth, and did worship, and said unto him, What saith my lord unto his servant?*
>
> *And the captain of the LORD'S host said unto Joshua, Loose thy shoe from off thy foot; for the place whereon thou standest is holy.*
>
> *And Joshua did so.*
>
> (Joshua 5:13-15)

Since we know that God did introduce Israel to his army, we have to be very careful about which nation we offend. We do not know what other nations may have also received this introduction, or which nation is under the protection of the LORD'S army; without introduction. The very nation that we offend, could be the one that is needed later to assist in the preservation of our own nation.

I'm having a flashback! This reminds me of something I learned when I was a college student: I was told how to behave when dropping a course. One thing that is very important is to never say anything bad about either the course or the instructor. Just because it may not have fit me, did not mean that it was not a good course.

Why was I taught this lesson?

I was taught this lesson because in college one never knows when one might once again face the same teacher in another classroom. It is not easy to come face to face with someone who we have criticized and made to feel worthless. It is particularly difficult when that person holds a part of our destiny in their hands; we will, then, live in a state of *constantly justified fear*. This is the fear of what they might do to us to get revenge. We should consider this as we interact with others, including those peoples of other nations. There are three considerations in this matter.

+=+=+=+=+=+=+=+=+=+=+=+=+=+=+=+=+=+=+

A key consideration is for us on this earth. We have every chance of needing something from that person or nation in the future. Wherefore we must be very careful about our actions toward them in the present. And if we have dealt harshly with them in the past; one of our actions must be to seek reconciliation with them.

> *Therefore if thou bring thy gift to the altar, and there rememberest that thy brother hath ought against thee; Leave there thy gift before the altar, and go thy way; first be reconciled to thy brother, and then come and offer thy gift.*
>
> *Agree with thine adversary quickly, whiles thou art in the way with him; lest at any time the adversary deliver thee to the judge, and the judge deliver thee to the officer, and thou be cast into prison. Verily I say unto thee, Thou shalt by no means come out thence, till thou hast paid the uttermost farthing.*

(Matthew 5:23-26)

For if we cannot get along with our brother, who is imperfect like us; how will we be able to get along with God, who is totally Perfect? When our brother's faults become so intolerable that we feel we have to destroy him, what does this say about our chances of enduring in the presence of the LORD? It takes far less than an instant for God to visit upon us the recompense for our faults.

Another flashback: a situation I was often in as a child. I was a very *active child*, as pertains to wanting to have my way. Sometimes I did not honor the civil rights of my fellow children. This causes those things known as fights. Unfortunately for me, as a child I was very good at winning fights; either physical or mental. Thus, there was usually someone else, other than me, who considered themselves the loser. Well, when you are a child and you lose--temporarily--you seek vengeance. And the best vengeance is to partake of that most pleasant of childhood activity called "telling your mother on you". This was sure to earn for me some form of a scolding; also known as a spanking. Ouch!

Well there came a day when it truly was not my fault. However, with my reputation at that time, my mother could no longer trust my petitions for mercy. She, therefore, had to mete out the punishment, also known as the spanking, that such actions merit. As I was subjected to discipline, I said to her one more time, "But Ma, I didn't do it." Her words after that will never be forgotten.

She said to me, "Well son, even if you didn't do it, there are undoubtedly many time when you did do it and were not punished. If you must; consider this a punishment for one of the times I missed."

And you know something, she was right. I had escaped the justice that should have been rendered to me for bad behavior several times before. This time could indeed fit that time of escape.

I share this, not to say that God does not know EVERY time that we have done something worthy of punishment. However, even though God knows, He does not chastise us every time. But if God chose to chastise us as we deserved, He would be more than justified.

Why do you imagine that God does not chasten us for each offense? Might it be so that we can learn from Him how to be longsuffering? That is, might it be that He wants us to know that there will be times when we should forgive our brothers offenses?

I think so!

> *For if ye forgive men their trespasses, your heavenly Father will also forgive you: But if ye forgive not men their trespasses, neither will your Father forgive your trespasses.*

(Matthew 6:14-15)

Know this, that if God reacted against us for every sin we commit, we would do nothing other than live in a constant state of punishment.

> *If thou, LORD, shouldest mark iniquities, O Lord, who shall stand? But there is forgiveness with thee, that thou mayest be feared.*
>
> (Psalm 130:3-4)

Let me not try to explain what has already been explained. The Bible tells us about another man who had a similar situation, of thinking that he had a right to chastise his brother for being insufficient. Furthermore, he did have a legal right to do so; but he lost the moral right to do so because of his own condition in life. Thus, being too intent on enforcing the legal right, he activated the exercise of the moral right against himself.

> *Then came Peter to him, and said, Lord, how oft shall my brother sin against me, and I forgive him? till seven times?*
>
> *Jesus saith unto him, I say not unto thee, Until seven times: but, Until seventy times seven.*
>
> *Therefore is the kingdom of heaven likened unto a certain king, which would take account of his servants. And when he had begun to reckon, one was brought unto him, which owed him ten thousand talents. But forasmuch as he had not to pay, his lord commanded him to be sold, and his wife, and children, and all that he had, and payment to be made.*
>
> *The servant therefore fell down, and worshipped him, saying, Lord, have patience with me, and I will pay thee all.*
>
> *Then the lord of that servant was moved with compassion, and loosed him, and forgave him the debt.*
>
> *But the same servant went out, and found one of his fellowservants, which owed him an hundred pence: and he laid hands on him, and took him by the throat, saying, Pay me that thou owest.*
>
> *And his fellowservant fell down at his feet, and besought him, saying, Have patience with me, and I will pay thee all.*

And he would not: but went and cast him into prison, till he should pay the debt. So when his fellowservants saw what was done, they were very sorry, and came and told unto their lord all that was done.

Then his lord, after that he had called him, said unto him, O thou wicked servant, I forgave thee all that debt, because thou desiredst me: Shouldest not thou also have had compassion on thy fellowservant, even as I had pity on thee? And his lord was wroth, and delivered him to the tormentors, till he should pay all that was due unto him.

So likewise shall my heavenly Father do also unto you, if ye from your hearts forgive not every one his brother their trespasses.

(Matthew 18:21-35)

+=+

It is time for the world to understand that God is not blind when it comes to the actions of other nations, and even of our *evil* neighbors. God is still God, and He will remove any offense to this world when He knows that it must be removed.

But of that day and hour knoweth no man, no, not the angels of heaven, but my Father only.

(Matthew 24:36)

Furthermore, it is God who must be allowed to remove such offenses--only God. Our job on this earth is not to select the people or places that must be removed from the earth, unless we own those places: we can never own people. We are created by God to dwell on this earth, in preparation for an existence different from this earthly one.

This earthly existence is only the first part of a very long training period. To understand this, I look at the words of Jesus of Nazareth and his apostles. Jesus was revealed to his disciples and the apostles to be the Son of God. In this manifestation Jesus came to establish salvation for us.

For God so loved the world, that he gave his only begotten Son, that whosoever believeth in him should not perish, but have everlasting life. For God sent not his Son into the world to condemn the world; but that the world through him might be saved.

(John 3:16-17)

But saved from what?

We do not need to be saved from God. We do not even need to be saved from Satan, for he is, according to Scripture, somewhat weak. The lingering deviousness of the force of Satan is not even anything that we have to be too aggressive about avoiding. We just need to apply light resistance, and this force will back down.

Submit yourselves therefore to God. Resist the devil, and he will flee from you.

(James 4:7)

But do not let this make you think that you can underestimate him; he is quite cunning and deceptive. Wherefore . . .

Draw nigh to God, and he will draw nigh to you. Cleanse your hands, ye sinners; and purify your hearts, ye double minded.

(James 4:8)

So what are we saved from? Might it be our own nature?

From whence come wars and fightings among you? come they not hence, even of your lusts that war in your members? Ye lust, and have not: ye kill, and desire to have, and cannot obtain: ye fight and war, yet ye have not, because ye ask not. Ye ask, and receive not, because ye ask amiss, that ye may consume it upon your lusts.

(James 4:1-3)

We delight in blaming Satan for the plight that we are in. We strive mightily to say that it is the Devil and the devils of the world that are causing us to be damaged, and to be lost. It is really convenient for us to point the finger away from ourselves at the other person or peoples, or things, and say that they are the problem.

I really like one of those neighborhood sayings that were told to me: "When you point a finger at another person there are even more pointing back at you". Try it, take your index finger and point it; you will find that in order to have an effective *point* you need to make a fist. When we do so, this causes the other fingers to point directly at you; specifically, your palm. This is a very interesting exercise; but the message is relayed better by the Bible.

> *Judge not, that ye be not judged. For with what judgment ye judge, ye shall be judged: and with what measure ye mete, it shall be measured to you again.*
>
> *And why beholdest thou the mote that is in thy brother's eye, but considerest not the beam that is in thine own eye? Or how wilt thou say to thy brother, Let me pull out the mote out of thine eye; and, behold, a beam is in thine own eye? Thou hypocrite, first cast out the beam out of thine own eye; and then shalt thou see clearly to cast out the mote out of thy brother's eye.*
>
> (Matthew 7:1-5)

+=+=+=+=+=+=+=+=+=+=+=+=+=+=+=+=+=+=+=+

God is over all: all nations will bow to Him. Indeed, all nations do bow to him, even now, and some do not even know that they are doing so. Would you ask God to create separate spaces in His presence? Would you ask God to make a separate space for those you call your enemy, so that you do not have to see them? Of course not!

God cannot be dictated to, nor can He be persuaded to take a separatist stance against any human, or any human population. God is the LORD of all. The LORD God has no respect of person. The LORD God cannot be persuaded to do anything that is not holy.

> *Let no man say when he is tempted, I am tempted of God: for God cannot be tempted with evil, neither tempteth he any man: But every man is tempted, when he is drawn away of his own lust, and enticed.*
>
> (James 1:13-14)

All of mankind will be ushered into the presence of God and His Son. When we come before His presence, none of us will have works or creations that we can present to Him and because of them say to Him that this is good. None of us can come before Him and say that we are, by ourselves, holy.

In the presence of God, every man is so small that we are smaller than an atom in the presence of the entire universe. No matter how radiant we thought we were on this earth, the light of our personal presence will not even be as bright as darkness.

> *For since the beginning of the world men have not heard, nor perceived by the ear, neither hath the eye seen, O God, beside thee, what he hath prepared for him that waiteth for him. Thou meetest him that rejoiceth and worketh righteousness, those that remember thee in thy ways: behold, thou art wroth; for we have sinned: in those is continuance, and we shall be saved. But we are all as an unclean thing, and all our righteousnesses are as filthy rags; and we all do fade as a leaf; and our iniquities, like the wind, have taken us away. And there is none that calleth upon thy name, that stirreth up himself to take hold of thee: for thou hast hid thy face from us, and hast consumed us, because of our iniquities.*

(Isaiah 64:4-7)

+=+=+=+=+=+=+=+=+=+=+=+=+=+=+=+=+=+=+=+

What do we do? What do we do?

We accept what God has provided for us. In the days of Moses, He provided the Law. The Law was not something that made the man perfect, nor did it justify his actions. The Law was a way man had of making a payment for his actions. This payment, however, was made in currency that came from God. The life of the animal was the currency of forgiveness. Man did not give birth to the animal, nor did he create the animal. The animals were, are, and always will be a creation according to the direct working of God on this earth. The same is true of man.

Oh, sorry, you thought that birth was automatic?

Nope, birth is under the direction of God. You were born because God designed you to be born.

Then, as time passed, God established a new currency for payment of our sins. In the fullness of time, when mankind could no longer say that he is too primitive to understand the working of God, He sent an eternal payment for our sins. This currency is established so that it is an internal personal payment. The animals were an external payment that had to be repeated. This is because the animal payment was only a sin at a time.

The final currency is a payment for all sins, of all mankind, for all time. This payment is never rescinded: it can never be undone. This payment was done in a similar fashion to the animal sacrifices, but this payment is human. This payment is by the life and the blood of Jesus Christ.

If I might be allowed some license here; the eternal payment seemed to be God's way of saying to us that we had matured. It seems to be His way of saying that now we can understand better this matter of good and evil. We are no longer children in the universe, as Adam was. Therefore, being no longer children, we can understand matters of compensation and gratitude. For this reason God sent the eternal currency, in the generation which received it, for the sake of all generations that surrounded it. This is the payment from God that was returned to God as payment for us all. For who else could prepare a payment for God, other than God? No one!

We should not be so amazed by the concept of God paying God. Our governments print currencies that we then return to them to pay our taxes. Except, our governments do not freely give us their currencies; we have to pay for it. God, however, gives the saving grace of Jesus Christ freely; for there is nothing we have that we could give in exchange for it: God owns everything.

Then, *what doth the LORD thy God require of thee?*

The LORD requires of us that we, too, give without any requirement. When a man does something good for you, usually you say, "Thank you". God requires no more than this. The LORD God is not greedy; indeed, He has no need to be, for the cattle on a thousand hills are His, and more. God requires from us only that we show gratitude for His provision for each of us. This gratitude is shown to God through our acknowledgment of Him, and by our righteous service to our fellow man; including all of mankind. This is the essence of believing in the Lord Jesus Christ: it is done to honor his gracious sacrifice on our behalf. When we do honor Jesus, we will perform actions, according to his model, which even when others attempt to kill them, they continually rise again to provide benefits to mankind. This is the expression of Jesus in us; and, through us.

This then is what we are saved from: we are saved from ourselves. We are saved from the strife that resides within us and around us. We are saved from the internal warring forces that would destroy, if they could, all mankind. God sent the payment for that strife, which He calls sin. What the LORD asks of us is that we show gratitude to Him, and that we share it with our brother in our nation, and among our nations. I think this is a small thing to ask for such a great salvation. I truly pray that you think so too. I further pray to the Father that if you do not, He will deliver you to the knowledge of this gratitude. This I ask in Jesus name and for his sake. Amen.

> *Let love be without dissimulation. Abhor that which is evil; cleave to that which is good.*
>
> *Be kindly affectioned one to another with brotherly love; in honour preferring one another; Not slothful in business; fervent in spirit; serving the Lord; Rejoicing in hope; patient in tribulation; continuing instant in prayer; Distributing to the necessity of saints; given to hospitality.*
>
> *Bless them which persecute you: bless, and curse not.*
>
> *Rejoice with them that do rejoice, and weep with them that weep.*
>
> *Be of the same mind one toward another. Mind not high things, but condescend to men of low estate. Be not wise in your own conceits.*
>
> *Recompense to no man evil for evil. Provide things honest in the sight of all men. If it be possible, as much as lieth in you, live peaceably with all men. Dearly beloved, avenge not yourselves, but rather give place unto wrath: for it is written, Vengeance is mine; I will repay, saith the Lord.*
>
> *Therefore if thine enemy hunger, feed him; if he thirst, give him drink: for in so doing thou shalt heap coals of fire on his head.*
>
> *Be not overcome of evil, but overcome evil with good.*
>
> (Romans 12:9-21)

Full circle is
Where we will go,
As we travel
In this kingdom below;

Built by God's will,
Not that of man,
Each of us a part
Of His excellent Plan.

Many strive to rise,
None wants to fall,
But too many seek
To have it all;

Each given a place
In God's great earth,
In a process that
Is called birth:

A process invoked
By our great LORD,
To produce beings,
Loved and adored.

The proof of God's love
Is all around;
From the sky above,
To deep underground.

His processes work,
They will not fail;
Standing, surely,
Against any gale.

His Laws are true,
They cannot change;
From morality to science,
A very wide range.

These things of God
Still hold true,

Pointing us to Him
In all that we do.

God, by His Holy Power,
Great love has shown;
Following His lead
May we let ours be known,

By returning to God,
Seeking His reconciliation:
For, us together in God,
This is The Great Consolidation.

A Matter of Obedience

Some things that do not make sense from one perspective are perfectly reasonable when viewed from another. Some may say that this is such an obvious statement that there is really no need to mention it. However, consider this: if you are called into action based on a principle that violates your view of reality, but which everyone else accepts; what do you do? This is a particularly relevant question when the conflict is caused by one who has authority over you. However, it becomes cloudier when the one with authority over you is far away. Let us step through this, one layer at a time; proceeding from near authority to far authority.

A near pattern of this is seen every day by parents and the parented. The parent tells the parented to do something. The parented questions whether this is relevant to them, and they then resist obeying. For instance, the parented may receive the command to clean their space. This may be protested as being unnecessary, since no one else will see it or enter it, at least not for any significant amount of time. The response: "Since it is *my space*; why should I comply?" The, "*Why*," has been raised.

First, we state that there is nothing wrong with this question. We are told to behave with a certain amount of caution; and this does involve validation. This is not just appropriate in the secular world, but is also endorsed by Scripture.

> *Beloved, believe not every spirit, but try the spirits whether they are of God: because many false prophets are gone out into the world.*

(1 John 4:1)

This Scriptural admonition does, however, have a prerequisite. No, it is not, necessarily, that we are believers; it is necessary, though, that we approach the message with an open mind. The prerequisite for validation is that thing which reasonably preceded the validation: it is simply that we receive something to validate. Furthermore, there are varying degrees of validation.

If, for instance, someone says that the earth does not exist, there is no need to provide more than a moment's validation. If the earth does not exist, there is no need to validate its lack of existence; we would not be here to do so. In this case, we have no reasonable precedent requiring validation.

However, if someone says that God require thus-and-so; then, we do have a reasonable thing that precedes a search for validation. The Scripture tells us how to do that.

> *And the brethren immediately sent away Paul and Silas by night unto Berea: who coming thither went into the synagogue of the Jews. These were more noble than those in Thessalonica, in that they received the word with all readiness of mind, and searched the scriptures daily, whether those things were so. Therefore many of them believed; also of honourable women which were Greeks, and of men, not a few.*

(Acts 17:10-12)

To make it even more difficult for parents; there is Scripture that directs them to be ready for the, *why*, question. Most often, we only apply this to our religious witness; but it is applicable in all areas of our lives. It is especially helpful, in this day, when the parent cannot control what the parented encounters, no matter how diligent they are. The public airway is an example of that place where anything can come to anyone, at any time. We must therefore be ready to provide answers, with all humility.

> *But and if ye suffer for righteousness' sake, happy are ye: and be not afraid of their terror, neither be troubled; But sanctify the Lord God in your hearts: and be ready always to give an answer to every man that asketh you a reason of the hope that is in you with meekness and fear: Having a good conscience; that, whereas they speak evil of you, as of evildoers, they may be ashamed that falsely accuse your good conversation in Christ. For it is better, if the will of God be so, that ye suffer for well doing, than for evil doing.*

(1 Peter 3:14-17)

The parent is not without assistance. The parent is not left alone. Probably the most difficult part of delivering the answer, is to stop and eliminate the anger that comes from such an outside intrusion; from, for example, the airways. The parent must be ready to avail themselves of the peace of God, especially in this area.

Does it seem that there are no situations in which the message of God cannot be found in our lives? Does it seem that there is no place that we can go to get away from the presence of God; where He cannot be found?

If this is your perception, then you are starting to get the total message. There is no area of life that is exempt from the working of God, and the need for the power of the Holy Ghost within us. Though this Scripture specifically addresses public persecution, it can also provide us with direction in dealing with private persecutions. For, intrusions by forces that seek to destroy the peace of our families, whether intentional, incidental or accidental; all are forms of persecution.

> *For nation shall rise against nation, and kingdom against kingdom: and there shall be famines, and pestilences, and earthquakes, in divers places. All these are the beginning of sorrows. Then shall they deliver you up to be afflicted, and shall kill you: and ye shall be hated of all nations for my name's sake. And then shall many be offended, and shall betray one another, and shall hate one another. And many false prophets shall rise, and shall deceive many. And because iniquity shall abound, the love of many shall wax cold. But he that shall endure unto the end, the same shall be saved.*

(Matthew 24:7-13)

Let us look at an example. If the parented is a child of four years of age, and the parent is old enough to provide the child with a space (whether this is an entire room to occupy, or just a corner of a room for sleep), the answer can be relatively straightforward. It can be the quick response: "Because I said so." At this age, in the vast majority of cases, this works.

If, however, the parented is much older than four years of age, then matters become more intricate. Typically we start to enter the realm of barter and exchange. The exchange of good behavior is closely tied to the receipt of benefit. The benefit can be either the creation of pleasure, or the opportunity to bypass pain; and sometimes both.

The children of Israel were faced with that interaction when they went in to possess the Promised Land. In their case, it involved both benefits. As the parented they were under pressure to do what they were told, in order to obtain the land under God's protection--this is the creation of pleasure. Also, they were to do it to prevent further loss of their lives and to prevent illnesses from breaking out in their community--this is bypassing the pain that is brought on by the wrath of God.

The parent in this case, God; had shown the nation that He had the *capital* necessary to deliver either of these things, and the will to do so. The sojourn of the children of Israel, in Egypt, had shown them this. No, the LORD had not, at that point, directly delivered the message of pain upon them. However, God had directed the message through the nation of Egypt, under Pharaoh.

Egypt had also been party to the negotiation of the Parent. Pharaoh and the people of Egypt had received God's good pleasure, for hosting His son, the mixed multitude of Israel. This is the congregation that God was bringing to full term in the womb of Egypt, in the body of the world. God's benefits were announced by Joseph, the son of the man Israel.

> *Now therefore let Pharaoh look out a man discreet and wise, and set him over the land of Egypt. Let Pharaoh do this, and let him appoint officers over the land, and take up the fifth part of the land of Egypt in the seven plenteous years. And let them gather all the food of those good years that come, and lay up corn under the hand of Pharaoh, and let them keep food in the cities. And that food shall be for store to the land against the seven years of famine, which shall be in the land of Egypt; that the land perish not through the famine.*
>
> *And the thing was good in the eyes of Pharaoh, and in the eyes of all his servants. And Pharaoh said unto his servants, Can we find such a one as this is, a man in whom the Spirit of God is? And Pharaoh said unto Joseph, Forasmuch as God hath shewed thee all this, there is none so discreet and wise as thou art: Thou shalt be over my*

> *house, and according unto thy word shall all my people be ruled: only in the throne will I be greater than thou.*
>
> *And Pharaoh said unto Joseph, See, I have set thee over all the land of Egypt. And Pharaoh took off his ring from his hand, and put it upon Joseph's hand, and arrayed him in vestures of fine linen, and put a gold chain about his neck; And he made him to ride in the second chariot which he had; and they cried before him, Bow the knee: and he made him ruler over all the land of Egypt.*
>
> (Genesis 41:33-43)
>
> *And the seven years of dearth began to come, according as Joseph had said: and the dearth was in all lands; but in all the land of Egypt there was bread. And when all the land of Egypt was famished, the people cried to Pharaoh for bread: and Pharaoh said unto all the Egyptians, Go unto Joseph; what he saith to you, do.*
>
> *And the famine was over all the face of the earth: and Joseph opened all the storehouses, and sold unto the Egyptians; and the famine waxed sore in the land of Egypt. And all countries came into Egypt to Joseph for to buy corn; because that the famine was so sore in all lands.*
>
> (Genesis 41:54-57)

For this service, Egypt had received benefit; comparable to those given to the man Israel, who is a party to a direct covenant from God. In fact, the children of Israel were brought to the point, along with much of the rest of the world, at which they depended on the graciousness of Egypt.

> *Now when Jacob saw that there was corn in Egypt, Jacob said unto his sons, Why do ye look one upon another? And he said, Behold, I have heard that there is corn in Egypt: get you down thither, and buy for us from thence; that we may live, and not die.*
>
> *And Joseph's ten brethren went down to buy corn in Egypt. But Benjamin, Joseph's brother, Jacob sent not with his brethren; for he said, Lest peradventure mischief befall him.*

> *And the sons of Israel came to buy corn among those that came: for the famine was in the land of Canaan.*

(Genesis 42:1-5)

So, the prosperity sent to Egypt continued; that is until the parented, Egypt, felt old enough to bypass the rules of the Parent. As with our natural children, this national child felt that it not only could, but that it must, establish its own rules. The memory of what was done for them and of what had been given to them faded away.

> *Now there arose up a new king over Egypt, which knew not Joseph. And he said unto his people, Behold, the people of the children of Israel are more and mightier than we: Come on, let us deal wisely with them; lest they multiply, and it come to pass, that, when there falleth out any war, they join also unto our enemies, and fight against us, and so get them up out of the land.*

(Exodus 1:8-10)

But God was patient and forbearing with Egypt. The nation of Egypt was, after all, a part of a MUCH bigger picture. The nation of Egypt was providing the pressure necessary to develop the strong son of the nation of Israel. As a certain saying goes, which we hear in this day: "that which does not kill you, makes you strong."

> *Therefore they did set over them taskmasters to afflict them with their burdens. And they built for Pharaoh treasure cities, Pithom and Raamses. But the more they afflicted them, the more they multiplied and grew. And they were grieved because of the children of Israel.*

(Exodus 1:11-12)

Yes, Egypt had it good. But, and let me throw in two very much overused adages, "all good things must come to and end" and it was "time to pay the piper." (I am really sorry I did that to you.) So, Pharaoh was directed by God to deliver to God what is His. Pharaoh refused; and the rest, as they say, is history. It is also a clear example for the world, then and now, of the power of God. It was quite effective in its tone, among the hearers in many of the nations of the world of that day. God had announced Himself as being directly active among the nations He possesses.

Having made this announcement, the LORD now ushered in the time of obedience. However, this is not just obedience, but rather OBEDIENCE (absolute obedience). You see, there is one *small* matter to consider: God is Perfect. Therefore, the first lessons in obedience had to be extremely precise, and powerful. These lessons would be relaxed later for the benefit of mankind; but the start had to be quite formal and rigid.

Egypt was not the only one to participate in the birth of the nation of Israel. Egypt prepared the people. The Canaanites, Amorites, Perrizites, Hittites, Jebusites, and some other nations were preparing the home for the nation. There was again a need for a Perfect example in the acquisition of the land.

The inhabitants of the land knew of the coming of the son of God, Israel. They knew that Israel was on the sure path to their location. They knew that God had demonstrated His power on behalf of this nation-to-be. Indeed, the second part of the move into the son's *house* was ushered in with a spectacular display of God's power. This display was broadcast to all the nations of the regions.

> *And it came to pass, when the people removed from their tents, to pass over Jordan, and the priests bearing the ark of the covenant before the people; And as they that bare the ark were come unto Jordan, and the feet of the priests that bare the ark were dipped in the brim of the water, (for Jordan overfloweth all his banks all the time of harvest,) That the waters which came down from above stood and rose up upon an heap very far from the city Adam, that is beside Zaretan: and those that came down toward the sea of the plain, even the salt sea, failed, and were cut off: and the people passed over right against Jericho. And the priests that bare the ark of the covenant of the LORD stood firm on dry ground in the midst of Jordan, and all the Israelites passed over on dry ground, until all the people were passed clean over Jordan.*

(Joshua 3:14-17)

> *And it came to pass, when all the kings of the Amorites, which were on the side of Jordan westward, and all the kings of the Canaanites, which were by the sea, heard that the LORD had dried up the waters of Jordan from before*

> *the children of Israel, until we were passed over, that their heart melted, neither was there spirit in them any more, because of the children of Israel.*

(Joshua 5:1)

But still there were only a few nations that came to Israel's table, to establish covenants. There was at least one that *persuaded* the new owners of the land to allow them to stay, in a small position. For this allowance they, and others like them, were made to give service.

Even the remaining nations of the prior powers of the land of promise were a part of the raising of the son, the nation of Israel.

> *Now these are the nations which the LORD left, to prove Israel by them, even as many of Israel as had not known all the wars of Canaan; Only that the generations of the children of Israel might know, to teach them war, at the least such as before knew nothing thereof; Namely, five lords of the Philistines, and all the Canaanites, and the Sidonians, and the Hivites that dwelt in mount Lebanon, from mount Baalhermon unto the entering in of Hamath. And they were to prove Israel by them, to know whether they would hearken unto the commandments of the LORD, which he commanded their fathers by the hand of Moses.*

(Judges 3:1-4)

Israel entered the land. The nation was born according to their obedience to the direct instructions of God. God had delivered on His parental promise. It was now time for the child to deliver on its promise, as well. This they did with varying degrees of success--over constant reminders. This did not amaze God, for the son is not the whole plan, but only a part of the total design of God for all nations. In this nation, the design had started to unfold.

Fast forward to now: The plan has been revealed, and fulfilled. No, I will not hedge my bets on this one. The plan is for a Messiah to bring the eventually mature nations into proper behavior with one another under God. The plan has been fulfilled in Jesus of Nazareth, the Christ, and the Messiah, who is, too, the Son of God. There was only one matter remaining; which is, for the will of God to be sealed and certified among men. This is what is called the time of the end. We still have an obligation; until God seals, certifies, and fully implants the evidence of His will; that obligation is, obedient service.

> *And as Jesus passed by, he saw a man which was blind from his birth. And his disciples asked him, saying, Master, who did sin, this man, or his parents, that he was born blind?*
>
> *Jesus answered, Neither hath this man sinned, nor his parents: but that the works of God should be made manifest in him. I must work the works of him that sent me, while it is day: the night cometh, when no man can work.*

(John 9:1-4)

There may be other nations, of old and of recent vintage, surviving until it is time for all nations to "pay the Divine Piper". But all nations will pay that Piper; even beyond just every knee bowing. The price is not excessive, nor is it odious; still, many will resist. This resistance will come from the top, down; from the heads of the nations, on through the people of the nations. But this price will be paid by all, in all nations.

> *A new commandment I give unto you, That ye love one another; as I have loved you, that ye also love one another. By this shall all men know that ye are my disciples, if ye have love one to another.*

(John 13:34-35)

This is where we seem to have a difficult time of it; especially, among the church. We have received the will of the Father; we call it the Bible. However, as the adolescent child might do, we now feel that it is up to us to rewrite it. I will give two examples. First, let me say this: either the Bible is true in all, or all will fall when even one part is separated. The much used statement about communities of men, applies to the structure of the Bible as well. You know; the one that says, "We must all hang together, or we will surely hang separately".

By the separation of certain doctrines of Scripture from the Bible, it is surely being destroyed in the remaining parts; in the minds of many who are proselytes--those who are newcomers to the faith. But more egregious than this, is that it is surely dying in the small part of the heart it once held in those who do not believe. This is our fault--we who believe, and yet still perform such separation. This is a violation of our promise to obey all; and not just, the convenient.

+=+=+=+=+=+=+=+=+=+=+=+=+=+=+=+=+=+=+

Two examples: this I promised you. Let us take the more politically sensitive one first. This is the matter of women's roles in the church and in the family. There are clear statements about what God has revealed on these matters. The arguments against accepting it includes the following (these are just a few among many):

- just for that time; we have grown enough to make it irrelevant
- a male dominated society, then; which we do not have and we do not need now
- just for that church to which it was written
- a waste of a great human resource, potentially more than half of the population (women)

All these are nice statements, and I will not disregard them. However, when we separate certain parts only, from the messages in which they were given, haven't we invalidated the entire message, the entire chapter, the entire book, and maybe even the entire Bible?

We do not agree with the notion of innocuous separation of Scripture from Scripture. For us, what the apostle Paul says, we believe as being true for now, as well as for then. We accept the message given in 1 Corinthians 7:40 as a footnote to all his writings. This message forms the capstone for wisdom that is specifically for husbands and wives. This is a subject that he covered in detail in the verses preceding the following ones. Please open your Bible and read the verses leading up to these.

> *The wife is bound by the law as long as her husband liveth; but if her husband be dead, she is at liberty to be married to whom she will; only in the Lord. But she is happier if she so abide, after my judgment: and*
>
> *I think also that*
>
> *I have the Spirit of God.*
>
> (1 Corinthians 7:39-40)

Since the Bible is from the Perfect God, it must all stand together.

The lingering effects of Satan, the adversary of God and man, are those that give a message covered in truth, but with a core of lie and irrelevance. God's messages are full, complete and all true; or they are not God's message.

> *For what if some did not believe? shall their unbelief make the faith of God without effect? God forbid: yea, let God be true, but every man a liar; as it is written, That thou mightest be justified in thy sayings, and mightest overcome when thou art judged.*
>
> (Romans 3:3-4)

This ends the uncloaking of the first of the separations.

+=+=+=+=+=+=+=+=+=+=+=+=+=+=+=+=+=+=+=+

The second separation attempts to roll back the theological timeline, in order to undo the promise of grace. This one tries to return us to the wrath of God, as demonstrated under the Law of God, given to Moses. Righteousness is being framed once again along legalistic lines. The dependence on ritual and the need for the intervention of man are replacing the price that was paid by the only begotten Son of God. The Son's place in the will of the Father is being usurped, on behalf of practices and principles of man. That usurpation is not according to Scripture.

> *Brethren, my heart's desire and prayer to God for Israel is, that they might be saved. For I bear them record that they have a zeal of God, but not according to knowledge. For they being ignorant of God's righteousness, and going about to establish their own righteousness, have not submitted themselves unto the righteousness of God. For Christ is the end of the law for righteousness to every one that believeth.*
>
> (Romans 10:1-4)

I am not just talking about an extremist wing of certain non-Christian religions; a group that insists that they can exact punishment on man according to their standards. Such extremists are known to be the sort that does not fully accept the price that Jesus paid for the sins of mankind. No, the ones I refer to, here, are those who say they accept the atoning sacrifice of Christ. Among these are some people and groups who are calling for the wrath of God against man, in every situation that you can imagine. And this call is being done in a self-serving way, to *command* others to "do it their way".

News flash (for some): there is no longer a "their way, our way"; there is only Christ's way; furthermore, Christ's way is NOT the way of wrath. This you know, and this you must return to in your preaching. This is not my command, but the proclamation of the representative of Jesus Christ.

> *And I, brethren, when I came to you, came not with excellency of speech or of wisdom, declaring unto you the testimony of God. For I determined not to know any thing among you, save Jesus Christ, and him crucified. And I was with you in weakness, and in fear, and in much trembling. And my speech and my preaching was not with enticing words of man's wisdom, but in demonstration of the Spirit and of power: That your faith should not stand in the wisdom of men, but in the power of God.*

(1 Corinthians 2:1-5)

This Scripture is losing--or in some cases has already lost--its emphasis among men. It is being replaced by spectacular arrays of events; among which are the rapture and the infallibility of a man (and this man is not Jesus of Nazareth). It could never be said, even of John the Baptist, that any man other than the Son of God is infallible. Even John the Baptist never claimed infallibility; and of anyone besides Christ, John comes closest to it. John is the one who was filled with the Holy Ghost *even from his mother's womb.*

> *But the angel said unto him, Fear not, Zacharias: for thy prayer is heard; and thy wife Elisabeth shall bear thee a son, and thou shalt call his name John. And thou shalt have joy and gladness; and many shall rejoice at his birth. For he shall be great in the sight of the Lord, and shall drink neither wine nor strong drink; and he shall be filled with the Holy Ghost, even from his mother's womb.*

(Luke 1:13-15)

Some of the reasons given for these errors of emphasis are listed below. But as you read them, please consider the Scripture below the *reasons*. This should show you that the *reasons* do not match with the teaching of the Scripture. Therefore, they are not reasons, but excuses.

To explain their error . . .

... They say
God is just, and cannot tolerate thus-and-so
But, the Bible says ...

But now the righteousness of God without the law is manifested, being witnessed by the law and the prophets; Even the righteousness of God which is by faith of Jesus Christ unto all and upon all them that believe: for there is no difference: For all have sinned, and come short of the glory of God; Being justified freely by his grace through the redemption that is in Christ Jesus: Whom God hath set forth to be a propitiation through faith in his blood, to declare his righteousness for the remission of sins that are past, through the forbearance of God;

(Romans 3:21-25)

... They say
Believers should not have to face strife
But, Jesus says ...

These things I have spoken unto you, that in me ye might have peace. In the world ye shall have tribulation: but be of good cheer; I have overcome the world.

(John 16:33)

... They say
All those who do not believe are eternally lost
But, Jesus says ...

Now is the judgment of this world: now shall the prince of this world be cast out. And I, if I be lifted up from the earth, will draw all men unto me.

(John 12:31-32)

... They say
Man needs a modern man to be the mediator

But, the Bible says . . .

For there is one God, and one mediator between God and men, the man Christ Jesus; Who gave himself a ransom for all, to be testified in due time.

(1 Timothy 2:5-6)

. . . They say
Suffering is required, in order to stand in the way of the Lord
But, Jesus says . . .

Come unto me, all ye that labour and are heavy laden, and I will give you rest. Take my yoke upon you, and learn of me; for I am meek and lowly in heart: and ye shall find rest unto your souls. For my yoke is easy, and my burden is light.

(Matthew 11:28-30)

. . . They say
Offices are **required**
But, the Bible says . . .

Behold, the days come, saith the LORD, that I will make a new covenant with the house of Israel, and with the house of Judah: Not according to the covenant that I made with their fathers in the day that I took them by the hand to bring them out of the land of Egypt; which my covenant they brake, although I was an husband unto them, saith the LORD: But this shall be the covenant that I will make with the house of Israel; After those days, saith the LORD, I will put my law in their inward parts, and write it in their hearts; and will be their God, and they shall be my people. And they shall teach no more every man his neighbour, and every man his brother, saying, Know the LORD: for they shall all know me, from the least of them unto the greatest of them, saith the LORD: for I will forgive their iniquity, and I will remember their sin no more.

(Jeremiah 31:31-34)

... They say
We are all born in sin
But, the Bible says ...

And they brought young children to him, that he should touch them: and his disciples rebuked those that brought them. But when Jesus saw it, he was much displeased, and said unto them, Suffer the little children to come unto me, and forbid them not: for of such is the kingdom of God. Verily I say unto you, Whosoever shall not receive the kingdom of God as a little child, he shall not enter therein. And he took them up in his arms, put his hands upon them, and blessed them.

(Mark 10:13-16)

Consider well, therefore, what you *expand* from the Scripture. There is no admonition, command, requirement, or any other such directive, telling anyone to expand the Scripture. We are told only to present it in the proper light of God, by our yielding to the Holy Ghost that is sent to dwell with us.

Study to show thyself approved unto God, a workman that needeth not to be ashamed, rightly dividing the word of truth. But shun profane and vain babblings: for they will increase unto more ungodliness.

(2 Timothy 2:15-16)

I close with the following; not to instill fear, but to illustrate the seriousness of what we do when we disobey God in this fashion. Consider well what you say, and what you do, with the Bible. It is to you either the Holy word of God, in print, or it is merely a convenient book of guidelines for life. In the Bible where a guideline is given--as in one of the statements of Christ Jesus, and a few of the apostle Paul--they are clearly stated as being such. If the Bible contains some things that are unstated guidelines, then it is not of God. But, since it is the word of God; there is no ambiguity about what must be absolutely lived in righteousness, and what is the permissive will of God, as stated in the Bible.

Furthermore, since it is the Holy word of God; remember that it is God who *avenges* the violation of his word, as it was given to us in the Scripture; and **NOT** man. He who hath an ear, let him hear.

> *I Jesus have sent mine angel to testify unto you these things in the churches. I am the root and the offspring of David, and the bright and morning star. And the Spirit and the bride say, Come. And let him that heareth say, Come. And let him that is athirst come. And whosoever will, let him take the water of life freely.*
>
> *For I testify unto every man that heareth the words of the prophecy of this book, If any man shall add unto these things, God shall add unto him the plagues that are written in this book: And if any man shall take away from the words of the book of this prophecy, God shall take away his part out of the book of life, and out of the holy city, and from the things which are written in this book. He which testifieth these things saith, Surely I come quickly. Amen.*
>
> *Even so, come, Lord Jesus. The grace of our Lord Jesus Christ be with you all. Amen.*

(Revelation 22:16-21)

Why I Can't Sing

The song is one of the most powerful gifts that was ever given by God to man. It is used by the Heavenly hosts to praise God, and to herald certain important celestial events. Its power is so pervasive that it can even eclipse that of prophecy in moving mankind toward God. For me, it is the special and sole property of God. And this is why I can't sing.

No, I do not mean that I do not have the ability to vocalize speech in the manner of a song; I can do this to a greater or lesser degree, depending on who is listening, and what is being attempted. When I say that I can't sing, I mean that I can't sing just for the sake of the rhythm and the rhyme. There are many songs that are very popular, and that have great power within them to move mankind to thoughts about God. These are useful for the child in the faith. But, we must all grow up some day.

> *For we know in part, and we prophesy in part. But when that which is perfect is come, then that which is in part shall be done away. When I was a child, I spake as a child, I understood as a child, I thought as a child: but when I became a man, I put away childish things.*

(1 Corinthians 13:9-11)

Therefore, since I am no longer a child, I must modify my behavior. For me, the content of the song is very important.

I have often been criticized for seeking 100% compliance in the things of God. In the few relationships that God has allowed me to have with humans in this world, I have been roundly criticized for this quest. In my search for a church home within which I will hang my Bible, I have been equally criticized. I, however, take literally the directive of Christ.

> *Be ye therefore perfect, even as your Father which is in heaven is perfect.*

(Matthew 5:48)

Will I ever make it to this level? In my mind the answer is, "No, not on this side of life". But this does not mean that I will stop trying.

So this is why I can't sing. I cannot justify singing a song that, in its lyrics, is 70% correct according to the Scripture. I cannot justify singing a song that is 80% correct, or even 90% correct, or even 95% correct in its representation of the things of God. The only reason I stop at 95% is because of the limitation of my own walk with God through Christ and in the Spirit. My ability to discern the fullness of God has not yet reached the 100% level--and no, it is not at the 95% level either, or the 80%, or even the 50% level, but I must set a standard. I must try, as best I can, to incorporate into my life, the wisdom of my brother Paul, the apostle.

> *Yea doubtless, and I count all things but loss for the excellency of the knowledge of Christ Jesus my Lord: for whom I have suffered the loss of all things, and do count them but dung, that I may win Christ, And be found in him, not having mine own righteousness, which is of the law, but that which is through the faith of Christ, the righteousness which is of God by faith: That I may know him, and the power of his resurrection, and the fellowship of his sufferings, being made conformable unto his death; If by any means I might attain unto the resurrection of the dead. Not as though I had already attained, either were already perfect: but I follow after, if that I may apprehend that for which also I am apprehended of Christ Jesus.*
>
> *Brethren, I count not myself to have apprehended: but this one thing I do, forgetting those things which are behind, and reaching forth unto those things which are before, I press toward the mark for the prize of the high calling of God in Christ Jesus.*

(Philippians 3:8-14)

I will not itemize the various songs that have entered the Christian faith that contain serious inaccuracies, but there are many. Generally, any song that does not recognize the words of Christ as he said them, but attempts to add grandeur to his life by escalating his position above that which he gave to himself is anathema to me. This also pertains to any song that does not recognize the nature of God as He chose to express it to mankind (in no way a complete picture, but enough for our feeble minds to grasp). These types of songs will not continue to be sung by me.

I have found myself stopping in the middle of a song, or even before that, because the Spirit of Truth within me has detected an anomaly. The Spirit then persuades me to evaluate this anomaly, to see if there is merit in bypassing a particular lyric or phrase.

"Why", I asked the Spirit of truth, "do you do this? Am not I protected from the content of this song, whether it is even outright wrong or not?"

In answer to my question the Spirit revealed the following:

"It is not for you that I stop the singing. It is for the sake of others with whom I will place you in contact. The song is a most powerful sword, piercing into the very soul of mankind. The song can shape the very essence of the messages that you give to others; not just the spoken messages, but also the ones illustrated by the way in which you live. The song can shape you in ways that will force you to shape others according to the same pattern. For this cause, I stop the song. On this matter, accept, as an example, the words that I presented to the world through the mind of my servant, Paul the apostle to the Corinthians.

> *All things are lawful unto me, but all things are not expedient: all things are lawful for me, but I will not be brought under the power of any.*

Though I would have the authors of songs listen more closely to me, and to write the songs accordingly; this is not the case. Guard yourself and your charges from even the most innocent of errors in the body of the song."

And this is what I will do. So there will be very few songs that I can sing to completion.

Thus, if you ever see me lifting my voice in song, and suddenly becoming silent; you will understand. It is not me who has determined this action, but it is He who dwells in me. Though I cannot sing all songs, the songs I do sing will carry the full power of the Spirit of God; even if they only come across with the sour resonance of my struggling and halting vocal cords. Why not think about trying it with your songs, whether singing or forming them.

Maybe if more of us only sing according to the word of God, we will have found the way to persuade God to come ever closer to our world to listen to His songs. And when we have his ear, let us not be shy about introducing other topics that are not contained in the song. Maybe, just maybe, with enough of this prayer to God in the midst of the song, we will have assisted mankind in coming one step closer to the prayer of Jesus. For, even though we may not use the actual words; the words that we use can contain the full power of the content of the words of Jesus, given to us as a pattern for our prayer.

> *After this manner therefore pray ye: Our Father which art in heaven, Hallowed be thy name. Thy kingdom come, Thy will be done in earth, as it is in heaven. Give us this day our daily bread. And forgive us our debts, as we forgive our debtors. And lead us not into temptation, but deliver us from evil: For thine is the kingdom, and the power, and the glory, for ever. Amen.*
>
> (Matthew 6:9-13)

I do not get really tense (anymore) about the matter, and you should not either. When you know Who you know, you can withstand even the inaccuracies in songs. And when you live the life that illustrates Christ, those around you who indulge in these, *not so correct* songs, will not damage the witness of Christ. So, ye, who are called according to God's purpose, embrace the Scripture, and fashion your message in song to the image of His Son.

> *Some indeed preach Christ even of envy and strife; and some also of good will: The one preach Christ of contention, not sincerely, supposing to add affliction to my bonds: But the other of love, knowing that I am set for the defence of the gospel. What then? notwithstanding, every way, whether in pretence, or in truth, Christ is preached; and I therein do rejoice, yea, and will rejoice. For I know that this shall turn to my salvation through your prayer, and the supply of the Spirit of Jesus Christ, According to my earnest expectation and my hope, that in nothing I shall be ashamed, but that with all boldness, as always, so now*

also Christ shall be magnified in my body, whether it be by life, or by death. For to me to live is Christ, and to die is gain.

(Philippians 1:15-21)

Amen.

As the Lightning Cometh

When I was a child my father and mother would chastise me when I misbehaved. I, therefore, expect nothing less from God when I sin. Oh surely, they forgave me once I showed the proper amount of remorse, and had passed the time of discipline: so it is also with God. Furthermore, my parents issued discipline speedily. They did not sit me in some area remote from them, to ponder the actions that they would do. Their actions were pretty much instant, and were meted out according to the gravity of the offense. It is as a result of this experience that I arrived at my first understanding of the ways of God. This is what allowed me to become absorbed in the discovery of the ways of Jesus Christ, the Son of God. Since I had a very good--no, excellent--relationship with my earthly father, it is my belief that Jesus has an even better relationship with our Heavenly Father.

With the above in mind, we should be able to discover the way Jesus Christ dispenses discipline to his charges. And lest you say that there is no similar example on the earth, let me go a little further with my family environment. In my family, if I, being the youngest son, and the youngest child, were to misbehave, it was the responsibility of those among my older siblings, the ones that had reached an age of sufficient reason, to correct me. The correction, of course, had limitations. One of the corrective measures was to grab me by whatever part would get my attention: arm, neck or even the leg (sometimes I'd *fall down*). Though, the most common way to get my attention was to simply say that my father was coming. Even in those times when I had *fallen down*, I suddenly found new strength, and rose to the occasion, so to speak. Thus, it is absolutely reasonable to me that Jesus Christ, being my brother, would have full rights from the Father to chasten me when it is necessary--also known as, often. Some Scripture might convince even you of this about Jesus.

> *And we know that all things work together for good to them that love God, to them who are the called according to his purpose. For whom he did foreknow, he also did*

> *predestinate to be conformed to the image of his Son, that he might be the firstborn among many brethren.*
>
> (Romans 8:28-29)
>
> *Behold, what manner of love the Father hath bestowed upon us, that we should be called the sons of God: therefore the world knoweth us not, because it knew him not. Beloved, now are we the sons of God, and it doth not yet appear what we shall be: but we know that, when he shall appear, we shall be like him; for we shall see him as he is.*
>
> (1 John 3:1-2)
>
> *And Jesus came and spake unto them, saying, All power is given unto me in heaven and in earth.*
>
> (Matthew 28:18)

Once it was established for me that Jesus Christ has the authority to issue discipline to me, and to anyone else, I wanted to know whether he would do so slowly or quickly. I have heard much talk about special times of suffering that will come on the earth, and that will even be visited on those who follow Jesus. The talk says that these times will be lingering times of extreme hopelessness and helplessness, even for Christians. This concerns me greatly, because when I read the Bible, and see where Jesus, before he returned to Heaven after his resurrection, said that those who follow him would never be hopeless, and they need never feel helpless.

> *Jesus answered and said unto him, If a man love me, he will keep my words: and my Father will love him, and we will come unto him, and make our abode with him. He that loveth me not keepeth not my sayings: and the word which ye hear is not mine, but the Father's which sent me. These things have I spoken unto you, being yet present with you. But the Comforter, which is the Holy Ghost, whom the Father will send in my name, he shall teach you all things, and bring all things to your remembrance, whatsoever I have said unto you. Peace I leave with you, my peace I give unto you: not as the world giveth, give I unto you. Let not your heart be troubled, neither let it be afraid.*
>
> (John 14:23-27)

So for this feeble mind of mine, which likes to take Jesus at his word, there can be no time when anyone can disrupt my peace; except me. To those who accept his death and resurrection, Jesus has promised that he will abide with them.

> *Behold, I stand at the door, and knock: if any man hear my voice, and open the door, I will come in to him, and will sup with him, and he with me. To him that overcometh will I grant to sit with me in my throne, even as I also overcame, and am set down with my Father in his throne. He that hath an ear, let him hear what the Spirit saith unto the churches.*
>
> (Revelation 3:20-22)

According to the Scripture, the abiding presence of Jesus will provide comfort. Yes, we have the Comforter to teach us and to plead for us; in words that we cannot even utter. However, sometimes the friend yearns for the presence of the friend. This, Jesus knew would happen with us. He did not say that he would appear physically, but that he would come and be a part of us. This is at the level of the spirit, and not of the flesh.

> *If ye love me, keep my commandments. And I will pray the Father, and he shall give you another Comforter, that he may abide with you for ever; Even the Spirit of truth; whom the world cannot receive, because it seeth him not, neither knoweth him: but ye know him; for he dwelleth with you, and shall be in you. I will not leave you comfortless: I will come to you.*
>
> (John 14:15-18)

There will be many forces that will try to disrupt the Christian from walking with the Lord. People may try; circumstances will intervene; consequences may even catch our eye; however, over all these God will prevail. For those who have accepted the ways of Jesus Christ, they will never be lost. Hear the words of the Lord.

> *My sheep hear my voice, and I know them, and they follow me: And I give unto them eternal life; and they shall never perish, neither shall any man pluck them out of my hand. My Father, which gave them me, is greater than all; and no man is able to pluck them out of my Father's hand.*
>
> (John 10:27-29)

Hear the confidence of the saints.

> *For God hath not given us the spirit of fear; but of power, and of love, and of a sound mind. Be not thou therefore ashamed of the testimony of our Lord, nor of me his prisoner: but be thou partaker of the afflictions of the gospel according to the power of God; Who hath saved us, and called us with an holy calling, not according to our works, but according to his own purpose and grace, which was given us in Christ Jesus before the world began, But is now made manifest by the appearing of our Saviour Jesus Christ, who hath abolished death, and hath brought life and immortality to light through the gospel: Whereunto I am appointed a preacher, and an apostle, and a teacher of the Gentiles. For the which cause I also suffer these things: nevertheless I am not ashamed: for I know whom I have believed, and am persuaded that he is able to keep that which I have committed unto him against that day. Hold fast the form of sound words, which thou hast heard of me, in faith and love which is in Christ Jesus.*

(2 Timothy 1:7-13)

Therefore, we who know the Lord are secure in him. I just wanted you to have an assurance of that before we go further.

But what of those who have not come to knowledge of the saving power of Jesus Christ? What about those who just have neither heard nor accepted? Is there a difference in his treatment of these two audiences? I think that there is, and we will cover that also, further on in the writing.

+=+=+=+=+=+=+=+=+=+=+=+=+=+=+=+=+=+=+=+

Our search, now, is for the way that God and his Son, Jesus Christ, will execute judgment on the inhabitants of the earth. As I mentioned before, some think that it will be done slowly: I do not.

Those who think it will be done slowly, read the book of Revelation as a spaced sequence of events. That is, they see one event occurring, and then some rest period happening, and then the next event occurring. This is the way they see things happening at the opening of the seals and the sounding of the trumpets. However, when in Revelation there is a timed event, it is stated as being timed; and the time of the event is given. The opening of the seals is more consistently viewed as happening one after the other, with no break in between. This is consistent with the rapid dispensing of judgment, and not a slow, lingering torture. God has no reason to torture anyone; instead, the Lord chastens us with purpose. The chastening of the Lord that brings torment is only torment according to man; it is designed by the Son and the Father to bring man to repentance. However, man will not always listen.

> *And the rest of the men which were not killed by these plagues yet repented not of the works of their hands, that they should not worship devils, and idols of gold, and silver, and brass, and stone, and of wood: which neither can see, nor hear, nor walk: Neither repented they of their murders, nor of their sorceries, nor of their fornication, nor of their thefts.*

(Revelation 9:20-21)

So what is the method used by Jesus to deliver the judgment of God? Well, according to the Bible, Jesus does this quickly.

> *And he said unto me, These sayings are faithful and true: and the Lord God of the holy prophets sent his angel to show unto his servants the things which must shortly be done. Behold, I come quickly: blessed is he that keepeth the sayings of the prophecy of this book.*

(Revelation 22:6-7)

Knowing that he does it quickly, the next question is: does he do it with stealth or in full view?

The Scripture tell us that when he comes, it is in full view. This is attested to by Jesus himself, as recorded in two of the first four books of the Bible that are generally referred to as, the Gospel writings; as opposed to the Letters of the Apostles.

> *Wherefore if they shall say unto you, Behold, he is in the desert; go not forth: behold, he is in the secret chambers; believe it not. For as the lightning cometh out of the east, and shineth even unto the west; so shall also the coming of the Son of man be. For wheresoever the carcase is, there will the eagles be gathered together.*

Immediately after the tribulation of those days shall the sun be darkened, and the moon shall not give her light, and the stars shall fall from heaven, and the powers of the heavens shall be shaken: And then shall appear the sign of the Son of man in heaven: and then shall all the tribes of the earth mourn, and they shall see the Son of man coming in the clouds of heaven with power and great glory. And he shall send his angels with a great sound of a trumpet, and they shall gather together his elect from the four winds, from one end of heaven to the other.

Now learn a parable of the fig tree; When his branch is yet tender, and putteth forth leaves, ye know that summer is nigh: So likewise ye, when ye shall see all these things, know that it is near, even at the doors. Verily I say unto you, This generation shall not pass, till all these things be fulfilled. Heaven and earth shall pass away, but my words shall not pass away.

But of that day and hour knoweth no man, no, not the angels of heaven, but my Father only.

But as the days of Noe were, so shall also the coming of the Son of man be. For as in the days that were before the flood they were eating and drinking, marrying and giving in marriage, until the day that Noe entered into the ark, And knew not until the flood came, and took them all away; so shall also the coming of the Son of man be.

Then shall two be in the field; the one shall be taken, and the other left. Two women shall be grinding at the mill; the one shall be taken, and the other left. Watch therefore: for ye know not what hour your Lord doth come. But know this, that if the goodman of the house had known in what watch the thief would come, he would have watched, and would not have suffered his house to be broken up. Therefore be ye also ready: for in such an hour as ye think not the Son of man cometh.

Who then is a faithful and wise servant, whom his lord hath made ruler over his household, to give them meat in due season? Blessed is that servant, whom his lord when he cometh shall find so doing. Verily I say unto you, That he shall make him ruler over all his goods.

But and if that evil servant shall say in his heart, My lord delayeth his coming; And shall begin to smite his fellowservants, and to eat and drink with the drunken; The lord of that servant shall come in a day when he looketh not for him, and in an hour that he is not aware of, And shall cut him asunder, and appoint him his portion with the hypocrites: there shall be weeping and gnashing of teeth.

(Matthew 24:26-51)

And when he was demanded of the Pharisees, when the kingdom of God should come, he answered them and said, The kingdom of God cometh not with observation: Neither shall they say, Lo here! or, lo there! for, behold, the kingdom of God is within you.

And he said unto the disciples, The days will come, when ye shall desire to see one of the days of the Son of man, and ye shall not see it. And they shall say to you, See here; or, see there: go not after them, nor follow them. For as the lightning, that lighteneth out of the one part under heaven, shineth unto the other part under heaven; so shall also the Son of man be in his day. But first must he suffer many things, and be rejected of this generation.

And as it was in the days of Noe, so shall it be also in the days of the Son of man. They did eat, they drank, they married wives, they were given in marriage, until the day that Noe entered into the ark, and the flood came, and destroyed them all. Likewise also as it was in the days of Lot; they did eat, they drank, they bought, they sold, they planted, they builded; But the same day that Lot went out of Sodom it rained fire and brimstone from heaven, and destroyed them all. Even thus shall it be in the day when the Son of man is revealed. In that day, he which shall be upon the housetop, and his stuff in the house, let him not come down to take it away: and he that is in the field, let him likewise not return back. Remember Lot's wife.

> *Whosoever shall seek to save his life shall lose it; and whosoever shall lose his life shall preserve it. I tell you, in that night there shall be two men in one bed; the one shall be taken, and the other shall be left. Two women shall be grinding together; the one shall be taken, and the other left. Two men shall be in the field; the one shall be taken, and the other left.*
>
> *And they answered and said unto him, Where, Lord?*
>
> *And he said unto them, Wheresoever the body is, thither will the eagles be gathered together.*

(Luke 17:20-37)

The two Scripture passages, above, refer to the coming destruction of Jerusalem, which Jesus foretold. This time is referred to as, *the coming of the Son of man*, and as, *the Son of man be in his day*.

There is another day that sees the Lord Jesus being very active. Jesus Christ is the one who opens the seals, and start the events of the latter day. This is a time that is referred to as, *things which must shortly come to pass*, and, *things which must shortly be done*. There is Scripture which tells of the way the things of God are done in that day, too.

> *John to the seven churches which are in Asia: Grace be unto you, and peace, from him which is, and which was, and which is to come; and from the seven Spirits which are before his throne; And from Jesus Christ, who is the faithful witness, and the first begotten of the dead, and the prince of the kings of the earth. Unto him that loved us, and washed us from our sins in his own blood, And hath made us kings and priests unto God and his Father; to him be glory and dominion for ever and ever. Amen.*
>
> *Behold, he cometh with clouds; and every eye shall see him, and they also which pierced him: and all kindreds of the earth shall wail because of him. Even so, Amen.*

(Revelation 1:4-7)

We must, therefore, not tell anyone that their life will be miserable on this earth if they do not accept Christ. God does not inflict misery to move us to His side; though, the LORD does chasten

His children. Therefore, there is a distinction between those who are in Christ, and those who are not. If a man sees one of his children misbehaving, he will surely chasten that child. However, if he sees someone else's child misbehaving, typically, he will not do so. We, who are the children of God, are subject to God's chastening; those who are not must be persuaded by the example of those who are.

God does not pull them by punishment; the LORD draws them by jealousy. Yes, this word, which is thought of as being negative, can actually have a positive effect. God mentions this word when he talks about His actions to move his son Israel back to Him.

> *But Jeshurun waxed fat, and kicked: thou art waxen fat, thou art grown thick, thou art covered with fatness; then he forsook God which made him, and lightly esteemed the Rock of his salvation. They provoked him to jealousy with strange gods, with abominations provoked they him to anger. They sacrificed unto devils, not to God; to gods whom they knew not, to new gods that came newly up, whom your fathers feared not. Of the Rock that begat thee thou art unmindful, and hast forgotten God that formed thee.*
>
> *And when the LORD saw it, he abhorred them, because of the provoking of his sons, and of his daughters. And he said, I will hide my face from them, I will see what their end shall be: for they are a very froward generation, children in whom is no faith. They have moved me to jealousy with that which is not God; they have provoked me to anger with their vanities: and I will move them to jealousy with those which are not a people; I will provoke them to anger with a foolish nation.*

(Deuteronomy 32:15-21)

Since jealousy can move a nation, made up of people; it must be effective in moving people, regardless of nation. We are told to live as examples that will cause others to want to know what we have that they do not. And perhaps, with the help of God and through our prayers on their behalf, in the name of Jesus, they will come to understand that they, too, can have it. This is the message spoken to the nation of Israel, and to the world.

> *For the scripture saith, Whosoever believeth on him shall not be ashamed. For there is no difference between the Jew*

and the Greek: for the same Lord over all is rich unto all that call upon him. For whosoever shall call upon the name of the Lord shall be saved.

How then shall they call on him in whom they have not believed? and how shall they believe in him of whom they have not heard? and how shall they hear without a preacher? And how shall they preach, except they be sent? as it is written, How beautiful are the feet of them that preach the gospel of peace, and bring glad tidings of good things! But they have not all obeyed the gospel. For Esaias saith, Lord, who hath believed our report? So then faith cometh by hearing, and hearing by the word of God.

But I say, Have they not heard? Yes verily, their sound went into all the earth, and their words unto the ends of the world.

But I say, Did not Israel know? First Moses saith, I will provoke you to jealousy by them that are no people, and by a foolish nation I will anger you.

(Romans 10:11-19)

Ye are the salt of the earth: but if the salt have lost his savour, wherewith shall it be salted? it is thenceforth good for nothing, but to be cast out, and to be trodden under foot of men. Ye are the light of the world. A city that is set on an hill cannot be hid. Neither do men light a candle, and put it under a bushel, but on a candlestick; and it giveth light unto all that are in the house. Let your light so shine before men, that they may see your good works, and glorify your Father which is in heaven.

(Matthew 5:13-16)

We do not give the increase, by either word or action; only God gives the increase. We are called, therefore, to rest in our words and examples; not to seek a hasty conversion of those around us.

+=+=+=+=+=+=+=+=+=+=+=+=+=+=+=+=+=+

There are some who feel that all who do not actively accept Christ are destined for a sojourn in hell. I mentioned before that I saw a difference between those who never knew to accept Christ and those who do. Here, this matter will be explored.

Many say that all those who are not introduced to the Gospel are lost. This is presumptuous of those who say it. God is not like the legal system; He does not penalize for ignorance. Consider His statement about the children in the nation of Israel.

> *And the LORD heard the voice of your words, and was wroth, and sware, saying, Surely there shall not one of these men of this evil generation see that good land, which I sware to give unto your fathers, Save Caleb the son of Jephunneh; he shall see it, and to him will I give the land that he hath trodden upon, and to his children, because he hath wholly followed the LORD.*
>
> *Also the LORD was angry with me for your sakes, saying, Thou also shalt not go in thither. But Joshua the son of Nun, which standeth before thee, he shall go in thither: encourage him: for he shall cause Israel to inherit it.*
>
> *Moreover your little ones, which ye said should be a prey, and your children, which in that day had no knowledge between good and evil, they shall go in thither, and unto them will I give it, and they shall possess it.*
>
> *But as for you, turn you, and take your journey into the wilderness by the way of the Red sea.*
>
> (Deuteronomy 1:34-40)

However, understand this fully: those who have been introduced to the Gospel and have turned away from it are condemned.

> *He that believeth on him is not condemned: but he that believeth not is condemned already, because he hath not believed in the name of the only begotten Son of God. And this is the condemnation, that light is come into the world, and men loved darkness rather than light, because their deeds were evil. For every one that doeth evil hateth the light, neither cometh to the light, lest his deeds should be reproved. But he that doeth truth cometh to the light, that his deeds may be made manifest, that they are wrought in God.*
>
> (John 3:18-21)

Jesus' coming is clear and brilliant. This applies not just to the coming that we view as an end time thing, but also to his coming into the life of an unbeliever. There is no need to fear that anyone will be separated from God because they never had a chance to know Him.

However, it is true that we who know Him will be chastened for not representing Him every time He directs us to do so.

> *But and if ye suffer for righteousness' sake, happy are ye: and be not afraid of their terror, neither be troubled; But sanctify the Lord God in your hearts: and be ready always to give an answer to every man that asketh you a reason of the hope that is in you with meekness and fear: Having a good conscience; that, whereas they speak evil of you, as of evildoers, they may be ashamed that falsely accuse your good conversation in Christ. For it is better, if the will of God be so, that ye suffer for well doing, than for evil doing.*

(1 Peter 3:14-17)

Let us, therefore, not just pray that God would hasten the *time of the end*; but let us pray that He would enhance His kingdom on this earth. This, too, is the lightening that can shine from one end of the world to the other. This, too, is the day of the Son of man. We must stop this concentration on what is called eschatology, and get back to preaching Jesus and him crucified. The *end* is already taken care of, from above.

Pray that the *time of the end* is not the only time that his brilliance will flow to the four corners of the earth. Pray that his brilliance will flow even now from one end of the world to the next, one soul at a time. As Jesus prayed, so must we.

> *And when thou prayest, thou shalt not be as the hypocrites are: for they love to pray standing in the synagogues and in the corners of the streets, that they may be seen of men. Verily I say unto you, They have their reward.*

> *But thou, when thou prayest, enter into thy closet, and when thou hast shut thy door, pray to thy Father which is in secret; and thy Father which seeth in secret shall reward thee openly.*

> *But when ye pray, use not vain repetitions, as the heathen do: for they think that they shall be heard for their much*

speaking. Be not ye therefore like unto them: for your Father knoweth what things ye have need of, before ye ask him.

After this manner therefore pray ye: Our Father which art in heaven, Hallowed be thy name. Thy kingdom come, Thy will be done in earth, as it is in heaven. Give us this day our daily bread. And forgive us our debts, as we forgive our debtors. And lead us not into temptation, but deliver us from evil: For thine is the kingdom, and the power, and the glory, for ever. Amen.

(Matthew 6:5-13)

Indeed, it is said to us as it was said to John the Revelator:

And, behold, I come quickly; and my reward is with me, to give every man according as his work shall be. I am Alpha and Omega, the beginning and the end, the first and the last. Blessed are they that do his commandments, that they may have right to the tree of life, and may enter in through the gates into the city. For without are dogs, and sorcerers, and whoremongers, and murderers, and idolaters, and whosoever loveth and maketh a lie. I Jesus have sent mine angel to testify unto you these things in the churches. I am the root and the offspring of David, and the bright and morning star.

And the Spirit and the bride say, Come. And let him that heareth say, Come. And let him that is athirst come. And whosoever will, let him take the water of life freely.

(Revelation 22:12-17)

Our concern must be not the beginning, nor the end, but the middle. It is very significant that both God and Christ say that they are alpha and omega, the beginning and the end. This leaves the middle for the servants of God to bring about. The Father and His Son have already taken care of the beginning, and the Father and His Son will take care of the end; wherefore let us proceed from the churches to take the witness of Christ into the world in the intervening time. Let us do this not just by words, but by actions and attitudes as well. Let us, especially, not do this by words of condemnation; but by words of hope.

I beseech you therefore, brethren, by the mercies of God, that ye present your bodies a living sacrifice, holy, acceptable unto God, which is your reasonable service. And be not conformed to this world: but be ye transformed by the renewing of your mind, that ye may prove what is that good, and acceptable, and perfect, will of God.

For I say, through the grace given unto me, to every man that is among you, not to think of himself more highly than he ought to think; but to think soberly, according as God hath dealt to every man the measure of faith.

(Romans 12:1-3)

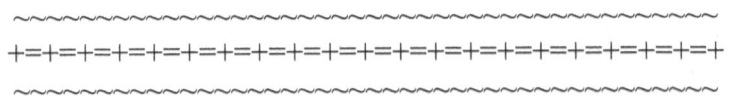

What is Jesus Christ?

This is a study/mystery for those who are persuaded to follow God. It will require that you petition God through the Holy Ghost, which is resident in you, for understanding. To any others who read this, it will be like reading someone else's mail; and that, written in an unknown language. You might understand some of it, but there is a lot of room for misunderstanding. This is not said to exclude you, but to persuade you to also go to God to request understanding. You see, God is not stingy. If you ask for wisdom, He will provide it for you; no matter what state you are in.

> *If any of you lack wisdom, let him ask of God, that giveth to all men liberally, and upbraideth not; and it shall be given him. But let him ask in faith, nothing wavering. For he that wavereth is like a wave of the sea driven with the wind and tossed. For let not that man think that he shall receive any thing of the Lord. A double minded man is unstable in all his ways.*
>
> (James 1:5-8)

But be ready; when He gives you wisdom, you may just find yourself believing in Christ Jesus the Lord as your personal savior as well. If so, I say, welcome to the family. If not, I say, eventually!

+=+=+=+=+=+=+=+=+=+=+=+=+=+=+=+=+=+=+

Acts 7:44-50

Our fathers had the tabernacle of witness in the wilderness, as he had appointed, speaking unto Moses, that he should make it according to the fashion that he had seen. Which also our fathers that came after brought in with Jesus into the possession of the Gentiles, whom God drave out before the face of our fathers, unto the days of David; Who found favour before God, and desired to find a tabernacle for the God of Jacob. But Solomon built him an house.

Howbeit the most High dwelleth not in temples made with hands; as saith the prophet, Heaven is my throne, and earth is my footstool: what house will ye build me? saith the Lord: or what is the place of my rest? Hath not my hand made all these things?

+=+=+=+=+=+=+=+=+=+=+=+=+=+=+=+=+=+=+=+

Revelation 1:1-7

The Revelation of Jesus Christ, which God gave unto him, to show unto his servants things which must shortly come to pass; and he sent and signified it by his angel unto his servant John: Who bare record of the word of God, and of the testimony of Jesus Christ, and of all things that he saw. Blessed is he that readeth, and they that hear the words of this prophecy, and keep those things which are written therein: for the time is at hand.

John to the seven churches which are in Asia: Grace be unto you, and peace, from him which is, and which was, and which is to come; and from the seven Spirits which are before his throne; And from Jesus Christ, who is the faithful witness, and the first begotten of the dead, and the prince of the kings of the earth. Unto him that loved us, and washed us from our sins in his own blood, And hath made us kings and priests unto God and his Father; to him be glory and dominion for ever and ever. Amen.

Behold, he cometh with clouds; and every eye shall see him, and they also which pierced him: and all kindreds of the earth shall wail because of him. Even so, Amen.

+=+=+=+=+=+=+=+=+=+=+=+=+=+=+=+=+=+=+=+

Revelation 1:11-13

Saying, I am Alpha and Omega, the first and the last: and, What thou seest, write in a book, and send it unto the seven churches which are in Asia; unto Ephesus, and unto Smyrna, and unto Pergamos, and unto Thyatira, and unto Sardis, and unto Philadelphia, and unto Laodicea. And I turned to see the voice that spake with me. And being turned, I saw seven golden candlesticks; And in the midst of the seven candlesticks one like unto the Son of man, clothed with a garment down to the foot, and girt about the paps with a golden girdle.

Revelation 1:17-18

And when I saw him, I fell at his feet as dead. And he laid his right hand upon me, saying unto me, Fear not; I am the first and the last: I am he that liveth, and was dead; and, behold, I am alive for evermore, Amen; and have the keys of hell and of death.

+=+=+=+=+=+=+=+=+=+=+=+=+=+=+=+=+=+=+=+

Revelation 5:1-14

And I saw in the right hand of him that sat on the throne a book written within and on the backside, sealed with seven seals. And I saw a strong angel proclaiming with a loud voice, Who is worthy to open the book, and to loose the seals thereof? And no man in heaven, nor in earth, neither under the earth, was able to open the book, neither to look thereon.

And I wept much, because no man was found worthy to open and to read the book, neither to look thereon.

And one of the elders saith unto me, Weep not: behold, the Lion of the tribe of Juda, the Root of David, hath prevailed to open the book, and to loose the seven seals thereof.

And I beheld, and, lo, in the midst of the throne and of the four beasts, and in the midst of the elders, stood a Lamb as it had been slain, having seven horns and seven eyes, which are the seven Spirits of God sent forth into all the earth. And he came and took the book out of the right hand of him that sat upon the throne. And when he had taken the book, the four beasts and four and twenty elders fell down before the Lamb, having every one of them harps, and golden vials full of odours, which are the prayers of saints. And they sung a new song, saying, Thou art worthy to take the book, and to open the seals thereof: for thou wast slain, and hast redeemed us to God by thy blood out of every kindred, and tongue, and people, and nation; And hast made us unto our God kings and priests: and we shall reign on the earth.

And I beheld, and I heard the voice of many angels round about the throne and the beasts and the elders: and the number of them was ten thousand times ten thousand, and thousands of thousands; Saying with a loud voice, Worthy is the Lamb that was slain to receive power, and riches, and wisdom, and strength, and honour, and glory, and blessing. And every creature which is in heaven, and on the earth, and under the earth, and such as are in the sea, and all that are in them, heard I saying, Blessing, and honour, and glory, and power, be unto him that sitteth upon the throne, and unto the Lamb for ever and ever. And the four beasts said, Amen. And the four and twenty elders fell down and worshipped him that liveth for ever and ever.

+=+=+=+=+=+=+=+=+=+=+=+=+=+=+=+=+=+=+=+

Revelation 22:7-14

Behold, I come quickly: blessed is he that keepeth the sayings of the prophecy of this book.

And I John saw these things, and heard them. And when I had heard and seen, I fell down to worship before the feet of the angel which showed me these things.

Then saith he unto me, See thou do it not: for I am thy fellowservant, and of thy brethren the prophets, and of them which keep the sayings of this book: worship God. And he saith unto me, Seal not the sayings of the prophecy of this book: for the time is at hand. He that is unjust, let him be unjust still: and he which is filthy, let him be filthy still: and he that is righteous, let him be righteous still: and he that is holy, let him be holy still.

And, behold, I come quickly; and my reward is with me, to give every man according as his work shall be. I am Alpha and Omega, the beginning and the end, the first and the last.

Blessed are they that do his commandments, that they may have right to the tree of life, and may enter in through the gates into the city.

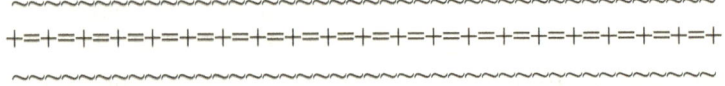

+=+=+=+=+=+=+=+=+=+=+=+=+=+=+=+=+=+=+=+

The Two Fires

I often wondered why the Scripture talks about death and hell giving up their dead. I asked myself, if all were lost from birth and could only escape hell by accepting Jesus Christ, then what is the use of the place called death? The Scripture clearly indicates that those who reject Christ's way will see condemnation. It also clearly says that those who accept his witness, once they die, are absent from the body and present with the Lord. So what about those who never knew to accept or reject Christ? Where do they go?

This question is particularly significant to me because before Jesus of Nazareth was born there was a whole world of many nations that did not know of the existence of Christ. Indeed, many in the nation of Israel did not fully understand what the Messiah was destined to do. So what about all these people; where are they *stored*?

According to the Bible, they are *stored* in death. These are they who are among those released, along with those in hell, and then they will be judged according to their works.

> *And I saw a great white throne, and him that sat on it, from whose face the earth and the heaven fled away; and there was found no place for them. And I saw the dead, small and great, stand before God; and the books were opened: and another book was opened, which is the book of life: and the dead were judged out of those things which were written in the books, according to their works. And the sea gave up the dead which were in it; and death and hell delivered up the dead which were in them: and they were judged every man according to their works.*
>
> (Revelation 20:11-13)

Let us look at these two places, so that we can clearly understand the difference. Once we understand the difference, we can share with others the true nature of the Kingdom of God with man, with greater clarity.

+=+

Hell

Let us use an earthly example to describe the purpose of this place. For purposes of this example, imagine that there are people who hate doctors and have cancer. Even though they know that they are sick, they will not spend their money on doctors. They feel that they can find their own remedy through herbs and by positive mental attitudes--but the cancer does not listen. They search and search through books and the Internet for solutions--meanwhile, the cancer continues to grow.

Finally they lose their ability to function, and are left with only pain. They wish for death, but the body hangs on to life. If they had the power, they would take their own life; but they do not have the power. Furthermore, because of their isolation, and of course the laws of the land, there is no one who will take their life from them. So they live in torment, waiting for the reprieve of death.

At least in this case, they know that death will some day come, and *relieve* them of this pain. But what if death never came? What if science found a *miracle*, which was spread in the air, preventing natural death? Think about them: they are living their lives in pain until someone found them and relieved them of their misery; either through death or through science. They are now totally dependent upon the very doctors that they had despised.

This is the state of those who receive the good news of the kingdom, and turn their backs. There are people who are so *involved* with their own view of life that they do not like to think of the ways of God and of His Son. They know that they have sinned; if they will sincerely admit it. They also know that this will separate them from anyone who is perfect: God is Perfect. Among these people are those who feel that they will find their own way in life. They will conquer their problem through moral and ethical means; but the sin nature, and the presence and problems of sin do not go away.

The Doctor of doctors appears with the solution to their sin problem: the Doctor is the Lord Jesus Christ. However, the sin sick person of this example still feels that, with time, they will find their own solution. They fully understand what is being offered to them.

They understand that their *ticket* to God's presence is fully paid for. They understand that the way of Jesus is the only solution to total remission and lasting healing. However, with full understanding, they still reject the offer of the Lord Jesus Christ. This is not an incidental matter of, not knowing; this is a willful rejection of the offer of God through Jesus Christ.

Let us say, for the sake of discussion, that there **are** other ways to God besides being called a Christian. Even if there are, these other methods will still end up facing the same gatekeeper, Jesus Christ. These other methods will still receive their power on the basis of the sacrifice of Christ. This was the case even of the Law of Moses.

The Law of Moses was a preview of the coming of the Messiah in Jesus Christ. Its power is fully contained in the Messiah, and without the Messiah it has no power.

> *Our fathers had the tabernacle of witness in the wilderness, as he had appointed, speaking unto Moses, that he should make it according to the fashion that he had seen. Which also our fathers that came after brought in with Jesus into the possession of the Gentiles, whom God drave out before the face of our fathers, unto the days of David; Who found favour before God, and desired to find a tabernacle for the God of Jacob.*

(Acts 7:44-46)

This is also the case with any other method.

> *Let not your heart be troubled: ye believe in God, believe also in me. In my Father's house are many mansions: if it were not so, I would have told you. I go to prepare a place for you. And if I go and prepare a place for you, I will come again, and receive you unto myself; that where I am, there ye may be also. And whither I go ye know, and the way ye know.*
>
> *Thomas saith unto him, Lord, we know not whither thou goest; and how can we know the way?*
>
> *Jesus saith unto him, I am the way, the truth, and the life: no man cometh unto the Father, but by me. If ye had known me, ye should have known my Father also: and from henceforth ye know him, and have seen him.*

(John 14:1-7)

One of the places of separation from God is the place called hell. In this place the pain of the cancer of willful sin is replaced by the pain of separation from God.

We often take too lightly just how much we depend on God. If we have health, it is from God. If we have family, it is from God. If we have opportunity, it is from God. If we have prosperity, it is from God. If we have even one friend, he or she is from God. Above all, our lives are from God; and this is from start to finish; from conception to death; from the fertilization of the egg to the cessation of the heart and brain functions. Even a sunshiny day is from God; in whatever fashion we describe a sunshiny day. None of this exists in hell.

Those who are in hell are separate and alone. Do not believe the jokes that some say about there being a party in hell. It is more like the parable of the inhabitants of hell who were fitted with six foot forks for hands, and plenty of food to eat. However, because they thought only of their own tormenting hunger, they spent their time trying to manipulate the forks to feed their own self. There was no thought about using the forks to feed one another. This is the state of those who are in hell. They are separated from one another by being contained exclusively in a torment of their own.

Even a second of torment in hell is more than a lifetime of agony on earth. Thus, even though hell is only temporary, it will feel like an eternity to those who walk themselves to it: one does not get assigned to hell, nor does one accidentally fall in. A person has to reject the things of God for God to release them to their choice. This is the downside of that thing known as, free will.

On the other hand, those who are believers in God through Jesus Christ are promised that they will neither see death nor hell.

> *For we that are in this tabernacle do groan, being burdened: not for that we would be unclothed, but clothed upon, that mortality might be swallowed up of life. Now he that hath wrought us for the selfsame thing is God, who also hath given unto us the earnest of the Spirit. Therefore we are always confident, knowing that, whilst we are at home in the body, we are absent from the Lord: (For we walk by faith, not by sight:) We are confident, I say, and willing rather to be absent from the body, and to be present with the Lord. Wherefore we labour, that, whether present or absent, we may be accepted of him. For we must all*

> *appear before the judgment seat of Christ; that every one may receive the things done in his body, according to that he hath done, whether it be good or bad.*

(2 Corinthians 5:4-10)

Those who do not accept the offering of God, especially that which was offered through Jesus Christ, will not be able to approach God; they will be separated from God. Once such a person dies, they will enter the hell of separation from God. However, God is merciful; this we will see better in a little while.

+=+

The Lake

There are some beings who will receive a special place of separation from God. These are they who did not just reject the offer of God, but who actively set out to defeat the coming of the Kingdom of God. Among these are some of the angels that formerly had access to Heaven.

> *And there appeared another wonder in heaven; and behold a great red dragon, having seven heads and ten horns, and seven crowns upon his heads. And his tail drew the third part of the stars of heaven, and did cast them to the earth: and the dragon stood before the woman which was ready to be delivered, for to devour her child as soon as it was born.*

(Revelation 12:3-4)

These are beings that fully understand the workings of God, but they actively will themselves to believe that there is a better way to follow. This way is the way of Satan. The Bible tells us of those who are deceived by Satan; and there is a great number of them.

> *And the great dragon was cast out, that old serpent, called the Devil, and Satan, which deceiveth the whole world: he was cast out into the earth, and his angels were cast out with him. And I heard a loud voice saying in heaven, Now is come salvation, and strength, and the kingdom of our God, and the power of his Christ: for the accuser of our brethren is cast down, which accused them before our God day and night.*

(Revelation 12:9-10)

Those who are deceived by Satan's methodology are not the ones referred to when we read about the Lake. The Lake is not a matter of deception, but of willful action. That which has a special place prepared for them in the lake, fully understand both the things of God and the things of Satan. These are the ones that, even with this understanding, chose to honor the things of Satan, and not the things of God. There is no accident, deception, ignorance, omission or excuse. They know full well the power that God gave to Christ to heal the nations, and they actively reject it. This is like the difference between premeditated murder and accidental homicide. God allowed a way **out of** destruction for accidental homicide: there is no reprieve for premeditated murder.

> *And the LORD spake unto Moses, saying, Speak unto the children of Israel, and say unto them, When ye be come over Jordan into the land of Canaan; Then ye shall appoint you cities to be cities of refuge for you; that the slayer may flee thither, which killeth any person at unawares. And they shall be unto you cities for refuge from the avenger; that the manslayer die not, until he stand before the congregation in judgment. And of these cities which ye shall give six cities shall ye have for refuge. Ye shall give three cities on this side Jordan, and three cities shall ye give in the land of Canaan, which shall be cities of refuge. These six cities shall be a refuge, both for the children of Israel, and for the stranger, and for the sojourner among them: that every one that killeth any person unawares may flee thither.*

(Numbers 35:9-15)

Ignorant violations have a remedy before God. There is no reprieve for premeditated violation of the will of God, accompanied by rejection of His grace. This goes far beyond choosing ones own course. This is the act of stabbing at the mind of God. Wherefore we must realize that the nature of the relationship between God and man is such that a mere mortal cannot achieve the kind of understanding that would place him at this level of violation. The devil will not give any human a true understanding of God, or of his will. This was seen with Eve in the garden, where the serpent--generally believed to have used the methods of Satan, if not actually being Satan--told a half-truth that deceived Eve.

> *And the serpent said unto the woman, Ye shall not surely die: For God doth know that in the day ye eat thereof, then your eyes shall be opened, and ye shall be as gods, knowing good and evil.*
>
> (Genesis 3:4-5)

Judas Iscariot's cooperation with Jesus' earthly adversaries, as recorded in the Bible, is generally viewed to be the closest hint of any human practicing willful conformance to the things of Satan. It can be said of Judas that he should have known the ways of God. Some think that even though Judas had knowledge of Christ's message, Satan was able to move him to a choice against the things of God. However, did Judas really make such a choice, or was he just used by Satan; again, according to deception? Maybe the end result will tell the middle happenings.

In the example, Judas could not be held to the level of violation that is done by the angels of Satan. Once Satan had used him to do his bidding, then the hold that the things of God had on Judas, returned to the forefront of his life. He was lost to them for a moment in time; but once he understood that this was a violation of God's principles, he repented. He does not have a spot in this special place for Satan and his angels, who are his true ambassadors.

To *earn* a spot in this place requires a large amount of knowledge. It seems that one would have to be ancient of days to fully acquire the will and the knowledge necessary to receive a place herein. This is something that fits the description of the angels who follow Satan. They were, after all, brought forth before the world began. God made sure that no humans could reach the point where they would have acquired sufficient knowledge to condemn themselves in that fashion. This is one of the other reasons why Adam was not allowed to partake of the tree of life.

> *And the LORD God said, Behold, the man is become as one of us, to know good and evil: and now, lest he put forth his hand, and take also of the tree of life, and eat, and live for ever: Therefore the LORD God sent him forth from the garden of Eden, to till the ground from whence he was taken.*
>
> (Genesis 3:22-23)

In general, God limited our scope of life to one that keeps us from acquiring such knowledge.

> *And it came to pass, when men began to multiply on the face of the earth, and daughters were born unto them, That the sons of God saw the daughters of men that they were fair; and they took them wives of all which they chose.*
>
> *And the LORD said, My spirit shall not always strive with man, for that he also is flesh: yet his days shall be an hundred and twenty years.*
>
> *There were giants in the earth in those days; and also after that, when the sons of God came in unto the daughters of men, and they bare children to them, the same became mighty men which were of old, men of renown. And God saw that the wickedness of man was great in the earth, and that every imagination of the thoughts of his heart was only evil continually.*
>
> (Genesis 6:1-5)

Thank You, God, for your blessing on mankind. By Your action of shortening his days on this earth, You prevented mankind from ever reaching such a state of total condemnation.

Thank You, God, that the judgment of mankind comes before the *disposal* of those ones and things not recorded in the book of life. This lets us know that those who are judged are recorded in your books and receive the recompense for their actions, as we all do. This was testified to by Your servant and Son, the Lord Jesus Christ.

> *When the Son of man shall come in his glory, and all the holy angels with him, then shall he sit upon the throne of his glory: And before him shall be gathered all nations: and he shall separate them one from another, as a shepherd divideth his sheep from the goats: And he shall set the sheep on his right hand, but the goats on the left. Then shall the King say unto them on his right hand, Come, ye blessed of my Father, inherit the kingdom prepared for you from the foundation of the world:*
>
> (Matthew 25:31-34)

> *Then shall he say also unto them on the left hand, Depart from me, ye cursed, into everlasting fire, prepared for the devil and his angels:*

(Matthew 25:41)

Thank You, God, that You do not see in mankind any need to extend the negative reach of Satan beyond those who already had sufficient knowledge to condemn themselves.

Thank You, God: You prepared the Lake of fire as a place which is only for the select group of those that actively fight against Your will and Your way.

> *And the devil that deceived them was cast into the lake of fire and brimstone, where the beast and the false prophet are, and shall be tormented day and night for ever and ever.*

(Revelation 20:10)

> *And death and hell were cast into the lake of fire. This is the second death.*

(Revelation 20:14)

Thank You, God, that Your word clearly identified the angels of Satan. These are they that were tossed from Heaven along with Satan when his accusations were stopped. These are they that were formerly given access to Heaven; not created beings on earth. Thank You for Your clarification.

> *And the great dragon was cast out, that old serpent, called the Devil, and Satan, which deceiveth the whole world: he was cast out into the earth, and his angels were cast out with him.*

(Revelation 12:9)

Also I thank You God that you do not lightly wipe out anyone's names from the book of life. I thank You for this because of the high consequences that come with not being listed in this book. Even though I am not sure if any human born of man can ever be blotted out, I thank You for not doing so. And if it is possible for me to ask, I ask that You never find a reason to remove anyone's name from this book, who is a living being born of man and woman; and further, I ask that all who have lived on this earth may have a part in the book of life. This is my prayer for all humanity, past, present and future. The price of removal from your book of life is great indeed.

And whosoever was not found written in the book of life was cast into the lake of fire.

(Revelation 20:15)

It is my prayer that no person ever created has to endure such punishment; whether they are the work of Your hand, or were they born by Your command to us, to be fruitful and multiply. This I ask in Jesus name, if I am allowed to do so, and for his sake.

Amen.

+=+=+=+=+=+=+=+=+=+=+=+=+=+=+=+=+=+=+=+

The Difference

Thus, we see that one of these places, the Lake, is eternal; the other, hell, is temporary. Therefore, we should not apply the expression "eternal punishment" to hell. Residence in hell will only be torment for a time. Then, there will be a release and judgment.

The Lake, however, is eternal.

Let us, therefore, be more precise in our statements about the functions of these two places. Particularly, let us not feel that we have to elevate the status of hell to an eternality that it does not have. We must believe that it is sufficient for us to share with others that hell is not a place to be; not even for a second. There are no parties there; and even if a party was ever held in hell, there would be no way to enjoy it.

I repeat to you what was written above: even a second of torment in hell is more than a lifetime of agony on earth. It is a place of torment; this is sufficient reason to persuade others to receive the free gift of God through Jesus Christ our Lord.

There was a certain rich man, which was clothed in purple and fine linen, and fared sumptuously every day: And there was a certain beggar named Lazarus, which was laid at his gate, full of sores, And desiring to be fed with the crumbs which fell from the rich man's table: moreover the dogs came and licked his sores.

And it came to pass, that the beggar died, and was carried by the angels into Abraham's bosom: the rich man also died, and was buried; And in hell he lift up his eyes, being in torments, and seeth Abraham afar off, and Lazarus in his bosom. And he cried and said, Father Abraham, have mercy on me, and send Lazarus, that he may dip the tip of his finger in water, and cool my tongue; for I am tormented in this flame.

But Abraham said, Son, remember that thou in thy lifetime receivedst thy good things, and likewise Lazarus evil things: but now he is comforted, and thou art tormented. And beside all this, between us and you there is a great gulf fixed: so that they which would pass from hence to you cannot; neither can they pass to us, that would come from thence.

Then he said, I pray thee therefore, father, that thou wouldest send him to my father's house: For I have five brethren; that he may testify unto them, lest they also come into this place of torment.

Abraham saith unto him, They have Moses and the prophets; let them hear them.

And he said, Nay, father Abraham: but if one went unto them from the dead, they will repent.

And he said unto him, If they hear not Moses and the prophets, neither will they be persuaded, though one rose from the dead.

(Mark 16:19-31)

To those who have not yet decided to acknowledge before God their acceptance of the message and sacrifice of Jesus Christ, I have a message.

One has risen from the dead, and this is Jesus Christ the Lord, who is, too, the Son of God. Please return to God so that you are not among those of whom it was said: *neither will they be persuaded, though one rose from the dead.*

To this, let the entire church of Christ, built on the rock of the truth that Jesus is the Christ, the Son of the Living God, say Amen. And may we, as the church of Christ, built upon the firm and sure foundation of Jesus Christ, rest in this confidence and release our being to the Holy Ghost.

And, with this release, O Holy Ghost, sent from God, in the name of Jesus Christ, seal us in you.

Selah.

References to hell in the New Testament

Matthew

+=+=+=+=+=+=+=+=+=+=+=+

5:21 Ye have heard that it was said of them of old time, Thou shalt not kill; and whosoever shall kill shall be in danger of the judgment:

5:22 But I say unto you, That whosoever is angry with his brother without a cause shall be in danger of the judgment: and whosoever shall say to his brother, *Raca*, shall be in danger of the council: but **whosoever shall say, Thou fool, shall be in danger of hell fire**.

+=+=+=+=+=+=+=+=+=+=+=+

5:29 And if thy right eye offend thee, pluck it out, and cast it from thee: for it is profitable for thee that one of thy members should perish, and not that thy whole body should be cast into hell.

5:30 And if thy right hand offend thee, cut it off, and cast it from thee: for it is profitable for thee that one of thy members should perish, and not that thy whole body should be cast into hell.

+=+=+=+=+=+=+=+=+=+=+=+

10:27 What I tell you in darkness, that speak ye in light: and what ye hear in the ear, that preach ye upon the housetops.

10:28 And fear not them which kill the body, but are not able to kill the soul: but rather fear him which is able to destroy both soul and body in hell.

+=+=+=+=+=+=+=+=+=+=+=+

11:22 But I say unto you, It shall be more tolerable for Tyre and Sidon at the day of judgment, than for you.

11:23 And thou, Capernaum, which art exalted unto heaven, shalt be brought down to hell: for if the mighty works, which have been done in thee, had been done in Sodom, it would have remained until this day.

11:24 But I say unto you, That it shall be more tolerable for the land of Sodom in the day of judgment, than for thee.

+=+=+=+=+=+=+=+=+=+=+=+

16:15 He saith unto them, But whom say ye that I am?

16:16 And Simon Peter answered and said, Thou art the Christ, the Son of the living God.

16:17 And Jesus answered and said unto him, **Blessed art thou, Simon Barjona**: for flesh and blood hath not revealed *it* unto thee, but my Father which is in heaven.

16:18 And I say also unto thee, **That thou art Peter, and upon this rock I will build my church**; and the gates of hell shall not prevail against it.

+=+=+=+=+=+=+=+=+=+=+=+

18:8 Wherefore if thy hand or thy foot offend thee, cut them off, and cast them from thee: it is better for thee to enter into life halt or maimed, rather than having two hands or two feet to be cast into everlasting fire.

18:9 And if thine eye offend thee, pluck it out, and cast it from thee: it is better for thee to enter into life with one eye, rather than having two eyes to be cast into hell fire.

+=+=+=+=+=+=+=+=+=+=+=+

23:14 Woe unto you, scribes and Pharisees, hypocrites! for ye devour widows' houses, and for a pretence make long prayer: therefore ye shall receive the greater damnation.

23:15 Woe unto you, scribes and Pharisees, hypocrites! for ye compass sea and land to make one proselyte, and when he is made, ye make him twofold more the child of hell than yourselves.

+=+=+=+=+=+=+=+=+=+=+

23:31 Wherefore ye be witnesses unto yourselves, that ye are the children of them which killed the prophets.

23:32 Fill ye up then the measure of your fathers.

23:33 Ye serpents, ye generation of vipers, how can ye escape the damnation of hell?

+=+=+=+=+=+=+=+=+=+=+=+=+=+=+=+

References to hell in the New Testament

Mark

+=+=+=+=+=+=+=+=+=+

9:43 And if thy hand offend thee, cut it off: it is better for thee to enter into life maimed, than having two hands to go into hell, into the fire that never shall be quenched:

9:44 Where their worm dieth not, and the fire is not quenched.

9:45 And if thy foot offend thee, cut it off: it is better for thee to enter halt into life, than having two feet to be cast into hell, into the fire that never shall be quenched:

9:46 Where their worm dieth not, and the fire is not quenched.

9:47 And if thine eye offend thee, pluck it out: it is better for thee to enter into the kingdom of God with one eye, than having two eyes to be cast into hell fire:

9:48 Where their worm dieth not, and the fire is not quenched.

+=+=+=+=+=+=+=+=+=+=+=+=+=+=+=+

Luke

+=+=+=+=+=+=+=+=+=+

10:13 Woe unto thee, Chorazin! woe unto thee, Bethsaida! for if the mighty works had been done in Tyre and Sidon, which have been done in you, they had a great while ago repented, sitting in sackcloth and ashes.

10:14 But it shall be more tolerable for Tyre and Sidon at the judgment, than for you.

10:15 And thou, Capernaum, which art exalted to heaven, shalt be thrust down to hell.

10:16 He that heareth you heareth me; and he that despiseth you despiseth me; and he that despiseth me despiseth him that sent me.

+=+=+=+=+=+=+=+=+=+=+

12:4 And I say unto you my friends, Be not afraid of them that kill the body, and after that have no more that they can do.

12:5 But I will forewarn you whom ye shall fear: Fear him, which after he hath killed hath power to cast into hell; yea, I say unto you, Fear him.

+=+=+=+=+=+=+=+=+=+=+

16:19 There was a certain rich man, which was clothed in purple and fine linen, and fared sumptuously every day:

16:20 And there was a certain beggar named Lazarus, which was laid at his gate, full of sores,

16:21 And desiring to be fed with the crumbs which fell from the rich man's table: moreover the dogs came and licked his sores.

16:22 And it came to pass, that the beggar died, and was carried by the angels into Abraham's bosom: the rich man also died, and was buried;

16:23 And in hell he lift up his eyes, being in torments, and seeth Abraham afar off, and Lazarus in his bosom.

+=+=+=+=+=+=+=+=+=+=+=+=+=+

References to hell in the New Testament

Acts

+=+=+=+=+=+=+=+=+=+=+

2:25 For David speaketh concerning him,

2:26 *Therefore did my heart rejoice, and my tongue was glad; moreover also my flesh shall rest in hope:*

2:27 *Because thou wilt not leave my soul in hell, neither wilt thou suffer thine Holy One to see corruption.*

2:28 *Thou hast made known to me the ways of life; thou shalt make me full of joy with thy countenance.*

2:29 Men and brethren, let me freely speak unto you of the patriarch David, that he is both dead and buried, and his sepulchre is with us unto this day.

2:30 Therefore being a prophet, and knowing that God had sworn with an oath to him, that of the fruit of his loins, according to the flesh, he would raise up Christ to sit on his throne;

2:31 He seeing this before spake of the resurrection of Christ, that his soul was not left in hell, neither his flesh did see corruption.

2:32 This Jesus hath God raised up, whereof we all are witnesses.

+=+=+=+=+=+=+=+=+=+=+=+=+=+=+=+

James

+=+=+=+=+=+=+=+=+

3:5 Even so the tongue is a little member, and boasteth great things. Behold, how great a matter a little fire kindleth!

3:6 And the tongue is a fire, a world of iniquity: so is the tongue among our members, that it defileth the whole body, and setteth on fire the course of nature; and it is set on fire of hell.

+=+

2 Peter

+=+=+=+=+=+=+=+=+=+

2:1 But there were false prophets also among the people, even as there shall be false teachers among you, who privily shall bring in damnable heresies, even denying the Lord that bought them, and bring upon themselves swift destruction.

2:2 And many shall follow their pernicious ways; by reason of whom the way of truth shall be evil spoken of.

2:3 And through covetousness shall they with feigned words make merchandise of you: whose judgment now of a long time lingereth not, and their damnation slumbereth not.

2:4 For if God spared not the angels that sinned, but cast them down to hell, and delivered them into chains of darkness, to be reserved unto judgment;

2:5 And spared not the old world, but saved Noah the eighth person, a preacher of righteousness, bringing in the flood upon the world of the ungodly;

2:6 And turning the cities of Sodom and Gomorrha into ashes condemned them with an overthrow, making them an ensample unto those that after should live ungodly;

2:7 And delivered just Lot, vexed with the filthy conversation of the wicked:

2:8 (For that righteous man dwelling among them, in seeing and hearing, vexed his righteous soul from day to day with their unlawful deeds;)

2:9 The Lord knoweth how to deliver the godly out of temptations, and to reserve the unjust unto the day of judgment to be punished:

2:10 But chiefly them that walk after the flesh in the lust of uncleanness, and despise government. Presumptuous are they, selfwilled, they are not afraid to speak evil of dignities.

+=+

References to hell in the New Testament

Revelation

+=+=+=+=+=+=+=+=+=+=+

1:12 And I turned to see the voice that spake with me. And being turned, I saw seven golden candlesticks;

1:13 And in the midst of the seven candlesticks one like unto the Son of man, clothed with a garment down to the foot, and girt about the paps with a golden girdle.

1:14 His head and his hairs were white like wool, as white as snow; and his eyes were as a flame of fire;

1:15 And his *feet like unto fine brass*, as if they burned in a furnace; and his voice as the sound of many waters.

1:16 And he had in his right hand seven stars: and *out of his mouth went a sharp twoedged sword*: and his countenance was as the sun shineth in his strength.

1:17 And when I saw him, I fell at his feet as dead.

And he laid his right hand upon me, saying unto me, Fear not; I am the first and the last:

1:18 I am he that liveth, and was dead; and, behold, I am alive for evermore, Amen; and have the keys of hell and of death.

+=+=+=+=+=+=+=+=+=+=+

6:7 And when he had opened the **fourth seal**, I heard the voice of the fourth beast say, Come and see.

6:8 And I looked, and behold a **pale horse**: and his name that sat on him was **Death, and Hell** followed with him. And power was given unto them **over the fourth part of the earth**, to kill with sword, and with hunger, and with death, and with the beasts of the earth.

+=+=+=+=+=+=+=+=+=+=+=+

20:11 And I saw a great white throne, and him that sat on it, from whose face the earth and the heaven fled away; and there was found no place for them.

20:12 And I saw the dead, small and great, stand before God; and the books were opened: and another book was opened, which is the book of life: and the dead were judged out of those things which were written in the books, according to their works.

20:13 And the **sea gave up the dead** which were in it; and **death and hell delivered up the dead** which were in them: and they were judged every man according to their works.

20:14 And **death and hell were cast into the lake of fire**. This is the second death.

+=+=+=+=+=+=+=+=+=+=+=+=+=+=+=+

The World to Come

What is it going be like when this creation, heaven and earth, has reached the end of its useful life? Will the earth be removed? Will both be replaced? Will they just hang here, continually tending toward a state of disorder? If they are removed or replaced, how will that be done? So many questions; and all that must be settled before we can decide who gets the property rights for the new existence. Moreover, is there still a, who, in the new existence?

Let me try my hand at explaining the things that occur at that time. To do this, I will have to draw on expert testimony. The only place I have been able to find this is in the Bible. Only those who have been in contact with God or His representatives wanted to be involved with these questions; there are just so many variables. The proclamation, which has been made by these few individuals, is that there is indeed a replacement.

To describe this stage of reality, we broke it down into five sections. The sections are presence, preparation, population, preservation and principalities.

+=+=+=+=+=+=+=+=+=+=+=+=+=+=+=+=+=+=+

Presence - the state of existence prior to the arrival of the world to come

The world and the universe are indeed tending toward a state of chaos.

As the race of man takes over more and more of the things of the universe, man's limitations are becoming obvious. The people of earth once believed in the concept of theocracy: "the chosen people of God," "one nation under God,", "in God we trust": these things are being strategically replaced.

Mankind is returning to the Adamaic state of grabbing for identity with God. Be sure you do not become confused about this: the word, *identity*, is not the same as the word, *identify*. The difference is more than one letter; it is a whole change of mentality, morality and everything else about the human condition. Those who identify with God are trying to understand Him, and incorporate the richness of His being into their own. Those who are striving for identity with God have once again reached for the fruit in the Garden of Eden from *that* tree.

> *And the serpent said unto the woman, Ye shall not surely die: For God doth know that in the day ye eat thereof, then your eyes shall be opened, and ye shall be as gods, knowing good and evil.*
>
> (Genesis 3:4-5)

Whenever there is an advancement that God allow man to make, there is a new pride-of-ownership trap that snaps shut. The creatures of *knowledge*, which we either make ourselves or discover, are given precedence over the One who engineered and allowed the knowledge that He is revealing. In truth, true knowledge is from God, and cannot be made by man. Man creates a synthetic form of knowledge that is built on reconstruction, or aberration, of God's knowledge. Furthermore, aberration is not true knowledge; it might be better called supposition or wish. However, much of this artificial knowledge has entered into the fields of science and morality, including religion, as if such knowledge were real.

> *For I am not ashamed of the gospel of Christ: for it is the power of God unto salvation to every one that believeth; to the Jew first, and also to the Greek. For therein is the righteousness of God revealed from faith to faith: as it is written, The just shall live by faith.*
>
> *For the wrath of God is revealed from heaven against all ungodliness and unrighteousness of men, who hold the truth in unrighteousness; Because that which may be known of God is manifest in them; for God hath showed it unto them. For the invisible things of him from the creation of the world are clearly seen, being understood by the things that are made, even his eternal power and Godhead; so that they are without excuse: Because that, when they knew God, they glorified him not as God, neither were thankful; but became vain in their*

> *imaginations, and their foolish heart was darkened. Professing themselves to be wise, they became fools, And changed the glory of the uncorruptible God into an image made like to corruptible man, and to birds, and fourfooted beasts, and creeping things. Wherefore God also gave them up to uncleanness through the lusts of their own hearts, to dishonour their own bodies between themselves: Who changed the truth of God into a lie, and worshipped and served the creature more than the Creator, who is blessed for ever. Amen.*

(Romans 1:16-25)

+=+=+=+=+=+=+=+=+=+=+=+=+=+=+=+=+=+=+=+

Preparation - all events leading up to final cleansing

Into this world, a change is coming. There is one who will flow from God into the midst of this existence and take control. This is not an evolutionary thing of political development and networking, delivering an ultimate human power source from the earth. This is one who arrives from Heaven with hosts that are not from this earth. He comes in a display of--well--Biblical proportions; and according to Biblical manifestation. This is the Messiah, the Son of God. This is not a closed meeting of a select few power mongers, but a display open to all and seen by all.

> *Behold, he cometh with clouds; and every eye shall see him, and they also which pierced him: and all kindreds of the earth shall wail because of him. Even so, Amen.*

(Revelation 1:7)

It is not just limited to those who are alive at that time. When it says that *every eye shall see him*, it does mean, **every**. This concept will be very difficult for those who see death as a cessation of existence, which it is not; God does not waste material in that fashion. The knowledge and issues collected in the soul of each individual are not placed there just to be arbitrarily discarded at death. Death is just a pause in the, "to everlasting," of an individual; a pause that is sometimes long, and sometimes instantaneously short.

To bring about the, *every eye*, scenario, all who exist in life and out of life will be gathered.

> *And the sea gave up the dead which were in it; and death and hell delivered up the dead which were in them: and they were judged every man according to their works.*
>
> (Revelation 20:13)

Then there is some cleanup. The old repositories of souls are of no more use; they have to go. This means the removal of death, hell, and the old ways of heaven and earth. A new reality is born.

> *The Lord is not slack concerning his promise, as some men count slackness; but is longsuffering to us-ward, not willing that any should perish, but that all should come to repentance. But the day of the Lord will come as a thief in the night; in the which the heavens shall pass away with a great noise, and the elements shall melt with fervent heat, the earth also and the works that are therein shall be burned up.*
>
> (2 Peter 3:9-10)

> *And death and hell were cast into the lake of fire. This is the second death.*
>
> (Revelation 20:14)

> *And I saw a great white throne, and him that sat on it, from whose face the earth and the heaven fled away; and there was found no place for them.*
>
> (Revelation 20:11)

After the cleanup, the new reality arrives.

> *And I will bring forth a seed out of Jacob, and out of Judah an inheritor of my mountains: and mine elect shall inherit it, and my servants shall dwell there. And Sharon shall be a fold of flocks, and the valley of Achor a place for the herds to lie down in, for my people that have sought me.*
>
> *But ye are they that forsake the LORD, that forget my holy mountain, that prepare a table for that troop, and that furnish the drink offering unto that number. Therefore will I number you to the sword, and ye shall all bow down to the slaughter: because when I called, ye did not answer; when*

I spake, ye did not hear; but did evil before mine eyes, and did choose that wherein I delighted not.

Therefore thus saith the Lord GOD, Behold, my servants shall eat, but ye shall be hungry: behold, my servants shall drink, but ye shall be thirsty: behold, my servants shall rejoice, but ye shall be ashamed: Behold, my servants shall sing for joy of heart, but ye shall cry for sorrow of heart, and shall howl for vexation of spirit. And ye shall leave your name for a curse unto my chosen: for the Lord GOD shall slay thee, and call his servants by another name: That he who blesseth himself in the earth shall bless himself in the God of truth; and he that sweareth in the earth shall swear by the God of truth; because the former troubles are forgotten, and because they are hid from mine eyes. For, behold, I create new heavens and a new earth: and the former shall not be remembered, nor come into mind.

But be ye glad and rejoice for ever in that which I create: for, behold, I create Jerusalem a rejoicing, and her people a joy. And I will rejoice in Jerusalem, and joy in my people: and the voice of weeping shall be no more heard in her, nor the voice of crying. There shall be no more thence an infant of days, nor an old man that hath not filled his days: for the child shall die an hundred years old; but the sinner being an hundred years old shall be accursed. And they shall build houses, and inhabit them; and they shall plant vineyards, and eat the fruit of them. They shall not build, and another inhabit; they shall not plant, and another eat: for as the days of a tree are the days of my people, and mine elect shall long enjoy the work of their hands. They shall not labour in vain, nor bring forth for trouble; for they are the seed of the blessed of the LORD, and their offspring with them.

And it shall come to pass, that before they call, I will answer; and while they are yet speaking, I will hear. The wolf and the lamb shall feed together, and the lion shall eat straw like the bullock: and dust shall be the serpent's meat. They shall not hurt nor destroy in all my holy mountain, saith the LORD.

(Isaiah 65:9-25)

> *And I saw a new heaven and a new earth: for the first heaven and the first earth were passed away; and there was no more sea. And I John saw the holy city, new Jerusalem, coming down from God out of heaven, prepared as a bride adorned for her husband.*
>
> *And I heard a great voice out of heaven saying, Behold, the tabernacle of God is with men, and he will dwell with them, and they shall be his people, and God himself shall be with them, and be their God. And God shall wipe away all tears from their eyes; and there shall be no more death, neither sorrow, nor crying, neither shall there be any more pain: for the former things are passed away.*
>
> *And he that sat upon the throne said, Behold, I make all things new. And he said unto me, Write: for these words are true and faithful.*
>
> (Revelation 21:1-5)

+=+=+=+=+=+=+=+=+=+=+=+=+=+=+=+=+=+=+=+

Population - gathered from the past, present and future, as referenced from the day of the Lord

Now we enter the most controversial of all the stages of the world to come. There are pieces of the controversy that are clearly understood from the Scripture, so we will introduce them first. We will center this around the person of Jesus Christ (if *chronology* could do it, we do not feel uncomfortable doing the same). *Really, we would not feel uncomfortable doing this, regardless of anything else.*

Among the populace are those who *rose to the occasion* to evidence Jesus' Lordship, at his death.

> *Jesus, when he had cried again with a loud voice, yielded up the ghost. And, behold, the veil of the temple was rent in twain from the top to the bottom; and the earth did quake, and the rocks rent; And the graves were opened; and many bodies of the saints which slept arose, And came out of the graves after his resurrection, and went into the holy city, and appeared unto many.*
>
> *Now when the centurion, and they that were with him, watching Jesus, saw the earthquake, and those things that*

were done, they feared greatly, saying, Truly this was the Son of God.

(Matthew 27:50-54)

These are they who knew that the resurrection is the icing on the cake. The deal with God for the redemption of mankind was sealed when Jesus died on the cross. Jesus told us this himself.

Now there stood by the cross of Jesus his mother, and his mother's sister, Mary the wife of Cleophas, and Mary Magdalene. When Jesus therefore saw his mother, and the disciple standing by, whom he loved, he saith unto his mother, Woman, behold thy son! Then saith he to the disciple, Behold thy mother! And from that hour that disciple took her unto his own home.

After this, Jesus knowing that all things were now accomplished, that the scripture might be fulfilled, saith, I thirst. Now there was set a vessel full of vinegar: and they filled a spunge with vinegar, and put it upon hyssop, and put it to his mouth. When Jesus therefore had received the vinegar, he said, It is finished: and he bowed his head, and gave up the ghost.

(John 19:25-30)

The apostle Paul confirmed it.

For if the blood of bulls and of goats, and the ashes of an heifer sprinkling the unclean, sanctifieth to the purifying of the flesh: How much more shall the blood of Christ, who through the eternal Spirit offered himself without spot to God, purge your conscience from dead works to serve the living God?

And for this cause he is the mediator of the new testament, that by means of death, for the redemption of the transgressions that were under the first testament, they which are called might receive the promise of eternal inheritance. For where a testament is, there must also of necessity be the death of the testator. For a testament is of force after men are dead: otherwise it is of no strength at all while the testator liveth. Whereupon neither the first

> *testament was dedicated without blood. For when Moses had spoken every precept to all the people according to the law, he took the blood of calves and of goats, with water, and scarlet wool, and hyssop, and sprinkled both the book, and all the people, Saying, This is the blood of the testament which God hath enjoined unto you. Moreover he sprinkled with blood both the tabernacle, and all the vessels of the ministry. And almost all things are by the law purged with blood; and without shedding of blood is no remission.*
>
> *It was therefore necessary that the patterns of things in the heavens should be purified with these; but the heavenly things themselves with better sacrifices than these. For Christ is not entered into the holy places made with hands, which are the figures of the true; but into heaven itself, now to appear in the presence of God for us: Nor yet that he should offer himself often, as the high priest entereth into the holy place every year with blood of others; For then must he often have suffered since the foundation of the world: but now once in the end of the world hath he appeared to put away sin by the sacrifice of himself. And as it is appointed unto men once to die, but after this the judgment: So Christ was once offered to bear the sins of many; and unto them that look for him shall he appear the second time without sin unto salvation.*

(Hebrews 9:13-28)

Additionally, there are those who experienced that instantaneous passage through death.

> *Therefore we are always confident, knowing that, whilst we are at home in the body, we are absent from the Lord: (For we walk by faith, not by sight:) We are confident, I say, and willing rather to be absent from the body, and to be present with the Lord.*

(2 Corinthians 5:6-8)

Of course, there are those who believe in Christ and were alive when the millennial reign of Christ started.

Oh, did I forget to mention the matter of the millennial kingdom? Let me quickly remedy that:

> *And he laid hold on the dragon, that old serpent, which is the Devil, and Satan, and bound him a thousand years, And cast him into the bottomless pit, and shut him up, and set a seal upon him, that he should deceive the nations no more, till the thousand years should be fulfilled: and after that he must be loosed a little season.*

(Revelation 20:2-3)

There are many others who do not see the grace of God through Jesus Christ during that time. These will be collected together, by the adversary, against him in a final futile attack. They will fail. This is done before the millennium starts. I guess the adversary and his army want to try to stop the inevitable arrival of the rule of Christ.

> *And the remnant were slain with the sword of him that sat upon the horse, which sword proceeded out of his mouth: and all the fowls were filled with their flesh.*

(Revelation 19:21)

God will allow Jesus Christ to give a preview of full eternity during the time of the millennial kingdom.

> *Blessed and holy is he that hath part in the first resurrection: on such the second death hath no power, but they shall be priests of God and of Christ, and shall reign with him a thousand years.*

(Revelation 20:6)

Once the preview is complete, the dead in Christ will join him.

> *And I saw thrones, and they sat upon them, and judgment was given unto them: and I saw the souls of them that were beheaded for the witness of Jesus, and for the word of God, and which had not worshipped the beast, neither his image, neither had received his mark upon their foreheads, or in their hands; and they lived and reigned with Christ a thousand years.*
>
> *But the rest of the dead lived not again until the thousand years were finished. This is the first resurrection.*

(Revelation 20:4-5)

Before the end of the preview, we have a potentially controversial vision: we will state the understanding that God has given us, without apology. Among those in the family of God in Christ will be those converted to or protected by Christ during his millennial reign. Chief among these are the children.

Another controversial part of the vision is the presence of those who are not of the family of God in Christ. These are they which are judged according to their works.

> *And I saw the dead, small and great, stand before God; and the books were opened: and another book was opened, which is the book of life: and the dead were judged out of those things which were written in the books, according to their works.*
>
> (Revelation 20:12)

Some of them may be allowed to enter into their rest, in the Lord. Later we will see where the others are.

+=+=+=+=+=+=+=+=+=+=+=+=+=+=+=+=+=+=+

Preservation

This is somewhat straightforward. There is no more death, so the soul goes on forever. Those who are in Christ will receive newness in body and in character.

> *The Spirit itself beareth witness with our spirit, that we are the children of God: And if children, then heirs; heirs of God, and joint-heirs with Christ; if so be that we suffer with him, that we may be also glorified together.*
>
> (Romans 8:16-17)

> *And we know that all things work together for good to them that love God, to them who are the called according to his purpose. For whom he did foreknow, he also did predestinate to be conformed to the image of his Son, that he might be the firstborn among many brethren. Moreover whom he did predestinate, them he also called: and whom he called, them he also justified: and whom he justified, them he also glorified.*
>
> (Romans 8:28-30)

> *And it came to pass, as he sat at meat with them, he took bread, and blessed it, and brake, and gave to them. And their eyes were opened, and they knew him; and he vanished out of their sight.*
>
> (Luke 24:30-31)

Those who are in Christ will have access to the tree of life.

> *And he showed me a pure river of water of life, clear as crystal, proceeding out of the throne of God and of the Lamb. In the midst of the street of it, and on either side of the river, was there the tree of life, which bare twelve manner of fruits, and yielded her fruit every month: and the leaves of the tree were for the healing of the nations.*
>
> *And there shall be no more curse: but the throne of God and of the Lamb shall be in it; and his servants shall serve him: And they shall see his face; and his name shall be in their foreheads.*
>
> (Revelation 22:1-4)

Those who are not in Christ will exist only as souls. No, they cannot go to hell, because this is not there in the new reality. They are just *without*: please read on.

+=+

Principalities

There are only two principalities remaining in the new heaven and earth (three, if you count Heaven as a principality unto itself; we do not, so we will only discuss the two).

The new Jerusalem

> *And there came unto me one of the seven angels which had the seven vials full of the seven last plagues, and talked with me, saying, Come hither, I will show thee the bride, the Lamb's wife.*
>
> *And he carried me away in the spirit to a great and high mountain, and showed me that great city, the holy Jerusalem, descending out of heaven from God, Having the glory of God: and her light was like unto a stone most*

precious, even like a jasper stone, clear as crystal; And had a wall great and high, and had twelve gates, and at the gates twelve angels, and names written thereon, which are the names of the twelve tribes of the children of Israel: On the east three gates; on the north three gates; on the south three gates; and on the west three gates. And the wall of the city had twelve foundations, and in them the names of the twelve apostles of the Lamb.

And he that talked with me had a golden reed to measure the city, and the gates thereof, and the wall thereof. And the city lieth foursquare, and the length is as large as the breadth: and he measured the city with the reed, twelve thousand furlongs. The length and the breadth and the height of it are equal. And he measured the wall thereof, an hundred and forty and four cubits, according to the measure of a man, that is, of the angel. And the building of the wall of it was of jasper: and the city was pure gold, like unto clear glass. And the foundations of the wall of the city were garnished with all manner of precious stones. The first foundation was jasper; the second, sapphire; the third, a chalcedony; the fourth, an emerald; The fifth, sardonyx; the sixth, sardius; the seventh, chrysolyte; the eighth, beryl; the ninth, a topaz; the tenth, a chrysoprasus; the eleventh, a jacinth; the twelfth, an amethyst. And the twelve gates were twelve pearls: every several gate was of one pearl: and the street of the city was pure gold, as it were transparent glass.

And I saw no temple therein: for the Lord God Almighty and the Lamb are the temple of it. And the city had no need of the sun, neither of the moon, to shine in it: for the glory of God did lighten it, and the Lamb is the light thereof.

(Revelation 21:9-23)

<u>Outside</u>

And there shall in no wise enter into it any thing that defileth, neither whatsoever worketh abomination, or maketh a lie: but they which are written in the Lamb's book of life.

(Revelation 21:27)

> *Blessed are they that do his commandments, that they may have right to the tree of life, and may enter in through the gates into the city. For without are dogs, and sorcerers, and whoremongers, and murderers, and idolaters, and whosoever loveth and maketh a lie.*
>
> (Revelation 22:14-15)

The universe is now a much simpler place. This may aggravate those scientists who thrive on complexity, but it is the way it is. Furthermore, even these scientists will find satisfaction in the Kingdom of God.

As we mentioned, the place of abode of God is still there, called Heaven. It is not a part of our reality, and it does not change.

There is, however, a new location that has been opened up in reality, if we can call it that; it is the *lake of fire and brimstone.*

> *And the devil that deceived them was cast into the lake of fire and brimstone, where the beast and the false prophet are, and shall be tormented day and night for ever and ever.*
>
> (Revelation 20:10)

+=+

Prayer

Lord Jesus, there are souls floating in a state outside. If you say that this is where they must forever be, your glory is undiminished. If you say that the Father will allow views into the city that allow them to see what they can be, your glory is undiminished. It is my prayer that you petition the Father to allow such views to occur, as was done with the rich man and Lazarus. It is further my prayer that you will shine your glory on them through the gates of the city, with an intensity that will lead to their conversion, even in the latter time; so that they will be moved to also share in your presence. This I pray in your name and for your sake.

Amen.

+=+

www.ingramcontent.com/pod-product-compliance
Lightning Source LLC
Chambersburg PA
CBHW021752230426
43669CB00006B/58